Sidney's Poetic Justice

Sidney's Poetic Justice

The Old Arcadia, Its Eclogues, and
Renaissance Pastoral Traditions

Robert E. Stillman

Lewisburg
Bucknell University Press
London and Toronto: Associated University Presses

© 1986 by Associated University Presses, Inc.

Associated University Presses
440 Forsgate Drive
Cranbury, NJ 08512

Associated University Presses
25 Sicilian Avenue
London WC1A 2QH, England

Associated University Presses
2133 Royal Windsor Drive
Unit 1
Mississauga, Ontario
Canada L5J 1K5

The paper used in this publication meets the requirements of the American National Standard for Permanence of Paper for Printed Library Materials Z39.48-1984.

Library of Congress Cataloging in Publication Data

Stillman, Robert E., 1954–
Sidney's poetic justice.

Bibliography: p.
Includes index.
1. Sidney, Philip, Sir, 1554–1586. Arcadia.
2. Pastoral poetry, English—History and criticism.
I. Title.
PR2342.A6S8   1986   823'.3   84-46096
ISBN 0-8387-5085-0 (alk. paper)

Printed in the United States of America

Contents

Preface 7

PART I Definition of Subject

1 Justice, Contentment, and the Idle Life 19

PART II Definition of Kind

2 Pastoralism and Generic Definition 47
3 As Critic and Poet, Sidney Defines *Pastoral* 64

PART III *The Old Arcadia* and Its Eclogues

4 From Prose to Poetry 81
5 Book One: The Divided Mind 98
6 Book Two: The Consequences of the Divided Mind 117
7 Book Three: Contentment and Justice 133
8 Book Four: "Discontentation" and Injustice 150

PART IV Poetic Justice

9 Nature and Art in *The Old Arcadia* 175

Notes 229
   Abbreviations 229
Works Cited 255
Index 268

Preface

In 1962 William A. Ringler observed that because Sidney's eclogues "are embedded in the prose of the *Arcadia* . . . , they have never been considered by themselves and Sidney has never received his due as a pastoral poet."[1] Ten years later, Jon S. Lawry wrote that "Sidney's eclogues are astounding performances. They await a full study in their own right—one that is almost certain to find infinitely more to praise for their accomplishment than to censure. . . ."[2] What was true in 1972 still obtains today. No serious attempt has been made to explore the world of the eclogues or to account for its function in *The Old Arcadia*.[3] These twenty-seven poems, totaling more than twenty-five hundred lines, are collected in four sets of entr'acte entertainments among the books of Sidney's romance. Difficult as much of this verse is, the eclogues consistently repay critical attention with the sophistication and intelligence of their design. The Arcadian eclogues *are* the astounding performances that Lawry describes, and they *are*, as Ringler knows, the right vehicles for giving Sidney his due as a pastoral poet. Great pastoralists are always great performers, and no Renaissance poet ever outdid Sidney in the skill and intelligence with which he reshapes traditional literary materials.

My study of Sidney's Arcadian eclogues imitates a conventional pastoral pattern: the poems merit attention in their own right, but they cannot be understood apart from the larger fictional world for which they were created, the prose of *The Old Arcadia*, or from the greater network of Renaissance pastoral traditions to which they persistently respond. The eclogues, then, in good Empsonian fashion, are a body of comparatively simple fictions in which more complex literary and cultural issues can be examined. A study of these entertainments carries far-reaching implications for our understanding of Sidney's poetics and the major intellectual and artistic preoccupations of his early career. The Sidney who emerges from this study is both more suspicious of his contemporaries' high claims for poetry than often has been thought, and more original in designing an aggressively optimistic program for poetry. He strives to lend the art a unique effectiveness in securing an inward state of justice and contentment for its readers, while remaining conscious, always, of the potential failure of that attempt, and the potential dangers arising from an abuse of poetic acts. *The Old Arcadia* is a special kind of fictive discourse that cannot be understood simply as the *expression* of one or more major themes. In its most important sense it is not a book about justice or contentment. Instead, as I shall argue, Sidney's romance is best conceived as a poetic *gesture* whose business is to make us into just and happy men.

The business of making men in Renaissance literature has recently become the subject of Stephen Greenblatt's *Renaissance Self-Fashioning*, and his argument is useful as a means of introducing my own. Greenblatt's thesis bears a strong and obvious relevance to Sidney's career as a whole and to *The Old Arcadia* in particular: "in the sixteenth century there appears to be an increased self-consciousness about the fashioning of human identity as a manipulable, artful process."[4] Insofar as *The Old Arcadia* can and should be read as a self-conscious gesture artfully designed to restructure the moral and psychological lives of its readers, my argument can be seen as a complement to Greenblatt's—a complement that makes room for some important exceptions. Unlike the writers who occupy Greenblatt's attention from More to Shakespeare, Sidney is one of the privileged few, not a member of the middle class, and he claims a measure of independence for himself that they do not enjoy; once more, the "self-fashioning" that *The Old Arcadia* both illustrates and promotes is not best interpreted as the product of "submission to an absolute . . . authority" such as church or state, or the result of attacking and destroying some "threatening Other" perceived as hostile to the self, as it is for Greenblatt's authors.[5] Instead, the important business of making men that is crucial to *The Old Arcadia* is better understood in conjunction with that historical process which Greenblatt sees enacted by literary works in relation to sixteenth-century society: "a shift from absorption by community, religious faith, or diplomacy toward the establishment of literary creation as a profession in its own right."[6] Sidney's *Defence* is the single most powerful argument during the sixteenth century for the preeminence of poetry among disciplines as a tool for promoting knowledge and reform; no surprise, then, that it is the poet who emerges in *The Old Arcadia* as the authority uniquely equipped with the skills required for what Greenblatt calls "self-fashioning," and that the "Other" whom the self confronts, most importantly, as a threatening alien is an image of the bad poet, a purveyor of dangerous fictions that corrupt the mind and destroy its health.

In his search for a "poetics of culture," Greenblatt articulates a primary concern not only of Renaissance poets but of their best recent critics: "art's concrete functions in relation to individuals. . . ."[7] This is a concern that actively motivates my study of Sidney as I seek to relate *The Old Arcadia* to the mind and life of its author and to the minds and lives of his readers. My description of Sidney's romance as a "poetic gesture"—as a literary device that "carries" action with it—is selected in order to further this process of relating. For like all gestures, *The Old Arcadia* arises from the desire of one man to make contact with other men, and to make contact (as so many gestures do) in an especially intimate and concrete way: for Sidney is interested in nothing less than reshaping the minds of his readers as he fashions them into just and happy men.

That justice should present itself as a central preoccupation of Sidney's early career makes sense in terms of the central events of these works. In *The Lady of May*, Queen Elizabeth holds court over the rival claims of Espilus and Therion for the hand of the May Lady; in *The Old Arcadia*, almost the entire fifth book is devoted to a trial of the princes; in the *Defence*, poetry's virtues are defended during a mock trial that has the poet triumph over his chief competitors, the historian and the philosopher. Sidney's early writings frequently imitate courtroom proceedings because Sidney is persistenty interested in problems of how to make judgments and how to secure a just life. Accounting for the unique relationship between justice and poetry in his early career is largely a matter of following Sidney in his typically eclectic range of interests: his fascination with the traditions of pastoralism, with Stoic conceptions of nature, with the ethical treatises of Aristotle, Cicero, and Plutarch, with the humanistic theology of Languet, and with Renaissance doctrines of the Fall of Man. Sidney is not a poet to whom labels come easily, and I make no apologies for failing to find one that fits.

A study of the eclogues has large implications for our understanding of *The Old Arcadia*, and a large portion of this book is devoted to a new reading of Sidney's romance in light of his interest in problems of justice and poetry. The pastoral entertainments supply the conceptual groundwork for the major themes of *The Old Arcadia* and the critical turning points in its symbolic action. They are simplified fictions in which the complex issues raised by the romance's main action can be evaluated and understood. How can justice be achieved in a world ruled by the seemingly arbitrary whims of fortune? How much power does the poet possess to produce the true contentment that is inseparable from justice? If these are the major questions posed by *The Old Arcadia*, Sidney's answers to them, I should indicate from the start, are tentative and few. He explores such problems without supplying easy resolutions to them.

Not only are the eclogues valuable guides to the interpretation of *The Old Arcadia*, but they are also reliable indicators of the major literary traditions to which the work as a whole responds—and those traditions, I am convinced, are predominantly pastoral. This is the first full-length study of *The Old Arcadia* as a pastoral romance, or rather as a new Elizabethan version of the pastoral romance, in which Sidney has availed himself of the pastoralist's traditional freedom to reshape literary materials in order to advance his own set of aesthetic, moral, and political values. Seen in the context of Renaissance pastoral traditions, Sidney's work becomes both more comprehensible, since its major themes derive from them, and more meaningful, since *The Old Arcadia* and its eclogues have a great deal to teach us about the nature of pastoralism and the pastoralist's negotiations between the literary past and the cultural present. As the product of critical thinking about literary traditions that are significant because they have real consequences for the way men live, *The Old Arcadia* is literature intended to have real effects on its author and his readers. Poetry matters to Sidney (a strange point to have to reemphasize about the author of the *Apology*), and it matters intensely not merely because it is a potential tool of abuse in alienating man from the justice and contentment that a life led in harmony with nature supplies, but also because it is the best means available to man for remedying the defects of his own infected mind.

One of the satisfactions of completing my study of *The Old Arcadia* and its eclogues has been to discover how well much of the recent criticism of Sidney and Renaissance pastoralism complements the arguments of this book. It is a pleasure to acknowledge alliances within a discipline better known for its warfare. Two recent studies of *The New Arcadia*, published after the main body of this book was finished, grow out of assumptions about Sidney's art similar to my own: Thelma N. Greenfield's *The Eye of Judgment* and Nancy Lindheim's *The Structures of Sidney's* Arcadia. Greenfield's book starts from the "premise that Sidney's high purpose in the *New Arcadia* was epistemological: its poetry meant to open the gates to understanding. . .;

caught up in its proffered delights, a reader could become both a learner and a student of the processes of his own learning."[8] Her argument is as useful for understanding *The Old Arcadia* as it is for the *New*, especially as it demands constant critical attention to the reader's experience of the text. As Greenfield writes, Sidney's art develops multiple "perceptions dramatizing the processes of the reader's own responses," a key point to remember in both versions of the romance since it should prevent us from simplifying the complex moral vision of these works (as we focus on the multiplicity of those perceptions), at the same time that it should encourage attention to the primary object of Sidney's concern: the experience of the reader.[9] This is an argument that can be effectively refined and elaborated in relation to *The Old Arcadia*, since, as I shall show, Sidney's pastoral is intended not merely to teach or to open gates to the understanding, but to create new readers as just men—a therapeutic gesture that results both from informing the reader's wit and from moving his will. Greenfield's study has a second, common ground with my own: her emphasis upon the persistent effort of Sidney's rhetoric, in teaching the reader how to make judgments, to render "the invisible visible."[10] Sidney's desire to embody abstract moral, psychological, and spiritual conditions in concrete speaking pictures is as essential to the poetry and prose of *The Old Arcadia* as it is to the *New*.

In Nancy Lindheim's study of *The New Arcadia*, "conscious structural complexity" emerges as "the hallmark of Sidney's writing."[11] This is a claim that my experience with *The Old Arcadia* makes me eager to support, especially in relation to the eclogues. For it is in these entertainments, as I shall demonstrate, that Sidney first experiments with the stylistic mode that Lindheim identifies as central to so much of *The New Arcadia's* "re-visionary" prose: "the disentanglement of a complex simultaneous perception[the voice of *The Old Arcadia's* narrator] into a sequence of unitary views."[12] When revising his original version of the romance, especially in book two, Sidney turned to the eclogues for those central stories which would serve as the foundation for much of the added material in *The New Arcadia* (the Plangus-Erona narrative and the tales of the princes' education and pre-Arcadian adventures); once more, he recovered from these entertainments a framework in which to contain those stories: the eclogues' colloquy of unmediated, individual voices singing songs and telling stories in such a way as to bring contrasting fictions and contrasting perspectives upon the world into harmonious relation. Sidney then incorporates in *The Old Arcadia* and its eclogues a structural sophistication (however much more limited in scope) parallel to that which

Lindheim locates in the *New*. Of equal importance in her study of *The New Arcadia* is Lindheim's emphasis upon "Sidney's tendency to see the world in terms of antithetical alternatives," and to do away with the antithesis once it has been established by "shifting perspective to a point where the differences no longer matter."[13] Stylistic complexity is a measure of the moral and intellectual complexity that Sidney brings to bear in his analysis of experience, and my account of how the seemingly antithetical alternatives of justice and contentment are reconciled over the course of *The Old Arcadia* should demonstrate how similar, in this regard, both versions of the romance are. My study of *The Old Arcadia* and its eclogues bears, then, a genuine alliance with Lindheim's work.

Two recent studies of Renaissance pastoral traditions also require some acknowledgment: Richard Mallette's *Spenser, Milton, and Renaissance Pastoral* and D. M. Rosenberg's *Oaten Reeds and Trumpets*. Mallette's book is the more recent and, for my purposes, the more important. At the heart of his argument is the claim that "Spenser and Milton develop in their pastorals profoundly self-conscious attitudes toward the poetic vocation and indeed toward the imaginative process itself."[14] Mallette is both conventional and correct in identifying as central to the pastoral experience issues about poetry and the capacity of song to reconcile man to this world; only when he claims that Spenser and Milton were "virtually alone among the English Renaissance poets" in making a self-conscious exploration of the imaginative process would I disagree.[15] As this book will demonstrate, in the course of fashioning *The Old Arcadia* into his most powerful and persuasive defense of poetry, Sidney undertakes an analysis of the poetic arts—their potential virtues and their possible perils—that rivals in its sophistication those analyses of his contemporaries. If Mallette does less justice to Sidney than he might (not to mention Shakespeare and Marvell!), he is right about a large number of the essential characteristics of pastoralism: about the reluctance of great pastoralists "to provide us with easy solutions to difficult questions" (and pastoralists *do* pose difficult questions);[16] about the refusal of great pastoral poetry to be "a merely belle-lettristic enterprise," as the readers are forced to confront "the designs of [their] lives which the poet's art illumines";[17] and, most telling in relation to Sidney, about the pastoralist's capability of "voicing his most individual concerns . . . within the confines of a relatively rigid and apparently limiting set of literary conventions."[18] *The Old Arcadia*, in spite of its conventional pastoral elements, must be regarded in ways as profoundly personal poetry. For Sidney shepherds the traditional resources of the pastoral genre as a means of procuring a special kind of contentment not only for his readers but for himself.

The major problems posed by the study of Renaissance pastoralism are those of generic definition: what kinds of fictions are we studying when we think critically about pastorals?; what kinds of formal properties do they display?; what aesthetic and ideological functions do they serve? (Critical questions about the genre multiply like sheep.) In spite of the large number of scholarly studies that pastoralism has inspired in the last few decades—and much of the best criticism of English Renaissance literature has been produced by critics of the pastoral from Empson to Poggioli—such questions remain problematic. Once more they will continue to prove problematic, given the protean nature of the genre and the impossibility of reducing it to some single, static definition. In light of these reflections, D. M. Rosenberg's survey of the increasing accommodation of the pastoral within the epic worlds of Vergil, Spenser, and Milton acquires some significance (beyond its own obvious merits) as a complement to my approach to the genre. For Rosenberg's historical perspective results from his understanding that "pastoral poems are made of other pastoral poems."[19] It is from the consequences of this fact that my reasoning about the genre begins. As I shall argue, Renaissance pastoralism has to be defined historically since the sense of history possessed by its authors is so acute, and the major Renaissance pastoralists are the best key and the only real key to understanding a genre so diverse because they are themselves constantly engaged in the very activity that has eluded so many contemporary scholars: generic definition. The literary traditions of the past are reinterpreted in the service of the present, as major pastoralists from Mantuan and Sannazaro to Spenser and Milton redefine the genre in order to promote their own sets of aesthetic, moral, and political values. It is to Sidney's redefinition of the pastoral in *The Old Arcadia* and its eclogues that I shall turn now. First, some acknowledgments.

No book of this kind gets written without its author's acquiring some sizable debts along the way, and I should like to acknowledge a few of those debts here. I want to thank Gary Schmidgall for his copious critical and stylistic comments on an earlier version of this study. I would also like to thank Richard C. McCoy for helping me to wrestle better with the critical issues raised in part I, and my colleague, Norman Sanders, for his criticism of the preface. My thanks to Carol A. Stillman for her professional advice on this study at nearly every stage of its composition. But my largest single debt is to Humphrey Tonkin, under whose visionary shepherding I began this study; what I know about pastoral I learned from a master.

I am grateful to the Society of Fellows in the Humanities at Columbia University for an Andrew Mellon Fellowship that allowed me to revise and complete this book, and I should like to thank *Studies in English Literature* for permitting me to reprint substantial portions of my essay, "Poetry and Justice in 'Ye goat-herd gods,'" *SEL* 22, no. 1 (Winter 1982): 39–50, and *Texas Studies in Literature and Language* for the right to republish "The Perils of Fancy: Poetry and Self-Love in *The Old Arcadia*," *TSLL* 26, no. 1 (Spring 1984): 1–17.

Sidney's Poetic Justice

PART I
Definition of Subject

1
Justice, Contentment, and the Idle Life

THE trial has ended. Pyrocles and Musidorus have been sentenced to death by an act of justice from which there appears to be no appeal. As Philanax approaches with his armed band, the princes exchange a farewell look, one last example (or so we are led to believe) of their "unappalled constancy" in the face of misfortune.[1] Suddenly Kerxenus rushes from the crowd, with arms flailing and mouth agape, in order to permit Kalodoulus to speak. For a moment our anxiety about the princes' fate is relieved.

With characteristic indirection, Sidney's narrator refuses at this point to report Kalodoulus's revelations, insisting instead that we first learn "what he was, and what cause and mean brought him thither" (408). Since our curiosity has been excited, there is a strong temptation to scan the digression hastily. A close reading would be wiser, however, since in *The Old Arcadia* it is frequently by indirection that we find direction out. Kalodoulus, we are informed, is Musidorus's servant. After faithfully performing his master's command to imprison Menalcas (the shepherd whose clothes Musidorus borrowed at the very outset of the romance), he determined to voyage to Arcadia for the following reasons:

> But as Kalodoulus performed the first part of his duty in doing the commandment of his prince, so was he with abundance of sincere loyalty extremely perplexed when he understood of Menalcas the strange disguising of his beloved master [his disguise as a shepherd]. For as the acts he and his cousin Pyrocles had done in Asia and Egypt had filled all the ears of the Thessalians and Macedonians with no less joy than admiration, so was the fear of their loss no less grievous unto them when by the noise of report they understood of their lonely committing themselves to the sea, the issue of which they had yet no way learned. But now that by Menalcas he perceived where he was [in Arcadia], guessing the like

of Pyrocles, comparing the unusedness of this act with the unripeness of their age, seeing in general conjecture they could do it for nothing that might not fall out dangerous, he was somewhile troubled with himself what to do, betwixt doubt of their hurt and doubt of their displeasure. Lastly he resolved his safest and honestest way was to reveal it to the king Euarchus, that both his authority might prevent any damage, and under his wings he himself might remain safe. Thitherward, therefore, he went. (409)

Coming immediately after the sentencing of the princes, this passage reminds us, in its own curiously oblique fashion, that much more has been at issue in the trial and the romance as a whole than the rape of one princess and the abdication of another, more even than the definition of such imponderables as love and virtue. *The Old Arcadia* asks us to consider a whole way of life, or, to be more precise, the work asks that we examine and judge several competing and contrasting ways of life, since Sidney is ultimately concerned with making us live justly. Kalodoulus is merely puzzled when he learns of Musidorus's disguise; he is more fearful when he hears of his sea journey; but upon discovering that his master has entered Arcadia (a pastoral landscape!), he is convinced that Musidorus has placed himself in danger. The reasons for his distrust of the Arcadian life are not hard to locate. A servant whose dutifulness is so evident could hardly have much sympathy for the *otium* (not to mention the dereliction) that ordinarily characterizes the pastoral life-style. Nor could a man who shares the general fear of his people for "lonely" commitments be expected to display any love for Arcadia's storied solitude. Kalodoulus's values are heroic, not pastoral; the admiration that he shares with the rest of the Thessalians for feats of arms in exotic Asia and Egypt marks him as a solid supporter of the active life, and helps, by implication, to explain his distaste for Arcadia—traditionally the province of contemplative shepherds who idle away the hours in making love and poetry. Arcadia is dangerous, as Kalodoulus realizes, because Arcadia implies a dangerous style of life.

His concern for the princes' safety is certainly not unwarranted. The last three books of *The Old Arcadia* in particular, with Musidorus's attempted rape of Pamela and Pyrocles' bedtime escapades with Philoclea, eventuating in the "murder" of Basilius and the apparent overthrow of moral and political order, provide ample evidence of the dangers attendant upon the life of idleness, the solitary life given over to love, contemplation, and poetry. Love can degenerate into lust; contemplation can disguise inaction; and poetry can create and perpetuate self-delusions. All of these dangers are brought into prominence by Kalodoulus's suspicions and by Philanax's feverish attacks upon the princes in the trial. The trial is the crucial episode in the romance since it is here that Sidney and the reader pass judgment upon the princes' pastoral experiences.

A narrowly moralistic reading of *The Old Arcadia* might be content with noticing Kalodoulus's immediate, almost instinctive distrust of the dangers of a pastoral life.[2] But the surface texture of the passage, with its insistently whimsical and ironic intonations, demands that we do much more than this; in fact, it asks that we carefully qualify any sympathy with his distaste for Arcadia.

From the outset of the digression, with its reference to his "appassionate exclaiming," Kalodoulus is made the object of the narrator's gentle but efficient ironies. We are amused by Kalodoulus's slightly excessive solicitude, by his "abundance of sincere loyalty," and particularly by the conflict between his desire to act honestly and his wish to preserve his own safety. Three centuries later he could easily have appeared as the good dull servant in a Dickens novel. In the last paragraph of *The Old Arcadia* he becomes the object of one final piece of irony, as a sequel to the romance is announced that will include the "shepherdish loves" of that very Vergilian-sounding Menalcas and Kalodoulus's daughter. Intensely suspicious of the unusual, of the "unusedness" of things, possessing a thoroughly conventional and obviously limited perspective on the world, Kalodoulus would not have been pleased by the affair.

Our response to this servant's-eye view of Arcadia measures the distance that we have traveled from the outset of the romance. Kalodoulus has presumably never been to Arcadia, and even if he had, his conviction that it is a morally dangerous place is precisely what can be expected from an ethically orthodox intellect, through whose sensibilities have passed whole heaps of clichés about the pastoral life. It is even possible that we more sophisticated readers began the romance with similar suspicions about or maybe hankerings for the dangers of Arcadia: for its amorous dalliance, relaxation, and relief. What is certain is that all of us come to the work with a set of expectations about the nature of pastoral, expectations that are deliberately and skillfully manipulated by Sidney to provide us with what is simultaneously an education in reading and a lesson in evaluating modes of life.

Pastoralism itself is on trial here, but in which of its versions? Our understanding of the expressive possibilities of the genre expands throughout *The Old Arcadia* as we are made to confront in the prose and in the eclogues various styles of the idle life. Geron, Dicus, Lalus, and the rest of the native shepherds (the shepherds who live in Arcadia) represent a version of pastoral quite different in its values, its methods of expression, and its philosophical and literary traditions from that which is represented either by the stranger shepherds (Philisides, Strephon, and Klaius), or by the princes. If Musidorus, Strephon, and Lalus all devote themselves to love, to contemplation, and to poetry (that particular complex of activities that comprise what can be called the idle life), they envision their mistresses, think about the natural world, and compose their songs in radically different ways. Sidney is far less concerned in *The Old Arcadia* with the conflict between action and contemplation, the heroic and the pastoral worlds, than he is with evaluating distinct versions of the idle life as competing models for living justly.

We smile at Kalodoulus's fears about his master's fate in Arcadia because in large part they represent such an inadequate recognition of the range of experiences that Musidorus confronts. Furthermore, our sympathy for the idle life, at least in some of its versions, is substantially greater precisely because of our recognition of that wider range. The marriage of Lalus and Kala, the yearning of Strephon and Klaius for Urania, even Pyrocles' adoration of Philoclea are experiences that reverberate with positive meanings scarcely dreamed of in Kalodoulus's less capacious, less resonant world. Exactly how much sympathy Sidney encourages us to have for these various versions of the idle life, exactly how we are to evaluate them, is one of the major critical problems posed by the prose books and the eclogues of *The Old Arcadia*. It should come as no surprise that a work that culminates in a trial should have as one large goal in that process of evaluation instructing the reader in how to make moral judgments; nor should we forget that whatever conclusions Sidney finally arrives at (if there are any final conclusions) are discoverable only by the most careful attention to the surface of the work, to its well-orchestrated ironies and its well-plotted narrative strategies. Our moral judgments are conditioned by our aesthetic responses.

It is necessary to return to Kalodoulus for a moment, since the most important function of this narrative interruption has yet to be mentioned. Placed between the princes' sentencing and Euarchus's astonishing refusal to revoke the order of execution even for his son and his nephew, the incident stands, with its high comic tone, as a kind of pastoral oasis in a desert of tragic gloom. There can be little doubt that Kalodoulus's interruptions and the subsequent digression before reporting his news are intended to tempt us into believing that a good, old-fashioned, romance ending is in store for the princes. The change in tone seems to guarantee such a conclusion. Our hopes are raised, immediately frustrated, and then, a few pages later, ultimately fulfilled as Basilius awakes from his deathlike sleep. What are we to make of this pattern? Undoubtedly, Sidney is generating suspense by these devices, but he is doing something more than that. This interruption, derived straight from the Greek Romance tradition, complete with a heavy-handed direct address to the reader ("But first you will be content . . .") is an obvious artistic ploy, a familiar gimmick from the romance writer's bag of tricks, and Sidney, I shall argue, expects us to recognize it as such.

Among Sidney's critics the ending of the romance has almost always been a source not only of dispute but of positive embarrassment. Rowe is convinced that it is ethically confusing; Lanham calls it "a contrived solution, applied to a problem that in life has no end and no painless solution"; Dipple believes that the conclusion is a mere sop to the readers, that the author simply wanted the work to end happily; and despite Dana's recent heroic efforts to prove otherwise, the conclusion has always seemed to its readers, no matter what interpretation they have given to it, an awkward narrative device. Its "awkwardness," it can be shown, is both indisputable and intentional.[3]

The events that Sidney permits Kerxenus to attribute, on the one hand, to the "good hap" provided by the gods, he encourages his readers, on the other, to perceive as the deliberate and open manipulations of an artist. What this peculiar juxtaposition of art and providence reveals about the meaning of Sidney's *Old Arcadia*, and how that juxtaposition contributes to our understanding of the meaning of justice, is a major critical issue that this study will address. Sidney's interest in problems of poetry, in how critical intelligence can serve to create moral intelligence, is as evident here as it is in his *Apology*.

Kerxenus's reference to the gods takes us one step closer to the subjects that lie at the heart of *The Old Arcadia*. Throughout the romance, Sidney asks that we refer the meaning of events to the tantalizingly ambiguous words of the oracle at its outset. The very fact that there is an oracle seems to guarantee that there will be a pattern to the events, although that pattern emerges only piecemeal and in slow order. At first we watch the characters involve themselves in what appears both to them and to us as the shifting intrigues of a mutable world. Sidney is especially concerned in *The Old Arcadia* that we learn how to measure the appropriateness of various styles of life as responses to an inconstant world.[4] One reason why Kalodoulus's interruption is of interest is that it serves as a bridge between two incidents designed to encourage exactly this kind of measurement. We admire the princes' "excellent courage" in the face of adversity as they exchange farewells, and we are astonished by Euarchus's integrity and quiet of mind as he learns of his prisoners' identities. In the final moments of *The Old Arcadia*, mutability's sway over the romance world appears particularly strong since our sense of justice comes so close to being outraged by the events of the trial. At first the dilemma posed by the dramatics of these proceedings seems to deny the possibility of a just resolution and, by implication, the possibility of any justice in the cosmos: how can princes of such apparent virtue and courage be executed by a king of such obvious integrity? Neither our admiration for the princes' response to adversity, nor our astonishment at Euarchus's refusal to pardon them is sufficient to resolve such a large and intricate question. Even as we concern ourselves with how characters respond to misfortune, Sidney forces us to deepen that concern by raising moral and metaphysical issues that complicate our experience of the text. The responses of admiration and wonder to old-fashioned romance are superseded by a tough-minded intellectual questioning that forces us to confront what for Sidney are the ultimate questions: what is justice? how does a man live justly? These are ultimate questions because by resolving them we discover in the face of inevitable misfortune how to achieve contentment and quiet of mind.[5] Only by means of a peculiarly Sidneian alliance of poetry and providence, as Basilius rises from the dead, does *The Old Arcadia* at last both confirm and fulfill our need for justice.

Sidney did not just happen upon his central theme. Justice is a major topic of pastoral literature from the genre's beginnings, and it makes sense that it should be so. Giving concrete expression to abstract virtues is one of the pastoralist's distinguishing skills: innocence is imaged in the features of a shepherdess, generosity in the exchange of presents at a shearing feast. In fact, it would be difficult to provide a concrete illustration of any state of pristine virtue without recourse to pastoral imagery. Even Socrates, the archetypal urbanite, forms his first image of the just society on the model of a simple pastoral community. Long before the Renaissance, the classical tradition had made the pastoral oasis and the golden age available as potential symbols of justice and contentment, of an essential rightness of things removed from the reader's situation in space and in time.

Justice is the central deity in the mythology of the golden age.[6] While she walked "proudly and joyfully in the midst of the people," man enjoyed peace and complete harmony with the natural world—or so the story goes.

> nondum vesanos rabies nudaverat ensis
> nec consanguineis fuerat discordia nota,
> ignotique maris cursus, privataque tellus
> grata satis, neque per dubios avidissima ventos
> spes procul amotas fabricata nave petebat
> divitias, fructusque dabat placata colono
> sponte sua tellus nec parvi terminus agri
> praestabat dominis, sine eo tutissima, rura.[7]

(Men were not yet so savage as to bare their swords in rage against each other; discord among blood relations was unknown; no one sailed the seas, men's own lands being satisfaction enough. Greed for wealth from far away did not cause them to build ships and entrust them to the hazards of the winds. The peaceful lands bore fruit unaided for those who dwelt in them. There were no boundary stones marking off their owners' small domains, for they were quite safe without them.)

These lines are taken from Aratus's *Phaenomena,* but the ideas belong to classical culture as a whole. The notion that the idyllic conditions of the golden age were not only accompanied but actually sustained by the justice of those who enjoyed them persists as a literary commonplace from Hesiod to Ovid. "Neither famine nor disaster ever haunt men who do true justice," Hesiod writes in *Works and Days,* "but lightheartedly they tend the fields which are all their care."[8] So conceived, Justice serves as a kind of shepherdess of the idyllic. In consequence it is not surprising that the beginning of our own period, the iron age, with its complete annihilation of "modesty and truth and faith," should be brought into being by the departure of Justice.[9] This is the hardest of time's metamorphoses. Ovid writes:

> victa iacet pietas, et virgo caede madentis
> ultima caelestum terras Astraea reliquit.[10]

(Piety lay vanquished, and the maiden Astraea, last of the immortals, abandoned the blood-soaked earth.)

The most important fact about the golden age for Hesiod and Aratus, indeed for every classical author before Vergil, is that it was over. Finished. In poem after poem, the justice of an irretrievable age of idyllicism becomes a device for excoriating the evils of contemporary society and for lending moral force to civilized man's nostalgia for lost happiness. In Vergil's hands, however, the golden age is transformed into something new and strange, a transformation of some consequence for the future of pastoral literature and of some help for understanding Sidney's early career. For in *The Lady of May*, *The Old Arcadia*, and the *Apology for Poetry*, Sidney's major moral and aesthetic concerns are shaped by a special understanding of the value of justice to remedy personal and public misfortunes.[11]

Vergil is no less conscious than Ovid of the realities of life in the modern iron age: "gaudent perfusi sanguine fratrum" ("Gleefully they steep themselves in their brothers' blood").[12] He, too, can catalogue its horrors. Vergil is also no less insistent than other writers in the tradition about Justice's role as the reigning deity of the golden age: she is the maiden hailed at the outset of Eclogue 4, and the consequences of her departure from earth are starkly detailed in Georgic 2. What marks his use of the myth as revolutionary is his transformation of the golden age from an unreachable past into a realizable future. Justice is invoked at the beginning of Eclogue 4 not as a deity whose age has passed, but as a returning goddess who will initiate a glorious age of peace and pastoral fecundity: "aspice venturo laetentur ut omnia saeclo!" ("Behold, how all things exult in the age that is at hand").[13] From the vantage of Sidney's early career and *The Old Arcadia* in particular, what is significant about Vergil's use of the myth is that he makes the golden age available as a poetic image to be realized in the future and that he represents its peace and prosperity—achieved under the reign of Justice—as an ultimate remedy for the misfortunes of life in the iron age: the earth will be released from its "perpetua . . . formidine" ("continual dread").[14]

Vergil's fourth eclogue can be interpreted, then, as an unusual and brilliant variation upon a more comprehensive and more frequently repeated theme of pastoral literature: that the rural life offers a defense against adversity or a remedy for its worst effects. The remedy that Vergil envisions as an event to be achieved in time is more commonly represented from the classical period to the Renaissance as a good to be discovered in a different place: "Are not these woods/More free from peril than the envious court?", asks the banished Duke Senior. By the sixteenth century, the claim that the pastoral life offers a defense against adversity or a remedy for its ills had been repeated so often in so many different varieties of pastoral as to achieve the status of a literary topos. The pastoral world promised contentment. In book 6, canto 9 of *The Faerie Queene*, no sooner has the courteous Calidore accepted the hospitality of old Meliboe than he begins to expostulate on his host's happy condition:

> . . . so free and fortunate
> From all the tempests of these worldly seas,
> Which tosse the rest in daungerous disease.[15]

The fact that the knight, not the shepherd, makes this speech, Spenser humorously reminds us, indicates the literary origin of these ideas. Calidore also happens to be dead wrong. As the invasion of the brigands illustrates, there is no protection against fortune, no therapy for its ill-effects in the world of Spenser's book 6. Some seventeen years earlier, in the course of examining the possibilities of justice and contentment in a mutable world, Sidney subjected the same literary topos to an extensive and penetrating critique. If his readers were well acquainted with the traditional claims of pastoral, they could hardly have anticipated such a thoroughgoing examination. Of course, keeping in mind Vergil's myth of the golden age might have helped them to understand how Sidney had come to link the themes of justice and contentment in representing the pastoral retreat as a place to find relief from misfortune.

In *The Old Arcadia* and the *Apology*, Sidney interests his readers in making use of moral and aesthetic tools for relieving the misfortunes of life in the iron age. His interest in relief, like his interest in justice, is entirely traditional. For the claim that the country life is a defense against adversity or a relief from it is made by writers of almost every kind of pastoral. How a pastoralist accounts for these special virtues (if he accounts for them at all) reveals a great deal about his values and about his place within the tradition, whether he is ancient or modern, native or Continental, bucolic, georgic, Horatian, or Christian. Each of these different kinds of poetry presents a different explanation for the happiness of the country dweller. A few examples will clarify the point. In the bucolic tradition, for instance, the shepherd receives good fortune—if he is fortunate—because of his poetic abilities and because of the harmony that those abilities establish between himself and the outside world.[16] Vergil addresses Tityrus in the first eclogue as "fortunate senex"; his delightful idleness is the gift of a "god," a gift that he merits, we are led to assume, because of his skills as a singer. In the georgic tradition, on the other hand, happy husbandmen ("fortunatos . . . agricolas") enjoy the good fortune of nature's bounty not because they sing, but because they labor for pious rewards.[17] As Vergil tells us, free from care, free from the obligation to pity other men's sufferings or to envy their wealth, the farmers relax in sound sleep beneath fruit-filled trees.[18] Horace explains the happiness of the country dweller in yet another way. In his version of the retired life, good fortune is a direct result of a specific kind of mental activity on the part of a specific kind of person: the country-house owner at leisure to contemplate his estates. "A man who prizes golden moderation" remains "safely clear" of filthy palaces: the outward modesty of the retired man's life-style reflects his more important inward commitment to the golden mean.[19] Horace's retired man is happy—far happier than we are—because he does not think the way that we do.[20] Or to give one last example, in Christian pastoral man is fortunate not because he leads an idle life, not because he labors, not even because he is able to achieve a quiet mind (though he may do any or all of these things in Christianized versions of bucolic, georgic, or Horatian poetry); he is fortunate, rather, because he stands in a harmonious relationship with God. His harmonious relationship with nature is simultaneously a symbol for and a benefit derived from that other more sacred relationship. It is such an appropriate symbol because of biblical stories like that of Cain and Abel, which lend special dignity to the shepherd's life and because of the New Testament's emphasis on Christ as the shepherd of the human flock. In Sidney's version of Psalm 1, after describing the blessed man as a "freshly planted tree" in a paradisal setting, he assures us:

> So all things whereto that man doth bend
> Shall prosper still, with well succeeding end.[21]

Song, labor, virtuous moderation, and Christian reverence—these are the major tools that the pastoral tradition from Vergil to Mantuan offered the Elizabethan writer for achieving contentment and good fortune.[22] But there is a more important literary tradition for the idea that the country life offers a defense against misfortune or a relief from its worst effects—more important, that is, for an understanding of *The Old Arcadia*. For this is an idea that plays a central role in Renaissance pastoral romances.

Sannazaro and his followers are the true inheritors of the classical bucolic tradition. It was undoubtedly in this light that the Italian author of the *Arcadia* saw himself, as his address to his *sampogna* at the end of the volume makes clear. He writes with the Petrarchan bravado of a great restorer:

> Io essere in questo secolo stata prima a risvegliare le adormentate selve, et a mostrare a' pastori di cantare le già dimenticate canzoni.[23]

> (you have been the first in this age to reawaken the slumbering woods, and to show the shepherds how to sing the songs that they had forgotten.)

As the inheritor of Vergil's mantle, Sannazaro concludes his work very much as one would expect him to do, by indicating the harmonious relationship with fortune enjoyed by the idle man.

> Onde per cosa vera et indubitata tener ti puoi, che chi più di nascoso e più lontano da la moltitudine vive, miglior vive; e colui tra' mortali si può con più verità chiamar beato, che senza invidia de le altrui grandezze, con modesto animo de la sua fortuna si contenta.[24]

> (Wherefore you may hold it as matter true and undoubted, that he who lives the more hidden, and the more removed from the multitude, lives better. And that man may with most truth be called blessed among mortal men who, without envy of the grandeurs of others, in modest spirit contents him with his fortune.)

It is Sannazaro who establishes contentment as the major theme of the Renaissance pastoral romance: how one achieves contentment in the face of life's inevitable misfortunes is a main source of interest not only in his *Arcadia*, but in the pastoral worlds of Montemayor, Gil Polo, and Sidney.

Sannazaro's *Arcadia* is a home for disappointed lovers. Some of them are native shepherds; most are exiled gentlemen fashioned on the model of Vergil's Gallus. What they all have in common is the desire to alleviate their amorous misfortunes, the wish to achieve contentment. This desire is given its most startling illustration in the eighth prose section. Here Carino attempts to console Sincero, Sannazaro's grieving protagonist, by telling him the story of his own near-tragic love adventures. He describes how his love-despair had driven him to the point of hurling himself from a cliff when the gods intervened to soften his lady's heart, thereby saving his life. The incident leads him to reflect upon the astonishing power of the gods, who bring peace when they most seem to threaten danger. If Sincero never sees his lady again, as Carino promised he would, he does return to his beloved homeland, and he returns after having received a substantial measure of comfort for his sorrows.

Sannazaro's Arcadia, it would be fair to point out, is much less a shield against fortune's blows than a place gifted with special capacities for the consolation of wounds already received. After all, Carino tells his story only as a way of consoling the lovesick Sincero. Sannazaro's major concern, like the concern of the pastoralists who follow him, including Sidney, is with relief rather than protection. This is one of his major innovations in the tradition, though as we shall see in part II, the consolation for misfortune that Sincero and the other shepherds attain in the *Arcadia* is derived, as it is in the classical bucolic, from special qualities inherent in the idle life itself, particularly from the power of song.[25]

In Montemayor's *Diana* and Gil Polo's *Diana Enamorada*, Spanish pastoral romances inspired by Sannazaro's, the fortune theme is extended and intensified, as is the emphasis upon relief and contentment. As Joseph Jones has indicated, the very first line of the *Diana*, with its reference to "Amor, la fortuna, el tiempo," defines the "awesome principles which preside over the lover's existence."[26] Gil Polo follows suit in giving fortune a central place in his fictional world. In both works, unrequited love is the greatest of all misfortunes, and in both, the climactic incident occurs when a group of unhappy lovers is brought into the pastoral center and restored to contentment by Felicia.[27] Just as directly as Sannazaro, Montemayor stresses the therapeutic value of the pastoral experience, the capacity of the idle life to provide consolations for misfortunes. Felicia's palace is a hospital, a Renaissance "Green Acres" for the amatorily ill. They journey there to find the contentment promised by her name.

The plot of Gil Polo's romance seems to suggest a similar point of view, but the final speech delivered by a moralizing Felicia indicates the divide separating his continuation from the works of his predecessors—a divide that prepares for Sidney's innovations in the tradition because of its direct moral criticism of earlier pastoral romances.[28] Felicia chides a portion of the assembled newlyweds for the anguish that they have brought upon themselves by falling into Cupid's bondage, and she explicitly forbids them (with a nod in the reader's direction) from risking such misfortunes in the future. This is not to suggest that Gil Polo repudiates his pastoral heroes or their idealized concepts of love—far from it. Felicia is careful to define the nature of "verdadero amor" as a refined and intellectual passion above suffering and sensuality, which leads men to delight in virtue and "cosas celestiales."²⁹ What she suggests, as a precedent for Sidney's handling of the topic, is that only the virtuous are able to find contentment; the amoral aestheticism of the Italianate tradition, which represents the satisfaction of amorous desires as a self-evident good, gives way to an austere, if rather unsophisticated brand of moral criticism that makes absolute but unclearly defined distinctions between varieties of lovers. Toward the end of her speech, Felicia asks the newlyweds to consider whether they have been slaves to Cupid or honest lovers. The latter, she says, should believe themselves fortunate and persevere ("tengase per dichoso, y procure perseverancia!"). Those in the former group (and the reader is left to decide which ones they are) are urged to reform. Intensely suspicious of the dangers of the idle life, Gil Polo forces the reader into a recognition of them. Nothing more than luck and romance traditions are responsible for rescuing those characters who have been Cupid's slaves from an anguished and morally dubious existence. If Gil Polo points the way toward a reconciliation of virtue and contentment, he fails to provide the kind of assured foundation for a happy life that Sidney sets out to achieve in *The Old Arcadia*—a foundation that Sidney discovers in a special understanding of justice and in a radically original program for poetry.

Sidney stands at the beginning of one tradition and at the end of another. His interest in the related ideas that the country life provides a defense against misfortune and a relief from its worst effects is scarcely idiosyncratic. The theme is one of central importance in the development of pastoral literature, and its presence here marks *The Old Arcadia* as deeply traditional. At one extreme, pastoral offered the example of the fortunate shepherd whose contentment is explained by the essentially amoral activities of an idle life—particularly by his activities as a singer; at the other end of the sheepcote stand the farmer, gentleman-landlord, and Christian swain, whose good fortunes are attributable to highly moral physical and intellectual labors or to pious exercises of the soul. In *The Old Arcadia* Sidney maintains his independence from both traditions as he reevaluates the notion of pastoral contentment and the means by which it is achieved in order to sharpen our understanding of how to lead a just life in an all too mutable world.³⁰

No one who is familiar with the main facts about his career between 1578 and 1580, the years in which *The Old Arcadia* was written, will be surprised to learn that Sidney's personal circumstances made it virtually inevitable that he should become interested in the idle life as a response to misfortune.[31] When Sidney returned from his successful German embassy in 1577, he entered a period of life that, in whatever light it is placed, can only be called unfortunate. As one reliable biographer informs us, these were times of "thwarted plans and disappointed hopes."[32] Sidney had financial troubles. Late in 1577 he appears to have invested in Frobisher's futile schemes to ship gold from the Indies—a characteristically impetuous investment that added to his already large debts. The importance and security of his family were also significantly endangered during these years. The powerful branch of the family, the Dudleys, went into sharp decline. The misfortunes of his uncles, with Warwick's failing health and Leicester's disastrous marriage, contributed to Sidney's own misfortunes. No wonder the tone of his correspondence with Languet is frequently somber. His solicitous and paternal mentor often chides Sidney for carelessness in attending to his frail constitution in evident concern over the number of his illnesses, and often advises him about his fits of melancholy.

In 1578 there was nothing new about Sidney's health problems or his tendency toward melancholy; if his family troubles were increasing in an alarming fashion, there had been worse periods in its history (including executions for treason); and if his creditors were more threatening than ever, such was the burden that the frugal Elizabeth's courtiers had to bear. His misfortunes were genuine, but they might not have seemed so oppressive had it not been for the one real change in his circumstances: his inability to find gainful employment, or what Greville calls more kindly "any fit stage for eminence to act upon."[33] Whether Sidney's failure to attain an important office was due to Elizabeth's aversion to his ambitiousness and militant Protestant politics, or to his own inability to compromise, as various scholars have argued, there can be no question about its toll in mental anguish.[34]

Sidney was no ordinary intellectual. The entire course of his adult education had been shaped by the loving attentions of Hubert Languet for one purpose: to mold him into a great Protestant statesman. His mentor never tired of reminding him of his hope that "your virtue may prove the salvation of you and your country."[35] In view of the severity of his disappointment and the suffering that was caused by having his personal aspirations continuously frustrated, it is not surprising to detect in the well-known letter to Languet of 1 March 1578 evidence of the mind's impatience at the loss of orientation:

For to what purpose should our thoughts be directed to various kinds of knowledge, unless room be afforded for putting it into practice, so that public advantage may be the result, which in a corrupt age we cannot hope for?[36]

It is of considerable interest that when Sidney addresses the topic again two years later in a letter to Edward Denny, he effectively answers his own question.

But first let me rejoyse with you, that since the unnoble constitution of our tyme, doth keepe us from fitte imployments, you doe yet keepe your selfe awake, with the delight of knowledge; one of the notablest effects of that, which makes us differ from beasts.[37]

In the years between these letters Sidney had written *The Old Arcadia*. If he is still convinced that the corruptions of the times rather than personal inadequacy are responsible for his lack of employment, and Sidney never abandoned his conviction that he lived in an unjust age, his tone shows no hint of its former stridency, for he seems to have discovered a renewed sense of pleasure in knowledge that can be employed for private, if not public ends. The process of writing his pastoral may have helped him to achieve this discovery. There is a quiet of mind evident here as Sidney reveals a genuine delight in intellectual attainments, which is remote from the March letter to Languet. By 1580 Sidney's fortunes had not improved; his future was still blocked, or to use Languet's expression, "a sort of cloud" continued to darken his affairs.[38]

If Sidney's personal misfortunes are well known, his acute sense of the political dangers, the public misfortunes facing the Protestant cause in Europe, has attracted far less attention. Over the course of his correspondence with Languet between 1574 and 1580 there is a marked change of tone in their references to the political scene, as a perceptible mood of pessimism, even desperation, begins to emerge. England's situation was thought to be particularly unsafe, as an island whose history had been marred by religious violence, and whose future appeared to promise still more bloodshed. In March of 1574 Languet wrote to Sidney about his apprehensions concerning England's destiny. After reminding him of the turmoil that raged between the reigns of Henry VIII and Elizabeth, he writes: "I fear that in your country such tragedies will soon return to the stage, since there are those who are working up material for that purpose."[39]

Sidney's fears were equally strong. In 1574 he wrote to Languet that "in your letters I fancy I see a picture of the age in which we live: an age that resembles a bow too long bent; it must be unstrung, or it will break."[40] A few months later he expresses further concern over the "rough storms . . . by which all Christendom has been agitated now these many years."[41] Sidney's chief anxieties appear to have centered on his Queen. After having spent a long period of time on the Continent, acquainting himself with governmental affairs in preparation for his own career, his first thoughts upon returning to England are drawn to the delicate nature of a peace that depends upon her life:

> On the last day of May, a fair wind wafted me to this our island nest, where I found all my family well, and the Queen, though somewhat advanced in years, yet hitherto vigorous in her health, which (as it is God's will that our safety should hang on so frail a thread), is with good reason earnestly commended to the care of Almighty God in the prayers of our people. She is to us a Meleager's brand; when it perishes, farewell to all our quietness.[42]

There is nothing mechanical or conventional about these fears. Sidney is articulating some of the deepest, most widespread anxieties of his countrymen in expressing his apprehension about the "quietness" of an England without Elizabeth.

In 1576, in an engagement that cost the lives of more than eight thousand people, the Spanish sacked the city of Antwerp. In 1577 the hero of Lepanto, Don John of Austria, was placed in charge of a "vast numbers of men" in the Netherlands, thereby increasing English fears of an invasion.[43] As Languet wrote to Sidney in June of the same year, "Your people must sleep with one ear open, especially if the Spaniards obtain their peace from the Turks, as I hear from many quarters that they will."[44] These events must have seemed intensely disturbing to Sidney, particularly in view of the failure of the Leicester party to win support for a militantly Protestant foreign policy and his own inability to play more than an insignificant role in these affairs. As Sidney himself realized as early as March of 1578, his cause at home and abroad was "withering away."[45] The situation grew worse. Elizabeth was entertaining marriage proposals from the Duke of Alençon with apparent seriousness—a fact of extreme repugnance to Sidney, whose presence at the Bartholomew's Day Massacre had already taught him what Protestants could expect from powerful French Catholics. The prospects of a papist marriage meant far more than political defeat and the ruination of the cause that his entire education had been directed to advance; a French marriage meant exile. The full peril of the situation is made evident in Languet's letter from Antwerp of 30 January 1580:

> Remember what Queen Mary, after King Edward's death, was enabled to effect, though at the first she had very few adherents, and your countrymen were then much more practised in war than they are now. The party and influence of Anjou is on the increase here, and if you should annoy him by your opposition in England, you will scarcely find a reception here, much less in France. . . . Germany would be your only refuge if you were compelled to leave your country.[46]

The misfortunes of the Protestant cause in Europe were fast threatening to become Sidney's personal misfortunes. In the years between 1578 and 1580 the public sphere weighed heavily upon what I have already described as an overburdened private life.

In 1578 Sir Henry Sidney was recalled from his post as the Lord Deputy of Ireland. This was a damaging setback for his family. Philip wrote to him in April of the same year with advice on how he might best manage his affairs in a letter that lies at the crossroads of his own public and private misfortunes. The nature of his advice is telling: Sidney counsels his father that it is "most noble to have allweyes one mynde and one constancy," urging him to keep "still yowr minde in one state of vertuouse quietnes."[47] *Quietnes* is an especially evocative word for Sidney, since it serves both as a standard of political harmony (it is England's quietness that Elizabeth's death will destroy) and as a measure of personal virtue (a mental condition to be achieved in the face of adversity): the term offers a ready vehicle for relating the private and public spheres of life.

Moreover, constancy and quietness are precisely the kind of principles that Languet had labored to instill in his charge. As early as 1574 we find him writing to Sidney on the effort to achieve virtue that: "that effort has no other goal than to live one's life honourably to the end. You must therefore press on towards your destiny and, be it happy or sad, temper it with virtue."[48] Once again, in 1577, Languet seized upon the opportunity to turn Sidney's headstrong involvement in Frobisher's voyages into a moral exemplum illustrating the virtues of the quiet mind and constancy:

> Whenever, therefore, any feeling new to yourself shall agitate your mind, do not hastily indulge it, even if the object to which it leads you seems to be a good one; but before you give it entrance, reflect carefully what it is that tempts you.[49]

The importance that his pupil attached to these ideas is adequately illustrated by a letter in which Sidney replies to one of Languet's frequent reproaches that he had been neglecting their friendship:

> One may condemn a friend for indolence, even without hearing his defence, or for carelessness, but to cast doubt on his constancy—that is, if there is any good in him at all—what is this but to announce that you wish to terminate our sacred friendship?[50]

Sidney's correspondence leaves no doubt about his high-mindedness: constancy and virtuous quietness are the responses to misfortune that Sidney had been taught to reverence as ideals. They are principles that guide his personal and political life, and they recur as important standards in *The Old Arcadia*.

In August of 1577 Sidney made the first of his increasingly frequent visits to his sister at her country estate at Wilton. By 1579 he had entered upon a sort of retirement there. No one cause can be singled out for Sidney's decision to retreat to the Countess's pastoral gardens. His letter to Elizabeth advising against the Alençon marriage played some role in his decision, but it is highly doubtful that Sidney was in any sense banished from court as a result of this or any other supposed indiscretion. His rustication can be explained only as a response to the whole complex of public and private misfortunes to which he had been subjected, and as a result of genuinely appealing aspects of life at Wilton. Sidney's retirement was in some measure the product of constraining circumstances—the inability to find gainful employment in particular—and in part the act of a man who could derive real pleasure from a life of idleness. Consider again his letter to Edward Denny. At its outset Sidney complains of his lack of employment, chafing against "the unnoble constitution of our tyme." By the closing lines, any thoughts of personal sorrows are absent as he urges his friend to:

> remember with your good voyce, to singe my songes for they will one well become an other. My Lord of Pembrook, my sister, and your charge thanke you with many thankes, and your cakes are reserved against all the parrish come to dinner.[51]

Songs, cakes, and parish dinners are pleasures to which Sidney obviously looks forward. There is no need to see the final sentence ("At Wilton This Witsondai. 1580.") to perceive the holiday spirit of the closing lines.

Cakes and dinners are pleasant, but songs belong to an entirely different order of experience, one whose pleasures Sidney discovered in his idle life at Wilton. For it was during this period that he became a poet, adopting what he calls so accurately in the *Apology* his "unelected vocation."[52] His major employment from 1578 to 1580 was *The Old Arcadia*. Sidney's writings are a response to the conditions of his life. On this point there can be no room for doubt. But what kind of response are they? For older scholars like Denkinger and Poirier, the issue could be resolved all too easily: the *Arcadia* is escapist pastoral, an "asylum . . . where he could forget dangerous religious struggles in England."[53] This heavily romanticized reading proved anathema to critics who had been reared on Greville's portrait of a moral and heroic Sidney. In its place there developed the second, more defensible position that *The Old Arcadia* is an extended argument in favor of heroic activity, a preparation for chivalric acts to come. A. C. Hamilton is the best and most recent exponent of this, the orthodox viewpoint on Sidney: "what began as a light-hearted pastoral romance developed in the two final books into a serious heroic poem."[54] While the proponents of this position stress the element of constraint in Sidney's rustication, Neil Rudenstine draws attention to its pleasures. In fact, he argues, *The Old Arcadia* "reveals itself . . . as a fictional extension of Sidney's letters in defense of relaxation, reflection, and a life of dignified ease."[55]

An escapist fiction, a preparation for heroic activity, a defense of relaxation: none of these critical descriptions does justice either to Sidney's complex response to the pleasures and constraints of his idle life or to the artistic boldness of his pastoral strategy. There is no need to commit ourselves to the position that Sidney felt entirely pleased or constrained by his idle life. *The Old Arcadia* is neither an argument for ease nor a defense of heroism. Sidney's pastoral is a radically original experiment in fiction that belongs to a different realm of discourse from that assumed by his critics. It cannot be understood as the *expression* of one or another set of related themes: in its most important sense it is neither an argument nor a defense. Instead, as I shall argue, *The Old Arcadia* is itself a special kind of poetic gesture. It lends expression to several important themes, but its main purpose is to procure special concrete benefits, personal and political, for its author and his readers: Sidney's pastoral is designed to bring relief from misfortune, to secure the contentment that only justice can supply. By drawing upon traditional materials of the pastoral genre and by reshaping them according to specific psychological principles derived from authorities as different as Plutarch and Languet, Sidney labors to create a "golden world" within—for himself and for his audience.

It is a golden world because his art acts to produce an inward state of virtuous contentment secure from the ravages of misfortune in the iron age. Some of these ravages are political and *The Old Arcadia* contains sharply focused political advice for their relief as well. Seen in a slightly different light, with the understanding that *The Old Arcadia* is a Renaissance fiction for Christian men in a Christian world, the action of his golden world assumes another kind of significance. By restoring man to a condition of virtuous pleasure, Sidney's pastoral seeks to remedy the secular consequences of a religious Fall, as damaging to himself as to his readers: the Adamic sin that turned man into a battleground between the erected wit and the infected will. *The Old Arcadia* is not a work about the wit and the will. It is "music" created to establish "jump concord" between them, as the poetic realization of a principle that Philisides expounds to his sheep:

> The song I sang old Languet had me taught,
> Languet, the shepherd best swift Ister knew,
> For clerkly rede, and hating what is naught,
> For faithful heart, clean hands, and mouth as true.
> With his sweet skill my skill-less youth he drew
>   To have a feeling taste of him that sits
>   Beyond the heav'n, far more beyond our wits.
>
> He said the music best thilke powers pleased
> Was jump concord between our wit and will,
> Where highest notes to godliness are raised,
> And lowest sink not down to jot of ill.
>
> (255, 15–25)

This is profoundly personal poetry, which aims to accomplish profound public goals. The Fall is universal, as is its remedy; the solution to one man's problems necessarily coincides with the solution to all men's.

What *The Old Arcadia* does is more important than what it *says*. If the romance poses questions about the competing demands of reason and passion, justice and contentment, it does so within a fictional structure designed not merely to answer but also to resolve them: the work tells us what it means to be reasonable and just, but its major business is in making us the reasonable and just men it describes.[56] This is not a thesis that I intend to support at once; it will be the labor of my entire book to demonstrate its validity, as I define its key terms, *justice* and *contentment*. I give the outlines of my argument here in order to prepare the reader for what lies ahead.

The Old Arcadia begins with one of the most sparkling pieces of prose that Sidney ever wrote, the dedicatory letter to the Countess of Pembroke. A beautifully articulated passage of fine wit and humor, its ironies, however well-expressed, have occasionally been lost upon the dull-minded. Kenneth Myrick is right to point to the special ambience of this letter as the product of Sidney's carefully cultivated *sprezzatura*.[57] If we need to recognize that the deprecatory references to his romance are not to be taken at face value, we should also not ignore the real clues that the letter affords concerning Sidney's artistic designs and the relevance of those designs to his personal life.

After assuring his sister that the work is nothing but a "trifle, and that triflingly handled," Sidney concludes the first portion of his dedicatory letter by writing:

> In sum, a young head not so well stayed as I would it were (and shall be when God will) having many many fancies begotten in it, if it had not been in some way delivered, would have grown a monster, and more sorry might I be that they came in than that they gat out. (3)

Sidney's lightness of touch is unmistakable. His manner of attributing a therapeutic function to his writings, suggesting that they serve as purgatives for his troubled mind, is clearly designed to amuse the Countess. No doubt his design succeeded. But it succeeded in large part because of the cultural context to which Sidney makes reference.

In the 1560s an unfortunate courtier who found himself out of favor with his monarch, or at any rate discovered himself unable to procure favor, would have had at least one conventionally approved course of behavior to follow: he could retire to a thick-walled castle and console himself by dieting upon moral philosophy or by partaking of a snack or two from the *Mirror for Magistrates*. If he were literarily inclined, he might even compose a tract in imitation of Seneca or verses in poulter's measure warning others against the dangers of ambition and inveighing against the evils of court life. By the late 1570s this kind of behavior was already unfashionably passé. As the English were rather late on the whole in discovering, the garden had long ago replaced the castle as the appropriate place to which the courtier could escape from worldly woes; and what is more significant, the pastoral (at least in the most cultured circles) had replaced the moral treatise and the lumbering reflective lyric as the appropriate aesthetic vehicle in which the gentleman could lament his misfortunes.

Of all of the twentieth-century theories of pastoral, the Renaissance man of letters would have been least surprised by the Freudian views of Renato Poggioli, a critic who argues that the bucolic is "an attempt to charm away the cares of the world through the sympathetic magic of a rustic disguise."[58] There is no need to accept the ideological basis of the remark in order to appreciate its applicability to Renaissance pastoral. Enough attention has already been given in this chapter to the topos representing the idle life as a defense against misfortune, to demonstrate just how central the therapeutic power of pastoral is as a theme within the tradition. What needs further emphasis here is that Tityrus, Sincero, Colin, and a host of other pastoral characters were commonly conceived during the sixteenth century as personae employed by Vergil, Sannazaro, and Spenser, at least in part for the purpose of giving vent to their personal sorrows. In short, not only would Sidney have been aware of the remedial value of the country life as a literary theme, but he would also have known that the act of writing a pastoral was itself often considered to be therapeutic.

In Abraham Fleming's Elizabethan translation of Vergil's *Eclogues*, the "general argument of the whole Booke" is summarized in this customarily biographical manner:

> By Shepheards, and by Shepheards homely songs,
> (contained in the summe of Virgils verse:)
> What harmes, what hurts, what injuries and wrongs
> The Poet had, lo, heer he dooth rehearse.[59]

The format of the usual sixteenth-century edition of Vergil, whether in Latin or English translation, made it impossible for the reader of the *Eclogues* to divorce the poems from the poet's biography. As Fleming assures us: "the poet in all his poetrie hath followed the order of his owne nature and life."[60] During the Renaissance the *Eclogues* were seldom read without some form of accompanying critical commentary (in England, never), and this fact had a decisive influence upon how they were interpreted. Whether one turns to Suetonian biographies of the poet (sometimes included at the front of the texts), to commentaries inspired by Servius (often interspersed among the poems themselves), or to arguments prefacing individual eclogues (essential components of most editions), the emphasis remains the same: the principal subject of Vergil's *Eclogues* is Vergil himself. To cite only a few examples from Fleming's Elizabethan translation: in the second eclogue Corydon's impassioned complaint for Alexis is understood as Vergil's love-plea to "*Alexander* the Lad of *Pollio*, whome he gave to *Coridon* afterward for a gyft"; Eclogue 10, we are told, is occasioned by Cornelius Gallus's unreciprocated love for a harlot named Cytheris ("*Virgil* therefore in this Ecloge comforteth him"); Eclogues 7 and 8 are allegorized as veiled requests to Augustus for personal favors.[61] This kind of interpretation is the rule, not the exception.

Personal motives determine not only the character of individual poems, Renaissance commentators insist, but the main purpose of the Eclogues as a whole. Fleming asserts that the poet's "cause of writing" was to get "peaceable possession of his lands and goods."[62] His is the standard explanation, deriving ultimately from a second-century *Life of Virgil* by Suetonius, where the story of the poet's loss and subsequent recovery of his Mantuan farm is given as his chief reason for writing the *Eclogues*. By writing, Suetonius explains, Vergil might "currie the Emperors favour."[63] Other explanations are sometimes provided for Vergil's decision to write the *Eclogues*, but whatever motive is assigned, whether it is a desire to imitate Theocritus or to give expression to particular moral or mystical ideas, the notion that these poems were written primarily to remedy genuine personal misfortunes enjoyed a long and important history.

Accounting for the *Eclogues* as an attempt to curry favor with the Emperor—to restate the position in its baldest form—is exactly the kind of reductive criticism that one comes to expect from classical and Renaissance commentaries on Vergil. But more sophisticated variations on this theme were possible and were sometimes explored. When Fleming summarizes the "general argument" of the work, Vergil's motives for rehearsing his "wronges" go unmentioned not because they are obscure, but because their consolatory character is so well known; by writing, he implies, the poet gains emotional relief. As we shall see, Sannazaro seizes effectively upon the theme of consolation in characterizing the entire function of Vergilian and Theocritean pastoral. In the Italian *Arcadia*, Vergil appears not as a Roman citizen attempting to achieve actual remedies for actual misfortunes—his traditional position in the commentaries—but as one pastoral poet among many striving to achieve relief from the mental anxieties of life in the iron age.

The therapeutic intent of the genre is also made apparent in E.K.'s prefatory epistle to the *Shepheardes Calendar*, that most perceptive of all Renaissance critiques of pastoral. Immediately after identifying Colin with Spenser, E. K. informs us:

Now, as touching the generall dryft and purpose of his Aeglogues, I mind not to say much, him selfe labouring to conceale it. Onely this appeareth, that his unstayed yougth had long wandred in the common labyrinth of Love; in which time, to mitigate and allay the heate of his passion, or els to warne (as he sayth) the young shepheards, sc. his equalls and companions, of his unfortunate folly, he complied these xii Aeglogues.[64]

The parenthesis, "as he sayth," makes E. K.'s private opinion clear: in this case, he prefers the plaintive to the moral reading. Whether or not Spenser was actually unfortunate in love is not at issue; the important point is that E. K. believes that his fledgling pastoralist must be said to have been so, just as it must be hinted that he is now poetically consoling himself for the ordeal, in order for Spenser to appear to be assuming a conventionally approved place on the tree of pastoral history. The same belief in the therapeutic value of pastoral poetry lies behind Edward Dyer's gloss on his version of Theocritus's famous Idyll 11:

Theocritus wrote this Idillion to Nicias a learned Physition, wherein he sheweth . . . that ther is no medecine so soveraigne against love, as is Poetry.[65]

Polyphemus, no doubt, would have agreed.

Thus the Countess of Pembroke would have been amused by Sidney's reference to his mental monsters because her brother is cleverly poking fun not only at himself, but at the kinds of projects in which cultured Italians and Spaniards had been engaged, with good classical precedents, for nearly a century. What this line of argument is intended to demonstrate is that Sidney's personal circumstances were remarkably akin to the conventional literary pattern that has been described, and that he recognized them as such. Out of favor with the Queen, oppressed by misfortune, and immersed in the pastorally sanctioned life of idleness, rather than making the expected defense of retirement as Rudenstine suggests, or the heroically defiant argument for the active life as Hamilton suggests, what Sidney does is to shepherd the traditional resources of the pastoral genre as a means of procuring a special kind of relief for himself and his readers: the attainment of justice and contentment is the major poetic action of the romance.

There is nothing strange in suggesting that Sidney should be interested in finding emotional relief. Languet was constantly urging him to shake off that "excessive melancholy of yours," and he gave him practical advice on how to go about doing so.[66] Sometimes he recommended a change of location, sometimes new friends and the avoidance of too much study. Sidney accepted much of this advice, though he maintained adamantly that "I am never less liable to moods of melancholy than while I am pitting my weak mental powers against some difficult challenge."[67] Rigorous intellectual activity, therefore, was one means that Sidney used to control his fits of melancholy. His correspondence with Languet was another. In 1574 Sidney wrote to his mentor: "But this is the true spice, or rather, the true fruit, of friendship: when the thought of a dear friend not only proves a great relief for all one's sorrows, but also forces one to let one's soul somehow relax."[68] The kind of relaxation that Sidney refers to here is the jesting that he does with Languet amidst the "fierce storms" of European politics. There is also one cure for anxiety that Sidney regretted he could not use. In 1580 we find him advising his brother Robert to "take a delight to keepe and increase your musick, you will not beleive what a want I finde of it in my melancholie times."[69] Languet's "jump concord," as we will see, is the music that Philip used to supply that "want."

The Old Arcadia is ultimately a defense of pastoral, but it is a defense of pastoral values that receive careful redefinition over the course of the romance. We should not be too surprised if the kind of contentment finally offered by *The Old Arcadia* is at odds with the amoral happiness enjoyed by those idle shepherds of the bucolic tradition. After all, Sidney wrote his romance with the awareness that Arcadia had offered more than one kind of poet relief from personal problems; his romance has the precedent of Vergil's fourth eclogue, in which pastoral contentment and ideal justice are reconciled in a new golden age. *The Old Arcadia* is, then, a deliberate gesture to obtain remedies for the misfortunes of life in the iron age. As the product of critical thinking about literary conventions that are important because they have real implications for the way men lead their lives, it is literature intended to have real effects upon its author and his readers.

In the first sentence of his dedicatory letter to the Countess, Sidney refers to his romance as "this idle work of mine." The descriptive phrase has an obvious double meaning: Sidney not only points with stylish humor to the *Arcadia* as a trifle, but marks it as the product of idle times. *Idleness* is a word that reverberates with significance throughout his career, in his fiction and nonfiction alike. Sidney usually reserves the term for contexts of the highest importance. In *The Lady of May*, Rixus sneers at the "idle Espilus," in a speech that attacks an elder shepherd's defense of the contemplative life.[70] Astrophil complains in the eighteenth sonnet about the effects of his amorous desires for Stella:

> . . .my wealth I have most idly spent.
> My youth doth waste, my knowledge brings forth toyes.[71]

In the *Apology*, Sidney reveals that he has slipped into the title of a poet "in these my not old years and idlest times. . . ."[72] As the banner term for a life devoted to love, poetry, and contemplation, the word carries complex and highly charged associations. It should not be forgotten as we read *The Old Arcadia* that Basilius, the princes, and the stranger shepherds are not the only ones who have chosen, at least temporarily, to lead an idle life. In the act of writing Sidney, too, has retired to Arcadia; and what is more important, as the reader picks up the volume, he himself has elected a kind of pastoral retreat. This is certainly what Sidney has in mind when he urges his sister: "Read it then at your idle times. . . ." Whatever judgments the poet finally renders upon the pastoral experience, favorable or not, it is clear that they must inevitably apply to ourselves and to his art, as well as to the major characters of the romance. As idle readers, we are all implicated in its verdicts.

In order to clarify the nature of Sidney's achievement as a pastoralist, I have begun by examining the broader reaches of the Arcadian horizon, that is, by defining what the romance as a whole is about, and by providing appropriate historical and biographical backgrounds for its subject. Understanding Sidney's *Old Arcadia* and its eclogues is primarily a matter of bringing the right contexts to bear upon their interpretation. Moreover, large contexts have been advanced here because the romance and its poems have large implications for them. As we shall see, the eclogues supply the conceptual ground plot for the themes of *The Old Arcadia* and the significant turning points in its poetic action. Of more immediate relevance are the insights that a study of these poems can provide into the nature and the conventions of Renaissance pastoralism. A definition of subject must be complemented by a definition of kind. We cannot hope to follow Sidney in his evaluation of various styles of life as responses to a seemingly mutable world unless we recognize the precise character of the modes of evaluation—the conventions—with which he is working.

PART II
Definition of Kind

2
Pastoralism and Generic Definition

IN Michael Drayton's *The Shepheards Garland*, a 1590s pastoral, Gorbo and Wynken lament the dead "Elphin," celebrating him as:

> A heavenly clowded in a humaine shape,
> Rare substance, in so rough a barcke Iclad,
> Of Pastorall, the lively springing sappe.[1]

Sidney's literary accomplishments are being honored here. He would have appreciated the humor of treating a pastoral writer as if he were a pastoral poem: rare substance in a rough bark. Drayton pays tribute to Sidney as the originator, the "springing sappe" of Elizabethan pastoral in a phrase that is both wonderfully evocative and nearly accurate as a historical statement—only "nearly" accurate because Drayton has failed to mention Spenser's contribution to this history. Wynken's remarks are typical of the praise that Sidney's writings received during the 1590s and throughout the first quarter of the seventeenth century. He enjoyed a reputation as a pastoralist that rivaled Spenser's—even, sometimes, among the Spenserians. In 1625, in an introductory poem to *Britannia's Pastorals*, Samuel Hardinge urged William Browne to:

> Go, go unto the oak
>   By yonder mound:
> Take Colin's pipe (there't hangs) in hand,
> Or if not that you may command,
> The whilom jolly swain's, Philisides.[2]

Colin is the preferred author, but Philisides' pipe, we are led to believe, hangs on an only slightly lower branch. The order of praise could just as easily be reversed, as it is in another contribution to the same volume. For Christopher Gewen, Sidney's accomplishments are "unparalleled."[3]

As an introduction to Sidney's use of the genre, it is helpful to account for his reputation as a pastoralist.[4] There are difficulties, however, in making that account, one of which is the lack of concern among the contemporaries who commented upon his writings about placing particular generic labels upon particular Sidneian works. As a result, it is not always easy to determine whether the praise given him as as pastoral author is due to the *Arcadia* as a whole, to the Arcadian poems and eclogues, to the few bucolic lyrics that occur in *Certain Sonnets* and *Astrophil and Stella*, to *The Lady of May*, or to all of these writings together. When Richard Barnfield hails Sidney in *The Affectionate Shepherd* as "the syren of this latter age," in a context that aligns him with Spenser and Drayton as a chief star in the pastoral heavens, it is without any reference, implied or stated, to the Sidney corpus.[5] Sometimes his contemporaries were more specific, however, and they were more specific often enough to reveal interesting facts about how a sixteenth-century reader would have valued the eclogues and about how he would have viewed the *Arcadia*'s genre.

In several instances Sidney's name has been attached to pastoral largely because of the Arcadian poems and eclogues. This appears to be the case in Francis Meres's *Palladis Tamia*. Sidney is placed among "the best for Pastorall" at the head of a list of authors including Spenser, Fraunce, and Barnfield, who were well known for their eclogues.[6] More clear cut is Puttenham's praise for Sidney in *The Arte of English Poesie* "For Eglogue and pastorall Poesie."[7] When Richard Carew wants to offer proofs of the "copiousnes" of the English language, he alludes to the Arcadian eclogues with their "Imitacione of all sortes of verses affoorded by any other Language. . . ."[8] Their variety impresses him. Elizabethan readers of the *Arcadia* in both of its versions seem to have been especially attentive to the presence and quality of these pastoral entertainments. The number of occasions on which these poems are referred to approvingly by Sidney's contemporaries is surprisingly and significantly large. Thomas Howell's poem on *The Old Arcadia* devotes a major portion of its praise to the eclogues'

> Discourse of Lovers, and such as folde sheepe,
> Whose sawes well mixed, shrowds misteries deepe.[9]

In *Pierce's Supererogation* Gabriel Harvey points to the "Pastorall exercises" as one of the most "notable" components of *The New Arcadia*.[10]

Angel Day displays a similar degree of appreciation of the role played by the eclogues in the *Arcadia* in a passage from his elegy, *Upon the Life and Death of Sir Philip Sidney:*

> Archadia now, where is thy soveraigne guide,
>   who stately Penbrooke erst did to thee knit,
> Where be the notes, his skill did earst devide,
>   In sondry meeters, wounde from finest wit.
> Which he so well in covert shapes could fit.
>   Where be the pypes, the deintiest shepheards sound:
> That ever erst, within thy woods were found.[11]

What all of this evidence suggests is that Elizabethans not only read Sidney's eclogues attentively but that they regarded them as an integral and particularly delightful part of the romance. These facts should help to explain, in turn, why the eclogues exercised such an important influence in establishing Sidney's reputation as a pastoral writer.

One other aspect of Angel Day's stanza merits attention. The lines do not specify a particular genre, but their language gives the impression that Day is inclined to treat the whole *Arcadia* as if it were a pastoral. Sidney guides us through Arcadian woods. Day is not alone in so doing. In poem after poem, bucolic imagery is consistently employed to describe the *Arcadia*.[12] The following stanza from Matthew Roydon's "An Elegie, or friends passion, for his Astrophill," is typical. On Sidney's career, Roydon writes:

> Within these woods of Arcadie,
> He cheefe delight and pleasure tooke,
> And on the mountaine Parthenie,
> Upon the chrystall liquid brooke,
>   The Muses met him ev'ry day,
>   That taught him sing, to write, and say.[13]

There can be no doubt about the bucolic nature of those Muses who first taught Sidney to sing. Roydon knows, as does every Elizabethan, that the fledgling poet begins on Vergil's example with pastoral. William Browne is even more specific: while celebrating his Elizabethan predecessors in *Britannia's Pastorals,* he offers an exclamation of praise for "Happy Arcadia!," a work he refers to as a "shepherd's lay, yet equaliz'd of none."[14] A few lines later, Browne again refers to Sidney's romance, asserting: "I sung the Past'ral next; his Muse, my mover."[15]

Particular generic labels attach themselves so infrequently to the *Arcadia*, I suspect, not because Sidney's readers were indifferent to such issues, but because the work's "kind" seemed so self-evident; only in recent years have critical disputes about its genre become important.[16] The title alone, with its deliberate evocation of the landscapes of Vergil and Sannazaro, invites us to view the work if not within, then at least against, pastoral traditions. This is an invitation that we had better accept. Serious objections have been raised against viewing the *Arcadia* as a pastoral, objections that concern the undeniably hierarchical character of its fictional world and values. How can it be explained that the events of Sidney's romance take place inside a political state, and a state so designedly unegalitarian? How can its strong ethical character be accounted for in view of the license ordinarily associated with the bucolic tradition? What are kings, princes, and trials doing in a pastoral romance?[17] It is my contention that these questions, and others like them, can be answered satisfactorily by referring *The Old Arcadia* to the traditions of Renaissance pastoralism.[18] Furthermore, an exploration into the character of those traditions will highlight the role of the eclogues in the romance, reinvesting them with the important position that they occupied during the Renaissance, while leading us, at the same time, to an understanding of Sidney's pastoralism.

There are almost as many different kinds of Renaissance pastorals as there are ways of testing the limits of aesthetic, moral, and social boundaries (sometimes reasserting and sometimes undermining the legitimacy of those boundaries).[19] It is no easy task to provide a definition for a genre so diverse as to include the ethical rigors of Mantuan's shepherds, the soft sentimentalism of Montemayor's pastoral gentlemen, and the complex courtesies of Spenser's Calidore. The values, modes of expression, and literary and philosophical traditions generating these pastoral characters are radically different. Faustus, Diana, and Pastorella would scarcely be on speaking terms; they belong to separate worlds. Given this degree of diversity, a completely satisfactory definition of Renaissance pastoralism may be unobtainable. Perhaps it is even undesirable. For no single static definition of the genre will produce an understanding of it. The consequences of this fact need to be carefully weighed.

The most distinctive characteristic of Renaissance pastoralism, considered as a whole and in its parts, is its diversity, the marvelously impure way elements from disparate traditions are brought together within continuously fluctuating boundaries. The study of Renaissance pastoral is necessarily an exercise in the demarcation of boundaries—the boundaries between city and country, between art and nature, and between generic types themselves. In our readings we are continuously made aware of the precarious balance that a Spenser or a Drayton delights in maintaining between pastoral and some other traditionally more exalted genre. Consider Motto's question: "Shepheard why creepe we in this lowly vaine,/as though our muse no store at all affordes?"[20] Its authority derives from Vergil's fourth eclogue, but it is one raised repeatedly by the practice and explicit pronouncements of Renaissance pastoralists. The pastoral poet forces the reader to be conscious of the dynamics of his art—the quality of his diction, the social status of his characters, the intellectual rigor of his arguments—by threatening to turn the work into something else, into something unpastoral, even antipastoral. Colin's "April" threatens to become royal panegyric; Rowland's songs are narrowly rescued from tragedy. The dynamism generated by this generic instability is one of the most distinctive features of sixteenth-century versions of the genre, including Sidney's.

A high degree of pretense is another constant in the pastoralist's presentation of his fiction, most visible perhaps in his insistence upon decorously simple diction. (What distinguishes his language is not its simpicity, but its imitation of simplicity, its calculated disingenuousness.) His subject is country matters, but his readers are city dwellers who would like to believe—if only for a short time—that they have something in common with those shepherds in their pastures. The pastoralist pretends to serve nature, while artfully constructing poetry in which the authority of nature is placed in the service of aesthetic, moral, and social ambitions. The pretense of presenting Elizabeth as the queen of shepherds permits Spenser to lend natural authority to her absolute sovereignty. Barclay pretends that all country dwellers are good, so that he can depict the good man as a country dweller, as a man in harmony with nature. Drayton writes with the pretense that his art is humble while elevating humility to a standard of literary excellence as a challenge to the pretensions of the epic: if epic is the tarnished product of an iron age, as Eglog 8 insists, pastoral retains the native innocence of the golden world. In all of these cases, pretense strengthens our awareness of boundaries, which is also a way of sharpening our understanding of the quality of experience as it is lived and as it is created on either side of the dividing line, between nature and art, country and city, bucolic and epic. As a by-product of pretense, pastoral includes self-consciousness of a kind that results in placing issues about poetry at or very near the center of attention.

Pretense and demarcation of aesthetic, moral, and social boundaries are essential tools of the Renaissance pastoralist, but they take us only so far in understanding the genre. For they do not explain how the Renaissance pastoralist understood his relationship to the literary tradition. This kind of understanding is essential, and it can be acquired only by considering boundaries of a more important kind: the historical divisions within Renaissance pastoralism, its repeated transformations over time. The fact that these transformations occurred so regularly is of more immediate significance than their character. From the fourteenth to the sixteenth centuries, pastoralists devised new possibilities of expression to supplement the classical and medieval inheritance: this is a basic fact of literary history. Breaking out of the confines of the eclogue, pastoral moved into romance, drama, court entertainments, and a variety of lyrical forms.[21] Always open to alien myths, themes, and styles, the genre proved flexible enough to incorporate within its shifting boundaries a seemingly incompatible assemblage of creatures from Christian shepherds and Platonic shepherdesses, to Epicurean fishermen and Stoical goatherders. Boccaccio, Petrarch, and Mantuan devised individual modes of allegorical and satiric pastoralism, shifting the boundaries of the pastoral and forcing the genre to be continuously and consciously redefined. By the sixteenth century the classical tradition of Theocritean and Vergilian pastoral had been split into several competing factions, with each one eager to demonstrate its own superiority, to lay claim to being the right kind of pastoral. As the means by which these claims are advanced, the activity of redefinition becomes the genre's most fascinating and distinctive mode—as well as its most neglected. For a primary task in which every major Renaissance pastoralist engages (and his success in accomplishing the task is what makes him major) is to reinterpret the traditions of his genre in order to establish the historical importance of his own aesthetic, moral, and social values. The past is remade in order to legitimize the present, or to open up new ways of writing and thinking for the future. Again and again, as founders of the bucolic tradition, Theocritus and Vergil have their portraits redrawn after the image desired by the artist. In some works, like Petrarch's *Bucolicum Carmen* and E. K.'s introduction to *The Shepheardes Calendar,* this process of historical transformation is carried out in explicit and readily comprehensible terms. In others, like Sidney's *Old Arcadia,* it occurs in a more subtle but equally effective manner. Renaissance pastoralism has to be defined historically because the sense of literary history possessed by its authors is so acute.

For an Elizabethan, writing pastoral could never have meant merely adopting a ready-made set of literary conventions: the genre had already become too diversified for that. At the very least an aspiring writer would have to choose among competing sets of conventions, herding his sheep with those of Mantuan or those of Sannazaro. At best, when that writer was a Spenser or a Sidney, he could make use of the traditional means afforded by the pastoral to redefine the genre from within in order to make room for his own way of understanding the world and giving expression to that understanding.

Who could understand the advantages of generic redefinition better than Petrarch? His tenth bucolic offers a good illustration of the device. The poem is an autobiography that records the poet's progress in what is at once a love quest (a search for Laura) and a pursuit after poetic fame (the laurel of the victorious poet). Each stage in that progress is marked by an encounter with a variety of rustics, in what quickly becomes evident to the reader is an allegory of Petrarch's education in Greek and Roman literature. He begins with Hesiod, but desiring to aim "tamen altius" ("somewhat higher"), he soon discovers "venetum . . . unum/Pastorem, agricolam bellatoremque vicissim" (a "Venetian, by turns a shepherd and farmer and warrior").[22] His encounter with Vergil strengthens him, we assume, for the next one-hundred-and-twenty or so meetings with the exalted literati of earlier ages. The cumulative weight of this new Renaissance erudition (or is it old medieval learning?) is overwhelming, but it is there to do more than to overwhelm. For Petrarch is locating a place in history for himself by rewriting Greek and Roman literature as if it were a preparation for his own poetic and amatory career, as if his literature and his love were the culmination of the entire course of Western civilization. By allegorizing the classical tradition in this way, Petrarch redefines the pastoral in order to make his own special autobiographical-allegorical version of it, the right kind. Petrarch's ambitions are not only aesthetic: his love for Laura is simultaneously a moral quest, an attempt to identify an ideal spiritual development for man within the context of Christian platonism, and an attempt to give that development greater authority by locating its roots in nature. As Sylvanus tells Socrates: "something divine . . ./Breathed in the boughs of that laurel."[23] It is also a political quest, an effort to highlight corruptions in church and state by contrasting Laura's pastoral purity to "Romulus' sons and their tribe . . . in their lordly/Togas of empire, all plucking green leaves from the sacred frondage."[24] Petrarch's approach to pastoral carried a clear message to his contemporaries: only the writer who knows *his* place in history, who is conscious of his Latin and Greek heritage, is worthy of assuming *a* place in history. No Renaissance pastoralist ever equaled Petrarch in the audacity with which he set out to clear avenues of fame for himself, but there can be no doubt that they understood his message.

Generic definition is the characteristic activity of Renaissance pastoralism.[25] In the process of reformulating the boundaries of the genre, while engaging in shepherdly negotiations between the literary past and the cultural present, the poet promotes his own aesthetic, moral, political, and religious interests. His theme, as Hallett Smith writes, is frequently "the rejection of the aspiring mind," but his fictions even more frequently are vehicles for the fulfillment of personal and public aspirations.[26] The pastoralist uses pretense even here: the humility of his pose as a shepherd is a disguise for his ambitions as a poet. This fact makes special demands on the critic, forcing him to examine not only what the pastoralist says, but what his fictions set out to accomplish. As George Puttenham makes clear in his *Arte of English Poesie*, it is not always prudent to say everything; the sophisticated Elizabethan turned to pastoral "not of purpose to counterfait or represent the rusticall manner of loves and communication, but under the vaile of homely persons and in rude speeches to insinuate and glaunce at greater matters, and such as perchance had not bene safe to have beene disclosed in any other sort."[27] It is useful to recall, while reading Puttenham, Howell's praise of the Arcadian eclogues as "misteries deepe" and Day's tribute to their "covert shapes." In these activities of veiling and shrouding lie the vital interests of the poet. Remove the veil, pierce the shroud, and there appears behind the pastoralist's pretense of humility a set of complex literary, moral, and social aspirations.

The major Renaissance pastoralists are the best key and the only real key to so diverse a genre because they are themselves so often engaged in the very activity that has eluded so many contemporary scholars: generic definition. Unless we are willing to point to Renaissance pastoralism as the "kind" that constantly reformulates its own boundaries, as different pastoralists construct different interpretations of nature, whatever definition we create for it is likely to distort its true character.

As a preparation for exploring Sidney's definition of "kind" in *The Old Arcadia*, it will be necessary to examine how two of his most radically dissimilar predecessors engage in the same activity. Jacopo Sannazaro, the sophisticated creator of Renaissance pastoral romance and Alexander Barclay, the more humble originator of English Christian pastoral, lend themselves so well to this kind of study because they both concern themselves explicitly with questions of literary history, and because they define two contrasting versions, which offer two very different sets of attitudes toward the central issues of pastoral contentment and relief from misfortune. Out of contrasting features from these two distinct varieties of pastoral, Sidney creates a new syncretic version of his own, a version unified, as we shall see, by a single animating conceit derived from a long philosophical tradition. By 1578, it would be fair to state, there was no third major version. Italianate and Christian pastoralists split the world between them.

At the beginning of the tenth prose section of Sannazaro's *Arcadia*, the company of shepherds journeys up a mountainside into what is described as "il reverendo e sacro bosco" ["the revered and sacred wood"].[28] Their findings are detailed in a leisurely narrative. The center of the grove is occupied, as we are told, by "una spelunca vecchissima e grande" ["a very ancient and roomy cave" (102)], where the shepherds discover a wooden statue "del selvatico Idio" ["of the forest Deity" (102)], and an altar from which "due grandi tavole di faggio" ["two long beechen scrolls" (102)] are extended (80). After a quick survey of its contents, their attention is drawn to the front of the cave where the sacred God's "grande e bella sampogna" ["large and beautiful sampogna" (103)] hangs from a pine tree (81). They are told how it came into being, how it later passed "ne le mani d'un pastore siracusano" ["into the hands of a shepherd of Syracuse" (104)] and that it was finally given as a gift "al mantuano Titiro" ["to Mantuan Tityrus" (104)] (81). After their tour, the company continues its progress.

As happens so frequently in pastoral, the shepherds' journey signals more than a change in geography: it marks a shift into a different order of discourse, as Sannazaro leads us out of the natural history that dominates the ninth prose, with its Plinean catalogues of the earth's magical resources, into the literary history of the tenth.[29] Far from being unexpected, this shift into a transparent allegory of pastoral history comes as the inevitable culmination of a work that from the first page betrays its literary debts.[30] The fact that the tenth prose and poem seem originally to have been intended to serve as the conclusion to the *Arcadia* indicates the significance that Sannazaro assigned to this history as a climactic statement of the romance's themes and his own aesthetic aspirations.

Sannazaro's allegory of the history of pastoral literature is easily deciphered. No one needs to be told that the great sampogna constructed out of seven reeds (the number of harmony, significantly enough) belongs to Pan, or that the Syracusan shepherd and Tityrus Mantuan refer to Theocritus and Vergil, or that those rustic scrolls recording seasonal changes and information about husbandry indicate pastoral's origins in agricultural poetry similar to that of Hesiod's *Works and Days*. In this instance it is a debt that Sannazaro acknowledges less openly that proves most helpful in understanding his version of the idle life.

The cave in the tenth chapter of the *Arcadia* is modeled upon a similar cavern in Longus's pastoral, *Daphnis and Chloe*.[31] Outside of both caverns there are pine trees sacred to Pan; both are bordered by springs; and in Longus's account, as in Sannazaro's, the cave is preserved as a sacred spot for the "offerings of old shepherds in times gone by."[32] The list of similarities could be extended, but it is the differences between the versions that mean the most, particularly since they reflect upon the nature of love in these two distinct pastoral worlds. Longus's cave serves as the appropriately innocent locale in which Chloe falls in love with Daphnis, as a place where she can learn about the delights of naked bodies while bathing him. Their love is sensuous, uncomplicated, and an entirely enviable source of pastoral pleasures: if Eros inflicts unsettling desires, the pastoral place satisfies them generously.[33] Love is something else entirely in Sannazaro's *Arcadia*. It is a passionate, complex, and all-consuming emotion, which far from reinforcing the repose of the bucolic life, as it does in Longus, constantly threatens its destruction. The impassioned amatory excesses of Theocritus's Daphnis and Vergil's Gallus anticipate those of the *Arcadia*'s exiled lovers, but Sannazaro had no precedent for situating passionate love at the center of pastoral to the exclusion of other kinds of love (and there *are* simple love affairs in Vergil and Theocritus), and of almost every other kind of human experience except song and death.[34] That peculiar complex of activities which distinguishes the idle life—poetry, love, and contemplation—instead of operating as a harmonious unit to create pastoral repose, is consistently interpreted by Sannazaro as containing the potential of destroying repose.

Drawing passionate love into the center of the bucolic experience had important consequences for Sannazaro's pastoral that are reflected both in his attitude toward poetry and in his relationship to the classical tradition. The ideal condition of the pastoral life is much the same in his *Arcadia* as it is in Theocritus's *Idylls*, the maintenance of quiet and the preservation of Epicurean delight in natural pleasures. In *Idyll* 7, Simichidas and his companions idle beneath the shady elms of Phrasidamus's farm, enjoying a harvest of country pleasures made available simultaneously by agricultural and poetic labors. This is a picture that would have appealed to Sannazaro, but it is not one that his art could often reproduce. By equating passionate love with pastoral love, Sannazaro shifts the emphasis away from a picture of repose attained to a concern with the activities needed in order to generate repose. To state the argument in Theocritean terms, the poetic harvests of *Idyll* 7 are abandoned for the therapeutic measures of Polyphemus's song in *Idyll* 11, where poetry cures the unrequited love of a Cyclops. If love, poetry, and contemplation were to provide the makings of a satisfactory idle life in this new Arcadian version, some balance had to be reached among them, and that balance was to be provided by poetry.

In Longus the cave serves as the locale for the beginnings of love; in Sannazaro it is the major point of interest on a journey that is designed to bring relief from love. Clonico's travels to find a remedy for his hopeless passion provide a miniature version of the action of the romance as a whole, a parallel to the larger plot in which Sincero (Sannazaro's double) struggles to find relief for the sorrow created by unreciprocated passion and the death of his mistress. Why, then, should Sannazaro lead this shepherd into a cave whose main purpose is to provide a lesson in the history of pastoral poetry? He does so in order to demonstrate that the function of pastoral, like the function of Pan's sampogna (literally the product of an unhappy passion), is to transform sufferings "in dolce suono" ["into sweet harmony" (103)] (81). Poetry is therapeutic; it assumes such importance in the idle life because of its special capacity to remedy the disruptive effects of love, to guarantee that sorrows never find expression without the softening effects of sentiment. In Sannazaro it is poetry that guarantees contentment and that explains the ability of the idle life to serve as a protection against misfortune.[35]

The fact that Sannazaro arranges his fable so that Pan's sampogna passes first into the hands of Theocritus and next into Vergil's signals the continuity of purpose with which he invests his history of pastoral. Of course, a sense of historical continuity works to his advantage. He attributes a therapeutic design to the pastorals of Theocritus and Vergil as a way of defining and justifying his own aesthetic values. His history is self-contained and exclusive: by recognizing no other possible versions of pastoral, Sannazaro convicts the rest of insignificance. As an account of classical pastorals, his insistence upon poetic therapy is distorting in its overemphasis, but it should be recognized that Sannazaro's celebration of the poet's powers is entirely traditional. Pastoralists spend a great deal of time telling us how important they are (almost as much time, in fact, as they devote to insisting upon their modesty). This is a basic fact about the genre that bears repeating every so often. Theocritus celebrates the harvests of poetry in his seventh Idyll (passages from which appear, significantly enough, in Sannazaro's tenth poem); Vergil signals the powers of the pastoral poet by ushering the dead Daphnis into heaven with an elegy (an event that Sannazaro reminds us of in the tenth prose); Petrarch's Tyrrhemus praises the consolatory effects of the lyre.[36] Whatever the justification, whether it is the art's extension of our imaginative horizons by prophecy, its capacity to provide immortality in the *aevum*, its virtue as an instrument of consolation or as a superior form of entertainment among a community of friends, the defense of poetry is a constant feature of classical and Renaissance pastoral.

A small piece of pastoral pretense allows an insight of considerable importance into the *Arcadia:* in no sense should we be misled by the Hesiodic overtones of the tenth prose to assume that Sannazaro is in any but the most minor way concerned with *ethical* "ammaestramenti de la pastorale vita" ["rules for conduct of the pastoral life" (102)] (80). The antique laws to which he makes reference are almost exclusively seasonal, animal, and vegetable. Like Spenser in the Garden of Adonis, Sannazaro has in mind the great generative processes of nature. There are no moral debates here or anywhere else in the work because there are no moral issues or crises. This is a crucial point. Love has no serious ethical dimensions as far as the *Arcadia's* author or his characters are concerned, apart from a faint Neoplatonic idealism occasionally attached to it. Its fruition, like its remedy, is a self-evident good. Sannazaro's pastoral is the kind of world that would horrify Kalodoulus.

The *Arcadia's* tenth chapter begins by describing how the woods sweetly echoed ["dolcissimamente rimbombato" (79)] to the singing of Elenco and Ofelio. Later Sannazaro reminds us by means of a literary echo how Tityrus "insegnò primeramente le selve di risonare il nome de la formosa Amarillida" ["first taught the woods to echo the name of the beautiful Amaryllis"(104)](82). These passages are interesting because they single out the most important feature of Sannazaro's landscape: its responsiveness. The meadows and springs of Arcadia are always willing to smile or to weep for the shepherd as his amatory conditions require. In fact, one has every reason to suspect that Sannazaro's characters would display little interest in nature if they did not find their private concerns sympathetically mirrored there. The meaning and value of events in the *Arcadia*, and Italianate pastoral as a whole, are determined ultimately and almost exclusively by the individual's personal experience. The question posed by Sannazaro (when, indeed, he poses any questions at all) is not, "Is this good for the individual as a member of society?" but, "Is this pleasurable or painful for the lover?" In this kind of fiction, parallels between individual worlds inevitably take the place of communications between them.

Sannazaro's pastoral is not a golden world, since Arcadia has some portion of beasts, bad weather, and suffering, but its setting is idyllic, as is the character of its idle life. If nature sometimes laments, it does so most often in response to man's wishes; and if there are some genuine ills in the world, agonies incurred by love and death, still, as Eugenio assures Clonico "ché al mondo mal non è senza rimedio" ["there is no ill in the world without a remedy" (89)] (67). In large measure Sannazaro's history of pastoral is designed to show how poetry functions to guarantee the truth of Eugenio's remark. In the *Arcadia* song secures the fortunate condition of the idle life by relieving the agonies of love and by providing the individual with access to a sympathetically responsive landscape.

What Sannazaro saves for the concluding portions of his work, as a definition of genre that explains and justifies all that comes before, Alexander Barclay situates at the outset of his *Eclogues*. Theory precedes fact in an effort to determine our response to the fictions that come after. This clearly conservative approach to pastoral reflects Barclay's anxiety about demonstrating the legitimacy of his literary project. As a way of marshaling authority, he displays his humanistic credentials eagerly, both in the prologue, with its citations from Horatian canons of style, and in the *Eclogues* themselves, with their frequent references to classical moral philosophers and complaints that "In this time courtiers will nothing have to do" with such ancients as Livy, Sallust, Plutarch, and Suetonius. Barclay's sense of history is acute.[37]

His account of the development of pastoral is not only more straightforwardly presented than Sannazaro's, appearing in nonfictional, nonallegorical form; it is noticeably more inclusive. As one might anticipate, "the famous Theocrite" and "Moste noble Virgill" head the list of ancient pastoralists (19, 27); to this group Barclay adds "the moste famous Baptist Mantuan," "Frauncis Petrarke," and Boccaccio (32, 35). The selection of authors is scarcely haphazard. Barclay singles out for praise the three most prominent writers of Christian pastoral as a means of indicating the aesthetic and ethical values of his own work. The manner in which their names are ordered is meaningful: as a sign of his greater prominence, Mantuan's is placed out of chronological sequence before Petrarch's and Boccaccio's (which is not directly mentioned). In fact, like many of Mantuan's zealous admirers, he elevates the "Christian Maro," as Erasmus called him, above not only the rest of the modern pastoralists but Theocritus and Vergil as well.[38] A single literary figure dominates Barclay's history in much the same way that a single theme (pastoral's therapeutic function) dominates Sannazaro's.

Barclay's methods of proceeding are not always so straightforward as they at first appear. By an act of pastoral pretense as calculated as any in Petrarch or Sannazaro, he establishes a close connection between his bucolics and those of his preferred author, Mantuan. After Barclay has concluded his catalogue of great pastoralists, he provides an account of how his *Eclogues* came to be written. He adopts a playful tone, solving the riddle of how he was able to find his "first youth agayne," by explaining that his *Eclogues* were conceived during his adolescence and were subsequently rediscovered and revised by him for printing (70). The entire account, masquerading as autobiography, is lifted straight from the dedicatory epistle to Mantuan's eclogues, almost detail for detail, including the very name given to the poems, "Egloges of youth" (76).[39] This cannot be explained as the act of a plagiarist or as an instance of mindless imitation: no one rifles passages out of a text so widely known. Instead, Barclay is superimposing his own riddle upon that of his master. He writes himself into Mantuan's life as a way of advertising whose literary footsteps he intends to follow. His is a bucolically approved way of announcing: "I am the English Mantuan." (His fourth and fifth *Eclogues* are derived from Mantuan.)[40]

Barclay is careful to separate his *Eclogues* from those of the "wrong" kind.[41] With characteristic pastoral pretense, he disclaims any desire to be considered a "Poet laureate" (104). Pretensions to modesty are made the prelude to literary assault, as he goes on to observe.

> That name [Poete laureate] unto them is mete and
>   doth agree
> Which writeth matters with curiositee.
> Mine habite blacke accordeth not with grene,

> Blacke betokeneth death as it is dayly sene,
> The grene is pleasour, freshe lust and jolite,
> These two in nature hath great diversitie.
> Then who would ascribe, except he were a foole,
> The pleasaunt laurer unto the mourning cowle.
>
> (105–12)

Barclay carries Sermon-on-the-Mount moralizing to the level of literary aesthetics: the first are made last and the last are made first. A plain style and moral gravity become the marks of true literary quality, as he explicitly places his fiction in opposition to the ethically suspect "grene" worlds of Italianate and classical pastoralists.[42]

Barclay redefines the history of pastoral in Christian terms as he rejects the reward of the poet's laurel in favor of:

> The glorious sight of God my saviour,
> Which is chiefe shepheard and head of other all.
>
> (114–15)

Pastoral pleasure is replaced by pastoral goodness (even holiness) as the ideal condition of the idle life. As a result, like all of the Christian pastoralists, Barclay has radically different notions about the kinds of songs that a shepherd ought to sing, about how, when, and indeed whether, he ought to make love, and about the way in which he ought to contemplate the natural world.

In Barclay's entirely commonplace conception, the function of pastoral poetry is to give profit and pleasure, providing "laudes of vertue," and informing man "misliving to eschue" (97–98). If he is nearly as eager to defend poetry as Sannazaro, he is, as we have already seen in his attacks upon other pastoralists, far more conscious of the abuses to which the art lends itself. As a consequence, the ethical half of this Horatian injunction receives the greatest emphasis. Barclay's first three eclogues are an adaptation of Aeneas Sylvius's anti-court prose treatise, *De Miserae Curialium*. Sound morality is poured into a fictional mold as a way of illustrating poetry's moral and religious utility within the human community.

To be sure, there is a well-developed sense of community in all of the Christian pastoralists, almost by definition. Normative standards of behavior keep our attention focused on the general concerns of the Christian flock rather than the private bleatings of Italianate sheep. In Barclay's version of pastoral, an individual's identity is determined not by his amatory condition, but by the fact that he belongs to the country, a social unit with moral and religious values in opposition to those of the city.⁴³ In the fifth eclogue, Faustus characterizes the latter as the

> . . . well and ground originall,
> Both first and last of deadly evils all.
>
> (977–98)

By contrast, the country is the source of simple pieties, of blessedness snatched from the jaws of the devil and virtue seized from the arms of vice. If the shepherds of the Italianate pastoralists give the impression of constantly putting off their chores, of avoiding their mythical responsibilities to their sheep, those of their Christian counterparts seem always to have just returned from the pastures exhausted by their labors. In short, we are constantly given the impression that behind their pastoral virtue and in some measure responsible for it, are some strenuous ethical exertions of a Georgic variety—exertions that are not shown because, after all, this *is* bucolic poetry.

It will not do to criticize the oppositions that Barclay and the other Christian pastoralists pose between the country and the city as a comically exaggerated distortion of social realities, without at least acknowledging that they were intended to function as such for good didactic reasons. A simplified moral landscape is created in order to clarify issues of primary concern to man's salvation. The real trouble inheres in the fact that there is so little complexity in the perspective on human issues that is placed in that landscape. Moral debates are almost as infrequent in Mantuan and his followers as they are in Sannazaro, for the simple reason that few spokesmen of the city life are permitted in their eclogues. There is no desire to achieve a balance of perspectives; the aim is to enforce an approved moral stand upon the audience.

Barclay's views on love supply a good example. He is neither openly misogynistic, as Mantuan is, nor so obsessed with the horrors of lust that he devotes an entire series of eclogues to the subject, as Googe does. Barclay is merely dully moralizing. "Venus disceatfull tiranny" is treated as no more than another sinful urban experience that country dwellers ought to avoid; and although he acknowledges the possibility of "love honest and laudable" as a part of marriage, neither Barclay nor any of the other Christian pastoralists gives sustained attention to it (132–33). No spokesmen for rival beliefs are introduced. Barclay's woods contain no echoes of Italianate love songs.

The Christian shepherd is allowed no pleasure in love and few pleasures in nature. Mantuan and his English followers attribute pleasant features to the countryside most often only when a contrast is being drawn with the harsh depravities of the city. Pleasure is simply too dangerous a commodity to be amassed in abundance, no matter how worthy the justification. Even in contrast with the city, the amount of pleasantness allowed to the country life is strictly limited. Cornis says to Coridon in the first eclogue:

> Here is a pleasaunt shadowe, here is a pleasaunt
>   coole,
> Take banke and floures for cushen and for stoole.
>
> (569–70)

Natural beauty is an infrequently used metaphor for holiness. (After all, this is a fallen world.) More often, shepherds complain about storms that ravage their pastures, cold weather, and plagues that infect their villages.[44] What the Christian shepherd sees in nature is not a symbolic reflection of his own psychological condition, or an idyllic pleasance whose beauties he can enjoy in contemplative repose, but a book of moral instructions to which he is obliged to pay the most careful attention. Every tree and animal has its lesson to teach the godly observer; for Minalcas, the "litle Emmet" is an instructive image of how "In youthes season to make provision" for old age (Ecl. 4, 247,246). The Christian pastoralist constantly threatens to crystallize the whole of nature into maxims, as wittily congealed pieces of scriptural wisdom. The world is fraught with divine purpose. When holiness replaces pleasure as the ideal of the idle life, the shepherd must be careful to sing morally inspired tunes, to limit his sexual desires within the approved boundaries, and to read God's book of nature with the right spirit, with a willingness to adhere closely to the text. Unlike Sannazaro, the Christian pastoralist provides no hope of finding relief from misfortune other than what is to be acquired from God's grace. As the central motive in a green world that is entirely rejected, contentment is simply too perilous a topic to explore.

3
As Critic and Poet, Sidney Defines *Pastoral*

RENAISSANCE pastoralism's growth in popularity coincided with the development of postclassical literary criticism. The self-consciousness of the one helped to stimulate and in turn must have been stimulated by the other. Poliziano's *Sylvae* (1489), a neo-Latin poem devoted in large part to the celebration of the rural life, also happens to be the first modern history of literature.[1] At the same time that pastoralists are discussing trees in their fictions as if they were poems, literary critics are writing about poems in their treatises as if they were trees. As a result, the pastoral writer and the literary critic frequently have a shared vocabulary. Insofar as the critic of pastoral poetry is interested in advancing the claims of a particular poet or a particular school of poets, as Vida and Scaliger are in the elevation of the Vergilian style above the Theocritean, or as E. K. is in his celebration of Spenser, they also have a shared purpose in generic redefinition.

During his career, Sidney provides two separate definitions of pastoral that are useful in understanding *The Old Arcadia*'s genre. On one occasion, he writes as a critic taking measure of the pastoral "hedge"; on the other, he writes as a poet inspired by "high conceits." In both instances he sets his definition of pastoral against a carefully conceived background of literary history. The usual Renaissance commerce between fiction and criticism is extended and transformed by him with an unanticipated richness of invention.

In the *Apology*, Sidney begins his defense of poetry's "parts, kinds, or species" in the traditionally approved manner by giving a short account of the "Pastoral poem."

> Is it then the Pastoral poem which is misliked? For perchance where the hedge is lowest they will soonest leap over. Is the poor pipe disdained, which sometime out of Meliboeus' mouth can show the

misery of people under hard lords or ravening soldiers? And again, by Tityrus, what blessedness is derived to them that lie lowest from the goodness of them that sit highest; sometimes, under the pretty tales of wolves and sheep, can include the whole considerations of wrongdoing and patience; sometimes show that contention for trifles can get but a trifling victory: where perchance a man may see that even Alexander and Darius, when they strave who should be cock of this world's dunghill, the benefit they got was that the afterlivers may say,

> *Haec memini et victum frustra contendere Thirsin:*
> *Ex illo Corydon, Corydon est tempore nobis.*[2]

Sidney restricts his remarks to the "right use" of pastoral: he knows more than he tells. Unlike E. K., he makes no explicit claims to inclusiveness. He will give no attention to all of the ways in which the genre can be employed, only to the manner in which it is properly employed. There is also no pretense of providing a history of pastoral literature, though his choice of allusions indicates clearly which authors and which aspects of the tradition Sidney believes are the most significant. Like other Renaissance literary critics, Sidney redefines the pastoral genre in terms of his own ethical and aesthetic aspirations.

Vergil dominates the entire paragraph, with the exception of what is possibly a reference to Spenser's pastoral in Sidney's mention of "the pretty tales of wolves and sheep." We begin with Tityrus and Meliboeus from *Eclogue* 1 and end with a quotation of the last lines of *Eclogue* 7. The Vergilian emphasis is not unusual, but there are as many Vergils in the Renaissance as there are Ovids, and this is one that we have not seen before. He is taken neither as the standard for an idyllic, therapeutically ameliorative version of pastoral as he is in Sannazaro (there is nothing especially idyllic about these scenes), nor as the precursor of a religiously pure plain style as he is in Barclay (there are no important Christian overtones in this passage). Instead, Sidney's Vergil is the founder of a pastoral tradition that has a clear ethical function, part of which concerns "considerations of wrongdoing," and a clearly defined subject: man's life considered in relation to fortune. It is possible to be more specific.

As the allusion to Meliboeus and Tityrus indicates, Sidney knows that political issues are traditional pastoral fare.[3] (His understanding of the genre is historically determined.) Sidney's purpose in interpreting Vergil's first eclogue is to show that pastoral is sometimes about the arbitrariness of the political fortunes to which communities are subjected: Meliboeus's "hard lords" balance those whose "blessedness" Tityrus praises. In the next part of the paragraph, he alludes to the moral-allegorical tradition of pastoral as a means of illustrating the genre's special concern with the quality of the individual's response to fortune. By identifying "patience" as the proper attitude to adopt against "wrong-doing," Sidney establishes it as a central pastoral virtue. Private concerns are balanced against public. He concludes the passage by making an extended comparison between the heroic struggles of Alexander and Darius for domination of the world and the singing contest between a pair of shepherds for two lines of poetic praise.[4] The wars of Alexander are a standard illustration in Stoically inspired ethical treatises and fictions of the vanity of worldly contentions. One remembers the graveyard scene in *Hamlet*. Alexander's chief conquest is referred to here for a similar purpose, as an argument that pastoral is sometimes written as a warning against fortune-seeking, a warning that recognizes that struggles for objects so valueless as this dunghill world are trifling, even when they are waged on the scale of the struggle between Alexander and Darius. Furthermore, this is an ethical position that Sidney attributes directly to Vergil as an allegorical interpretation of the singing contest between Thyris and Corydon in *Eclogue 7*, an event characterized in the original as a "certamen . . . magnum."[5] What Sidney implies is that Vergil's contending shepherds parody, by means of their strife over amorous and poetic trifles, the actions of the great men of the world. The "right" use of pastoral employs the shepherd as moral critic.

In Sidney's conception, Vergil's shepherds, and by extension, those of the central pastoral tradition, enforce a set of ethical notions about how man ought to adjust his private and his public lives to the lures and snares of fortune. Once more, the distinctive organization of the definition provides an important insight into his attitude toward the genre: by balancing Meliboeus's "hard lords" against those whose "blessedness" Tityrus cites, "wrongdoing" against "patience," and the trifling contentions of Alexander and Darius against those of Thyrsis and Corydon, Sidney shows a preference for an inclusive version of pastoral, one that takes into account a full range of experiences. The *Apology*'s illustrations of the proper concerns and characteristics of the genre are not exhaustive; any complete discussion of Sidney's pastoralism would need to place them in the wider context of his whole aesthetic, as I shall do when I consider the relationship of art and nature in part IV, but this critique of the "right use" of pastoral will help to clarify how he defines the nature of his "kind" at the beginning of *The Old Arcadia*.

Sidney is as anxious as Barclay to set the reader straight from the outset about the kind of pastoral world that he is entering. For this reason it will be necessary to examine its opening sentences with some care.

> Arcadia among all the provinces of Greece was ever had in singular reputation, partly for the sweetness of the air and other natural benefits, but principally for the moderate and well tempered minds of the people who (finding how true a contentation is gotten by following the course of nature, and how the shining title of glory, so much affected by other nations, doth indeed help little to the happiness of life) were the only people which, as by their justice and providence gave neither cause nor hope to their neighbours to annoy them, so were they not stirred with false praise to trouble others' quiet, thinking it a small reward for the wasting of their own lives in ravening that their posterity should long after say they had done so. Even the muses seemed to approve their good determination by choosing that country as their chiefest repairing place, and by bestowing their perfections so largely there that the very shepherds themselves had their fancies opened to so high conceits as the most learned of other nations have been long time since content both to borrow their names and imitate their cunning. In this place some time there dwelled a mighty duke named Basilius, a prince of sufficient skill to govern so quiet a country where the good minds of the former princes had set down good laws, and the well bringing up of the people did serve as a most sure bond to keep them. (4)

We are in the midst of fiction openly talking about fiction, as Sidney sets out to establish his place within a tradition and to redefine that tradition from within. He proceeds to create his own version of pastoral by reminding us that there have been other pastorals written for a "long time" by men of "other nations." Sidney looks back to Vergil and to Sannazaro, among others. By doing so, he simultaneously advertises his own membership in the company of the "most learned" pastoralists, while hinting that if poets from "other nations" can imitate the Arcadians' "cunning," an English poet not only can, but should do so as well. This is the purpose of borrowing "names" from the earlier poets: it signals a readiness to make use of the best literary traditions. Of course, those names have a special source: they are not the aesthetic products of learned writers, nor even—one step closer to nature—the creation of the "very shepherds" whom those writers imitate; they originate with the muses themselves, at the fountainhead of creative "perfections." Arcadia, as we are told, is the muses' "chiefest repairing place." There is a point to this elaborate pastoral pretense: Sidney enlists himself in the company of learned poets who imitate the high conceits of native shepherds, who, in turn, are inspired by the muses, as a way of signaling something important about the appeal of pastoral: pastoral not only makes accessible sophisticated literary skills and literary skills grounded in nature, but, more important still, it allows access to the very source of creative expression—what he names here as the repairing place of the muses and what he describes in the *Apology* as the golden world of the imagination.

There is no bucolic trembling before heroic trumpets here. We are already at a considerable distance from the ironic self-effacing remarks of the dedicatory letter to the Countess, and we are carried even further with the recognition that his introduction includes echoes from Polybius's account of Arcadia.[6] Sidney's decision to use a historical source as a framework for introducing his fiction is significant because it indicates from the start that he intends to part company with those "most learned" writers from the past. Drawing from history is one way of stating that his Arcadia, as opposed to Vergil's or Sannazaro's, is the *real* one—presumably both because it acknowledges the existence of the actual place and poetically improves upon it. As in Petrarch, Sannazaro, and Barclay, erudition becomes a means of advancing the writer's personal stature, of gaining a "singular reputation" for himself.

This introduction shares with the definition of pastoral in the *Apology* an inclusive interpretation of the genre's boundaries. Arcadia is not merely a landscape, it is a province, a political entity in which affairs of state will assume considerable importance. But while the *Apology* provides a view of the pastoral life set amidst a background of misfortune, complete with ravening soldiers, wrongdoings, and trifling martial contentions, *The Old Arcadia*'s first three sentences conjure up a picture of the idle life as the perfect image of good fortune. With its "sweetness of . . . air" and other "benefits," the landscape is noticeably more idyllic—a fact that promises a genuine degree of kinship with Italianate bucolics. Sidney's reminder of the muses' choice of Arcadia as "their chiefest repairing place," is responsible for a second difference in emphasis: in the romance, poetry is immediately established as an experience of central importance in the pastoral life.[7]

The idyllic features of the romance passage are carefully subordinated to a concern with the Arcadians' character of mind. This is the crucial point. One suspects that Sidney makes use of Polybius's account here principally because it offers him a historical justification for pointing to the virtue of the Arcadians' simple life-style as the distinguishing feature of his pastoral world. (As in Christian pastoral, we discover a community of shepherds.) Polybius writes: "the Arcadian nation on the whole has a very high reputation for virtue among the Greeks, due not only to their humane and hospitable character and usages, but especially to their piety to the gods. . . ."[8] Sidney's passage creates the image of a just and pious quiet life produced by "moderate and well tempered minds" as a standard of human happiness. Again and again he points to their "contentation," their "happiness of life," describing Arcadia as "so quiet a country," free from warlike aspirations. (To be happy, of course, is to have "good hap"—good fortune.) As in the *Apology*, an attack is included upon fortune-seekers, who pursue a "shining title of glory" at the expense of true contentment. Even the vocabulary of the two passages is similar: "ravening" soldiers appear in both accounts—an indication, it appears, that Sidney recalled his earlier definition of the bucolic mode while writing the *Apology*. No other description in his works so closely approximates the golden-world aesthetic of his *Apology*: in the quiet life of the Arcadians, with its special combination of justice and contentment, we are presented, not with the realism of what is, but with an ideal of what should be. It is the Arcadians' justice that Sidney mentions first.

In Theocritus, Sannazaro, and what has been called the Epicurean tradition of pastoral, pleasurable repose achieves the status of a virtue: "contentation" is the true business of the shepherd. In Barclay and the Christian tradition, repose is largely ignored or condemned in the interests of virtue. Sidney's approach is different. What he is attempting in *The Old Arcadia*, if we judge by his introduction, is the transformation of virtue into an image of pleasurable repose. This is the main point of his generic redefinition. Viewed from a historical vantage, his purpose is syncretic and conciliatory. Pastoral pleasure will not be rejected, it will be redefined. Sidney combines the emphasis upon contentment in Italianate pastoral with the moral concern of the Christian bucolic, creating a new brand of critical poetry that deepens our sense of pleasure as it sharpens our ethical understanding. Our pleasure is deepened because of the additional satisfaction derived from its goodness; our morals are sharpened because the complex ethical issues posed by the fiction are developed within a literary structure that does justice to their complexity. This is not simply a gesture of good will. Because his version of pastoral is more inclusive than the versions of his predecessors, Sidney clearly implies, it is a better version.

In Italianate pastoral, poetry provides relief from misfortune: Sincero sings in order to console himself for the loss of his mistress. In the Christian bucolic, a shepherd obtains comfort in adversity (if he obtains it at all) because of God's grace. Sidney is no less concerned than Sannazaro or Barclay with the question of pastoral relief: his personal misfortunes in private and public life took care of that. But he had very different ideas about how relief could be obtained, ideas that will ultimately explain his desire to fashion a new kind of poetry able to combine Italianate contentment with the Christian bucolic's moral concern.

In *The Old Arcadia* the idle life, as it is lived by the native Arcadians, serves as a metaphor for goodness—at least until the fall of Basilius, that is. Like all golden worlds, this one is tragically short lived. The native shepherds who populate the eclogues are not idealized, even though they frequently articulate primary values of the romance. Patience and fortitude are the moral responses to bad fortune; justice and temperance are the guarantees (if there can be such a thing in an absolute sense) of good fortune. The two sets of virtues are closely related. For the native Arcadians, the ideal remains constant: the preservation of a quiet mind. In the years intervening between the romance and the *Apology,* Sidney's beliefs about the principal subject of pastoral underwent no major changes: a good Arcadian poet concerns himself with man's life in relation to fortune.

The *Arcadia*'s image of the quiet life needs further probing in order to measure the full weight of Sidney's redefinition of pastoral. The most important phrase in the passage appears, characteristically enough, in a parenthesis, as the narrator observes "how true a contentation is gotten by following the course of nature." The kind of nature that Sidney has in mind is quite different from the trees and shrubs evoked by the term *natural benefits.* As Basil Willey points out in *The Religion of Nature,* the appeal to this extraordinarily slippery abstraction "has generally been an appeal to certain human values, aspirations or ethical standards, to which men have tried to impart compulsive authority by ascribing them to Nature—whether or not they are actually to be found realized in physical nature or human nature."[9] Which particular set of values happens to be singled out as the "natural" is subject to considerable variation. In fact, one could construct a reasonably comprehensive history of Western ethics since the fifth century B.C. by describing the attempts that have been made to provide a fixed meaning for Nature as a moral norm.[10] Largely because of the influence of Cicero and the Stoic philosophers, who adapted and defined the "law of nature" according to their own philosophical persuasions, the term came to have a far more definite significance for the Elizabethans.[11] For those who believed in what has been called an "optimistic view of Nature," who regarded the universe as divinely ordered and hierarchically constructed, to follow the law of nature was to live in accordance with the responsibilities dictated by man's place as a rational creature on the scale of being.[12] *The Old Arcadia* leaves few doubts concerning the genuineness of Sidney's faith that "nature's works be good" (373).[13]

Thus, when Sidney announces at the beginning of the *Arcadia* that his shepherds' "contentation" results from following the "course of nature," he depends upon a wider fictional and cultural context to clarify the meaning of his statement: these "unfallen" Arcadians are happy because they employ their reason in accordance with virtue. It is because of this interpretation of the course of nature, and its pervasiveness as a concept in the romance as a whole, that *The Old Arcadia* can best be referred to as a "Stoic pastoral."[14] This term requires careful explanation.

The principle that it is man's nature, and therefore his moral duty, to follow the dictates of reason and virtue is central to a variety of important philosophical schools, and can be found in the ethical treatises of writers like Aristotle, Cicero, and Plutarch, who differ fundamentally in many other respects. In his essay *On Moral Virtue*, Plutarch gives clear and succinct expression to the idea when he writes: "For, in accordance with Nature, it is proper that reason, which is divine, should lead and rule. . . ."[15] Robert Hoopes has demonstrated how widespread this concept of "right reason" is in the Renaissance, in which "the exercise of virtue is itself an indispensable part of the proper use of reason," and how many different philosophical traditions—Platonic, Aristotelian, Stoic, and neo-Stoic—played an important role in its formation and transmission.[16] But in spite of the variety of contexts in which it is found, this is a "philosophy" that can appropriately be called "Stoic," since it is framed upon a concept that has been inextricably associated with the Stoics since the time of Cicero: the law of nature dictates reason and virtue.[17] From the *De Officiis*, the educated Elizabethan would have learned:

> quod summum bonum a Stoicis dicitur, convenienter naturae vivere, id habet hanc, ut opinor, sententiam: cum virtute congruere semper.[18]
> (". . . when the Stoics speak of the supreme good as 'living com-

formably to Nature,' they mean, as I take it, something like this: that we are always to be in accord with virtue.")

In no sense should this term, *Stoic pastoral*, be taken to imply that the *Arcadia* embodies the complex system of ethics, logic, and cosmology that constitutes philosophical Stoicism: those tenets which are peculiar to the school's followers, such as the equal viciousness of all crimes and the corruptness of all passions, are of no relevance here. Without exception, the conceptual elements that distinguish Sidney's Stoic version of pastoral can also be found as a logical extension of this interpretation of the law of nature in several other schools of ancient philosophy—in Aristotle, Cicero, or Plutarch, and usually in all three.

Sidney was not, then, a philosophical Stoic. In fact, on several occasions during his career, he isolated the members of this school as the objects of special amusement. A particularly waggish persona in the *Certain Sonnets* asks pardon for not appearing before his lady in the manner of some hypocrites: "Stoick-like in clowdie hew" (*CS* 17, 48); and when Sidney attacks the moral philosophers in the *Apology*, in that wonderfully pointed passage ridiculing their "sullen gravity," their rude clothing worn "to witness outwardly their contempt of outward things," and their duplicity in being "angry with any man in whom they see the foul fault of anger," it is mainly of the Stoics that he appears to be thinking.[19]

At the same time Sidney was just as capable of bestowing high praise upon the style and "notable morality" of Seneca, that most famous of all the Roman Stoics, and of translating a portion of Seneca's *Oedipus* in the *Certain Sonnets*.[20] He included another translation in the same work that is also important in measuring the depth of his interest in Stoic ideas, since it deals with a subject of profound personal interest: the country life as a protection against misfortune. His version of Horace's "Rectius vives" reads in part:

> You better sure shall live, not evermore
>   Trying high seas, nor while Sea rage you flee,
>   Pressing too much upon ill harbourd shore.
>
> The golden meane who loves, lives safely free
>   From filth of foreworne house, and quiet lives,
>   Releast from Court, where envie needes must be.
>   (*CS* 12, 1–6)

By altering the last line of the second stanza from an assertion about *not needing* the Court to a statement about his release from it, Sidney transforms Horace's poem into a more autobiographically relevant monologue of a disappointed courtier.[21] His translation provides one more indication that the Stoic virtues of the quiet life held a large personal appeal to him and there can be no question that he identified those simple virtues as specifically Stoic in kind. In his well-known letter to Languet of 1 March 1578 (part of which I must quote again because of its importance in this context) Sidney writes:

> For to what purpose should our thoughts be directed to various kinds of knowledge, unless room be afforded for putting it into practice, so that public advantage may be the result, which in a corrupt age we cannot hope for? . . . But the mind itself, you will say. . . , is cultivated in this manner. This indeed, if we allow it to be the case, is a very great advantage: but let us see whether we are not giving a beautiful but false appearance to our splendid errors. For while the mind is thus, as it were, drawn out of itself, it cannot turn its powers inward for thorough self-examination; to which employment no labour that men can undertake is in any way to be compared. Do you not see that I am cleverly playing the stoic? Yea, and I shall be a cynic too, unless you reclaim me.[22]

Languet never did reclaim him, not entirely at any rate. His defense of relaxation and of contemplation, like his defense of retirement in a corrupt age, is traditional Stoic fare.[23] Sidney's letter leaves no doubt about the depth of his familiarity with philosophical Stoicism, of his sympathy (however ambivalent) with some of its positions, or of his knowledge of its applicability to and historical support of the quiet life in the country.

It was not by accident that I selected Aristotle, Cicero, and Plutarch as examples of authors who endorse right reason as a principle of natural responsibility. At the time he was writing *The Old Arcadia*, these are the very philosophers in whom Sidney was most interested. We know this from his correspondence. When Edward Denny asked for advice about how to educate himself, he received a letter from Sidney recommending that he read, among the moral treatises, "Aristotles Ethickes," "Tullyes offices," and "some of Plutarcks discourses, as of Refreining anger, of curiosity, of the Tranquillity of the minde, of the Flatterer, and the Friende, of Morall vertew, and soe by peeces as your leysure serves."[24] (Sidney tells Denny to read at his leisure; like *The Old Arcadia*, these works are for idle times.) This is an eclectic choice of philosophers, and Sidney recommends Cicero, the most eclectic member of the group, as the "foundation" upon which to study the rest. What provides a solid center of coherence for his selection is the commitment shared by these writers to a rationalistic interpretation of natural law.[25]

It is helpful to think of Aristotle, Cicero, and Plutarch as providing the raw materials out of which Sidney derived the animating "*Idea* or fore-conceit" of *The Old Arcadia*.[26] This interpretation places a heavy emphasis upon the conceptual nature of Sidney's creative process, but it is an emphasis that stands in basic agreement both with his own focus in the *Apology* upon the governing "*Idea*" in a poem as the chief factor determining the "skill of the artificer," and with the best recent criticism of Elizabethan prose fiction, which has indicated the variety of methods available for transforming imaginative ideas into creative acts.[27] There is nothing mechanical about this process of creation. He is not a Christian pastoralist transmuting morally and religiously approved doctrines into sugar-coated fictions. *The Old Arcadia* has no philosophy to promote. Instead, it lends imaginative embodiment to a concept of the idle life grounded in a Stoic interpretation of the course of nature.

Sidney's *Old Arcadia* offers a superb example of pastoral pretense. It is a grand act of impudence, a fiction grounded upon a pun. Sidney asks that we agree to pretend that a life led according to the laws of Nature (Stoically interpreted) is equivalent to a life lived in nature. In short, he requests our complicity in his purposeful confusion of Nature as a reason and virtue with nature as shrubs and trees. His pun is conceptual, not verbal. Reason and virtue are made to belong to the individual even more essentially than food, clothing, or shelter.[28] By encouraging a confusion between two different natures, the moral and the physical, Sidney establishes a precedent for much of the best Elizabethan pastoral from Drayton to Shakespeare.

Stoicism can be adapted so readily to a pastoral context because it concerns itself in such great measure with satisfying the individual's longing to feel at home in the world: as a reasonable creature, man is provided with a reasonable society and a reasonable universe to which he can relate himself. For the Stoic, the world is instinct with divine purpose and meaning, and is under the direct control of a benevolent providence.[29] Like the Epicureans, the Stoics argued for the virtue of leading a simple life, carefully restricting one's needs and desires to those things which are easily obtained.[30] As Seneca writes in his *Moral Epistles:* "Simplici cura constant necessaria; in delicias laboratur"[31] ("The things that are indispensable require no elaborate pains for acquisition; it is only the luxuries that call for labour"). Again, like the Epicureans, they believed in the wisdom of self-sufficiency. The good life was to be achieved not by acquiring anything, but by abandoning everything that was inessential, while preserving the inner happiness of a quiet mind.[32] It is obvious with what ease standards of these kinds could be transformed by Theocritus and Sannazaro on the one hand and by Sidney on the other into an image of pastoral repose.[33] Petrarch's portrait of the solitary life of the retired man expresses in compact form an ideal that would have appealed to both parties:

> Nulli penitus invidet, nullum odit, sorte contentus sua, et fortunae iniuriis inaccessus, nihil cupit; . . . scit vitae hominum pauca sufficere, et summas verasque divitias nil optare, summum imperium nil timere, laetum agit atque tranquillum aevum, placidas noctes, ociosos dies, et secura convivia.

> (Content with his own lot and inaccessible to the injuries of Fortune, he feels himself above all fears and all desires. . . . He understands that a few things suffice for the life of man, that the greatest and truest wealth is to have no wishes, the greatest power to have no fears. He passes his life happily and tranquilly, with peaceful nights, serene days, and undisturbed recreation.)[34]

What distinguishes an Epicurean from a Stoic, and ultimately what separates an Epicurean pastoralist from a Stoic pastoralist, concerns the means recommended by each for attaining a quiet mind: the Epicurean pursues pleasure as his ultimate goal; the Stoic chooses instead to follow reason and virtue. In the one, nature is license; in the other, it is law. What this fact determines at the level of individual pastoral fictions is the difference between the amoral bucolic sentiments of Sannazaro's lovers and the sharp ethical distinctions of Sidney's Arcadian shepherds.

It is reasonable to anticipate that a community of shepherds in Stoic pastoral as a reflection of a rationally ordered nature would hold a common set of standards in a society whose lines of authority are clearly and hierarchically defined. (A political unit would constitute only a more complex extension of such a community.) At the center of Stoic pastoral, it is also reasonable to assume that one would discover such virtues as patience, temperance, fortitude, and justice—the very ones that Sidney emphasizes so strongly in his definitions of pastoral in the *Apology* and at the outset of *The Old Arcadia*. The native Arcadians offer an example of such a community, just as they frequently express values that are a logical consequence of a Stoical interpretation of nature. This gives them an especially important role in the work. The ethical standards of the Arcadian shepherds provide a central core of values against which we measure the behavior of the rest of the characters. As the princes, the royal family, and the stranger shepherds make love, sing, and contemplate a world governed by the seemingly arbitrary fluctuations of fortune, Geron, Dicus, and the other Arcadians guide us in evaluating their actions.

It is important to recognize that although the native shepherds occupy a central place in *The Old Arcadia*, there are at least two other varieties of the idle life with which they must compete for sympathy and approval—those of the princes and the stranger shepherds. As central as their values are within the romance, Sidney constantly demands that we be aware of their limitations. The native Arcadians do not possess the sophistication of Pyrocles and Musidorus, and there is something to be said for sophistication. They are not capable of the exalted imaginative vision of Strephon and Klaius, and in Sidney's world there is much to be said for imaginative vision. These are flawed shepherds. Their precepts are a body of moral commonplaces that served as the cornerstone of Sidney's education and that reappear in the *Arcadia* in order to be tested both by experience and by rival ethical systems. It is most helpful to think of the Arcadians not as an ideal, but as a kind of solid middle against which we can evaluate other sorts of extreme experiences—better and worse. This is a hypothesis, a working theory about *The Old Arcadia* that must be substantiated in part III as we examine the eclogues and their relationship to the work as a whole.

Sidney was praised by his contemporaries as among "the best for pastoral." The Arcadian eclogues were valued as an integral and particularly delightful part of a romance that itself was read within the same tradition. In spite of these facts, twentieth-century critics of *The Old Arcadia* have been reluctant to consider the work in relation to its pastoral context. This reluctance stems mainly from misunderstandings about the nature of Renaissance pastoralism, perhaps the most damaging of which is the notion that *The Old Arcadia*'s genre can be assessed according to an exclusive and arbitrarily devised definition of "real" pastoralism: Sidney's *Arcadia* does not resemble Sannazaro's, but unless we assume without historical or theoretical justification that the Italianate version is the only true kind, this does not make it antipastoral or even unpastoral.

Renaissance pastoralism is composed of a diverse group of distinct traditions with equally distinctive expressive possibilities. Its diversity is its most characteristic feature, particularly because of the freedom assumed by the major pastoralists to engage in generic redefinition. The traditions of the past are regularly reshaped in order to advance both the writer's reputation and new sets of aesthetic, moral, and social ideals. In 1578, when Sidney set out to write *The Old Arcadia*, he would have been conscious of two major traditions of Renaissance pastoralism: the Italianate and the Christian. As representatives of these groups, Sannazaro and Barclay had radically different conceptions of the idle life: they disagreed about the functions of poetry, about the value of love and about the rationale for contemplating the natural world. At the basis of all these disagreements was the emphasis of the Italianate writer upon pleasure as the end of life and art, and the Christian writer's unequivocal rejection of that end in favor of a religious vision of Christ the shepherd. As I have argued, what Sidney sets out to do in *The Old Arcadia* is to create a new version of pastoral that merges the emphasis upon contentment in the Italianate tradition with the ethical concern of the Christian bucolic. He does so while seeking to maintain one of the traditional functions of Renaissance pastoral in supplying relief from misfortune. Sidney succeeds in bringing these two traditions together in the romance's animating fore-conceit: the Stoically derived notion that the happy man leads his life in accordance with nature—in accordance, that is, with the dictates of reason and virtue. At the conceptual center of *The Old Arcadia*, pleasure and virtue are reconciled, and it is Sidney's Stoical fore-conceit that makes that reconciliation possible.

Prior to Sidney there had been other writers who had given a Stoic coloring to fictional passages set in one kind of rural landscape or another, but there are no genuine literary precedents for the creation of a Stoic pastoral, no other works that embody the rational law of nature as a bucolic image. Rather than speculating that the idea for a literary work of this kind could have been generated in the remote landscapes of Horace, Seneca, or the Christian pastoralists, it seems more prudent to assume, as the *Apology* encourages us to do, that *The Old Arcadia* owes its inspiration directly to a single animating fore-conceit: the law of nature as reason and virtue.

PART III
The Old Arcadia and Its Eclogues

4
From Prose to Poetry

THE *Old Arcadia* is constructed out of divided and distinguished worlds, the prose world of the books and the poetic world of the eclogues. There is no more important fact about the pastoral, since it is in the movement from the narrative to the eclogues that Sidney establishes the characteristic rhythm of its style and themes. Reading *The Old Arcadia* is a lesson in navigation, for learning to navigate between the fictions of the Arcadian narratives and its entr'acte entertainments is ultimately to understand how Sidney succeeds in creating a single, well-balanced, Stoic pastoral. The business of part III of my study is to account for that success, especially as far as Sidney's thematic intention is concerned: his desire to instruct the reader in how to lead a just life within a cosmos ruled by the seemingly arbitrary whims of fortune. To make that account, I shall begin by examining one of the romance's primary characteristics: its division into largely distinct units of prose and poetry. A new pastoral vision required a new pastoral form, capable of realizing Sidney's generic design to reconcile Italianate contentment with the moral fervor of the Christian bucolic. My intention is to isolate the eclogues from the romance's design in order to clarify their contributions to its unity. I shall focus first upon Sidney's motives for constructing distinct worlds of prose and poetry, and then upon the consequences of that structure for the character of his fiction. In the remaining chapters of part III, a reading of the first four books of *The Old Arcadia* and their corresponding entr'acte entertainments will clarify the coherence of the pastoral's themes.

Sidney's inclusion of poems in *The Old Arcadia* is scarcely surprising. No pastoral romance in the sixteenth century could have done without its portion of lyrics. Sannazaro's *Arcadia* had made sure of that by setting a precedent for the combination of elegantly lyrical poetry with equally elegant prose. As Sidney remarks in the *Apology*, "if severed they be good, the conjunction cannot be hurtful."[1] What is surprising about the poems in *The Old Arcadia* is their placement. Although he continues to include lyrics within the prose books, as Montemayor and Gil Polo do, Sidney is the first writer of pastoral romance to incorporate sets of eclogues as entertainments separate from the rest of the action.[2]

Out of *The Old Arcadia*'s division between prose books and poetic eclogues, Sidney fashions distinct fictional worlds by exploiting the expressive potential of a contrast between fictional modes. As the pastoral moves from prose into poetry, the reader is brought out of a forward-moving, logically patterned narrative into static, emblematically significant eclogues. In one world individual events are scrutinized from the outside by the narrator; in the other, general concerns are subjectively voiced by particular singers. The characteristic rhythm of *The Old Arcadia* is a movement from the individual to the universal.

Finding motives for Sidney's decision to separate his eclogues from the prose books begins properly with a look at *The Old Arcadia*'s narrative style, for particular styles of prose have particular consequences both for the character of a fictional world and for the nature of its poetry. The prose style of *The Old Arcadia* is as logical as it is urbane. Its main function is to guarantee a regular, causally determined flow of events.[3] Unlike other pastoral romances, Sidney's contains no magical, rationally inexplicable happenings (with the rather large exception of its ending); its narrative is perfectly intelligible because its main purpose is to encourage intelligent judgments upon the causes and effects of events.[4] In the first, fourth, and fifth books in particular, the triumph of a forward-moving narrative style is nearly complete, almost novelistic in its proportions. The princes suffer love's agonies, seduce their mistresses, and fall prey to Euarchus's judgments. Their passions press onward with a logically patterned momentum. If the twenty-six poems scattered throughout book three, as the princes' love adventures achieve their greatest successes, produce a prose texture more reminiscent of Montemayor and Sannazaro, that is to say, more lyrical, this can be explained as a deliberate interruption—dictated by the logic of events—in a cause-and-effect-momentum.

The really memorable prose of *The Old Arcadia* is found in Philanax's reasoned attacks upon the princes, in the orderly balance of Philoclea's pleas for patience, and in the shrewd, ironic commentaries of Sidney's narrator. What makes the prose style of these passages memorable is an especially significant deployment of those qualities that distinguish the style of the narrative as a whole. Consider one example. When the Arcadian shepherds have captured Gynecia after discovering Basilius' "murdered corpse," Sidney writes: "Now all together, and having Gynecia among them (who, to make herself the more odious, did continually record to their minds the excess of their loss), they yielded themselves over to all those forms of lamentation that doleful images do imprint in the honest but over-tender hearts, especially when they think the rebound of the evil falls to their own smart" (283). In a single sentence Sidney displays much of his characteristic manner. This is difficult, intricately wrought prose: it cannot be read in one breath (we are forced to dwell amidst parentheses). Passing in and out of its winding clauses, we are asked to pause over subtle distinctions (the shepherds' hearts are "honest" but "over-tender") and to marvel at puzzling behavior (Gynecia's desire to "make herself the more odious"). The narrative analyzes events as it reports them. What Sidney thinks about tender-hearted shepherds who fail to qualify their passions by reason is as apparent as the judgmental character of the prose. His narrative presses on toward conclusions, illuminating the intricate psychological connections between events and responses to events. Across the divide that separates the tragic Gynecia from the foolish shepherds, Sidney erects a single instructive bridge. Even amidst public suffering, the self-loathing duchess and the timid shepherds can think of nothing but themselves. What the syntax weaves together, Sidney's art relates intelligently. His narrative is in the business of thinking—and in persuading the reader to think.

A narrative style of Sidney's type has consequences for the kind of pastoral world that can be created within it. The mode of expression makes demands upon its contents. *The Old Arcadia* is one among several Renaissance pastorals, like Gil Polo's *Diana Enamorada* and Spenser's book 6 in which the triumph of narrative is accompanied by an increased emphasis upon the fragility and the dangers of the pastoral place. Lustful dalliance brings disruptive passions into Felicia's retreat; murderous brigands destroy Pastorella's rural oasis. In *The Old Arcadia* the "murder" of Basilius threatens moral and political chaos. Events of this type, which inevitably undermine our sense of the security of the pastoral place, are a logical accompaniment of narrative movement. For narratives like Sidney's guarantee instability and impermanence, inescapably undermining the idyllic qualities traditionally associated with the genre. Pastoral happiness depends upon a measure of stasis, the kind of stasis that lyric best supplies.

There are no brigands or murderers in Theocritus's Coan pastorals; freed from the pressures of narrative, from the misfortunes of acting and being acted upon, his shepherds bask contentedly in the pastoral sunshine. Even though it is theoretically possible for a bucolic narrative to take place entirely within the boundaries of an idyllic Arcadia, the temporal dimension inherent in narration would inevitably work against that happiness. When the pastoral locale becomes a landscape that characters have to travel *to* (rather than an already established setting in which they are discovered), that same locale is transformed into a place that they eventually have to travel away *from*.[5]

There are narrative elements in Vergil's *Eclogues*, including travel between the country and the city—Meliboeus is forced out of his farm; Moeris and Lycidas journey toward a town that sounds suspiciously like Rome; Gallus exiles himself to Arcadia—but these elements play a minor role in the work as a whole in comparison to the fully developed narrative schemes of Renaissance pastorals. Vergil confines such details largely to the opening and closing portions of the *Eclogues*, on the boundaries of the pastoral world, as an indication of the kinds of experiences that the bucolic life is designed to exclude. If Vergil had anticipated Renaissance writers in his concern for the effects of time and fortune upon the idle life, the movement of pastoral into a narrative mode made a continuing obsession with such effects a structural necessity. Evanescence was no longer merely a possible topic of pastoral (one option among many conventional bucolic subjects); it became a necessary topic (a concern dictated by the mechanics of the work). At the same time, in the movement between places, a comparison between different kinds of settings, and, consequently, between different kinds of imaginative and ethical worlds was made equally inevitable. The two writers who value rational control most highly and who are most critical of the ethos of Italianate pastoral, Gil Polo and Sidney, are the same writers who are so concerned with the development of a causally determined, forward-moving style of narration. The critical perspectives of their romances can be accounted for as a logical accompaniment of the Renaissance pastoral's single most important transformation, the movement from lyric into narrative.

My retreat into the larger context of the Renaissance pastoral romance, with its triumph of a logically patterned style of narration, is useful not only in accounting for the fragility of the pastoral place but for clarifying Sidney's motives in separating his eclogues from his prose books. Prose of this kind has special consequences for poetry; this is especially apparent in the poems situated within the narrative.

For Sidney's lyrics bear little resemblance to those of the traditional pastoral romance.[6] In the poems of book one, for instance, we are confronted by the sexual paradoxes of an oracle ("Thou with thy wife adult'ry shalt commit"), a humorous anti-Petrarchan blazon on an ugly shepherdess ("What length of verse can serve brave Mopsa's good to show"), the comic boasts of a rustic fool ("Now thanked be the great God Pan"), and the laments of a princely shepherd and an Amazonian transvestite upon the inconveniences of their sartorial metamorphoses. These are hardly what one would call sentimental lyric effusions. Sidney's poems are brief, sudden interruptions of the narrative movement that provide plot details (as the oracle does), comic relief (as Dametas does), and information about the characters' states of mind (as Cleophila and Dorus do). At other stages of the narrative they are introduced to supply ironic comments on abandoned piety ("Apollo great . . ."), evidence of recollected virtue ("Since nature's works be good . . ."), humorous erotic exposition ("What tongue can her perfections tell"), to name only a few of their multiple functions. The dominant lyrical mode of *The Old Arcadia* is irony.

An unsentimental style of narration demands an equally unsentimental style of lyric. After adopting the dress of an Amazon, Cleophila sings:

> Transformed in show, but more transformed in mind,
> I cease to strive, with double conquest foiled;
> For (woe is me) my powers all I find
> With outward force and inward treason spoiled.
>
> (28, 30–33)

His verses afford an instructive illustration of his mental condition: in the witty parallels between the prince's outward changes and his inward treasons, Sidney creates a speaking picture of the divided mind. His picture speaks so clearly and eloquently because of all those characteristics of the *Arcadia*'s lyrical style which by now are well known: its logical symmetry, reinforced by medial caesuras; its carefully patterned alliteration; and its orderly progression of iambs.[7] Cleophila's lyric is not designed for the forceful expression of emotion: it has no personal voice because it makes no effort to express personal feeling. There is nothing spontaneous about his sentiments. As a picture of Cleophila's state of mind, a picture isolated from the movement of the prose, the lyric is best described as an emblematic representation of experience—emblematic, because the particulars of

Cleophila's private emotions are refined into a public depiction of passion's universal causes and effects. By understanding Cleophila's poem, we understand how passion of this kind works. Sidney imposes a tight organization upon the prince's feelings from above as hot pastoral passions are cooled by analysis within the sonnet's symmetrical parts. Like all of *The Old Arcadia*'s lyrics, "Transformed in show . . ." is an appropriate addition to the narrative because it, too, is in the business of thinking.

Thoughtful prose, thoughtful poetry—if severed they be good, the conjunction cannot be hurtful. So the *Apology* says. However, the marriage between *The Old Arcadia*'s narrative and its lyrics is less comfortable than at first appears. For among the special demands that the prose books make upon the poems included within their boundaries are a set of important constraints upon Sidney's range of expression. These constraints are important because they supplied his primary motives for creating a separate world for the eclogues. Clarifying the nature of those constraints and their corresponding effect in motivating the construction of a special kind of poetic world is the main business of my argument.

The narrative style of *The Old Arcadia* can tolerate only brief, fairly infrequent interruptions. As a result it is all but impossible to include in the prose books the usually extended debates, song-contests, and amorous complaints of the traditional pastoral—a sizable limitation upon the poet's range of expression. The great majority of the narrative's lyrics are sonnets. Sidney employs the sonnet form frequently, not merely because it is an apt vehicle for clarifying the psychological states of his characters, but also because it is brief enough to punctuate the narrative movement without retarding its flow. If Sidney wanted to exploit the expressive possibilities of a greater number of poetic forms and styles (and there can be no doubt that he did), he would have had to create a separate fictional world in which to do so—a world distinct from the narrative in which shepherds could debate moral issues, engage in song-contests, and delight in amorous complaints, freed from the pressures of a forward-moving plot. Writing eclogues was Sidney's pastoral retreat from the responsibilities of narrative.

Creating a separate fictional world for the eclogues offered Sidney an escape from another kind of constraint imposed by his narrative. The sonnets of the prose books are effective tools for clarifying the mental condition of his characters, but they are limited modes of expression insofar as they provide only a single range of perspectives upon the speaker's state of mind. In the poems of the prose books, we overhear a single character (usually one of the princes) giving voice to a single set of sentiments (usually of an amorous kind) that Sidney's ironic narrator has a singular fondness for undercutting. Narrative rationality has a way of deflating lyric passion. When Cleophila concludes his lyric upon his transformations in mind, the narrator comments characteristically: "I might entertain you, fair ladies, a great while, if I should make as many interruptions in the repeating as she did in the singing. For no verse did pass out of her mouth but that it was waited on with such abundance of sighs, and, as it were, witnessed with her flowing tears, that, though the words were few, yet the time was long she employed in uttering them" (29). Eager to get on with his story and obviously annoyed with Cleophila's feminine sighs and sobs, the narrator works a further transformation upon the prince by making him the butt of his sarcasm.

Constraints of this kind, and narration of this sort, are absent from the eclogues. Moral debates and song contests between characters with radically different ideas about reason, love, and the nature of the cosmos multiply, rather than limit, the range of perspectives we are given upon the characters, events, and themes of the narrative world. Once more, in the virtual absence of the narrator, we are allowed to make our own judgments by choosing among rival points of view—a freedom essential to the success of Sidney's pastoral strategy since he is interested in teaching us how to judge. No narrator intrudes to undercut sarcastically Dorus's amorous idealism or Dicus's moral fury. As we pass between the prose books and the verse eclogues, from the ironies of the narrator to unmediated song contests and debates, the range of perspectives on *The Old Arcadia*'s events is multiplied significantly. One of Sidney's primary motives for creating entr'acte entertainments was to make multiplication of this kind possible.

The eclogues freed Sidney from one last constraint imposed by the character of his narrative world: the need to show individuals acting upon other individuals in a verisimilar landscape. The prose world is a realm of events in which we interest ourselves in the causes and effects of human actions, in the consequences of Basilius's withdrawal to Arcadia, in the success of Musidorus's flight with Pamela. The focus is upon individual characters engaged in particular activities that have unique results (rebellion, capture, death sentences). The eclogues are different. We move from the realm of events to the realm of ideas, where individuals derive their chief dignity from how justly they conceive their world and from how skillfully they express those conceptions in song. The poems do not advance the plot of *The Old Arcadia;* they provide a relief from it. The very fact that all of the eclogues, except for those of Lalus and Kala, take place during the evening or at night, indicates their separateness from the sphere of action. During these entertainments, as we witness the debate between Philisides and Geron, or the laments of Agelastus for Basilius, we focus upon characters whose status within a community is more important than their individual identities, and upon experiences like love, death, and marriage, whose general human consequences are more important than their unique results. In the song contests and debates of the eclogues, Sidney succeeds in refining the particular concerns of the prose world—Gynecia's lust for Cleophila and Dorus's yearning for Pamela—into moral and intellectual abstractions (such as Passion and Love) that can be understood and evaluated in comparison with rival abstractions (such as Reason and Anger). The individual themes of the forward-moving narrative are isolated and immobilized in the static realm of the eclogues—set out on display, so to speak, with other valuables whose worth is a test of their own.

As Sidney retreats from prose into poetry, he moves simultaneously from a volatile landscape filled with amorous intrigues, rebellion, and "murder," into a far more orderly world dominated by a superior brand of orderly shepherd. Given the character of *The Old Arcadia's* prose style, it is no accident that this change in the character of Sidney's fictional worlds should parallel the movement from narrative into lyric. The Arcadian shepherds articulate many of the pastoral's primary values with a directness and power found nowhere else in the romance. Sidney takes advantage of the static, emblematic mode of expression in the eclogues to fashion out of the life-style of the native Arcadians *The Old Arcadia's* most persuasive image of contentment and justice: the marriage of Lalus and Kala. His shepherds gesture significantly towards ideals. Only within the lyrical world of the eclogues does Sidney attempt to depict such virtue and pleasure.

Sidney had, therefore, a variety of motives for establishing a separate world for his eclogues. As an escape from the constraints of his narrative, he fashions lyrical fictions in which to exploit a more extensive range of poetic forms and styles; he creates song contests, debates, and amorous complaints designed to multiply the number of perspectives upon *The Old Arcadia's* characters, events, and themes, while educating the reader in how to make judgments for himself; and he finds relief from the prose books' march of events by designing a static realm of ideas in which moral abstractions can be evaluated and in which images of contentment and justice can be preserved. Given these opportunities for expanding the interest and significance of his pastoral, by the inclusion of separate sets of entertainments, Sidney's innovation in establishing eclogues within *The Old Arcadia* must be judged as one of primary stylistic and thematic importance.

Sidney's eclogues do not closely resemble Vergil's, Sannazaro's, or Spenser's, and they stand in sharp contrast to them, in large part, because they were designed to appear within a narrative. Their placement between extended prose books accounts for many of Sidney's innovations in the form, innovations essential in shaping them into unified components within *The Old Arcadia*. Consider the kinds of characters who inhabit the eclogue world. When Spenser introduces a shepherd named "Cuddie" into the "February" eclogue, he is perfectly entitled in terms of the decorum of the bucolic poem to include another possibly unrelated Cuddie in "October." The Corydon who appears in Vergil's *Eclogue* 2 is not the same Corydon who defeats Meliboeus in *Eclogue* 7; the Tityrus who appears in *Idyll* 7 bears no resemblance to the goatish swain of *Idyll* 4. Sidney never takes this liberty. Applying the same standards of coherence that exist for narrative figures, Sidney lends a consistency of character to the entire body of his eclogue shepherds that is ordinarily reserved for one or two major shepherds. The Lalus, Dicus, and Geron who appear in the opening entertainments are the same Lalus, Dicus, and Geron who take part in the third eclogues.

Not only are the characters more consistent; they are also more familiar. The fact that these poems occur within a narrative structure guarantees that even before approaching them we know far more about the figures who take part in the entertainments and the kind of world in which they are set than we do about such matters before reading Vergil or Theocritus. By the time they enter the pastorals of the first book, Dorus and Cleophilia are far from strangers to us. As a result, we are engaged in Sidney's eclogues to a much greater extent than in those of his predecessors in a continuous process of measuring familiar aspects of the fictional world against new, sometimes unsettling revelations.

The novelty of establishing eclogues within a narrative scheme is only one indication of the freedom that Sidney takes with pastoral conventions. With characteristic independence of mind, Sidney includes a variety of poems that are foreign to the bucolic tradition. In his eclogues we find a beast fable, a Petarchan sonnet, a fabliau, an echo poem, and a dream vision. The very fact that they are able to stand alongside works cast in a more purely classical mold without creating a sense of disharmony indicates the elasticity of the conventions with which he is working. A list of the meters and stanzaic types that he employs in his *eclogae*, or "selected pieces," reads very much like an English redaction of an Italian neoclassical handbook of prosody. Sidney had no precedent for innovation on this scale. Terza rima, rhyme royal, Alexandrine couplets, single and double sestinas, sixain and dizain stanzas, and a variety of other polymetrical forms and classical meters find a place in this collection. Many of these devices were new to the native literature, and Sidney's use of them indicates his desire to fashion an English poetry capable of rivaling both classical and Continental verse. In part he sets out in these eclogues to give concrete proof of what he was later to maintain in his *Apology:* that the English language "for the uttering sweetly and properly the conceits of the mind, which is the end of speech . . . hath it equally with any other tongue in the world."[8]

It is not simply narrative that produces changes in the eclogues but a particular histrionic mode of narration. There is no more revealing difference between Sidney's entertainments and the bucolics of his classical and Continental predecessors, than the dramatic form imposed upon the poems. The first two groups of eclogues are records of theatrical performances, revised by pens that "having more leisure than their tongues, might perchance polish a little the rudeness of an unthought-on song"—a humorous reflection upon the pastoralist's usual pretensions to spontaneity (56). Although the third and fourth sets of eclogues take place in separate, nontheatrical settings, the ritualistic nature of the occasions that inspire them, marriage and death, guarantees a nearly equal amount of attention to them as performances. Sidney demands that we interest ourselves not only in the relationship between various singers, as we do in Sannazaro and Barclay, but in the interchange between the singers and the audience witnessing the action. As a consequence, his eclogues possess a dialectical complexity that is unrivaled in earlier pastorals. Again, in the *Arcadia,* we are able to contrast the world of the eclogues not only with our own world, as we do in the bucolic tradition, but with another fictional realm largely distinct from it: that of the prose books. A further measure of the complexity of these entertainments is supplied by the number of different kinds of characters who are allowed to participate in them. In the Italianate tradition the world is split between the native shepherds and the outsiders; in Christian pastorals there are country dwellers and city dwellers. Sidney's Stoic pastoral is different. His eclogues place three rather than the usual two groups of characters in opposition: the princes, the native Arcadians, and the stranger shepherds. The dynamic interaction among these spokesmen for various versions of the idle life is what captures our attention.

The sophisticated structure that Sidney creates for his eclogues affords a good indication of his rhetorical intentions. The form multiples rather than limits the number of perspectives upon experience, and lends itself much more readily to the production of ironies and ambiguities—in the complex interaction among singers, between singers and audience, and between the worlds of the prose and the poetry—than to didactic certainties. As a result Christian pastoralists would have found little use for it. The dialectical character of Sidney's eclogue form offers plenty of possibilities for contrast between opposing points of view, and criticism of particular moral positions.[9] As a consequence Italianate pastoralists would have been baffled by its expressive possibilities. A new pastoral vision required a new pastoral mode, one whose expressive potential could complement the logical rigor of Sidney's narrative. The dramatic structure of the Arcadian eclogues is an apt vehicle for a poetry of criticism, for a Stoic pastoral attempting to confront human issues of profound significance without diminishing their complexity.

The dramatic structure of *The Old Arcadia* needs further probing since this structure offers the best explanation for the peculiar grouping of the poems. The eclogues are situated at the end of each of the romance's first four books or acts, on the model of the *intermedii* of Continental Terentian comedies. As the name implies, the *intermedii* were elaborate entertainments devised for performance between the acts of a comedy. Most of them were allegorical and mythological spectacles, which because of their phenomenal popularity became a standard feature in sixteenth-century Continental drama. Often transferred unchanged from one comedy to another, the *intermedii* were used principally to satisfy the audience's taste for lavish display.[10] Trissino complains in his *Poetica* that they obscure the meaning of the comedies and another contemporary dramatist, Grazzini, laments (1582): "Già si solevono fare gl'intermedi che servivono alle commedie, ma ora si fanno le commedie che servono agl'intermedi. . . ."[11] Some of them were pastorals, utilizing the methods and materials of the classical bucolic. In between the first two acts of Antonio Landi's *Il commodo* (1539), six shepherd couples sing a song to Apollo; after the third act, a version of Vergil's sixth eclogue is performed.[12] Even in these examples, however, the subjects are so arbitrarily selected that their relationship to the *Arcadia*'s entertainments seems remote. If the Continental *intermedii* provided Sidney with a fashionable precedent for extended entertainments within a Terentian structure, he was unimpressed and uninfluenced by their contents.

English Renaissance comedies never developed *intermedii* on the scale of the Continental variety. Entr'acte songs and dances were regular features within the performances of the children's companies, and may also have occasionally been included in popular comedies, but they were never allowed to compete for the audience's attention with the work at hand. In the early Elizabethan period the tragedies contain the significant entr'acte entertainments and provide the most important dramatic precedent for Sidney's eclogues.[13] In *Jocasta, Gismonde of Salerne, Locrine,* and *The Misfortunes of Arthur,* dumb shows are included between the acts as a way of clarifying the drama's themes. (In *Gorboduc,* the dumb shows precede the acts.) According to Dieter Mehl it was the function of these shows "to make abstract spiritual experiences and conflicts visible as concrete scenes and to impress a moral idea on the spectators by appealing directly to the senses."[14] For instance, when six wild men enter the stage at the beginning of *Gorboduc* and proceed to break sticks individually that could not be broken as a group, they dramatize an important lesson about the need of unity within the state.

Although Sidney's eclogues are only fictionally dramatic (rather than scripts for actual dramas), and although Sidney is not engaged in the simplistic didactic enterprise of enforcing ethical ideas upon an audience, his entertainments do possess a similar purpose and often manifest a similar emblematic method. Like the dumb shows, the Arcadian entertainments are an attempt to give concrete expression to moral and intellectual abstractions. They offer a sustained attempt to transform psychological events into speaking pictures, which in their variety and inclusiveness create a single, unified picture of the life of the mind as it responds to the inconstancies of fortune. (Unlike the dumb shows, of course, Sidney's pictures really do speak.) This is an emphasis that agrees with both the entr'actes of Elizabethan tragedy and with Sidney's focus in the *Apology* upon the unique effectiveness of the speaking picture in illuminating the mind's imaginative and judging power.

Not all of the Arcadian eclogues are so straightforwardly emblematic as the contest between the passionate and the reasonable shepherds, or Dicus's anti-Cupid tirade, but the poems never carry us far from this fictional level. In Plangus's lament, for instance, we are confronted not simply by the grief of an impassioned lover (a particular individual in a particular setting), but by the passion of frustrated love itself (a timeless emotion in a timeless context). The eclogues stand on the boundary line between mimetic and iconographic fiction, leaning much more heavily in the direction of the latter than the former. The very fact that Sidney provides many of his eclogue characters with allegorical names—Geron, Dicus, Mastix, and the rest—while allowing them to be perceived simultaneously as individual shepherds is an indication of the degree to which we are expected in these entertainments to measure the particular by the general, and to pass suddenly between them. The movement from the individual to the universal defines the characteristic rhythm of particular eclogues just as it defines the rhythm of *The Old Arcadia*'s larger movement from prose books to poetic entertainments.

These facts are important for our understanding of the romance. The dramatic structure of *The Old Arcadia* functions as a device for structuring the ordinarily unruly materials of pastoral romance and as an invitation to the reader to picture the events of the work, to recreate the fiction actively in his imagination. By rendering moral and intellectual abstractions in visual images, by balancing one image against another, and by encouraging the reader to reenact that psychomachia in his own mind, Sidney attempts both to delight and to instill in his audience a complex moral vision. The eclogues are given a Continental appearance by means of their placement in a Terentian structure, but their kinship with the entr'actes of English tragedy provides a more telling indication of their function.

In the process of my describing what happens as Sidney moves from prose into poetry in *The Old Arcadia* and my recounting how the eclogues are altered by being set within a narrative framework, some of the major contrasts between the fictional worlds of the books and the entr'acte entertainments have already been clarified.[15] Sidney leads us to expect irony and ambivalence in his entertainments by the character of the poems that he includes in the narrative and by the dramatic structure that he creates for the eclogues, a structure designed to maximize such effects. In the transition from books that are dominated by an extremely slippery narrator to pastorals in which there is an almost total absence of overt stage-managing, there is not so much an increase in the level of irony as a change in its character. Rather than being imposed upon the action from above, as they are in the prose books, the ironies of Sidney's eclogues are allowed to emerge without editorial comment from the juxtaposition of various styles and ideas within the dialectic of the poetry.

At the same time, as we have seen, the two worlds of Sidney's fiction are distinguished according to the predominance of their particular narrative and lyric functions; the prose is more persistently verisimilar, the eclogues more frequently emblematic. Another way of defining this contrast is to describe the prose world as a realm of events in which we interest ourselves in the causes and effects of human actions, and the eclogues as a realm of ideas, where individuals derive their chief dignity from how justly they conceive their world and from how skillfully they express those conceptions in song.

Sidney's Arcadian entertainments constitute, then, a kind of pastoral-within-a-pastoral. At the end of each major portion of the action we retreat into a new bucolic place from a world that is itself a place of retreat. The new pastoral movement is accompanied, as one might anticipate, by new pastoral pretense. Sidney's entertainments promise relaxation and diversion from the multiple entanglements of the plot. If they make good on part of this promise, they also require unexpected intellectual activity as we are forced from within a place of retreat to measure the validity of the very activity in which we ourselves are engaged: pastoral withdrawal. In good Empsonian fashion, the complex issues of the *Arcadia*'s prose books reappear as the simplified moral emblems balanced within the eclogues' sophisticated dialectical structure. They appear in simplified form so that they can be understood more readily; they appear within a sophisticated structure so that we remember their complexity. Writing a pastoral-within-a-pastoral allowed Sidney to establish a hermeneutic center from which the rest of its action could be interpreted. He creates what might be called a reader's paradise, a place in which we are equipped with the right tools for literary analysis, the skills for moral judgment, and the means for securing not only justice but contentment. The calculated disingenuousness with which this process occurs is a triumph of Sidney's artistry. As we first move into the eclogues we are made conscious of a whole series of fresh limitations. We are aware of having passed into the narrow confines of a theatrical setting, where we will confront much simpler rustic characters in entertainments that "being dedicated only to pastorals," (the accent is on "only") will leave "all . . . princely motions" aside (57). Our awareness of the limits imposed upon the landscape, people, and subject matter of the eclogues is reinforced by the poems' physical placement in the fiction, wedged as they are between longer, more imposing prose sections. What results from all these limitations, from this conscious pastoral pretense, is, as we have seen, a tremendous expansion of meaning and applicability in the romance. As in the double plots of Elizabethan drama, this secondary action has the effect of making us believe that the fiction is dealing with life as a whole.[16]

One more instance of Sidney's subterfuge is worth drawing attention to here. The retreat from one place of withdrawal to another is accompanied not, as we might expect, by further distance from the "real" world, but, paradoxically, by closer ties to it. Philisides' presence within the eclogues guarantees this. When he delivers Languet's fable to his sheep in the third eclogues and an autobiographical narration in the fourth, he establishes important political and personal connections with the actual world that are without parallel in the narrative. Sidney measures the validity of his pastoral withdrawal just as we do.

As pastorals-within-a-pastoral, simplified fictions designed to clarify the complex issues of *The Old Arcadia*'s plot, the eclogues required an intellectual coherence both equivalent and parallel to that of the narrative. Each set of poems had to be unified in itself and the four sets of pastorals had to cohere as a group in complementary development with the narrative. A complete account of their unity would yield, as a result, a nearly complete reading of *The Old Arcadia*'s themes—the kind of reading that I shall supply in the remainder of part III. In order to prepare for that account, it will be useful to outline, in general terms, the nature of the eclogues' unity.

Several different kinds of coherence are evident in *The Old Arcadia*'s entertainments, some of which are particularly conspicuous by reason of their absence from the classical and Continental eclogue. For instance, in contrast to Vergil's bucolics, each set of Arcadian poems gains in unity by having all of its songs take a place within a particular location (not just Arcadia, but a theater, a bower, and a hillside), and within a particular time span (at night, in the daytime, in the evening). The very fact that these songs are performed one after another by singers who are conscious of each other's presence, leads the reader to expect a considerable degree of relatedness from them. Another kind of coherence is provided to the eclogues as a consequence of Sidney's greater consistency of characterization. The use of similar sets of characters from one group of eclogues to the next helps in defining a fictional world peculiar to the poems. The fact that Geron and Dicus participate in all four sets of eclogues guarantees the presence of other more important kinds of unity. The native Arcadians never leave the scene, and as a result, their Stoical values persist in the fiction as a dominant ethos. There is only one other character who appears with equal regularity, and that, appropriately enough, is Sidney's fictive double, Philisides. (In fact, Philisides is the sole figure to deliver a song in all four groups of eclogues.) The presence of the poet gives unity to his poems.

The eclogues maintain a high degree of structural coherence. Into the twenty-seven songs of *The Old Arcadia*'s entr'acts entertainments, introduced and followed by prose passages of varying lengths, Sidney instills a purposeful organization. Philisides' lyrics help to provide unity not simply because they occur in all four groups but because they occupy important places within them. His confrontations with Geron and Echo, his beast fable, and his love laments for Mira occupy the central portions of the four sets of eclogues. The medial placement of Philisides' songs supplies the key to an understanding of their structure. Each set of Arcadian entertainments is organized in three specially related parts.[17] In the eclogues of books one and two, we move from songs that directly involve the princes, to lyrics of greater general relevance by Philisides and the native Arcadians, only to return in the last few poems to the particular experiences of Dorus and Cleophila. In a similar fashion the eclogues of the third book begin and end with explorations of the marriage problems that are endowed with peculiar universal significance in Philisides' song to his sheep. In the fourth eclogues we pass from the private misfortunes of Strephon and Klaius to the public mishaps of Agelastus and the native Arcadians; in the intervening poems on Mira, private and public concerns establish an uneasy balance. As one might anticipate, in the central poems of each set of eclogues the central thematic issues of *The Old Arcadia* receive their most direct and significant treatments. The three-part dialectical structure of the entertainments encourages a balanced argumentative progression, one capable of producing new understandings but few final resolutions.

Sidney's eclogues have a carefully planned thematic coherence. They echo, by means of their structural parallels, both each other and the themes of the *Arcadia*'s narrative. Their skillfully contrived surface unity has been obvious to nearly everyone who has considered them in any detail.[18] It is appropriate after the princes have been introduced to Arcadia and to love that the first book should conclude with poems on the reciprocation of amorous desires. After Pyrocles and Musidorus have revealed their identities to their respective mistresses in the second book, the theme of the eclogues undergoes a corresponding change; the struggle between reason and passion becomes a principal focus of attention. The third eclogues constitute a celebration of marital love and fidelity, a subject of great importance in a book that finds Basilius committing "adultery" with his wife in a cave. In the fourth and final eclogues, the duke's supposed murder occasions a series of poems on the twin calamities of unrequited love and death.

These connections are easy to establish, but they tell us little about the deeper underlying unity of the eclogues, about those infinitely more significant matters that the shepherds utter "under hidden forms," and it is in this unity that I am primarily interested. As a rule there are few allegories to be explicated here; but the poems do focus persistently and obliquely upon issues other than those with which they initially appear to be dealing. The eclogues have more thematic coherence than has been recognized. All four sets of poems examine a single complex topic, contentment and the just life; contentment (or "quietness," as it is sometimes called) is a goal of each of these pastoral life-styles and, as one might expect, it is a goal subject to multiple interpretations. In the first eclogues, our interest is centered upon the divided mind and the frustrations attendant upon its search for contentment. In the second eclogues, we are chiefly concerned with the consequences of division, definitions of pastoral quiet, and debates over how it is obtained. The eclogues of the third book present us with an image of contentment achieved as an ideal of justice, and in the fourth eclogues we witness the catastrophic effects of the mind's loss of tranquillity and the loss of justice in the individual and the state in what is simultaneously an exploration into the limits of quiet as an ideal of human behavior.

The next four chapters will be devoted to an examination of Sidney's rigorous and impressively exhaustive treatment of this theme, as it appears, first, in each of the prose books, and then as it is extended and developed in the subsequent eclogues. It should be pointed out that it is because Sidney links his discussion of contentment and justice with his characters' conceptions about love that I shall focus so heavily upon this particular feature of the idle life. In part four Sidney's concern with how the natural world is contemplated and how it is represented in poetry will serve as the focus for analyzing his redefinition of pastoral, and his effort to use the genre to obtain justice and contentment for himself and his readers.

5
Book One: The Divided Mind

NO sooner has the idealized image of Stoic quiet been presented in the opening sentences of *The Old Arcadia* than it is destroyed by Basilius's determination to relinquish his responsibilities as a duke. He withdraws to a pastoral oasis, forging the first link on the chain of follies and mishaps that comprises the romance's plot. Basilius is guilty of two mistakes: he shows curiosity in consulting an oracle in a world "wherein there is nothing so certain as our continual uncertainty" (5), and fear, when he believes himself "so cruelly menaced by fortune" that he needs to withdraw from public life "to avoid her blows" (6). By dividing himself from his dukedom, he sets a precedent for the ensuing drama of self-divisions, preparing the way for what Sidney calls at the end of the first book, "a very stage-play of love"—a play framed, of course, by "fortune" (54).

Basilius is the victim of the literary convention whose history was traced above in chapter 1, since it is a pastoral life on which he depends for protection against fortune's "inconveniences" (6). So thoroughly has this particular notion colored his senses that he places his eldest daughter, Pamela, with Dametas, "thinking it a contrary salve against the destiny threatening her mishap . . . to place her with a shepherd" (6). There is no difficulty in knowing what to think of Basilius. Within a few sentences, Philanax, his trusty counselor, is introduced for the purpose of delivering a Stoically inspired critique of Basilius's irresponsibility, one that receives explicit authorial approval. Philanax chides his inconstancy, asserting that "wisdom and virtue be the only destinies appointed to man to follow" (7), while making it clear that these are the only real protections offered to man against misfortune: ". . . either standing or falling with virtue, a man is never in evil case" (7). The virtue that Philanax is most concerned about is justice: "neither your subjects have wanted justice in you, nor you obedience in them," he tells Basilius; "let them see the benefits of your justice daily more and more" (7–8). Its loss will mean disaster for the state. Philanax's emphasis on reasoned self-reliance and justice looks ahead to the arguments of the native shepherds in the eclogues. To enforce the moral of his opening exemplum even more pointedly, Sidney introduces a short character sketch of Euarchus, "a prince of such justice" that he never "did measure greatness by anything but by goodness" (10). Basilius's folly is highlighted by the virtue that enables Euarchus to carry "a heart prepared for all extremities," to respond justly to the full range of fortune's vagaries (10).

The opening pages of *The Old Arcadia* have all of the simplicity of an apologue. A foolish duke meets a wise counselor and fails to heed his lesson in Stoic constancy. Sidney presents a simplified fiction as a way of clarifying the pastoral's major question, "how can a man lead a just life in an inconstant world?," and to advance what can accurately be called the conventional wisdom on the topic. But this is not a simple question to be answered by pat precepts. As Philanax himself will learn by the end of *The Old Arcadia*, the world of experience is far too unpredictable to be measured by moral commonplaces. Sidney quickly complicates the ethical scheme of the romance, overgoing his initial exemplum with the arrival of Pyrocles and Musidorus in Arcadia.

Even though it is the princes' desire for "virtue" and "experience" that leads them to Arcadia, their movements at every stage of the plot are attributed to fortune's influence. Fortune drives the princes into Asia; "fortune" is held responsible for Pyrocles' amorous fall as he gazes at Philoclea's portrait (11); "fortune" is blamed for metamorphosing Musidorus into a lover (39); "fortune" is made accountable for the passions of Basilius, Gynecia, and Philoclea for Cleophila (48), for the attack of the lion and the bear, and even for Dorus's ability to kill the invading beast (52). In fact, nothing of any importance takes place in the first book without in some way being linked to fortune. Rather than resulting in the absolution of the princes from moral responsibility (an evasion of ethical implications that an Italianate pastoralist would gladly have adopted), what this pattern guarantees is the constant need to evaluate the princes' choices as responses to the world *sub specie fortunae*, providing, in the process, a specific cosmic context in which to understand their actions.[1]

After the princes embark on their sea voyage, Sidney writes that they will experience "good and evil fortune" (10), but he is unwilling to paste on the moral labels for us. When Pyrocles falls in love, as we are told, he does so by "either evil or good fortune" (11). Just as Basilius's had been, his resolve to withdraw into the royal retreat is greeted by immediate criticism, only this time the critique of pastoral withdrawal takes the form of a contest between points of view whose merits are nearly equal.[2] Musidorus's reasoned contempt for the pastoral life, scorning contemplation as a smokescreen for idleness, coupled with his assault upon love as a masquerade for lust, links him with Philanax as a purveyor of textbook ethics. He is obviously at home in what he believes to be a well-ordered universe: passions are to be suppressed, just as women are to be kept in their place. Like a good schoolbook Stoic, Musidorus centers the major thrust of his argument upon the need for virtuous constancy. In a passage highly reminiscent of Sidney's letter to his father in Ireland, he argues: "A mind well trained and long exercised in virtue . . . doth not easily change any course it once undertakes but upon well grounded and well weighed causes; for being witness to itself of his own inward good, it finds nothing without it of so high a price for which it should be altered" (13).

Musidorus is right on target. As he knows, Pyrocles' "good or evil" fortunes stem from his enthrallment by a variety of desires for the world "without" himself: the delights of relaxation, a fondness for pastoral contemplation, and, most important, his love for Philoclea. Because we have Musidorus as a foil we can comprehend what happens to Pyrocles as his comfortable Elizabethan world picture is shattered and replaced by a dangerously inviting universe in which the satisfaction of amorous desires becomes the ultimate goal. Pyrocles' special pleadings, sighs, and tears win less approval for his arguments, but they also gain more sympathy than Musidorus's easy rationalism and petty misogyny. (After all, as we well know, he too is about to fall in love.) If Pyrocles' Amazon costume is laughable, so is his cousin's pedantry. If we acknowledge the virtues of Musidorus's constancy, we are also aware that it would be a mistake to dismiss out of hand the high claims for love advanced by Pyrocles.

As Musidorus details the dangers of love, the narrator informs us:

> Pyrocles' mind was all this while so fixed upon another devotion that he no more attentively marked his friend's discourse than the child that hath leave to play marks the last part of his lesson, or the diligent pilot in a dangerous tempest doth attend to the unskilful words of a passenger. (20–21)

This is Sidney in his most characteristic style. Pyrocles is portrayed first as a truant child, then as a diligent pilot; Musidorus is represented first as a teacher, then as a busybody. Contradictory images are simultaneously balanced in order to increase the number of viewpoints that we have upon the experience, thereby improving the quality of our understanding of it. Pyrocles is not a child or a pilot; he is both child and pilot. The simple didacticism of Philanax is supplanted by a more sophisticated mode of rendering judgments.

Pyrocles and Musidorus are lured into the Arcadian retreat by a set of motives quite different from Basilius's. They withdraw to the lodges not to protect themselves in good pastoral fashion against fortune's blows, but to pursue their fortunes in love; their contentment—or so they think—depends upon the success of their pursuit. They seek relief, not protection; as Pyrocles tells Musidorus: "the question is not now whether I shall love or no, but whether loving, I shall live or die" (17). When Pyrocles expounds the delights of the Arcadian landscape, he reminds us of the lovers in Italianate pastoral, just as Musidorus does when he appears for the first time after acquiring his passion for Pamela, "in the apparel of a shepherd, with his arms hanging down, going a kind of languishing pace, with his eyes sometimes cast up to heaven as though his fancies strave to mount up higher, sometimes thrown down to the ground as if the earth could not bear the burden of his pains" (39–40). The literary origins of his behavior are unmistakable. What clinches the princes' connection with the Epicurean characters of the Italianate tradition is the climax of Pyrocles' debate with his cousin: when asked to describe the "end" to which his love for Philoclea is directed, he answers with a deep sigh, "Enjoying" (23).[3]

Like the lovers of Sannazaro's *Arcadia*, Pyrocles and Musidorus are bent on achieving pleasure, and are confronted, instead, by the agonies of divisive passion. Again and again we are told how love produces "unquiet longings" in their "troubled brains" (12, 23). Just as Basilius's divided mind leads to improper divisions in the state and the royal family, the unquiet passions of the princes separate them from their country, their estates, and in Pyrocles' case, even from his sex. What keeps our sympathy for them, in addition to our admiration for the constancy of their friendship and our confidence in the innate nobility of their characters (they are princes "born to the exercise of virtue"), is their awareness of the dangerous consequences of the divided mind (10). Once again, this consciousness is accompanied by a knowledge of fortune's sway over human events. Pyrocles and Musidorus lament:

> Alas! What further evil hath fortune reserved for us, or what shall be the end of this our tragical pilgrimage? Shipwrecks, daily dan-

gers, absence from our country, have at length brought forth this captiving of us within ourselves which hath transformed the one in sex, and the other in state, as much as the uttermost work of changeable fortune can be extended unto. (43)

At the conclusion of the first book, during the very moment in which preparations are being made for the eclogues, Sidney introduces a conventional twist into his pastoral plot by arranging for the intrusion of the lion and the bear. As the agents of fortune the beasts supply uncomfortably concrete evidence of the vulnerability of the pastoral oasis: Basilius is not going to find protection in his lodges, at least not the kind of protection he had hoped for, just as the princes will be forced to suffer constant mishaps in their attempts to achieve contentment in pastoral dalliance.[4] What Sidney has succeeded in doing in this episode and in the first book as a whole is to qualify the Italianate pastoral's sentimental image of man by a critical look at his susceptibility to unquiet longings. In a book that focuses so heavily upon divisions in the self, the family, and the state, one goal of human behavior emerges unequivocally as a good to be pursued: "the contentment of the mind, which once obtained, no state is miserable; and without that, no prince's seat restful" (45).

Sidney introduces his first eclogues with a brief description of the "manner" of the shepherds' songs and games. The details of his account are derived from Polybius as a way, once more, of attaining historical authenticity for the fiction and as a means of reasserting the image of Stoic quiet with which *The Old Arcadia* began. We are reminded of the native shepherds' "goodness of . . . wit" and of the "thrifty world" that they inhabit (56). Still more important is the renewed attention given to "the peace wherein they did so notably flourish" and "the sweet enjoying of their peace" employed "to so pleasant uses" (56). Their tranquil life-style and their quiet of mind receive the greatest portion of Sidney's attention. Balanced against these qualities are the "inward melancholies" troubling the stranger shepherds, and the "ambassade of . . . passions" and "unlawful desires" tormenting the royal audience (56, 57). Stoic quiet becomes the standard of measurement for the disturbances of a divided mind.

Sidney begins with a dance, with an emblem of what Lalus will later call "love['s] condition": an amatory state whose extremes are defined by a division between fortunate and unfortunate shepherds (63, 19). One half of the dancers sing, "We love, and have our loves rewarded," as the other half replies, "We love, and are no whit regarded" (57, 58). Sidney reinforces the image of love created in the narrative: by juxtaposing the lines of the rival groups without attempting to account for the differences between their "conditions," he gives renewed strength to the picture of love as an independent, highly arbitrary power akin to fortune. There seems to be no reason, and indeed, no possibility of finding a reason for why one group is loved and the other scorned.[5]

Dorus takes part in the opening performance, presumably as a member of the unfortunate shepherds. He is singled out by a young Arcadian named Lalus, significantly enough, because of the "extreme tokens of a troubled mind" evident in his dancing, and provoked to "a more large expressing of his passions" (58). Dorus is actively baited for the entertainment and the instruction of the rest.

The princes achieve several advantages by entering the eclogues. They participate in the entertainments after accomplishing their most notable feats of valor: the killing of the marauding beasts and the quelling of the rebellion. At the height of their heroism, they are provided with their best opportunities in the romance to give extended expression to their love for the princesses and to convince us of the genuineness of their idealized passions. The princes are also provided with a stage on which to dramatize their superiority of wit and artistic skill as they compete with shepherds in a variety of songs and games.[6] These are real advantages. At the same time, there is a significant degree to which clever rustics and conventionally determined disguises can foil the courtier's ability to control the drama in which he participates. An initially advantageous situation can quickly become a platform for exposure.

When the princes move from the verisimilar world of the prose into the highly conventional, emblematic world of the eclogues, there is an instructive and entertaining clash between kinds of fictions. For the first time in *The Old Arcadia*, we are given an extended look at Dorus and Cleophila in the act of behaving as a shepherd and an Amazon. As Dorus competes with Lalus in the opening contest of the first eclogues, we are continually pressured to adjust our knowledge of him as a particular character with a particular history and temperament against the new conventionalized identity that he assumes in the course of the song. He is very much like the Connecticut Yankee in King Arthur's Court, a "normal" character who walks into a world populated by fictional beings inhabiting a separate dimension of experience. The fact that Dorus takes on one of these fictional roles, forcing his complex personality within the boundaries of a simple literary construct, that of the Italianate shepherd, is both amusing and revealing. We are amused by the synecdoche-writ-large: Musidorus, as we know, is considerably more complicated than his disguise suggests, the whole larger than the part that is taken for it; but in the course of the poem we are made aware that he has important features in common with the lovelorn shepherds of pastoral convention.[7] By juxtaposing Dorus and his literary stereotype we establish our knowledge of his character. What this process inevitably entails for the princes, at least for the duration of the eclogues, is the loss of the special, nearly archetypal status that they possess in the narrative world. They are no longer the only young lovers in the romance, nor is their variety of love the only or even the most admirable variety to be found. With the multiplication of parallels, both with other characters and other traditions, there is an inevitable increase in critical awareness—literary and moral.

The competition between Lalus and Dorus is a fine example of pastoral indirection. The surface rhetoric of the contestants is so polite that there is some danger of forgetting that this really is a *contest*. One indication that all is not as it seems is provided by the poem's rhyme scheme: the singers engage in a fierce competition to keep pace with the increasingly complex patterns of the opponent.[8] Lalus has ulterior motives in provoking Dorus to sing. By debating which of the two "deserveth most compassion" from their mistresses, they also debate the merits of two different styles of life (59, 6).

Lalus and his healthy love for Kala come as the fulfillment of a promise made at the *Arcadia*'s outset: the creation of a Stoic version of pastoral. As one of the "very owners of the sheep themselves," Lalus is clearly in a class above the shepherds whom we have previously encountered: the low-minded Dametas and his decorously ridiculous wife and daughter, and the cowardly shepherds who run away from the lion and the bear (56).[9] But this superiority does not entirely rescue him from comic limitations—a constant in our dealings with the native Arcadians. An ugly shepherd who "babbles" about the hard heart of his beauteous and buxom shepherdess is likely to provoke a smile or two. What his status as a native shepherd does guarantee is his commitment to a set of standards whose value is largely independent of the personal eccentricities of the shepherds who are its spokesmen. The community he belongs to supplies him with a measure of dignity.

To be sure, Lalus is as conscious as any shepherd in the Christian bucolic of belonging to a community, and he knows how to bring its pressures to bear upon others. When Dorus tells him in good Italianate fashion that no "true love loves his loves with others mingled be," he is rebuked as the shepherd replies sharply: "Be none of us, or else maintain our fashion" (58, 34; 59, 2). The prince gives in by agreeing to sing. The contrasts between the two are extended further. When Dorus tells Lalus that "Thy health [is] too mean a match for my infection," he announces the principal point of comparison around which the poem is organized (59, 9). We are impressed by the shepherd's thriftiness when he boasts about the "many hundred sheep" that he will provide to Kala as a marriage gift (61, 33)—a boast that finds no parallel in Dorus's more aristocratic promises. But the more important contrast to be drawn between them concerns the simplicity of Lalus's affection for Kala and Dorus's complex metaphysical passion for Pamela. When Lalus's mistress is praised, it is because she resembles a lamb or a cony; when Dorus's princess becomes the subject of song, it is because "She is herself of best things the collection" (59, 36). Although it is difficult not to admire the prince's conviction that his love is ennobling, that Pamela's virtue will raise his "mind to high erection," his penchant for sexual puns is troubling (60, 22). Dorus's desire to "reach . . . beyond humanity" is a potentially dangerous and frustrating passion (60, 16). In contrast, the appeal of Lalus's love is immediate; like Rixus in *The Lady of May*, he may limit his reward by limiting his desires to what is obtainable, but he also assures his contentment.

Lalus assumes his most persuasive stance as he makes his marriage offer to Kala:

> Such as you see, such still you shall me find:
> Constant and kind. My sheep your food shall breed,
> Their wool your weed: I will you music yield
> In flow'ry field; and as the day begins
> With twenty gins we will the small birds take,
> And pastimes make, as nature things hath made.
> But when in shade we meet of myrtle boughs,
> Then love allows, our pleasures to enrich,
> The thought of which doth pass all worldly pelf.
>
> (62, 3–11)

The standards to which he appeals are those of a Stoic pastoral: constancy and kindness. In this rejection of worldliness and the aspiring mind, Lalus glorifies a version of the idle life in which pleasure and goodness have been so completely interwoven that it is difficult to distinguish which is employed as a metaphor for the other. He offers Kala the wool from his sheep not as "worldly pelf"—an alternative that is explicitly rejected—but as an emblem of virtuous pleasure.

Final clarification is given to the shepherd's health and the prince's infection by the eclogue's concluding emblems. In Lalus's complaint that he grows "like the beast/Which bears the bit a weaker force doth guide,/Yet patient must abide," we have a miniature allegory of reason's continued control over the passions, while Dorus's lament that his identity has become as insubstantial as a vision in another's mind is employed as an image of the major theme of the first eclogues: the "wretched state of man in self-division" (63, 6–8, 15).[10] Even though the eclogue has no winner since no clear evidence is presented as to which of the two "deserveth most compassion," we are left with no doubt that Lalus is the more likely of the pair to dance with the fortunate shepherds.

The entrance of Geron and Dicus, with their protests against love, provides a sudden change of tone. Pastoral song contest collides head-on with didactic emblematic poetry. Geron and Dicus are the eldest members of the Arcadian community, and as such, within the natural hierarchy of the social system, they are made the most important purveyors of the ethos of the native shepherds. (Even Dicus's name, meaning "custom" or "justice," is an indication of his authority among the Arcadians.) Sidney treats these shepherds with an amused skepticism. Geron's animosity toward love is attributed to the spite of a provincial old man who "wished all the world proportioned to himself," and Dicus's hatred is represented ambiguously either as the product of "certain mischances of his own," or as the result of "better judgement" (64). Again, Sidney refuses to pass simple judgments. In the process of watching Dicus rail against love, impassioned against the foul fault of passion, we recall Sidney's humorously critical description of the moral philosophers in the *Apology*.[11] It is easy to share Basilius's laughter as Dicus enters the stage after transforming himself into a walking-talking-rag-tag emblem of beastly Cupid, but there is a measure in which both we and the duke are obliged to consider his performance seriously.

The most important point to be grasped about Dicus's assault on Cupid is that it is directed not so much against love as against "flatt'ring of desire," that far more comprehensive power which creates what I have been calling "the divided mind" (66, 14). His rebukes are aimed at "those fools that will have all they see" (66, 22). He chides those greedy "narrow breasts" who seek out "gain" and those ambitious "swelling hearts" who pursue "honour's fire," as well as the lustful (66, 11, 12). Sidney's decision to transform Cupid into a speaking picture of the full range of human passions derives from the one provided in the immediate and as yet unnoticed source of the poem: in the first book of Gil Polo's *Diana Enamorada* the cynical Alcida delivers a double attack in poetry and prose on the god of love. In the course of her prose assault, Alcida makes it clear that Cupid is more than an image of lust; he is the principal and universal cause of "temores, cuidados, recelos, mundanças y otras infinitas passiones. . . ."[12]

Sidney's poem is inspired by Gil Polo, but the idea of wittily and satirically reworking the traditional image of Cupid, like the details of the emblem itself, is entirely his own. Dicus's assault is more comic and more outrageously exaggerated than Alcida's, just as it is more meaningful. Cupid is transformed into a half-man, half-beast, as a way of emphasizing the unnatural divisions of the impassioned mind. The fact that the god should also be the product of divisions within the Olympian royal family, having been begot by Argus on Io, "What time for her Juno her Jove did miss," is a hint that the eclogue has a special relevance for the laughing Basilius (65, 23). At the conclusion of *The Old Arcadia*, in an event already predicted by the oracle, the same passions will eventuate in another "father's death, and mother's guilty shame" (65, 27).

Frightened by Dicus's attack, a young Arcadian named Histor relates a prose tale illustrating how "revengeful a god" Cupid is, a tale that provides the opening eclogues' third and most disturbing look at the divided mind (66). The very fact that the community of Arcadian shepherds should contain a historian is significant, particularly one who puns shamelessly upon his own name, asserting at one point about the princes that "all Asia was full of their histories" (70). Histor supplies a good indication, together with Dicus ("custom") and Geron ("old man"), of the retrospective character of Stoic pastoral; like Sannazaro in his tenth prose, Sidney hints at pastoral's access to the accumulated experience of the culture, to the storehouse of native wisdom enduring through time.[13]

Histor's story is a Greek romance in miniature: the correspondence extends even to the medium in which he speaks. The prosaic historian is placed in his native element as a way of signaling our temporary reentry into a narrative world of forward-moving, causally determined events. The stylistic jolt that carries us back into that world heightens our awareness of the contrast between the narrative movements of the prose books and the lyrical progression of the eclogues. Sidney reduces the scale and accelerates the pace of the action, as the details of the unfortunate loves of Plangus and Erona are narrated, in order to accentuate the customary effect of such romances: an increased emphasis upon destiny's control over human events. Love and fortune again become associated as Cupid is transformed by Histor's narrative into a reigning tyrant. Cupid takes revenge upon Erona for having scorned his worship. (Both her name, which suggests "eros," and her age—she is fourteen—supply further indications of the degree to which her fall into passion is determined by forces seemingly beyond her control.) It is Cupid who is responsible for the jealous Otanes' decision to make war on Lydia, who is held accountable for Antiphilus's treacherous passion for Artaxia, and who is blamed for leading Plangus into his apparently hopeless passion for Erona. He controls a world gone mad with eroticism.[14]

Histor's romance adds a new dimension to our understanding of love, one that serves to complicate our sympathies further. In his tale of Plangus and Erona, love is given an increased intensity that wins our admiration; it is also made to appear more paradoxical, as Erona weds Antiphilus, having "love against love" (68); most important, however, is the new force given to our appreciation of its dangers. In Erona's world we witness the destructive consequences of a divided mind, which are as yet unrealized in Basilius's dukedom. Her passion for Antiphilus leads to hardship for the state, as Otanes makes war against Lydia, to irreparable divisions in her family, as her father's heart is broken with grief, and to unnatural divisions in herself as she weds a man of "mean parentage" (67).

Histor's tale also complicates our sympathy for Dorus and Cleophila. (Dorus, too, had boasted against love that "all the heavens cannot bring me to such a thraldom" [40]). As an account of their first heroic adventure, while coming to the aid of Erona in her battle against the Persians, it is an important episode in supplying "historical" proof of the princes' "incomparable valour" and "matchless courage" (68, 69). From beginning to end, Histor speaks of them as the "two excellent . . . princes," the "two heroical princes," the "two rare princes" (68, 70, 71); his narrative is filled with descriptions of their "notablest adventures," their "courage," and the "notable proofs . . . of their virtue" (69, 70). If such an unusual amount of praise is calculated to increase our admiration for them, that admiration is qualified by our knowledge of their truancy: Erona suffers in prison, threatened with death, while the princes bask idly in Arcadia. (They plan to help her but, as Sidney informs us, even "that fancy was stopped" [71].) It is clear, therefore, that one function of Histor's narrative is to provide a concrete image of the princes' past virtue as a way of measuring the distance that they have traveled from it. At the same time, his narrative also makes their truancy partially understandable. In a world dominated by Cupid, even the most heroic princes are vulnerable to the woundings of desire. The intensity of Erona's passion goes some way, if not in justifying then at least in explaining the princes' presence in Arcadia.[15]

An emblematic dance, a pastoral song-contest, a moral satire, and a miniature Greek romance: the diversity of fictional kinds presented in the first section of Sidney's opening entertainments points to the inclusiveness of his pastoral strategy. Each new eclogue raises new questions about the nature of love, and more important still, about the mind's capacity to control experience, to secure its own contentment in a world ruled by the seemingly arbitrary whims of fortune. To accept the view of love presented in the shepherds' dance as an arbitrary power akin to fortune is to understand something of importance about it, but it is also to overlook the degree to which a lover's good and bad fortunes stem from his mental condition. Good fortune, of course, is exactly what Dicus would deny to anyone under the influence of passion, but his assumption that the mind can escape from passion is challenged not only by his own ambiguous motives for singing, but by Erona's disastrous experience in attempting to flee from it.

Passion is an inescapable part of the human condition; it is the psychological agent through which fortune operates to produce division and discontent. If contentment is to be achieved, then desire must be reckoned with. This much seems clear. But is this a real possibility in terms of Sidney's understanding of the mind? If so, what kind of activity would make such a fortunate reckoning possible? The opening entertainments raise more questions than they answer. In the poems that follow, Sidney provides no answers to these questions, but he does supply greater clarity to the issues. The central songs of the first eclogues move us beyond particular considerations of the attractions and dangers of love into a broader landscape where a set of related confrontations—between youth and old age, man and emblematic beasts, shepherds and satirists—presents a speaking picture of the divided mind itself. This picture is of particular importance because it provides Sidney's first lesson in how to read the pastoral and in how to pass judgments.

Just as it seems that Sidney is about to permit a heroic ethos to dominate the eclogues, the pastoral perspective is restored. We are introduced to one of the stranger shepherds, Philisides. After dramatizing Cupid's tyranny over Erona's world, Sidney could bring only one character onstage to rival these others in misfortune: a despairing lover from the Italianate tradition. (What creature could be more hopeless?) In this posture Philisides is first presented to us as he lies "at the foot of a cypress tree" in deep melancholic contemplation (71).

"Up, up, Philisides, let sorrows go": with Geron's challenge to the languourous lover, the eclogues change course. For the first time in the entertainments, the suggestion is made that there are remedies for misfortunes and protections against "plaintful custom" (72, 6). Geron does not need to be told, any more than the reader, that Philisides is a frustrated lover. This is a world in which all young foreigners are despairing and impassioned. His approach is as openly didactic as that of a Christian pastoralist as he attempts to raise Philisides' "fancies" (72, 8), admonishing the youth to acquire "virtue" and a "constant temper" (72, 16, 18). As an unbending rationalist with a firm faith in the orderliness of his world, Geron proceeds to chide Philisides for his passions:

> He is a beast that beast's use will allow
> For proof of man who, sprung of heav'nly fire,
> Hath strongest soul when most his reins do bow.
> (74, 34–36)

His most telling gesture is his advice to him "upon thyself to stand" (73, 20). Reason, virtue, piety, constancy, and self-reliance: his speeches contain all of the major tenets of Stoic pastoral. Most of Geron's arguments have been anticipated by Philanax and the other native shepherds. (Even his misogyny is recognizable from Musidorus's debate with Pyrocles.) Their appearance here is significant because of the proof they supply of the coherence of the Arcadian shepherds' central core of values and of Sidney's intention to ground those values in a life led according to the laws of nature.

What is genuinely new about Geron's remarks is his emphasis upon the mind's ability to shape its own destiny—new, that is, in *The Old Arcadia*. Geron adopts a traditionally approved point of view as he shifts from assuring Philisides that "fortune may change thy hap," to informing him how to use his reason to suppress "Those rebel thoughts which are thy slaves by kind" (72, 28; 73, 15). The old shepherd advises Philisides about the kinds of songs he ought to sing and about the kinds of country labors he ought to pursue. At the heart of all of his shepherdly remedies for passion, "How thou from foolish love mayst purge thy sense," is his admonition:

> Then virtue try, if she can work in thee
> That which we see in many time hath wrought,
> And weakest hearts to constant temper brought.
>
> (72, 16–18)

On his side of the debate, it is well to recognize, Philisides does not reject virtue, piety, and constancy as standards of behavior; he redefines them. To make a "causeful moan" for one's mistress is consonant with "Sweet virtue's law" (72, 21); to devote oneself to a female saint indicates "holy fear" (74, 30). In place of the constancy of reason, he substitutes as an ideal, like the lovers in Montemayor's *Diana*, the constancy of amorous devotion:

> If fortune's lap became my dwelling place,
> And all the stars conspired to my good,
> Still were I one, this still should be my case,
> Ruin's relic, care's web, and sorrow's food.
>
> (72, 29–32)

He glorifies his suffering for a beloved "Whose wit the stars, whose fortune fortune thralls" (72, 34). Love becomes an absolute standard of value.

In the process of redefining virtue, piety, and constancy as ethical standards best realized in the devotion to one's mistress, Philisides clarifies exactly what is wrong with Geron's platitudes about how to achieve a "constant temper." To argue, as the old shepherd does, that virtue's law provides a remedy for misfortune is not very helpful unless one knows what virtue is—and it is exactly this knowledge that is at issue here. The old shepherd and the young lover are not debating about the importance of virtue; they are arguing about its meaning. Does virtue consist in the suppression of passion or in the realization of idealized amorous desires? Once more, the eclogues return to the central question: how are passions to be reckoned with in order to assure the mind's contentment? Once more, Sidney refuses to provide a final answer.

Geron tangles with a tougher opponent than he had anticipated. Philisides refuses to fit into simple categories.[16] If he resembles a despairing Italianate shepherd, his violent emotions and acute intelligence quickly distance him from even the most desperate of Sannazaro's shepherds. If his literary roots place him in the company of persona shepherds, such as Vergil's Tityrus, Sannazaro's Sincero, and Spenser's Colin, Philisides is more vigorous and more comic. He is also more ambiguously situated in relation to his creator; we see much less of him than we do of most other personae, and what we do see is sometimes colored by ironies from the rival authorial voice of a narrator. He is Sidney's representative in the eclogues, but not his spokesman.

Philisides must also be distinguished from Dorus and Cleophila. The very fact that he perseveres in his worship of his mistress is an indication of the value that he attaches to love, an indication that reinforces the princes' high estimation of their passions. At the same time, Philisides is made to suffer extraordinary hardships due to the frustration of desire, hardships that reveal the princes' folly in naively idealizing an emotion capable of inflicting serious pain. His experience allows him to articulate values as yet unimagined in Dorus and Cleophila's more limited world and unimaginable in the restrictive universe of the native shepherds.

Put "out of countenance" by Philisides' scorn, Geron attempts to find relief from his passions, "to restore himself to his countenance," first by railing at his dogs and then by approaching an old acquaintance named Mastix (76). In this eclogue Sidney makes his most significant exploration of the divided mind. Geron is more than an angry man, he is a speaking picture of anger, aroused as "practically all" angry men are, according to Plutarch, by scorn and neglect. In his essay "On the Control of Anger" (one that Sidney recommends to Edward Denny), Plutarch marvels that "we even rage against dogs that bark."[17] But these are no ordinary dogs that Geron chides. Melampus and Laelaps are named after two of the animals who tear the mythical Actaeon to pieces. They might even be called blatantly emblematic beasts since they are standard participants in Elizabethan allegories of passion's assault upon reason.[18] When Geron rebukes his curs for their "envy" and "pride" as they fight over food, he draws an analogy between their strife and his conflict with Philisides; more important still, by chiding his curs, he supplies a telling dramatic image of his own "divided weakness" (76, 24). The dogs have a clear symbolic function in alerting us to the state of his passions and the difficulty that he has in establishing control over them. In Sidney's world the gap between precept and performance, the capacity to know the good and the ability to act upon that knowledge, is a large one—even for the native shepherds.

As Geron shifts his attention from his dogs to Mastix, "one of the repiningest fellows in the world," Sidney moves from the private passion of an individual to the anger of a satirist against the public. Mastix's appearance onstage (his name means "scourge") is accompanied by a sudden change in diction as both shepherds proceed to load their speeches with rustic terms:

> Come nar, good Mastix, 'tis now full tway score
> Of years (alas) since I good Mastix knew.
> Thou heardst e'en now a young man sneb me sore.
> (77, 6–8)

The abrupt shift in language is telling. Sidney evokes the diction and style of the native Christian pastoralists, with typically allusive economy, as the prelude to another clash between kinds of fictions. Geron confronts an exaggerated portrait of himself in the literary Mastix—a huffing-puffing fictional being who appears to have walked straight out of the pages of a Barclay or a Turberville. Geron's private passions, emblematically mirrored in Actaeon's snarling curs, are mirrored at another level in the excessively bitter satiric ire of Mastix. By means of this pattern of reflections, Sidney attributes to the satirist psychological motives that mark his literary productions as one more expression of the divided mind. Satire, Sidney clearly implies, in a challenge to its legitimacy as a literary mode, is the creation of an impassioned intellect, an aesthetic version of a psychological disorder. (No doubt, this is the poem that Thomas Moffett had in mind when he praised Sidney for so composing "satires that he nicely ridiculed satyrs full of vices. . .").[19] Barclay and the Christian tradition are no more acceptable than Sannazaro and the Italianate pastoralists. In the movement, then, from Geron's attempt to reconcile his wrangling dogs (his passions) to his rejection of Mastix's undiscriminating malice (a literary mode arising from similar passions), Sidney passes from moral criticism to literary criticism, only to return in the last portion of the eclogue to indicate what these moral and aesthetic issues have to do with us as readers.

Geron provides us with an essential lesson in how to read and how to make moral judgments. By confronting an exaggerated portrait of his own anger in Mastix and by realizing its applicability to himself ("Yet thou art mickle warse than ere was I"), Geron is taught a fundamental lesson about his own and other men's behavior (78, 12):

> Let our unpartial eyes a little watch
> Our own demean, and soon we wonder shall
> That, hunting faults, ourselves we do not catch.
> Into our minds let us a little fall,

> And we shall find more spots than leopard's skin.
> Then who makes us such judges over all?
>
> (79, 5–10)

Because we are all flawed, because we are all in some measure victims of the divided mind, with our reasons at war with our passions, the only valid judgments to be made are those which acknowledge even the best judge's liability to error. It is altogether characteristic of Sidney's native shepherds that Geron should proceed to dump most of the blame onto Mastix, as he turns a personal lesson into an opportunity for moralizing; even a triumph of ethical understanding in this all-too-fallen world can provide the occasion for new follies. If Geron does not respond just as the reader ought to, by demonstrating the need to recognize in the images with which we are confronted our own liability to folly, he does at least point the way to a right response.

In the last three poems of the first eclogues, our attention is refocused directly on Dorus and Cleophila. After having the chance to compare their complex Italianate love for the princesses with other romances, with the simplicity of Lalus's devotion to Kala, the intensity of Plangus's hopeless passion for Erona, and the frustrated idealism of Philisides, we have a better understanding of the princes' nobility and naiveté. Dicus, Histor, and Geron have also made us aware of the dangers of a divided mind and the misfortunes to which passionate excess leads. At the same time, while witnessing how difficult it is even for an old shepherd to maintain rational control, we have been exposed to the attractions of idealized eroticism.

Throughout most of the performance, if we judge by their concluding lyrics, Dorus and Cleophila have not given much attention to the events onstage—though, as Geron reminds us, we had better avoid judging them too harshly for this. Neither their nobility nor their naiveté has diminished. They do not misunderstand their situation. When Dorus singles out "desire" as the principal cause of his "Infernal agonies," he is perfectly correct in doing so (80, 5–6). Nonetheless, the same aesthetic reserve and studied artificiality that allow us to delight in a lyric like "Fortune, Nature, Love," are also what serve to convince us that Dorus is toying with concepts that he does not fully understand, for the simple reason that he has not yet fully experienced the effects of the divided mind. He creates an elegantly crafted allegory in which he is transformed into the passive victim of a cosmic triumvirate, without comprehending the consequences of his literary posturing.[20]

A similar argument could be made about Cleophila's lyric. In his only solo performance of the first eclogues (women are ordinarily excluded from bucolics altogether), equally elegant sapphic stanzas are employed to supply additional force to a sentiment advanced earlier in his debate with Musidorus: "love it is that hath joined/Life to this our soul" (82, 9–10). This is not an idea that we are likely to dismiss very quickly, though it is one, with its consequent idealization of love, that we will need to see substantiated by the rest of the romance. The very fact that both lyrics are accompanied by a sudden heightening of aesthetic pleasure, as classical meters replace the plainer measures of the shepherds, obtains a renewed admiration for the princes.

The final poem in the first eclogues is an extended "provoking" song, in which Dorus and Cleophila debate which of them is the more unfortunate in love. In this context the eclogue is important chiefly as a summary of the major themes of Sidney's opening entertainments. We are reminded of the "strange operation of love," which as a comprehensive power akin to fortune "Neither . . . bears reverence to a prince nor pity to beggar" (82, 27, 29). While the princes tend to insist upon the difference between their experiences, the eclogue's rhetoric asserts the similarity. Both continue to blame fortune for the fact that they are "wholly diseased," while looking to their mistresses to restore their minds' contentment (86, 18). What the contrast between their estates as shepherd and Amazon does provide for, significantly enough, is the elevation of pastoral above courtly values. Dorus exclaims "what a blessing/Is chanced to my life," in escaping from "marble bowers, many times the gay harbour of anguish" (85, 30–31, 27).[21] If he understands that "sorrow's torments" may continue in the country, he also believes that it is better to have "scope" to breathe out griefs in private, than to be "tied to the pomps of a palace" (86, 7–8). No one steps forward to contradict his idealizing image of the idle life's remedies against misfortune. For the time being, Italianate pastoral seems to have achieved the ascendant position. After all, the princes have the last word.

In the first book of *The Old Arcadia* Sidney explores the divisions that uncontrolled passions create in the individual, the family, and the state. By balancing the rival viewpoints of the eclogues' characters, as Dorus competes with Lalus and Philisides rails against Geron, he succeeds in highlighting the possible virtues and the certain perils of the aspiring mind's response to a treacherously mutable world. Love is capable of frustration, and the princes' claims for its values are of uncertain authority. If there can be no question that the good to be pursued as a just response to fortune is a quiet mind, no single fictional image has yet been offered to show how real quiet can be obtained.

6
Book Two: The Consequences of the Divided Mind

NEW light gives new directions. As the sun rises at the outset of the second book, Sidney sets about "manifesting" passion's "venomous work" in Gynecia (91). The first sentence, with its notice of her "unquiet motions," announces his major theme. This is Sidney's book of seductions. In the pursuit of Basilius and Gynecia for Pyrocles, Dorus's wooing of Pamela, and Cleophila's exchange of vows with Philoclea, Sidney details a complex network of desire. Passion is deployed with copulative variety: the foolish lust of a duke, the murderous jealousy of a mother, the sexually ambiguous longings of one princess, the imprudent passions of another, the idealized eroticism of the princes—all of these "unquiet motions" are represented as the consequence of a single evil, what Sidney continues to call, throughout book two, the divided mind.

Sidney opens the book with Gynecia's complaint, rather than with Basilius's or Cleophila's, as an indication of the new seriousness with which he represents the princes' experiences in love, just as Gynecia's exclamation against the imperfections of reason, "which can too much foresee, and so little prevent," gives new clarity to the difficulties of achieving self-control and contentment (92). At the same time, a larger cosmic context is supplied for these considerations. There is nothing unusual about Gynecia's blaming the "destinies" for her misfortunes (92), but when she appeals to the "heavens" to prevail in making her virtuous, she introduces a larger providential dimension into the romance, a dimension that assumes increasing importance as the work proceeds.

In the first of the two central wooing scenes of the second book, we watch Dorus advance his amorous fortunes. He is by far the cleverer of the two princes, as he demonstrates by seducing Pamela while pretending to make love to Mopsa. Dorus strives to make good on the fortunes of falling. (In the first eclogues he thanked the gods who to "my advancement . . . have me abased" [83, 31].) That is, he makes use of his fall into a shepherd's estate to win Pamela's favors with his unusual knack of procuring practical benefits from fancy metaphors. Almost the whole of their conversation is couched as a witty exchange about fortune. As vigorously as Dorus complains about the hindrances it erects against his love, he knows, just as Pamela does, that the only fortune that matters in this instance is the much more mundane fact of his estate.

Dorus's access to Pamela depends upon his disguise as a shepherd, but he succeeds in wooing her only because she comes to recognize that he is a prince—a recognition made possible by his literary skills. As is often the case in Sidney, an impassioned mind is an ingenious mind. Taking his cue from Histor, Dorus spins out of his more prosaic princely biography a Greek romance about his courageous struggles against destiny:

> Arcadia, Arcadia was the place prepared to be the stage of his endless overthrow; Arcadia was (alas, well might I say it is) the charmed circle where all his spirits should for ever be enchanted. (105)

Much of the scene's pleasure derives from the ironic recognition that Dorus really is fortune's victim, at least insofar as his passion has made him abandon control of himself. As Pamela chides him, speaking more wisely than she knows, "the fault is not in fortune but in you that cannot frame yourself to your fortune . . ." (100). Geron would certainly agree.

In the prelude to the second wooing scene, Philoclea struggles with the "impossible desires" of her divided mind in one of *The Old Arcadia*'s most idyllic groves (111). Typical of Sidney, the pleasance is employed as a defining image with important moral and psychological ramifications. For the pastoral place becomes, in Philoclea's mind, a measurement for divisions in time and self as she confronts an image of her own lost innocence: "there had she enjoyed herself . . . [prior to loving Cleophila] and had no other thoughts but such as might arise out of quiet senses" (109). Present agonies stand in contrast to past contentment, as the grove serves "as an accuser of her change" (110). What Sidney is at some pains to indicate, as other critics have noticed, is that her fall into passion results from the weakness of untaught innocence.[1] But Philoclea's fall separates her from something as important as a quiet mind: her grove also consists of "living powers enclosed in stately shrine/Of growing trees . . ." (109, 30–31). Philoclea's pastoral oasis is a symbol of innocence lost, but, more important, it is also a place of "fearful devotion," a sign of the providential order of the universe (109). The impassioned mind is endangered by its isolation from the living powers of a divinely inspired nature.

By the time Cleophila appears, only a few laments on his "unfortunate fortune" and "most perplexed mind" are required to win her promise of marriage (118–19). (Of course, he does inform her that he is prince of Macedon.) If we are impressed by the simplicity of Philoclea's frank confession of her love and "divided mind," we are also interested in the outcome of her earnest command to Cleophila: "Thou hast then the victory; use it now with virtue . . ." (121).

Just as at the end of the first book, pastoral quiet is suddenly interrupted at the conclusion of book two—this time by the uprising of the Phagonian shepherds. The princes are given a second chance to display their "virtuous courage" and "excellent valour" as they help to suppress the rebels (124, 128).[2] Sidney has several reasons for including this interruption at the end of the second book. As the result of Basilius's injustice in separating himself from his dukedom, the uprising of the Phagonians comes as the most striking of book two's consequences of the divided mind. More serious than the attack of the lion and the bear, the uprising reinforces the more ominous tone of the narrative, just as it pictures, once again, the public results of private passions.

Moreover, just before the attack, Dorus is found idling in a grove with a group of shepherds, doing what shepherds of his ilk generally do; he sings a lyric about the pastoral life's protections against misfortune.

> Feed on my sheep, possess your fruitful field,
> No wolves dare howl, no murrain can prevail,
> And from the storms our sweetest sun will shield.
>
> (125, 4–6)

Whatever its power against storms and murrains, as the Phagonian rebellion makes plain, the Arcadian retreat is no help against unhappy peasants. Fortune reigns over the events of *The Old Arcadia,* largely, one suspects, because men allow it to do so.

The one new element of importance that Sidney introduces into the conclusion of the second book is the royal family's "yearly-used hymn" (134). Basilius remembers the song as thanksgiving for his good fortune in having the oracle fulfilled (or so he thinks) to the satisfaction of his desires. After the intrigues at the lodges, the piety of their prayer to "Apollo great, whose beams the greater world do light," comes as an abrupt piece of irony (134, 7). Basilius, Gynecia, and the princesses certainly do not act as if they believed "That nothing wins the heav'n but what doth earth forsake" (134, 22). The providential perspective on events achieves increasing significance.

What is most striking about Sidney's second eclogues is their similarity to the opening entertainments. As Ringler has pointed out, the first two eclogues, comprised of eight songs each, are nearly mirror images of each other. Both begin with a dance announcing a major theme; in the second song that theme is developed and explored, and in the third it is the subject of a comic treatment.[3] The symmetry is even more pervasive than has been indicated. In both sets of eclogues, Dorus develops the major theme while contending with a native shepherd. At approximately the same moment, Histor relates a prose story concerning the past adventures of Pyrocles and Musidorus. In the first two eclogues the fourth song is reserved for highly serious matters, the near-tragic love complaints of Philisides and Plangus. In the fifth songs Sidney makes use of the Ovidian myths of Actaeon and Echo, respectively, to provide speaking pictures of the divided mind. A solitary lover's lament is delivered by one of the princes in the sixth poems, while Cleophila bemoans his fortunes in the seventh. The two eclogues end with an assertion of the positive values of a pastoral life.

What are we to make of this pattern? Is it merely a private system for ordering the poems that Sidney devised for his own convenience and artistic discipline? Or does the pattern have a significance independent of the individual eclogues?

The continuity of structure between the two groups argues for a continuity of purpose. As we read the second eclogues, marking their similarities to the first group of entertainments, any sense of arbitrariness that we may have believed to be present in the structure of the first eclogues gradually disappears. Beneath the seeming flux of the fictional surface, with its apparently random placement of songs, we are made to discover a significant pattern. A structural device of this kind, pointing to the continuity of the princes' experiences in Arcadia, has obvious relevance for a book in which we find our perspective on events shifting increasingly away from a vision of fortune's arbitrary power toward an understanding of the controlling order of providence. The device also serves a didactic purpose: in case we did not understand the disagreements among the princes, the native Arcadians, and the stranger shepherds, we are given a chance to examine them again.[4] The second eclogues bring a new, stronger sense of the orderliness of things, along with new, stronger challenges to that order.

The Arcadian shepherds are inveterate emblem makers. As Sidney informs us, the "rude tumult of the Phagonians gave occasion to the honest shepherds to begin their pastorals this day with . . . the skirmish betwixt Reason and Passion" (135). The shepherds make the connection, not Sidney. That the Arcadians should transform the world of events into a morally symbolic dance, abstracting the invasion of the Phagonian rebels into a warfare between reason and passion, is an entirely characteristic activity that might serve as a model for the function of the eclogues as a whole. Our understanding of the skirmish's relevance to the public concerns of *The Old Arcadia* is complemented by our awareness that we are witnessing simultaneously a personal psychomachia. The pastoral contains no better illustration of Sidney's treatment of public and private events as parallel variations upon a single theme. In his essay "On Moral Virtue," Plutarch writes about the lover:

> neither through passion has he done away with reason, nor through reason is he rid of passion, but being borne back and forth from one to the other he lies between them and participates in both.[5]

Sidney's dance illustrates the condition that Plutarch describes, as a speaking picture of the divided mind's most important conflict: the debate between reason and passion. As the two sides exchange charges, moving "back and forth from one to the other," a single standard of value dominates: the attainment of "content," or what Sidney elsewhere calls quiet of mind (135, 23). Reason complains, "Who Passion doth ensue lives in annoy," as Passion responds, "Who Passion doth forsake lives void of joy" (135, 26, 27). Later in the dance Reason argues "our strife sure peace in end doth breed," as Passion answers skeptically, "We now have peace, your peace we do not need" (136, 13–14). What Reason fails to do is to convince Passion to relinquish "present joys" for future "bliss" (136, 26, 25). Neither side wins a victory in the debate because neither is able to vindicate its claim to supply contentment. In the end, both camps agree to give way to "heav'nly rules": "Which Passions kill, and Reason do deface" (136, 29, 30).

In typically Sidneian fashion, the dance's conclusion creates more problems than it solves.[6] The final lines are comprehensible as an expression of the native shepherds' traditional piety, but they leave us wondering about the nature of those divine laws. In the course of analyzing the various debates between reason and passion in the second eclogues, together with the disputes over how to define and how to achieve the quiet mind, we shall also confront several accounts of how one abides by "heav'nly rules."

Just as the skirmish between Reason and Passion is more violent than the opposition between the fortunate and unfortunate shepherds in the first eclogues, so Dorus's impassioned confrontation with the reasonable Dicus is more heated than his friendly competition with Lalus. The change in tone is easily accounted for if we remember that this new open criticism of the princes occurs in a book in which there are no Philanaxes and unfallen Musidoruses to serve as spokesmen for orthodox moral positions. As a result, the more vigorous arguments of the native shepherds reflect their increased importance as critics who aid us in evaluating the events and characters of the narrative world.

Dicus invites Dorus to sing in spite of, not because of his moral disapproval of impassioned young shepherds. As the narrator remarks, he had "a delight to taste the fruits of his wit—though in a subject which he himself most of all other despised" (137). The conflict between Dicus's aesthetic tastes and his didactic inclinations provides much of the eclogue's entertainment as we watch him struggle to suppress his moral indignation. Even while attempting to disguise the fact, Dicus betrays his allegiance to the reasonable shepherds by his amusingly schematic manner of proceeding. He asks Dorus at regular intervals questions about how he fell in love, how his love grew stronger, and how his mistress "framed is/To help or hurt in thee her own infection" (139, 1–2). When Dorus praises "love's most high vocation," Dicus pretends to be swayed almost enough "to love love's contemplation" (138, 3, 11); Dicus is even able to keep calm as Dorus explains that love's "wings" are "desire oft clipped with desperation" (138, 23). But when the young "shepherd" goes so far as to claim that love is his "protection" against misfortune, Dicus is no longer able to restrain himself (139, 21). He immediately stuns Dorus with the reply that "Thy safety sure is wrapped in destruction," because he has permitted "reason" to be enslaved to "servile sense" (139, 22, 25). The native shepherd urges him, predictably enough, to adopt "A quiet mind" (140, 19).

If there has never been much doubt about how the princes intend to achieve contentment, Dorus's redefinition of pastoral quiet at the end of his debate with Dicus is the most explicit statement of these intentions that has yet appeared in *The Old Arcadia:*

> The quiet mind (whereof myself impairer is,
>   As thou dost think) should most of all disquiet me
> Without her love than any mind who fairer is.
> Her only cure from surfeit woes can diet me:
>   She holds the balance of my contentation:
> Her cleared looks (naught else) in storms can quiet me.
>   (141, 3–8)

Dorus has been hobnobbing with the Italianate shepherds again. He redefines quiet as success in love, at the same time that he shows a willingness (taking his cue from Philisides) to abandon quiet altogether if it should threaten "grief" to his mistress (141, 11). It is undignified but humorously appropriate that a prince of Musidorus's stature is compelled not only to submit to verbal bludgeoning by a wily old shepherd, but to become the victim of a literary convention that denies him even the privilege of being unique in his follies; he looks very much like any other pleasure-seeking youth in a debate with old age. The criticism implied by his fictional role is appropriate because Dorus has also been *behaving* very much like any other pleasure-seeking young shepherd.

With the entrance of Nico and Pas into the entertainments, "lads to climb any tree in the world," Sidney provides what on the surface, at least, is comic relief from the weightier concerns of the divided mind (141). The relief offered is of a special kind. The same bias that makes it possible to delight in the suppression of the Phagonian rebels enables us to take pleasure in the antics of Sidney's rustics: a clear sense of the "proper" hierarchies of society. Even laughter assumes political overtones in *The Old Arcadia.* In the *Apology*'s definition of pastoral, Sidney praises Vergil's use of the song contest to parody the aspirations of great men in the world. The "contention for trifles" between Nico and Pas (they compete for the prizes of a dog and a cat) supplies an oblique parody of the *Arcadia*'s great men, Pyrocles and Musidorus.[7]

Among the follies that the young shepherds commit while wooing Cosma and Leuca, we recognize aspects of the princes' behavior. In part we are able to do so because of the rustics' attempts to pattern themselves after courtiers. When Nico accuses his rival of theft for stealing Cosma's glove, Pas defends himself by appealing to the standards of a more sophisticated world, "Ah fool, so courtiers do" (142, 3). Any criticism of their manners or language could be met by the same response. When Nico approached Leuca, "She ran away and threw at me a ball"; when Pas attempted to woo Cosma, she suggested by means of a well-placed rope that he hang himself (144, 18). Their humiliations in love remind us of those which the princes continue to experience at the hands of Basilius, Gynecia, and the native shepherds even in their success. If we leave this eclogue uncertain as to how much of Nico and Pas's folly is shared by the princes, we are at least forced to wonder whether their pursuit of the princesses is not simply a more exalted version of a contention over trifles. (The concluding line of the second book continues to reverberate through the eclogues: ". . . nothing wins the heavens but what doth earth forsake.")

Serious speculations like these are swept away by the eclogue's ending as Nico and Pas pose separate riddles, a traditional conclusion to the song contest. Ringler has suggested that Nico's monster, "That hath four eyes, and only two can frame," is a man on crutches wearing glasses.[8] This is a good guess but "a pregnant woman" might provide a better solution in light of the bawdy answer to Pas's conundrum:

>   . . . what monster grows
> With so strong lives that body cannot rest
> In ease until that body life forgoes?
>
>   (146, 7–9)

As any Elizabethan could have told you out of his familiarity with puns on death and orgasm, Pas is indelicately pointing to a "penis." No wonder Dicus hurries him offstage. Pas's amusing reduction of the causes of the divided mind to gross biological terms is a breach in the Arcadians' decorum.

The fictions at the center of the second eclogues are immediately distanced both from its introductory lyrics and from the particular concerns of the prose books. By returning to the remote landscape of

Erona's romance world, in the love complaints of Plangus and Histor's tales of the princes' pre-Arcadian adventures, Sidney designs complementary fictions that clarify as they broaden the narrative's interest in the consequences of the divided mind. Even within these central fictions, there is a corresponding movement from the individual to the universal as we pass from stories about the unique experiences of Pyrocles and Musidorus to a speaking picture of the mind divided by passion in Philisides' contest with Echo. As in the opening entertainments, the central poems and tales of the second eclogues present the reader with a lesson in how to interpret the work. But unlike the first eclogues, that lesson is contained within a group of ambitiously unsettling fictions. Sidney dramatizes the limitations of heroic activity while permitting Plangus to challenge the validity of *The Old Arcadia*'s most prized standards—justice and contentment.

The violence of Plangus's complaint comes as a sudden and calculated change of pace. The intensity of his lament is increased by the fact that it is unexpected, particularly after the comedy of the bumpkins' song contest. Plangus's lyric is not a love poem, nor is it, in its fundamental sense, a poem about the conflict between reason and passion. To restrict his song to these boundaries is to trivialize Sidney's concerns. Plangus's eclogue is about the nature of man, about man's relationship to fortune and to providence, and about his struggle to lead a just life. In short, as one of the central poems of the second eclogues, it concerns itself with those subjects which are at the center of *The Old Arcadia,* and it gives voice to those concerns with an eloquence and directness that is found only in a handful of other eclogues and at the trial concluding the romance. This is also a lyric about desperation, one whose peculiar and haunting poetic resonance reflects its expansion of interest and theme.

The divided mind has resulted in more desperation than we thought possible in Sidney's world. Passion has the potential of eventuating not only in the sloppy inanities of Dametas and his family but in the stark intelligence that informs Plangus's assault upon cosmic injustice. He complains that men are nothing more than "Balls to the stars, and thralls to Fortune's reign," the victims of a grand conspiracy in which misery is biologically determined:

> So diverse be the elements disposed
> In this weak work that it can never be
> Made uniform to any state reposed.
> (147, 26–28)

Contentment and quiet of mind are spurned by Plangus both because they are unobtainable and because grief alone allows dignity to "this talking beast, this walking tree" (147, 31). In a world of such suffering, "who grieves not hath but a blockish brain" (147, 33). Plangus creates for himself the only possible "shield" against misfortune that can be sustained in such a universe: "despair," transforming desperation into a heroic posture against life as he disassembles the great chain of being link by link (148, 5–6). The thought of Erona's possible death makes him skeptical about the very existence of heaven, at the same time that it convinces him that "if heav'n there be," only "dolts" could worship its monstrously unjust powers (148, 22, 25).

Plangus is opposed throughout his complaint by a "wise" shepherd named Boulon. There is more than a touch of local pride in Histor's bestowing the role of prudent counselor upon a shepherd. In a wonderful bucolic reversal, pastoral reason opposes heroic passion. Boulon has a number of features in common with Sidney's native Arcadians: he shares their faith in the beneficent order of the cosmos, a faith that he displays in chiding Plangus for the "Blasphemous words" inspired by deceptive "passions" (148, 30, 32). We are reminded of Philanax's rebukes to Basilius as Boulon warns him not to provoke the gods to "causeful wrath" by prejudging their intentions and questioning their justice (148, 29).[9] Like the native shepherds, he is also an advocate of the Stoical values of rational self-control and patience in adversity:

> Yet reason saith, reason should have ability
> To hold these worldy things in such proportion
> As let them come or go with e'en facility.
> (150, 24–26).

What distinguishes Boulon from native Arcadians like Dicus and Geron is his greater compassion, his better understanding of the limitations of reason, and his profound awareness of human weakness. Boulon knows that men lack "perfect rightfulness," that they will continue to expose themselves to the consequences of the divided mind by placing their chief delight in transitory goods, "Where but a baiting place is all our portion"; nonetheless, he also realizes that in spite of its limitations, reason is still the best instrument "to tame these childish superfluities" (150, 30, 29, 31). Man is weak yet morally responsible for strengthening himself. In Boulon's perspective, even the compassion that we experience for Plangus becomes a sign of our corruption:

> Betwixt the good and shade of good divided,
> We pity deem that which but weakness is;
> So are we from our high creation slided.
>   (152, 7–9).

There is more than a touch of Calvinism here, as Sidney provides one more lesson to the reader in how to interpret *The Old Arcadia*'s fictions. The understanding that Boulon obtains while listening to Plangus's complaints is one that the reader must achieve for himself:

> Thy wailing words do much my spirits move,
> They uttered are in such a feeling fashion
> That sorrow's work against my will I prove.
> Methinks I am partaker of thy passion,
> And in thy case do glass mine own debility—
> Self-guilty folk most prone to feel compassion.
>   (150, 18–23)

We are all "self-guilty folk": the emotional impact of the lyric implicates us all in its judgments. Geron's lesson is reinforced by Boulon's revelations.

If there is no winner in this dispute, there can be no question that Plangus is right when he argues that "raging woes" will not be contained by "moral rules" (151, 11).[10] Boulon understands the dangers of frustrated passion, but not the value of love. In the process of worshiping "such a saint disgraced," of delighting in the "flower/That sweetens all" the world, Plangus has had access to experiences whose intensity and significance lie well beyond even a wise shepherd's ken (149, 26–28). The eclogue offers no solution to the problem of how to lead a just life or how to acquire a quiet mind. Indeed, it even forces us to wonder whether such things are obtainable.

The transition from Plangus's debate with Boulon to Histor's stories of the princes' adventures in Asia and Africa is easily accomplished: after all, both sets of characters belong to the romance world of Erona. Histor returns with his inevitable puns: the heroism of Pyrocles and Musidorus is said to be sufficient for "full works to excellent historiographers" (153). As a schematic historian with well-developed didactic inclinations, Histor relates four selected adventures of Pyrocles and Musidorus, each of which is concerned with their increasingly limited success in applying heroic action as a remedy for a dangerous division caused by passion. Just as desire overcomes the heroic Plangus, so Sidney illustrates in Histor's tales the ultimate impotence of courageous activity against the assaults of passion.

The closer Pyrocles and Musidorus move to Arcadia and to pastoral, the more complicated their adventures and their victories become. The princes develop from storybook heroes who slay a giant and his "trusty dragon" in the childish dramatics of the first episode into wise conciliatory agents in the second, as they reunite a pair of divided and disputing brothers (153). In the third story, as they become for the first time the objects of passion, their success is more ambiguous and limited when they find themselves victimized by Queen Andromana's "divided desire," and have to be rescued from prison by a sympathetic populace (155). (Andromana, we are informed in another humorously aristocratic aside, eventually marries an apple-monger.) In the fourth episode the princes again emerge victorious as they reunite the Egyptian king with his son and a remorseful servant with his master, for whose divisions a lustful Phaedra-like stepmother had been responsible. (The warning contained in these events for Basilius and his family is obvious.) But even this "success" is severely qualified by "historical" ironies since it is Amassis, Queen Artaxia's lover, whose life is saved by Pyrocles and Musidorus—the same Queen who is threatening to execute Erona.[11] Implicated in a complex network of desire whose intricacies no amount of heroic activity can unravel, they create worse divisions than they resolve.

The princes' heroism will hardly supply us with the "unmeasurable . . . contentment" experienced by the princesses in hearing these tales (158). Their courage does provide concrete examples of the power of acts of virtue to restore quiet to the state, the family, and the individual, but even Histor would have to acknowledge that there are limits to heroism. Before their arrival in Arcadia, the princes' virtuous activity had received more than one setback. As Plangus has already shown, courage is of little use against Cupid. The heroic ethos is too limited and too unsophisticated to provide an adequate response to the new pastoral experiences of Arcadia: in *The Old Arcadia*, courageous activity is the province of adolescents who have yet to experience the inroads of desire. It neither forestalls those inroads nor supplies a remedy for their worst effects. Contentment is to be found elsewhere, inside the pastoral experience itself.

In the last of the central fictions of the second eclogues, we move from chivalric romance to pastoral myth as Sidney's fictive double becomes the principal agent, once again, for dramatizing the work's most important concerns. In the division between Philisides' insistent questions and Echo's blunt replies, we are provided with one of *The Old Arcadia*'s most graphic pictures of the divided mind's struggle between reason and passion. The eclogue's form is also its meaning.

Sidney's Echo is not the ordinarily sympathetic nymph of traditional Ovidian mythology: this is no sentimental moaner. A sarcastic, inflexibly rationalistic creature, she delights in mocking Philisides' agonies. Sidney derived the main outlines of his portrait of Echo from a poem by Joachim Du Bellay, entitled "Dialogue d'un amoreux et d'Echo." In Du Bellay, as in Sidney, we find a lover attempting to reason his way through passion by posing a series of questions about its origin, growth, and eventual conclusion. Although he expects to find a "Piteuse Echo," Du Bellay's lover discovers instead a blunt, unsympathetic nymph who informs him that his love will come to nothing: "Sent-elle bien la douleur qui me poignt? Point."[12] Philisides asks, "Then, then what do I gain, since unto her will I do wind? Wind" (161, 32–33); in Du Bellay's poem, the lover wants to know, "Qu'est-ce qu'aimer, et s'en plaindre souvent? Vent." There can be no question either that Sidney knew Du Bellay's "Dialogue" or that he improved upon it. The Echo who confronts Philisides is a livelier and more entertaining character principally because she is more spiteful.

Sidney gains his chief effects by means of the rhymes. They are given a special significance as the eclogue makes us aware, line after line, that passions generate their own contradictions. Their special significance is the product of a special technique. Sidney does not confine Echo, as Gascoigne does when using this device at Kenilworth, to repeating the exact words of the speaker. The will's "desire" brings "ire"; the "disease" brought about by love is produced by "ease" (162, 2; 160, 18). At each stage of the poem, linguistic similarities are used to suggest unavoidable and disastrous causal relationships between various aspects of the lover's experience. Philisides is portrayed as the victim of passion's insidious logic:

> What is it that may be a salve to my love?   Love.
> What do lovers seek for, long seeking for to
>   enjoy?   Joy.
> What be the joys for which to enjoy they went
>   to the pains?   Pains.
> Then to an earnest love what doth best victory lend?
>   End.
>   (160, 25–30)

The nymph's replies have an impressive finality.

Sidney's eclogue is without a hint of love's nobility. Philisides begins the poem by looking for quiet of mind, as he asks "when shall I see peace?"; by the conclusion, Echo and the logic of his passions, transforming the lover's hope for contentment into comic agonies, have sent him packing to the "Dev'ls" (160, 6–7; 162, 26).[13] His folly does not augur well for the princes, with whom we inevitably connect this poem if only because Philisides also displays a skill in manipulating classical meters. After all, they speak the same language.

The concluding lyrics of the second eclogues are given to Dorus and Cleophila just as they are in the opening entertainments. Instead of one song, Cleophila sings two: "My muse what ails this ardour," and "Reason, tell me thy mind. . . ." (Perhaps the shepherds were getting used to having a woman participate in the eclogues.) Dorus sings the final poem in the group, "O sweet woods. . . ." The most noticeable fact about these lyrics is their quality. Sidney saves the best until last—he never wrote better quantitative poetry—and he must have known what he was doing. After Dorus's mild embarrassment at the hands of Dicus, the comic parody of their passionate folly in Nico and Pas's song contest, and the increased attention given to the dangers of love in the complaints of Plangus and Philisides, the princes resume the stage and dazzle us with their noble passions and artistic skills. Heightened artistic powers are also one consequence of the divided mind: the princes, Philisides, Strephon, and Klaius are Arcadia's best singers.

Cleophila's songs advance steadily toward an epic victory over reason:

> Reason sighs, but in end he thus doth answer:
> 'Naught can reason avail in heav'nly matters'.
> (165, 28–29)

If the conclusion seems a bit too comfortably arranged, a bit too contrived, Cleophila does manage to clarify the major issue in the second eclogues' debate between reason and passion. For the native shepherds and Boulon, impassioned love is a dangerous threat to the individual's quiet of mind, a sign of his descent from reason, the noblest of human qualities, toward beastliness; for Plangus, Philisides, and the princes, their devotion to their mistresses is ennobling, a token of heavenliness, since the mistress is the source of all value in the world.

Dorus's lyric is more pastoral and more important. His celebration of solitariness comes as the last in a series of sudden reversals spread throughout the second eclogues. The change in mood is less dramatic than the one brought about by Plangus's complaint but it is an important change nonetheless, as Cleophila's Petrarchan heroics are replaced by praise of the idle life on a scale that we have not seen before and that we scarcely have thought likely in Sidney's *Old Arcadia.*

Dorus sings the delights of "solitariness," idealizing the "Sweet birds" and "Fair trees' shade," but saves the greatest number of his praises for the protections that the Arcadian life-style offers against misfortune (166, 20, 21). In the first stanza he praises the contentment of its "sweet woods," where "Naught disturbs thy quiet," and where there is no "danger to thyself, if be not in thyself" (166, 18, 22). ("Your If," as Touchstone reminds us, "is the only peacemaker. Much virtue in If.") The whole middle section of the poem is given over to an extended list of evils at court that are absent from the country, implying clearly not only that Arcadia is a shield against them, but that it is a kind of therapy for their worst effects: "Keep thy sprite from abuse, here no abuse doth haunt" (167, 1). In the third stanza he returns once more to the same theme by pointing to the "safety" of the Arcadian "shade," and its freedom from "danger" (167, 8). It has not been since the early portion of the first book, in the debate between Pyrocles and Musidorus, that we have heard either of the princes refer to the idle life in such highminded terms. Like Dorcas in *The Lady of May,* Dorus celebrates the opportunities in the Arcadian landscape for "Contemplation," where the mind can climb "even unto the stars," and where the senses can "behold th' order of heav'nly host" (166, 15, 17, 13). He has a greater, more pious regard for "heav'nly rules" than the religious language of his love lyrics would suggest.[14]

Do we believe Dorus's celebration of the idle life? Does Sidney want us to believe it? The answers to these questions should tell us something about our response to the first two books of the romance as a whole. "Solitariness" is hardly an unfamiliar word in *The Old Arcadia;* in fact, the word appears in a variety of forms so frequently in the narrative that it is made practically synonymous with the pastoral life—at least as it is led by Basilius and the princes. Within the first few pages of the romance alone, we are told about the "solitary place of the two lodges," the Duke's "solitary life," the "strange solitariness" that "had possessed Basilius," and the "solitary dwelling of the duke" (9–11). It is also a word that figures prominently in the debate between the princes. Cleophila praises "solitariness" as the "nurse" of his "contemplations" (15). The fact that Musidorus had warned his cousin that this "nurse" is also "the sly enemy that doth most separate a man from well doing," indicates the extraordinary reversal that has taken place in his character and beliefs as a consequence of his divided mind (14).

There are ironies in his lyric that would tend to make his earlier hostility toward the solitary life appear to be the wiser posture. The fiction provides little evidence to support a belief in Dorus's idealizing assertions. The attack of the lion and the bear and the invasion of the rebels have shown that there are real misfortunes and dangers in the woods, just as Mastix has demonstrated that envy, flattery, hypocrisy, and many such "courtly" evils also exist in the pastoral world. But, these ironies exist independently of other more significant responses to the lyric.

For the first time in *The Old Arcadia*, Sidney has pulled out all the stops, fulfilling our expectations of what a "real" pastoral romance ought to be like by providing a highly lyrical, sentimental idealization of the bucolic life-style. The power and meaning of this dramatic ploy should not be underestimated. There are important ways in which we are willing and expected to believe Dorus's assertions about the idle life in spite of all the evidence: perhaps Sidney is hinting that all idealizing occurs in spite of the facts of life. We believe because we want to, because a world of such pleasure and goodness ought to exist. The lyric's structural symmetry and the carefully modulated rhythms of its falling classical meter supply the aesthetic relaxation that Dorus is praising; the poetry itself is persuasive. We want to see these noble young princes succeed in the virtuous pursuit of their mistresses because we want the world to answer, in good pastoral fashion, to our desires. In short, by the end of the second book we are far from discounting the value or the viability of the idle life in any of its versions, no matter how many limitations in those life-styles Sidney makes us conscious of. In spite of our knowledge of the agonies of Plangus and Erona and the perils of uncontrolled passion, we are not inclined to scorn the princes' hopes for contentment. The reader engages in his own conflict between reason and passion. Once more, that conflict is itself an indication that no certain means has yet been suggested for achieving the quiet mind and the just life.

7
Book Three: Contentment and Justice

THE third book of *The Old Arcadia* is Sidney's Italianate pastoral in miniature. It is almost as if Dorus's idealization of the delights of solitariness at the conclusion of the second eclogues were the magic key to a new greenhouse of bucolic pleasures. The emphasis is upon "almost." There are more songs and pastoral pleasures in book three than we have found in the first two prose portions of the romance, but there is little backing away from a critical stance toward the events. After focusing our attention upon the divided mind and the unfortunate political and psychological consequences following from it, Sidney interests us in contentment—how it is defined, and how men attempt to achieve it. In the third book all of the major characters—the princes, Basilius and the ruling family, Dametas and his clan—aspire to and come closest to achieving (even if it is only in their imaginations) the height of good fortune. For a change, Dame Fortuna appears to be smiling.

An old setting offers a new beginning. At the outset of book three, Dorus and Cleophila return to the idyllic grove where they had their debate over the merits of the idle life, but this time there are no moral conflicts. The discussion turns, as it usually does, to their fortunes in love. Dorus thanks the "motherly destinies" for his good haps, while boasting that "My joys are such . . . as neither suffer in themselves uncertainty, nor are in danger by inconstancy" (170). True to his shepherd's role, he believes himself protected against misfortune. Cleophila is unnerved by Dorus's claims, "lest envious fortune should spite at the too much boasting of your blessedness," but he too must admit that "the stars have not held wholly an angry aspect towards me" (171). Their rhetoric should not obscure the fact that the princes' meeting has practical goals. When mapping strategy with Cleophila, Dorus plans to return with Pamela to Thessaly, where he will muster an army to procure "the fortunate hour" of his own and his friend's "contentment" (173).

Dorus's adventures supply the clearest indication of Sidney's strategy in the third book and the ends to which it is employed.[1] In three successive incidents the prince ensures the safety of his escape with Pamela by deceiving Dametas, Miso, and Mopsa. He succeeds in paving the way for his own fortunate contentment, appropriately enough, by convincing the rustics that they are about to receive good fortunes of their own. When Dorus lures Dametas away from the lodges in the hope of finding buried treasure, he does so with the ironically expressed wish that "your fortune may be of equal balance with your deserts" (187). Miso presents a greater challenge. As a woman who is incapable of nourishing "a quiet thought," and who "having long since hated each thing else, began now to hate herself," she is promised the only kind of contentment that she is capable of receiving: the pleasure of spitefulness (189). Miso is led to believe that she will have the joy of beating an unfaithful husband, "content," as the prince remarks, "to be revenged on others with your own harms" (190). Mopsa's removal is accomplished by similar means. She is made to climb a tree with the expectation that Apollo will come to satisfy her wish to be "the greatest lady of the world, and never after to feed on worse than furmenty" (196).

The meaning of this pattern is clear. All three characters are led into folly by aspiring to achieve a false kind of contentment, after having been aroused by passion: Dametas's greed, Miso's spite, and Mopsa's sexual ambition. What Dorus has created is a small allegory of how fortune operates in the world: fortune rules because men allow themselves to be seduced by passion. Sidney intended this pattern, at least in part, as a parody of the princes' fortune-seeking. When Dametas hurries away to dig up his gold, imagining "what money to employ in making coffers to keep his money," we are reminded of Dorus's confidence in his good fortune, just as the stoical-sounding note that he discovers in the process augurs badly both for his own success and that of the princes (188):

> Seek then, and see what man esteemeth best,
> All is but this, this is our labour's hire,
> Of this we live, in this we find our rest. . . .
>
> (188, 32–34)

As Dorus rides off with Pamela into "the wildest part of the desert," he renews his promise to preserve her chastity, one that he made, highmindedly enough, "by the eternal givers of virtue" (196–97). He assures her that "Your contentment is dearer to me than mine own," displaying the same confidence in his invulnerability to desire as he previously has shown in the protections of the pastoral life (197). The setting is bucolic, but the nature of the occasion is that of a heroic test: "What I am," Dorus says, "the gods, I hope, will shortly make your own eyes judges" (197). The idyllic grove that they happen upon is an appropriate locale for the test, since it is not only Dorus who is on trial but the ethos of the Italianate pastoral, with its sentimental conception of man and its idealization of love as an appropriate kind of contentment. The succeeding events provide a disturbing comment on that ethos. "Overmastered with the fury of delight," Dorus fails his test as he attempts to extract sexual favors from the sleeping Pamela (202).

Even a prince is vulnerable to the inroads of desire. His lust tarnishes our belief in his nobility just as it lessens our admiration for the idealistic aspirations of his love, unrealizable as they are made to appear. Dorus's attempted rape of Pamela is *The Old Arcadia*'s plainest illustration that an attempt to "reach beyond humanity" can lead to behavior more appropriate for beasts. It is important to note, however, that Sidney does not encourage severe moral judgments upon Dorus's failure. When the rebels interrupt his approach to Pamela, the narrator's response mirrors the division in our own feelings, as he points to the interruption as a "just punishment of his broken promise, and most infortunate bar of his long-pursued and almost-achieved desires" (202). Even when attempting to rape his beloved, Dorus wins part of our sympathy; we want to see him achieve "contentment" because, as Sidney will eventually make us aware, we too are vulnerable to the same desires.[2] In a deliberate dramatic ploy maintained until the trial's conclusion, our reasoned judgments upon events are placed in direct conflict with our emotional responses: wit combats will.

Cleophila undergoes a similar set of experiences while pursuing his fortunes in love. Like Dorus he happens into an idyllic location, an "easeful" cave instead of a pleasant grove, only in this instance Cleophila dallies not with his beloved but with Gynecia, an event that he imputes to his "continual mishaps" (184). The discovery that he makes in the cave is important. Dorus confronts in Dametas a parody of the passion driving him toward a false kind of contentment; what Cleophila finds in the darkness, as Davis indicates, is a horrifying image of "his own potential lust."[3] For the princes, passion is alternately foolish and terrifying.

Having learned very little from his experiences in the cave, Cleophila proceeds to remove the obstacles to his desires. Like Dorus, he smooths the way for his own contentment by promising contentment to others. He convinces Gynecia that he has disguised himself as an Amazon in order to procure her love, that he has experienced a fortunate fall to achieve "inward contentation" (206). When Cleophila arranges his rendezvous with Gynecia in the cave, he assures her ironically that "I have found out a way by which your contentment shall draw on my happiness" (213). Before Basilius sets out for his love tryst in the dark, he sings a lyric "as a fairing of his contentment" (226). Lust makes the royal couple vulnerable to deception, encouraging their hopes in a false kind of happiness. Almost immediately after hearing Basilius's boasts about his good hap, "how each thing seemed vile in his sight, in comparison of his fortune," we come upon Pyrocles at Philoclea's bedroom door, "rapt from himself with the excessive forefeeling of his near coming contentment" (226, 228).

Dorus has already failed to realize his happiness; Dametas, Miso, and Mopsa, we know, are well along the road to disappointment; Gynecia and Basilius will have their desires frustrated. In light of this pattern, it comes as no small surprise that Cleophila succeeds in achieving, as he takes Philoclea to bed, the full measure of "contentment." Sidney is at his best in this scene, as he establishes an unequal balance between criticism of the prince for his passionate indulgence, and a more important admiration for and identification with his display of idealized eroticism.[4] We are impressed by his assertions of "unspotted faith" and undoubted constancy, just as we are moved by his willingness to abandon everything for Philoclea (233): "All the great estate of his father seemed unto him but a trifling pomp, whose good stands in other men's conceit, in comparison of the true comfort he found in the depth of his mind" (228–29). Sidney ensures our sympathetic participation in this scene by an ingenious device; as Pyrocles makes love to Philoclea, he recalls one of Philisides' extended erotic blazons, "What tongue can her perfections tell?" The prince contents himself with his beloved while we are contented by a delightfully titillating lyric.[5] If our knowledge that it is Philisides' song reinforces our awareness of the impermanence of such delights, Sidney deliberately mutes the ironies of the episode, refusing to "grudge at the due bliss of these poor lovers whose loyalty had but small respite of their fiery agonies" (243). The reader is again given the opportunity to indulge his sentimental appetites. In the gulf that divides the third book from its eclogues, new ideas about contentment come into view.

Book Three: Contentment and Justice   137

The third eclogues are different. We enter a simpler fiction that is at once more innocent and more limited than the histrionic world of the first two sets of entertainments. There are no performances as such here, and no fancy rhyme schemes or refined quantitative meters to which we need to attend, or, to emphasize the point in a slightly different way, in which we can be delighted. As in Christian pastoral, a plain style is employed as a means of expressing plain moral truths, only in Sidney's case the truth is rarely plain except to schoolboys and Stoic shepherds. The greatest difference between the third eclogues and the preceding entertainments is that they are dominated almost entirely by the native Arcadians. Since the princes are "otherwise occupied," as Sidney's narrator so aptly puts it, they are excluded from the celebrations, and only one song, Philisides' beast fable, is given to a stranger shepherd (245). With the antagonists removed there is much less juxtaposing of rival attitudes within and between individual eclogues, and consequently there are no real debates. Geron and Histor disagree for a time about the merits of weddings, just as Pas and Nico quarrel about jealousy, but these are not disputes representing fundamental conflicts between distinct sets of values. After all, it is a holiday world into which we are invited, a fact that helps to explain the poems' noticeably more relaxed, more joyful mood. The third eclogues are considerably shorter than the first two sets of entertainments. In place of eight songs and a prose narrative, there are only five poems. It is altogether characteristic of Sidney's brand of pastoral pretense that these increased limitations in style, characters, and length should result in the creation of a powerfully concentrated fiction. The third eclogues provide a single, expansive, speaking picture of the Stoic ideal of contentment. Marriage becomes the vehicle for supplying an image of the quiet mind and the just life, as an institution that supplies *The Old Arcadia*'s most available social tool for reconciling the competing demands of reason and passion.

At the conclusion of Gil Polo's *Diana Enamorada,* well-bred, highly refined young ladies and gentlemen are married in a formal garden setting outside the walls of Felicia's palace. They spend the entire fifth book of the romance fulfilling Felicia's injunctions:

> moved regozijados juegos, tañed los concertados instrumentos, entonad apazibles cantares y entended en agradables conversaciones, por honra y memoria de estos alegres desengaños y venturosos casamientos.[6]
> (make merie pastimes; play upon your tuned instruments; sing sweete Ditties, and exercise your selves in delightfull sports and

conversation, in honour and memory of these joyfull meetings, and happie marriages.)

Their games are elegant and aristocratic, including contests between elaborately costumed nymphs and savages, ingenious riddles, and emblematically significant dances. The celebrations are idealizing and didactic, designed as they are to illustrate the virtues of "el sossegado contentamiento" ("quiet content").[7]

Like Gil Polo's marriage festivities, the third eclogues are ultimately intended as aristocratic entertainments, and like Gil Polo, Sidney uses the wedding to supply a speaking picture of the quiet mind. But Sidney's entertainments are hardly so refined as his predecessor's. His characters are shepherds, not gentlemen. As such, they achieve the measure of dignity accorded them in the first two Arcadian eclogues, but they are also subject, often simultaneously, to laughter of a mildly ridiculing kind. The ideal contentment imaged in the marriage of Lalus and Kala is a shepherd's ideal, which only approximates that of the author. Just as surely as any courtly bystander watching a country wedding, Sidney realizes that there are limitations to a rustic's imagined perfection of simple piety and contentment.

Marriage is a community event, and at no point in *The Old Arcadia* does Sidney give us a fuller or more complimentary portrait of the native Arcadian community. We are provided with a concrete example of their thrift, as the Arcadians bring pigs, sheep, and geese as marriage gifts for Lalus and Kala. We see their piety as they "talk of the holiness of marriage" (245). Of greatest importance is the stress Sidney places upon the justice of their hierarchical social order in which a "painful modesty" restrains women from interfering in men's affairs and in which every one is "placed according to his age" (245). These values are hardly new to the romance, but Sidney brings them to the foreground again in order to provide a solid moral foundation for the contentment of the Arcadian life-style.

Lalus and Kala stand at the center of this Stoic celebration. The narrator informs us that the young shepherd won his beloved "with a true and simple making her know he loved her; not forcing himself beyond his reach to buy her affection, but giving her such pretty presents as neither could weary him with the giving nor shame her for the taking" (244). The balance of the sentence structure reinforces our sense of his balanced affections and temperate life-style. Lalus is a pious, hard-working shepherd with a proper regard for his parents who gains "content" for himself and his bride by the constancy of his love and the virtuous moderation of his desires (244). As we anticipated at the end of his song contest with Dorus, Lalus can now dance with the fortunate shepherds.

There can be no question about the appeal of Lalus and Kala's simple, sincere love or the superiority of Stoic contentment to the base pleasures pursued, for instance, by Dametas, Miso, and Mopsa. The virtuous constancy of their marriage is a criticism of the adulterous behavior of Basilius and Gynecia. There can also be no doubt that their honest affection supplies oblique criticism of the manner in which Pyrocles and Musidorus pursue contentment. The fact that Lalus gains Kala's favors "not with many painted words, nor false-hearted promises," reflects badly upon the princes, especially after a book in which they have employed so many deceptions to gain sensual satisfaction (244).[8] This is an issue that Sidney has already raised in the narrative on several different occasions; when Philoclea believes that Cleophila has been unfaithful, she asks herself how she could expect "plain proceeding in him that still goes disguised?," accusing him at the same time of displaying "painted passions" (209, 210). Confronted in the marriage of Lalus and Kala by a pastoral image of such innocence and appeal, it becomes clear that we have been made the victims of what can only be described as an artistic trap. After having given us the chance to indulge our sentimental appetites in the bedroom scene at the end of the third book, Sidney makes us conscious by the wedding of our weakness, of our vulnerability in accepting a cheap version of sexual contentment in place of the more genuine happiness of virtuous moderation. Sidney betrays us (and not for the last time), but it should be remembered that although the princes have employed deceptive strategies throughout the third book, they are forced to do so by Basilius's strictures against suitors, and that their wiles, like their author's, are a source of positive pleasure for the reader.[9]

Before we turn to the poems, one more difference between the third eclogues and the first two sets of Arcadian entertainments needs to be pointed out. Sidney supplements the usual three-part rhetorical structure of the eclogues with a traditional symbolic method of organization. It is no accident that there are five poems here. Five is the marriage number, as Sir Thomas Browne indicates in *The Garden of Cyrus,* because it is "made out by two and three, the first parity and imparity, the active and passive digits, the materiall and formall principles in generative Societies."[10] There is nothing unusual about Sidney's practice. The number five plays an important symbolic role in Spenser's *Epithalamion* and Chapman's *Hero and Leander;* as

Alastair Fowler writes, "numerology was particularly common in the epithalamic genre."[11] The connection between the two is easily accounted for. God "hast ordered all things in measure, and number, and weight" (Wisdom 11:20). For the Christian Renaissance, numerological patterns are a sign of the harmonious order of a providentially controlled cosmos, an order that is mirrored and sustained by the harmony of marriage.

Dicus sings the opening song of the third eclogues, an epithalamium that begins, "Let mother earth now deck herself in flowers." The marriage song is customary, as the singer's name shows.[12] Dicus's eclogue is structured with meticulous care. There are five introductory and five concluding stanzas centered around a medial paean. In the opening stanza Dicus defines the major theme of the epithalamium and the third eclogues as a whole when he praises the "justest love," in which "war of thoughts is swallowed up in peace," asking Hymen to ensure that "no chance" will stain their marriage (245, 31, 32; 246, 3). Dicus's poem has the rhetorical structure of a magical charm, with its pattern of invocations and exorcisms. In the next four stanzas, he calls upon heaven, the muses, the nymphs, and Pan to supply a series of protections and favors to the couple. He requests that their "mutual embracements" be tinged with "delightful pain," that their "chaste love" remain "spotless," that they have long life and children "In number like the herd" (246, 11, 12, 16, 20; 247, 4).

The center of the poem belongs, appropriately enough within this community of native Arcadians with their Stoical values, to "Virtue, if not a god, yet God's chief part" (247, 8). This quality is to be:

> . . . the knot of this their open vow:
> That still he be her head, she be his heart,
> He lean to her, she unto him do bow.
>
> (247, 9–11)

The balanced movement of the verse, like the balanced structure of the poem as a whole, points to the ideal reciprocity of their affections, each spouse receiving, according to the laws of justice, what is due to him. This is a principle of major importance in the Arcadian version of the idle life; as Dicus later makes clear, it is by keeping a "wholesome mean" between extremes that the shepherds maintain justice and contentment (248, 8).

Symmetry is preserved in the second half of the epithalamium. Dicus turns his attention in the next four stanzas to exorcizing a series of evils from their marriage. He banishes "lawless lust," "churlish words," "peacock pride," and "vile jealousy" (247, 17, 26; 248, 1, 10). In light of his emblematic performance in the first eclogues, Dicus is an appropriate author for this new assault upon "foul Cupid"; it is lust, not chaste love, to which the elder Arcadian shepherds have been opposed (247, 17).[13] In the final stanza of the poem, after all of the invocations and exorcisms come to an end, Dicus asserts that his charms have been successful: "For Hymen will their coupled joys maintain" (248, 27). No wonder he calls them, "Happy man, happy wife" (248, 23). Good hap is good fortune.

Sidney had no desire to sustain the high level of didactic and lyric intensity of Dicus's performance. He moves from the Continental epithalamium into a more rugged and entertaining native form, the traditional English fabliau. Pastoral "variableness" continues to operate as a formal principle in the eclogues. Nico sings the poem because he needs to vindicate his artistic skills after Pas's fresh assault on them, and also because he wants to give further support to Dicus's attack on "jealousy, the filthy traitor to true affection" (249). Why Sidney should devote such a large portion of his attention to jealousy is not immediately apparent. (Two of the five poems are entirely concerned with this issue.) Part of the explanation for his interest rests in the fact that Gynecia's ruling passion is constantly referred to in the narrative as jealousy. But to suggest this much is only to beg the question further. A better reason for Sidney's concern over this issue is provided, once again, by a passage from Gil Polo's *Diana Enamorada*, a work that displays almost an obsession with the topic. In book two, Marcelio delivers a long diatribe against the passion, one that reveals that jealousies differ from other dangerous emotions because: "Porque en fin, todos, sino él, pueden y suelen parar en admirables dulçuras y contentos. . . ." ("all the rest [saving they] may be converted in the end to a great sweetnes, and content . . .").[14] As a result, jealousy is represented as the greatest threat to the quiet mind. This is an interpretation in harmony both with Sidney's treatment of Gynecia (she is clearly the romance's most violently impassioned character) and with the importance that he assigns to the passion in a group of eclogues intended to serve as a speaking picture of Stoical contentment. Sidney goes one step farther than Gil Polo in having Dicus supply an explanation for jealousy's power to corrupt the quiet mind. The passion is so dangerous because it gives the individual "just cause to be unjust," undermining the principal virtue on which the Arcadian life-style is grounded (248, 11).

Nico's fabliau is an appropriate vehicle for treating the subject of jealousy. As Charles Muscatine points out, "The triangle of the dull-witted or jealous husband, the sensual wife, and the lecherous priest or clever clerk reappears so often as to have almost an *a priori* status."[15] Sidney has cleverly adapted this triangle to a pastoral situation. The gullible, jealous husband and the lustful wife are transformed, as Nico's neighbors, into rustics. A more interesting change occurs in the replacement of the traditional priest or clerk by a courtly shepherd. Nico is a shrewd poet, one who realizes that an audience prefers heroes who are like themselves. In spite of the pastoral transformation (perhaps because of it), much of the original vigor of the native fabliau remains. Nico is a blunt, abrupt narrator who keeps the story moving without sentimentalizing its contents; he creates a world as uncomplicated as his transitions, "And so she was," "And thus she did," "And this was all," "Thus may you see" (250, 11, 29; 252, 31; 253, 9). This is jealousy seen from a shepherd's-eye view.

Nico's fabliau has ramifications for a variety of *The Old Arcadia*'s characters. Its most obvious relevance is the warning that it contains for Lalus and Kala. Like the husband in the story, "a foul unhandsome groom," Lalus is described as "none of the fairest" (249, 24; 244). He, too, will be exposed to the temptations of jealousy by being married to another "trick and bonny lass" (249, 22). At the fabliau's outset, the rustic wife, "yet was good," like Philoclea, "because she knew none ill" (249, 33). Nico's point, of course, is that Lalus could change himself into a cuckold and his wife into a similarly deceptive wench by jealousy. The adulterous behavior of the wife also carries an oblique reminder of the adulteries of Basilius and Gynecia. There is one further connection with the narrative. The mere mention of a "courtier shepherd" involved in illicit sexual activities inevitably calls Musidorus to mind. Additional criticism is directed against his wiles, as well as his cousin's, as we watch the wife's deceptive manipulations. The "sweet content" she offers and the "full content" the courtier shepherd receives parody the sensual contentment into which the princes descend (252, 28; 253, 14).

Pas is unimpressed by Nico's performance, particularly in his view since it is more likely by attributing so many "subtleties" to the "feminine gender" to create than to suppress jealousy (253). As a response to his rival's fabliau and as a deliberate act of literary one-upmanship (his comically inflated diction prepares for the event), Pas lets loose with the "wise words" of a sonnet (253). The poem's first three quatrains are a tangle of didactic precepts giving renewed emphasis to the need for justice in preserving chastity and preventing jealousy: "First be he true, for truth doth truth deserve" (253, 22).

Again, a proper moral response is equated with the discovery of a mean between extremes; Pas states that the husband must be:

> Not toying kind, nor causelessly unkind,
> Not stirring thoughts, not yet denying right,
> Not spying faults, nor in plain errors blind;
> Never hard hand, nor ever reins too light.
>
> (253, 25–28)

Not until the sonnet's final couplet are we rescued from the monotony of his moralizing. Pas ends the poem by singing:

> This done, thou hast no more, but leave the rest
> To virtue, fortune, time, and woman's breast.
>
> (254, 3–4)

With one quick ironic stroke, the sonnet's comfortable moral structure comes tumbling down. (The sudden demolition looks forward to Astrophil's strategy in sonnets such as "Who will in fairest book. . . .") In *The Old Arcadia*, anyone who trusts to fortune, time, or woman's breast is in for a bad fall. Whether the irony is Pas's or Sidney's, and it is impossible to know for sure, the couplet is important in rekindling our awareness of the inadequacy of such pat moral responses to life and the limitations of such simple shepherdly notions of justice and contentment. No matter how steadfastly Basilius pursued such a program, it would be impossible to conceive of Gynecia's resolving upon chastity or abandoning jealousy.[16]

The third eclogues move quickly beyond these shepherdly conceptions of justice and contentment as Philisides takes the stage. He sings a beast fable as a peculiar interruption of the marriage celebrations. Geron spitefully remarks that "he never saw thing worse proportioned than to bring in a tale of he knew not what beasts at such a banquet" (259). The old shepherd's sense of decorum is offended, and rightfully so, since no amount of rationalizing can or should dispel our sense of the poem's peculiarity. There are important ways in which the beast fable does *not* fit into the third eclogues. This is as it should be, given the character of its author. (The stranger shepherds are not merely "foreign," they are also "strange" in the sense of being "peculiar": the youth tells philosophical tales to sheep as a way of easing his fear of the dark.) Philisides behaves indecorously because he is the victim of a divided mind.

The style of the beast fable is as peculiar as its author's mind set and dramatic situation. It is chock full of English archaisms of the kind employed by Spenser in *The Shepheardes Calender*. All of a sudden stars are "ycleped" rather than named, just as they enclose a "welkin" rather than a sky. The archaic diction is incorporated, suitably enough for a beast fable, into the native measures of rhyme royal, a stanzaic form employed by Chaucer in *The Parliament of Fowles*. Sidney's reasons for utilizing archaic diction and a native verse form are not difficult to comprehend. A literary style is used metaphorically, in this case to signal Philisides' very different psychological condition, the pristine "archaic" mental state enjoyed by him prior to his metamorphosis into a lover. The implied connection is delightfully whimsical, supplying a good indication that poetic rules, even Sidney's injunction in the *Apology* against archaic diction, are sometimes made to be broken.

When Dicus asks him to join in the wedding celebrations, at first Philisides is squeamish, "loath either in time of marriage to sing his sorrows . . . or by any outward matter to be drawn to such mirth," but at length he agrees after resolving to take "a mean way betwixt both" (254). The hint is small but clear. Philisides' token gesture of support for the golden mean announces indirectly the eclogue's subject. His poem is about justice, "the chief of virtues" according to Sidney's *Apology* and the central virtue in the Arcadian lifestyle.[17] (Appropriately enough, his beast fable appears almost at the very center of the romance, placed as it is in the middle of the third eclogues.) A process of refinement brings about an expansion of meaning: after all of the inessential elements of the marriage discussions are removed, justice establishes itself as the cornerstone of the quiet life. The connection between the two is virtually assured by the numerological structure of the third eclogues: five is not only the number of marriage, it is also, as Sir Thomas Browne writes, "the middle point and Central Seat of justice."[18] This connection helps to explain the importance that Sidney assigns to marriage in the third eclogues, and that is supplied to it by Euarchus in the romance's concluding trial: "marriage . . . [is] the most holy conjunction that falls to mankind, out of which all families, and so consequently all societies, do proceed, which not only by community of goods but community of children is to knit the minds in a most perfect union . . ." (383). Marriage is a metaphor for the operation of justice within the family and the community: its "perfect union" is a cure for the divided mind.

Philisides purports to have learned his song from "old Languet," whom he affectionately calls "the shepherd best swift Ister knew" (255, 15, 16). As fictions multiply inside fictions, with Sidney writing about Philisides' performing a song learned by a young Philisides, paradoxically the poem moves closer to the world of real events. The Languet of the beast fable sounds very much like the Languet whom we know from Sidney's correspondence. He advances a set of principles in accord with the letters' emphasis on constancy and quiet of mind, and consequently with the ethos of the Arcadian shepherds. The key stanza of the beast fable, whether by accident or design, is the fifth; it was Languet's belief, Philisides informs us, that:

> . . .the music best thilke [heavenly] powers pleased
> Was jump concord between our wit and will,
> Where highest notes to godliness are raised,
> And lowest sink not down to jot of ill.
>
> (255, 22–25)

By achieving a mean between extremes, a just balance is maintained between reason and passion in the individual, between husband and wife in marriage, and between monarch and populace in the state. In the center of a wedding celebration we find a new myth of man's creation and his subsequent tyranny over nature, one employed as a metaphor for the creation of kings who arrogate the whole power of the state to themselves. One context inevitably implies the other, as our attention moves rapidly from the individual to the family to the state.

Sidney's purpose is not to show Languet's principle in action but to demonstrate what happens when concord is violated. Any creature constructed on the model of Philisides' man is likely to be in some need of balance. Although Jove lends him "part of my heav'nly fire," the beastly portion of his nature is, at best, ambiguously composed (257, 5); he receives "heart" and "active might" from the lion and the lynx at the same time that he acquires "craft" and "flattery" from the fox and the dog (257, 10, 15). There is no golden age for Philisides' man, only a temporary period of concord followed by an unjust epoch of warring factions.

Sidney engages in a bit of pastoral pretense by attributing the authorship of his beast fable to Languet, at least insofar as that act tends to obscure other equally important authorities behind the eclogue. For example, as Ringler has noted, Ovid's *Metamorphoses* and Isaiah are used to supply significant details about the golden age enjoyed by the beasts.[19] Far more important sources of the eclogue have been overlooked, including Aristotle's *Nichomachean Ethics*. In the eighth book, while drawing analogies between various kinds of political systems and various sorts of friendships, Aristotle argues that "the relation of husband to wife seems to be in the nature of an aristocracy: the husband rules in virtue of fitness, and in matters that belong to a man's sphere; matters suited to a woman he hands over to his wife. When the husband controls everything, he transforms the relationship into an oligarchy, for he governs in violation of fitness, and not in virtue of superiority. And sometimes when the wife is an heiress it is she who rules. In these cases then authority goes not by virtue but by wealth and power, as in an oligarchy."[20] He praises the same kind of balance in marriage and the state that Sidney does, while providing an important precedent for linking the discussion of marital affairs to the role of the aristocracy in government. But the best evidence of Aristotle's influence on Sidney's beast fable and the third eclogues as a whole is supplied by his claim that

> The question what rules of conduct should govern the relations between husband and wife, and generally between friend and friend, seems to be ultimately a question of justice.[21]

Languet would certainly have agreed.

The implications of one more equally important source for Philisides' beast fable have also gone unnoticed.[22] In the first book of Samuel, "Otherwise called The First Book of the Kings," the origins of the Hebrew monarchy are explained (8:5–22). The Jews petition for a king and are warned by God through Samuel of the fatal consequences of their choice; in spite of his efforts, "the people refused to obey the voice of Samuel; and they said, Nay; but we will have a king over us" (8:19). The dramatic situation is almost identical to that in Philisides' poem, in which the beasts insist on having a monarch despite similar warnings from the owl and Jove. In the biblical passage the petition is motivated by the impious and willful pride of the "elders of Israel" (8:4). Sidney alters the motivation and the social status of the petitioners to suit his own ends. In Philisides' beast fable, it is the "multitude," led on by frivolous discontent and unjust envy of the "senators," that asks for a king (256, 24, 19). The consequences of the beasts' request are strikingly similar to the ones predicted by Samuel. He warns that the king will transform the Israelites into his servants, taking their fields, vineyards, and oliveyards for himself and his favorites. The king "will appoint him captains over thousands, and captains over fifties; and *will set them* to ear his ground, and to reap his harvest, and to make his instruments of war . . ." (8:12). Sidney's fable develops to a larger extent than the passage in Samuel the king's exploitation of social factions for his own unjust ends. He reports that the nobler beasts are forced to seek "their rests" in "deserts," and that the "smallest birds" and "meanest herd" are eventually murdered (258, 18; 259, 3). The point is obvious: only a strong aristocracy, as a balance against the power of the king and the ignorance of the multitude, can ensure the common good.[23] Sidney displays considerable artistic and political acumen in modeling his fable on a biblical story. By making use of a scriptural source, he gains religious authority for his representation of monarchy as the potentially dangerous product of a fallen world, one in need of just constraints from noble beasts.

Although certainty about the full extent of Sidney's political aims in this poem is impossible, the beast fable is clearly something more than the rhythmical grumblings of a disappointed nobleman. Sidney gives sharply focused political advice to those enlightened few who are capable of piercing the eclogue's allegorical veil. (The "veil," of course, is a matter of prudent self-protection.) His warning against the potential abuses of monarchy and his support of a strong aristocracy are political gestures with real implications for an age that had witnessed the rapid consolidation of state power at the hands of the Tudors. It is not a fable that would have delighted Elizabeth.

In the last poem of the third eclogues, Sidney returns to the marriage theme in the debate between Geron and Histor. As the narrator remarks, the young shepherd "having been long in love with the fair bride, Kala, and now prevented, was grown into a detestation of marriage" (260). (Sidney's decision to award Kala to the poet rather than the historian is a small joke at the expense of those tied to the truth of a foolish world.) The debate between Geron and Histor is important, in part because it supplies a summary of the arguments of the third eclogues. From Geron, we learn once again of "the quiet joy of loving wife," the ideal contentment supplied by marriage (260, 14). He places particular emphasis upon its therapeutic value and effectiveness in helping to ensure a just life as the "sweet and surest mean/ Our foolish lusts in honest rules to stay" (260, 8–9). There is a marked utilitarian quality to the kind of love praised by both Geron and Dicus; marriage's benefits in providing good citizens for the state are major considerations in their approval of it.

But the eclogue's importance is not confined to recapitulation. When Geron supplies a portrait of his happy marriage of "fifty winters," praising his "wife worthy to be a queen," he succeeds in creating a persuasive image that embodies in concrete form the precepts advanced elsewhere in the eclogues (262, 25, 27). His experience is a promise of continued contentment for the marriage of Lalus and Kala.

Sidney allows Histor to pose a series of objections to marriage. His complaints are the traditional fare of anti-feminist satire: wives are guilty either of "dull silence, or eternal chat"; they are too frivolous, always looking for "some new-found ware" (261, 4, 13). But these are superficial concerns. At the heart of Histor's complaint is his belief that "Phoenix but one, of crows we millions have" (260, 26). He is a victim of a common fallacy of the *Arcadia*'s refined lovers: the fallacy of uniqueness (to adopt Geron's perspective for a moment). No matter what Histor thinks, Sidney makes it clear that there is nothing special about Kala except that Lalus happens to think that she is special. This is chiefly why Geron's marriage is such a vital element in the third eclogues, since it demonstrates that the contentment achieved in the union of Lalus and Kala is enjoyed by other shepherds and is able to be enjoyed by anyone who will enter into marriage with a quiet mind. We are not witnessing a unique event; their wedding is entirely typical of the pastoral life and values of the Arcadian shepherds.[24] Its contentment is universally available.

Geron frames his advice to Histor in terms of selecting an appropriate response to fortune:

> No mortal man the cup of surety drinks.
> The heav'ns do not good haps in handfuls bring,
> But let us pick our good from out much bad;
> That still our little world may know his king.
> (261, 33–34; 262, 1–2)

The old man realizes that there are no absolute guarantees against misfortune, but at the same time he assures Histor that as long as we preserve a mean between extremes, according to the laws of nature "we never ought be sad" (262, 5). Geron's advice is more intelligent than we might have anticipated from his earlier bouts with Philisides. He does not recommend that passions be destroyed or suppressed; what he attempts to persuade Histor is to "use desire" in proper balance with reason: "Cupid now apply/. . .And thou shalt find in women virtues lie" (263, 4, 6). He may not have understood the politics of Philisides' beast fable, but Geron has an intuitive grasp of Languet's central principle: real contentment is a matter of achieving a just balance between extremes.

The marriage of Lalus and Kala is an image of that other more important wedding at the center of the Stoic ideal of the good life: the union of contentment and justice. It is a useful image, as we have seen, in evaluating competing ideals of contentment found in the narrative. It is also an effective means of imitating, though only at a distance, the ideal concord that Sidney establishes in *The Old Arcadia* between pleasure and virtue. The native shepherds imitate this ideal at a "distance" because their didacticism often leads them to divorce justice (thereby distorting it) from the balance that Sidney's notion of jump concord requires. What this means for our approach to the pastoral is that Sidney's ideal must be rigorously distinguished from the one presented by the native Arcadians. After all, Philisides, his representative in the eclogues, not Geron or Dicus, advances concord as a central standard in the third eclogues and makes it into a central concept in the work as a whole. As we shall find in part four, after examining the limitations of quiet in the next chapter, "jump concord" has more implications for the meaning of justice than Dicus and the rest of the native shepherds would either recognize or approve.

8
Book Four: "Discontentation" and Injustice

FORTUNE frowns in the fourth book of *The Old Arcadia*. One by one, all of the characters have their hopes for contentment thwarted. In Pyrocles' case, the full content that he has experienced is destroyed by a disastrous turn of events. Even Arcadia suffers misfortune as Basilius's apparent death throws the state into violent political turmoil. The loss of contentment is a sign of the injustice reigning in the private and public spheres. It is no accident that the narrative begins with a reference not to God, providence, or Apollo but to the "everlasting justice" (265). In the fourth book our attention is focused mainly on how men respond to misfortune and what happens to the mind at the loss of quiet.

The design of book four is strikingly schematic. There is such a succession of falls into adversity that it seems for a time as if we have moved from the hot groves of Italianate pastoral into the chillier confines of *Mirror for Magistrates* poetry. In grandiloquent fashion Dametas is comically transformed by the book's opening sentence into a providential "instrument of revealing the secretest cunning" (265). A few pages later Sidney's narrator is considerably more wary of assigning a cause to Dametas's discovery of Pyrocles and Philoclea in the bedchamber. He offers three possible explanations for the event, providential, physiological, and amorous: "whether it were they were so divinely surprised to bring their fault to open punishment; or that the too high degree of their joys had overthrown the wakeful use of their senses; or that their souls, lifted up with extremity of love after mutual satisfaction, had left their bodies dearly joined to unite themselves together so much more freely . . ."; in the end, he disclaims any knowledge of how the discovery came about, insisting only that the couple offers "a perfect model of affection" (273). If we do not doubt the role of providence in these events, Sidney's narrative strategy sharpens our awareness of how difficult it is to determine the progress and nature of everlasting justice. Of course, Geron has already warned us about hasty judgments.

Dametas's "discontentation" sets the pattern for those in the rest of the book, as a simplified fiction against which we can measure more complex events. When his hopes of finding gold are frustrated, he becomes disconsolate, for "so far had he fed his foolish soul with the expectation of that which he reputed felicity that he no less accounted himself miserable than if he had fallen from such an estate his fancy had embraced" (266). In Sidney's world almost all misfortunes are self-induced as the product of uncontrolled passions.

Dametas quickly finds his discontents compounded, first as he watches Mopsa fall out of a tree and then as he becomes the object of Miso's wrath, in what the narrator describes as "a picture of a rude discord" (270). Worse still, Dametas discovers that Pamela is missing from the lodges. His behavior on learning about this last and greatest misfortune supplies, appropriately enough, an instance of the least admirable kind of response to adversity; Dametas becomes "the right pattern of a wretch dejected with fear. For crying and howling, knocking his head to the wall, he began to make pitiful complaints where nobody could hear him . . ." (266).

Basilius's fall is nearly as swift. For the dull-minded, Sidney provides yet another illustration of how an impassioned aspiration to false felicity leads to discontent. Basilius awakens after a night of pleasant "adulteries," still confident in pastoral protections against misfortune, praising the night as a "sure refuge": "My soul is blest, sense joyed, and fortune raised" (275, 9–10). Gynecia overhears his exultations, and, amazed to discover "how much fancy doth not only darken reason but beguile sense," delivers a strong and impressive assault upon the injustices that he has committed both against her and against his "children," his "country," and himself (276–77). (Of course, she conveniently overlooks her own injustices.) Basilius's initial response to misfortune is that of a fool. He attempts to evade responsibility for his adulteries by "swearing it was the very force of Apollo's destiny which had carried him thus from his own bias" (277). A moment later, before drinking the apparently fatal "cup of gold," an action guided by his "hard hap," Basilius thanks the "destinies . . . that had made his own striving to go amiss to be the best mean ever after to hold him in the right path" (278). For a change, the duke has better success in predicting the course of future events but, as usual, he does so with the wrong expectations.[1]

Basilius's death supplies another sudden reversal of fortune as romance appears to be shading into tragedy. The first important effect of his death is to thrust Gynecia into "a necessary downfall of inward wretchedness" (279). The duchess finds herself the victim of a dilemma, realizing that the courts will eventually lay Basilius's "shameful death upon her—which being for that action undeserved, made it the more insupportable; and yet in depth of her soul most deserved, made it more miserable" (279). As a result, Gynecia kindles in herself a "furious fire of self-detestation" (280). When confronted by adversity, she despairs with a ferocity so great that it generates sympathy nearly equal to the moral criticism to which she is exposed.

Philanax's situation offers another variation upon the same theme. He also has suffered a loss of contentment because of Basilius's death, but unlike Dametas and his family and unlike the royal couple, there had been nothing misguided about his aspirations to serve the duke. The fact that Philanax has his "constancy of . . . mind surprised before he might call together his best rules," shows how much more complicated the world of *The Old Arcadia* has become since its opening pages (286). The good Stoic counselor who initially advised Basilius to preserve constancy and quiet of mind is himself overcome by passion. Not even the best moral rules are always sufficient. Enraged by the duke's death, Philanax vows "just revenge upon your unjust and unnatural enemies," as he begins to pursue what the narrator afterward calls "an unjust justice" (287).

The central episode of the fourth book takes place in Philoclea's bedchamber. When Pyrocles discovers that his amorous adventures have been found out, "his excellent wit, strengthened with virtue but guided by love" determines upon suicide as a means of preserving the princess's honor (290). After his one frustrated attempt she awakens and, in the course of a lengthy debate, is able to persuade him to relent only by threatening injuries to herself.

Dametas's response to misfortune is fear; Basilius's, self-serving evasiveness, Gynecia's, despair; Philanax's, vengeful rage. Sidney has taken considerable pains in the first portion of the book to provide a series of examples of how not to respond to adversity. The behavior of Pyrocles and Philoclea is of a different kind. We admire Philoclea's quiet of mind and are astonished by the strength of Pyrocles' fortitude. No trace of Amazonian effeminacy remains; Pyrocles displays nobility and courage on a scale even loftier than the one supplied by Histor's tales, and there is nothing in his adolescent heroics to suggest the moral virtue displayed here. Sidney does not inform us whether Pyrocles' new display of virtue is the product of a fortunate fall (has he, as Boulon might say, been beaten on to bliss?), or whether it results from the ennobling power of his love. What

Sidney does make clear—his critics to the contrary—is that it is Pyrocles who demonstrates to the princess the right response to adversity: "helped with the true loving of Pyrocles, which made her think no life without him," Philoclea "did almost bring her mind to as quiet attending all accidents as the unmastered virtue of Pyrocles" (294).[2] The prince is unquestionably taking the lead.

Pyrocles has been transformed into an impressive image of Stoic constancy, exemplifying nearly the whole range of virtues praised by the native Arcadians. He displays a pious regard for the "great maker and great ruler of this world," self-sufficiency, unshakable dedication to "everliving rightfulness," and a regard for the contentment achieved by "true fortitude" (292, 298), a state of mind that,

> carried away neither with wonder of pleasing things nor astonishment of unpleasant, doth not yet deprive itself of the discerning the difference of evils, but rather is the only virtue with which an assured tranquillity shuns the greater by valiant entering into the less. (296)

Pyrocles' metamorphosis cannot be explained as a return to or justification of the heroic ethos (whatever that might be in *The Old Arcadia*); indeed, it could be interpreted with much better accuracy as a vindication of the pastoral ideal, at least as that ideal is conceived by the native shepherds: his fortitude is designed to achieve an assured tranquillity. At the same time, the prince continues to be divided from the native Arcadians by the intensity of his valor, by his innate nobility, and by his idealizing love for Philoclea. At no point does he reject his pastoral experience. Although he admits to some unspecified "errors of . . . youth," he never repudiates the value of the idle life that he shared with Musidorus (292).

Pyrocles' virtue is "unmastered" in part because he has not yet achieved mastery over it. He is as impassioned in honor as he is in love, setting a precedent for the cavalier heroes of Beaumont and Fletcher. The prince has fortitude, but there is little temperance in his character—a fact that the bedroom setting keeps us ironically aware of. Determining how successful he is in the debate over suicide is difficult. Sidney shared the admiration of Lipsius and de Mornay for Stoic doctrines encouraging self-inflicted death when the opportunity to live virtuously is denied.[3] But admiration for Pyrocles' arguments is not the same thing as approval. Supported by the opinions of "wise men," Philoclea suggests that his resolution to die "is but a false colour of true courage . . . " (294). No final solution is offered to the problem of suicide, but events in *The Old Arcadia* ultimately do vindicate the justice of Philoclea's belief that "it is not for us to appoint that mighty majesty what time he will help us. The uttermost instant is scope enough for him to revoke everything to one's own desire" (297).[4] Far more significant than the details of their debate is the quality of Pyrocles' response to adversity. He is able to leave the discussion "with as much tranquillity . . . as before he had gone unto it, like a man that had set the keeping or leaving of the body as a thing without himself, and so had thereof a freed and untroubled consideration" (299). He is achieving quiet of mind.

Musidorus undergoes a similar set of experiences in the fourth book. Oppressed by rebels who have been "guided by the everlasting justice to be chastisers of Musidorus's broken vow," he displays an equal amount of courage in responding to misfortune (307). Again, there is little evidence that the prince learns anything from his beloved; as Sidney writes, "the cause of his courage grew in himself, but the effect was only employed in her defence" (307). Once he is captured, Musidorus experiences his own metamorphosis into an exemplar of Stoic fortitude. Like Pyrocles, he declares: "For my part, the image of death is nothing fearful unto me . . ." (313). Pamela is a spokesman for the same set of values. She gives voice to an ideal of Stoic self-sufficiency, "For how can I want comfort that have the true and living comfort of my unblemished virtue," at the same time that she follows her sister in acknowledging the inscrutability of divine justice: "What is prepared for us we know not, but that with sorrow we cannot prevent it, we know" (312). Soon afterward she falls into an "extremity of weeping," and is comforted by her stronger lover (314).

Musidorus's transformation from Italianate shepherd into noble prince is accomplished, like Pyrocles' without rejecting any part of the shepherd's experiences. His change is particularly important, since it signals a sudden reversal in the downward progress of his character. Until the concluding trial, Sidney's narrator provides nothing but praise for both princes. In this episode he cites his courage, the "brave . . . welcome" that Musidorus gave to the rebels, and the virtuous constancy of his love (307). Sidney undertakes the large task of transforming a potential rapist into an image of Stoic virtue (too large, in the view of some readers), but there can be no question that this is the task that he sets out to accomplish. When Musidorus is greeted by his cousin at his return to the lodges, Pyrocles exclaims: "Let us prove our minds are no slaves to fortune, but in adversity can

Book Four: "Discontentation" and Injustice

triumph over adversity" (318). This is one boast on which Sidney permits the princes to make good.

In the final portion of the fourth book we witness the "discontentation" of the state as Arcadia falls "into confused and dangerous divisions" (320). Injustice in the private sphere has led to public injustice. Sidney's political theme is even more pointed. As in Philisides' beast fable, he gives a "notable example how great dissipations monarchal governments are subject unto," while showing that the confusion is the direct result of Basilius's failure to provide his counselors and the nobility with a suitable role in the government: "Public matters had ever been privately governed, so that they had no lively taste what was good for themselves . . ." (320). In a world in which "all well doing stands so in the middle betwixt his two contrary evils," in which justice and contentment depend on a carefully maintained equilibrium, the state, like so many of the characters in the fourth book, is in need of a more certain balance (324).

The fourth eclogues take place in the evening and are distinct, correspondingly, both from the impassioned nighttime entertainments of the first two sets of poems and from the daylight celebrations of Lalus's wedding. A serene elegiac mood is created for the shepherds' complaints as they withdraw to "the western side of a hill," separating themselves from "the clamorous multitude" (327). Their laments are made in isolation from the mainstream of narrative events, an isolation reinforced by the fact, as in the previous set of poems, that none of the *Arcadia*'s main characters joins in the songs. The fourth eclogues are relatively brief; there are only six poems here, and once again, like the marriage celebrations, they are dominated by a single set of characters. In this case the stranger shepherds occupy the center of attention. The complaints of Philisides, Strephon, and Klaius were "many times occasion to beautify more than otherwise it would have been this pastoral exercise" (56). In addition to having more "beauty," the fourth eclogues also have more complexity. There is no hint of a limitation in perspectives here, since the stranger shepherds display a capacity for imaginative vision as superior to the princes' as the princes' range of understanding is to the native shepherds'. The poetry of marriage gives way to the poetry of death and loss, a sign of Sidney's attempt to foster pastoral inclusiveness and a preparation for his exploration into the limits of the quiet mind as an ideal of contentment. In three separate myths, the absence of

Urania, the banishment of Philisides from Samothea, and the death of Basilius (this too is mythic), the poetry of justice is replaced by an extended dirge on the loss of justice in the individual and the state.

The evening setting of Sidney's fourth eclogues recalls the twilight poetry of Vergilian pastoral. When "good old Geron" complains to his flock, we are reminded of the laments of Meliboeus, Moeris, and Lycidas in the first and ninth *Eclogues:* "Alas, poor sheep . . . which hitherto have enjoyed your fruitful pasture in such quietness as your wool, among other things, hath made this country famous, your best days are now passed. Now must you become the victual of an army, and perchance an army of foreign enemies" (327).[5] We also think ahead to the "ravening soldiers" of the *Apology*. Sidney includes these allusions for a special purpose. He declares his allegiance to the Vergilian tradition while gaining the benefit of its superb elegiac tones. At the same time, just as he does in the *Apology*'s definition of pastoral, Sidney enlists Vergil's support for his contrast between the "quiet hearts" of the shepherds and the "ambitions" of the romance's warring factions. There is nothing new about injustice in Arcadia.

The fourth eclogues begin with Sidney's magnificent double sestina, "Ye goat-herd gods." This is deservedly the best known of *The Old Arcadia*'s poems and it is the eclogue most frequently written about. Although some of this criticism has been extremely helpful— Empson's and Kalstone's in particular—Sidney's sestina has suffered both by its treatment outside of the original context for which it was written and by an oversight that has allowed its most important source to go unrecognized.[6]

The fact of greatest importance about "Ye goat-herd gods," is not that Urania has gone away, but that Strephon and Klaius, struggling to obtain quiet of mind, "tarry in Arcadia" in expectation of her return.[7] Sidney informs us, "they bare it out as well as such evil might be" (328). As their faithful devotion to her "strait commandment" indicates, Strephon and Klaius are speaking pictures of constancy in misfortune (328). Furthermore, the shepherds supply a lesson in temperance, a lesson that Sidney prepares for by means of what appears to be a biblically inspired emblem.[8] Strephon and Klaius, he writes, "continued their pursuit, like two true runners both employing their best speed, but one not hindering the other" (328). In Paul's letter to the Corinthians, similar language is used to describe the need to keep passionate desires in check: "Know ye not that they which run in a race run all, but one receiveth the prize? So run, that ye may obtain. And every man that striveth for the mastery is temperate in all things.

Now they *do it* to obtain a corruptible crown; but we an incorruptible" (1 Cor. 9:24–25). With her dual status as fair maid and heavenly beauty (Urania is the muse of astronomy), she is a reminder simultaneously of the corruptible and incorruptible crowns mentioned by Paul, just as Strephon and Klaius are at one and the same time pictures of the struggle to obtain temperance and warnings of the need for it. The very complexity of the double sestina form, the narrowness of the confines in which the two shepherds attempt to contain their passions supplies the best indication of the mastery they are striving to achieve over their emotions. In "Ye goat-herd gods" and in the fourth eclogues as a whole, Sidney fulfills both functions of "the lamenting Elegiac" as they are described in the *Apology;* he provides "compassionate accompanying [to] just causes of lamentation" while "rightly painting out how weak be the passions of woefulness."[9]

It has long been recognized that Sidney modeled his poem in part upon Sannazaro's fourth eclogue. The similarities between the two songs are numerous and striking, ranging from the likeness of their poetic forms (both are double sestinas) to the resemblance of their subject matter (both are amorous complaints). What has escaped the attention of Sidney's critics is that "Ye goat-herd gods" has a more important model in a song included in Gil Polo's *Diana Enamorada*. At the end of the first book, Tauriso and Berardo sing a complaint that begins "Pues ya se esconde el sol tras las montañas." The dramatic situation is almost identical to that in Sidney's poem. Like Strephon and Klaius, Gil Polo's shepherds are both in love with the same woman, a woman who scorns them, and, again, like Strephon and Klaius, they are described as being "commonly wont to go togither in company, and sing in emulation the one against the other" ("tenían costumbre de andar siempre de compañía y cantar en competencia").[10] As is true of Sidney's shepherds, their appearances in the romance are confined to the sets of poems found at the end of each book. Even the setting is the same; "Pues ya se esconde el sol" is sung during the evening just as "Ye goat-herd gods" is.

Gil Polo's poem is not a sestina. Although written largely in ottava rima, it is best described as a polymetrical song since it contains a variety of other stanzaic types. What we find Sidney setting out to do in "Ye goat-herd gods" is to superimpose a rhetorical device employed by Gil Polo upon Sannazaro's sestina form. The elaborate network of syntactic parallels incorporated into the paired stanzas of Sidney's sestina is a device borrowed from "Pues ya se esconde el sol." Just as Strephon and Klaius do, Tauriso and Berardo give vent to their agonized passions and hopeless devotion in matched alternating stanzas, and, again like Sidney's shepherds, Gil Polo's never speak directly to each other: their laments are self-contained.

>   Cuando imagina el triste pensamiento
>   la perfición tan rara y escogida,
>   la alma se enciende assí, que claro siento
>   ir siempre deshazíendose la vida.
>   Amor esfuerça el débil sufrimiento,
>   y ariva la esperança consumida,
>   para que dure en mí el ardiente fuego,
>   que no me otorga una hora de sossiego.
>
>   Cuando me paro a ver mi baxo estado
>   y l'alta perficíon de mi pastora,
>   se arriedra el coraçón amedrentado,
>   y un frío yelo en la alma triste mora.
>   Amor quiere que viva confiado,
>   y estoilo alguna vez, pero a deshora
>   al vil temor me vuelvo tan subjeto,
>   que un hora de salud no me prometo.[11]
>
>   (When that my painefull thoughts and pensive minde
>   Doe but imagine of her comely graces,
>   Then burnes my soule so strangely, that I finde
>   My vitall spirits to leave their proper places:
>   Love doth inforce this suffrance, weake by kinde,
>   And hope, that's flowne away with feathered paces,
>   To make my flames still burning in my brest,
>   Which gives me not one hower of wished rest.
>
>   When I consider of my base estate,
>   And high perfections of my Shepherdesse,
>   Then doth my hart retire with fearefull gate,
>   And pinching frost my timorous soule possesse:
>   Love wills I live in hope of happinesse,
>   And so I doe sometimes, but fortunes hate
>   To quaking feare subjecteth every power,
>   Which makes me not enjoy one happy hower.)

What happens in Gil Polo's poem and in Sidney's is that two solo laments are intertwined in such a way as to increase our awareness of the painful monotony suffered by the lover in the prison of his desires. Sidney succeeds in generating more intensity in "Ye goat-herd gods" than is produced in either of his models because he combines in an entirely unprecedented fashion the built-in repetitive devices of the sestina form, doubled for double effect, with the rhetorical symmetry of syntactic parallelism. This creative synthesis is chiefly responsible for the poem's unique power, and ultimately explains its meaning.

"Pues ya se esconde el sol" is the most important source for "Ye goat-herd gods" not only because of the similarities of its dramatic situation and rhetorical structures, but because Gil Polo's thematic intentions resemble Sidney's. Like Strephon and Klaius, Berardo and Tauriso exemplify "constant faith and true love" ("fe constante y amor verdadero") at the same time that their behavior provides a warning against the ferocity of uncontrolled passion. This is not to suggest that "Ye goat-herd gods" has the didactic simplicity of Gil Polo's song. It does not. By making a series of alterations in his source, Sidney incorporated into his double sestina an altogether new set of complex symbolic meanings.

Sidney does not follow Gil Polo in drawing careful distinctions between his shepherds; Berardo is bold and passionate, Tauriso is timid and modest. The characters and behavior of Strephon and Klaius are made as uniform as the syntactic parallels between stanzas, principally as a means of reinforcing our awareness of the painful monotony of the lover's psychological state.[12] Strephon and Klaius are gentlemen in disguise as shepherds, not real shepherds like Berardo and Tauriso. At the beginning of their sestina, they address the forest gods, nymphs, and heavenly deities, not their sheep. They occupy a considerably more exalted plane of experience. At the conclusion of Gil Polo's poem, Berardo and Tauriso provide alternate reminiscences of their beloved Diana as she dallies with her husband. Sidney's sestina ends with parallel accounts of the beloved, but the vision of Strephon and Klaius is of an entirely different kind. In spite of her "alta perficíon," Diana is a real woman living in a real world; her absence has no consequence for anyone besides the shepherds. (In any case she is only hiding behind the next bush.) Urania is not a woman to be dallied with, nor is she the kind of lady a bush is likely to conceal. She is not a lady at all, but a complex literary image. Her absence from Arcadia is symbolic of the discontentation and injustice reigning throughout the state.

Not only is Urania, as the muse of astronomy, an image of heavenliness—a heavenliness that has vanished from Arcadia—but she is also, as other critics have noted, Venus Urania, the object of idealized love.[13] After seeing the princes descend into lust, we have no difficulty understanding her absence. The celestial Venus, as Panofsky writes: "dwells in the highest supercelestial zone of the universe, i.e., in the zone of the Cosmic Mind, and the beauty symbolized by her is the primary and universal splendour of divinity."[14] These commonplace Renaissance associations with Urania are evoked by Sidney's sestina, but they cannot account for all or even the most important of her symbolic functions. Venus Urania *dwells* in the cosmic regions; Sidney's Urania has *departed*, presumably to them, leaving in her wake "eternal evening" and "spoiled forests, / Turning to deserts our best pastured mountains" (330, 23, 29–30). What Sidney has set out to do by bestowing this role upon Urania is to merge her with Astraea, the goddess of justice, whose departure from the world signaled the beginning of the iron age. As Ovid writes at the conclusion of his description of the four ages of man:

> victa iacet pietas, et virgo caede madentis
> ultima caelestum terras Astraea reliquit.
>
> (Piety lay vanquished, and the maiden Astraea, last
> of the immortals, abandoned the blood-soaked earth.)[15]

The link that Sidney establishes between the muse and the goddess is not an arbitrary one. As Frances Yates points out, the female deity whom Astraea most resembles is the "Virgo Caelestis . . . associated with Urania";[16] and according to Bernard Silvestris, a medieval commentator, some writers refer to Venus Urania as Astraea, others as natural justice.[17] The readiness with which both could be associated with Virgo, the sixth sign of the zodiac, made the conflation even easier. The frontispiece of Riccioli's astrological treatise, *Almagestum novum* (1651), contains a picture of Astraea as Urania.

Strephon and Klaius's mistress is called Urania rather than Astraea, for one reason, because the subject of the eclogue is not justice, but "everlasting justice." Sidney wants the action of the romance to be viewed from a providential perspective. The sestina's apocalyptic imagery serves a similar purpose. When Klaius laments "Long since my thoughts chase me like beasts in forests, / And make me wish myself laid under mountains," the Actaeon myth is brought into contact with the book of Revelation, as the shepherd joins "every bondman, and every free man" who calls (329, 25–26): "to the mountains and rocks, Fall on us, and hide us from the face of him that sitteth on the throne, and from the wrath of the Lamb" (Rev. 6:15–16). When

Strephon replies in the immediately adjacent verses, "Meseems I see the high and stately mountains / Transform themselves to low dejected valleys," Sidney alludes to another eschatological passage, this time from Isaiah (329, 27–28): "The voice of him that crieth in the wilderness, Prepare ye the way of the Lord, make straight in the desert a highway for our God. Every valley shall be exalted, and every mountain and hill shall be made low: and the crooked shall be made straight, and the rough places plain" (Isa. 40:3–4).[18] The religious events are the vehicle, not the tenor, in Sidney's metaphor of everlasting justice. This is not a poem about the apocalypse or about man's fall from grace. It is not even what needs to be called a Christian poem. The apocalyptic passages are introduced to heighten our awareness of the profound injustice suffered by the individual and the state in Urania's absence. But they do something more than that as well. After the apocalypse comes the heavenly Jerusalem and divine justice. Like the anticipation of Strephon and Klaius for the return of Urania, these passages are instrumental in transferring the golden age from a past image recollected in the present into a myth of everlasting justice to be fulfilled in the future. In light of these facts, new meaning is given to the Vergilian echoes with which the fourth eclogues begin. Sidney, too, can sing in a slightly higher key ("paulo maiora"). For a time he follows in the messianic tradition of Vergil's fourth eclogue by creating his own prophetic allegory of man's aspiration for a golden age of piety and justice.

This discussion of "Ye goat-herd gods" began by examining the Pauline emblem with which Sidney introduces the sestina. Now that we have seen the poem placed in its important literary contexts, it may be helpful to reexamine the emblem as a paradoxical image suggesting (as opposed to supplying) a resolution to an important problem of *The Old Arcadia*. The concept of a race for temperance is very nearly oxymoronic, and in terms of Sidney's conception of justice as a mean between extremes, Strephon and Klaius's frenetic pursuit of the muse of everlasting justice must be regarded as equally paradoxical. They aspire feverishly toward an ideal that is ultimately distinguished by its moderation, and in the process of doing so, Sidney makes them suggest a way of harmonizing the temperate minds of the native shepherds with the princes' aspiring intellects. The mean and the extreme coalesce in a single literary image whose power of imaginative persuasion is sufficient both to render the Arcadians' ideal of contentment almost joyless and the princes' amorous hopes severely limited. Strephon and Klaius have cosmic vision. This is a resolution that Sidney suggests rather than supplies because Urania, after all, never does make it back to Arcadia. The vision remains an image; the myth of justice stays a distant longing.

In Strephon and Klaius's second complaint, "I joy in grief, and do detest all joys," the shepherds continue their lament for the absent Urania. This is an impressive but considerably more earthbound poem than "Ye goat-herd gods." The eclogue's main focus is upon the mind's loss of quiet and the terrifying paradoxes of frustrated passion. Its structure supplies the surest pointer to its meaning. Strephon and Klaius lament their agonies in alternating dizain stanzas connected by "that kind of verse which is called the crown"; the last line of each strophe becomes the first line of the next (331).[19] The corona verse imparts a strong impression of circularity to the lyric, an impression reinforced by the fact that it begins and ends with the same line; Strephon speaks the verse at the outset and Klaius at the conclusion, as a token of the identity of their experiences. The shepherds run with agonizing monotony upon the same wheel of frustrated desire.

What is particularly unsettling about their experiences is the circular logic of the paradox in which they are trapped. Grief takes over the self with such large-scale force that it becomes indistinguishable from it, as Strephon laments;

> So close unto my self my wracks do lie,
> Both cause, effect, beginning, and the end
> Are all in me: what help then can I try?
>
> (332, 11–13)

The only delight that remains possible is a delight in despair, what Klaius calls "the burial of my bliss" (332, 21). Content is made inseparable from discontent. Sidney pursues the logic of their passions with striking thoroughness, creating in the process the first genuinely metaphysical style of Elizabethan poetry. In Strephon's complaint the dark lyric voice of Donne's "A Nocturnall upon S. Lucies day" can already be heard:

> If I myself will save,
> Then must I save what in me chiefly reigns,
> Which is the hateful web of sorrow's pains.
> Sorrow then cherish me, for I am sorrow;
> No being now but sorrow I can have;
> Then deck me as thine own; thy help I borrow,

> Since thou my riches art, and that thou hast
> Enough to make a fertile mind lie waste.
>
> (331, 26–33)

The shepherd's sorrow is absolute. But however dangerous it may be, this is not the immoral despair of Gynecia; little or no disapproval is implied by the lyric. Strephon and Klaius endure a loss so complete that their laments acquire a nobility rivaling that of the princes' newfound fortitude. At the extreme of despair, despair begins to achieve the appearance of fortitude. This, too, is one of the eclogue's paradoxes, and one of the best proofs of Sidney's pastoral inclusiveness, his willingness to question the limitations even of those values which are most central to *The Old Arcadia*'s narrative. The circular structure, which emphasizes the painful monotony of Strephon and Klaius's sufferings, is also an indication that they manage to achieve some amount of control over them, perhaps even some amount of relief.

Once again, the central portion of the eclogues is given to Philisides. We encounter our second myth of the loss of justice. It is appropriate that Sidney postpones having him disclose his full misfortunes until the conclusion of the book, in which everyone in *The Old Arcadia* suffers misfortune. It is even more appropriate that Philisides, "who by no entreaty of the duke would be brought unto it," is persuaded by Strephon and Klaius to sing (334). We do not need to be told that he agrees to give vent to his pains because he recognizes his kinship with them: all of the stranger shepherds have been victimized by the loss of quiet. If Philisides' separation from Mira is ultimately of less consequence than the absence of Urania, he has, at least from one perspective, more cause for desperation than Strephon and Klaius: his separation is permanent.

In the first of Philisides' two eclogues, Sidney brings pastoral to the limits of inclusiveness. This is mutton-stew poetry: it contains a little of everything. His fiction begins with a detailed personal reminiscence in the style of Sannazaro's mournful Sincero. Sidney forces autobiography into harmony with Italianate romance in prose that subsequently merges with medieval dream-vision poetry. Philisides relates his adventures in a mythical British kingdom named Samothea, populated by slightly dowdy classical goddesses, Venus and Diana—adventures that begin as epic, with a reenactment of the Judgment of Paris, and that eventuate in hot pastoral as the hero lights out for an Arcadian retreat. As in many of the Ovidian mythological poems of the 1590s, for which Sidney is clearly setting a precedent, the tone of the eclogue stays consistently playful, as Sidney moves back and forth in great bounds between the mundane and the visionary, the fictional and the actual. When Philisides sees the "moon asunder rent," and a chariot appear in the heavens "by doves and sparrows guided," he imagines that he is in the center of a grand apocalyptic cataclysm:

> I, wretch, astonished was, and thought the
>   deathful doom
> Of heav'n, of earth, of hell, of time and
>   place was come.
>
> (337, 7–8)

Upon discovering that he has only seen what by comparison is a singularly unimpressive pair of goddesses, Philisides, comically enough, is disappointed:

> When I such guests did see come out of such
>   a house,
> The mountains great with child I thought
>   brought forth a mouse.
>
> (337, 21–22)

It would be a mistake to assume that such playfulness exists for its own sake. Sidney deliberately confuses the boundaries between the worlds of fiction and fact in order to provide us with a better understanding of the real.

Of course, the poem's strategy being what it is, we are hardly likely to mistake its intentions. In line after line Sidney reinforces his central point. He tells us about the "benefits of a quiet mind" that Philisides enjoyed in his youth, and about how love "diverted this course of tranquillity" (335). We hear about his "careful musing," about "they which quiet live," and about his disdain for "aught whereto their minds aspire / Who under courtly pomps do hatch a base desire" (335, 20, 24, 27–28). We learn about his "unentangled mind," his "wakeful mind," his "calmy thoughts," and his "single mind" (336, 3, 9, 18, 29). Sidney overdoes it, but after all, this is a poem about excess that is simultaneously a reminder and a test of our aesthetic capacity to respond to its pleasures.

The key to an understanding of Philisides' dream vision lies in his symbolic use of Samothea, which, as Katherine Duncan-Jones has discovered, is a name given to England in its golden age.[20] The eclogue is a fine example of nationalistic primitivism. Under the rule of the just King Samothes, the inhabitants of Britain displayed a series of only slightly more exalted virtues than those possessed by Sidney's native shepherds. The line of descent is clear.

As Holinshed writes, the Samotheans were "exceedinglie given to religion," and dedicated to "the understanding of the sundrie courses of the starres, the order of inferiour things, with manie other matters incident to the morall and politike government of mans life."[21] Their principal concern is justice. As usual, the golden world that attracts Sidney's attention is distinguished by its ethical rather than its physical beauty.

Sidney's use of the myth is fascinating. In a bold, comic gesture, he equates the golden age of Samothea with Philisides' pristine condition prior to meeting Mira. The history of England is merged with his personal history. As Philisides falls into passion, his descent is transformed into a criticism of England's fall from its past glory. Sidney had good historical authority for positing a relationship between the two events since the explanation assigned by Holinshed for the Samotheans' destruction is nearly identical to the one used to account for Philisides' fall. The Samotheans are able to be conquered by Albion: "without finding any great resistance, for that . . . they had given over the practise of all warlike and other painefull exercises, and through use of effeminate pleasures, whereunto they had given themselves over, they were become now unapt to withstand the force of their enimies."[22] Philisides informs us that as an adolescent "my strength was exercised with horsemanship, weapons, and suchlike other qualities . . ." (334). In both instances, for the state and for the individual, effeminate pleasures bring about a loss of quiet and justice. However radical his metaphor might seem, there is nothing arbitrary about the analogy that Sidney draws between Philisides' misfortunes and those of Samothea; throughout *The Old Arcadia*, he has struggled to relate the private sphere to the public, to demonstrate that actions in one have consequences for the other.

Although Katherine Duncan-Jones is right in calling this a "rather baffling" eclogue, it is likely that the poem would have seemed even more baffling to its contemporary audience.[23] Sidney again frustrates conventional expectations about the nature of pastoral romance. This time he does so by transforming the nature of its politics. Vergil set the precedent for a marked patriotic strain in subsequent pastoral literature by creating such allegorical panegyrics as the one on Daphnis-Caesar in the fifth *Eclogue*. Sannazaro includes generously full passages of praise for Naples in the *Arcadia*, and in both Gil Polo and

Montemayor the trip to Felicia's palace is combined with elaborate paeans on the glories of Spain. In England, Spenser follows the tradition by lavishing praise upon Elizabeth in his "April" eclogue. Even Barclay remembers to flatter Henry VIII. In light of these facts, it is sufficiently surprising that *The Old Arcadia* contains not a single hint of praise either for England or for Elizabeth. But for Sidney's pastoral romance to include a myth of England's fall into effeminate wantonness is unprecedented and startling.[24] Philisides' dream vision complements the evidence provided by his correspondence with Languet of Sidney's disdain for his "corrupt age" and for what he calls elsewhere the "unnoble constitution of our time."

It is appropriate that the Samothean myth should be incorporated into the framework of the Judgment of Paris story. Since the time of Athenaeus, Paris's momentous choice, resulting in the fall of another civilization, was interpreted as a trial of pleasure against virtue.[25] Even as it was refined by Ficino and the Florentine Neoplatonists, the myth continued to center upon a decision among alternative modes of life, the active, the contemplative, and the pleasurable. The story is ironically as well as thematically appropriate as the framework of the eclogue. In 1579 Daniel Rogers, one of Sidney's friends among the Leiden humanists, addressed an especially complimentary verse epistle to him, filled with praise for his eloquence, virtue, and notable future as a Protestant hero. In the course of the poem Rogers makes Sidney the recipient of virtues from his own slightly modified set of competing goddesses: "Each vied with the other to adorn you with her gift, to leave all her tributes in your cradle. Gracious Venus gave you beauty, the Graces wit, and Pallas took care of your judgment and eloquence."[26] Although it is impossible to determine exactly how much autobiographical material there is in the eclogue, Sidney's estimation of his career's success is clearly as different from Rogers's as the "gifts" that Diana and Venus bestow, by way of Mira, upon Philisides. In place of beauty, wit, and eloquence, he receives the torments of frustrated passion. Whether that passion represents his love for Penelope Devereux, his desire for Queen Elizabeth's favors, a subtle compliment to his sister, or an entirely fictional event is a difficult and ultimately unanswerable question.[27] Of more significance is the fact that Philisides' perspective upon these events is identical to the one assumed by Sidney in writing about his career to Languet and Edward Denny. By making a few important alterations in the myth, Sidney complicates his portrait of Philisides as a wantonly indulgent lover by transforming him into the victim of a humorously cosmic

Book Four: "Discontentation" and Injustice

injustice. Unlike Paris, he is not even given the opportunity to choose a course of virtue. Forced to decide between meager chastity and dowdy lust, Philisides does the best he can by awarding the victory to Mira, a maiden who embodies, as a mean between extremes, the beauty of Venus and the purity of Diana. The subsequent torments heaped on him by the goddesses are the unmerited products of divine spleen. To make matters even more unfair, all of this takes place in a dream. One meaning of the allegory is clear: there are no protections against the inroads of desire; biology, as Plangus well knows, is manifestly unjust. It is difficult not to believe that these events also represent a protest on Sidney's part against the unjust treatment that he has received, perhaps from the Queen, perhaps merely from fortune.

Sidney continues to make use of literary styles as metaphors for psychological states in Philisides' eclogues. We move from the bouncy native iambs of the dream vision, describing his fall into passion, into the elegant quantitative meters of the verse epistle sent to Mira upon his banishment from her affections. The passage from innocence to experience is accompanied by an abrupt change of mood as the playful blending of literary traditions in the dream vision is replaced by the uniformly plaintive tones of classical elegiacs. One of the chief reasons why this metaphorical use of styles is significant is that it prevents us from making overly simple moral assumptions about the nature of Philisides' love experiences. Merely pointing to his loss of quiet is insufficient. Discontent and love carry benefits as palpable as the heightened eloquence he displays. Love, as Philisides knows, will not "learn temp'rance" (343, 23). If Geron would argue that this is precisely why it must be avoided, like any other passion of the aspiring mind, it is unlikely that the old shepherd would win our agreement. Philisides admits that he was "faulty" in allowing reason to yield to passion, but, as he asks his beloved:

> . . . what's this for a fault, for which such
>   faith be abolished,
> such faith, so stainless, inviolate, violent?
>
> (343, 28–30)

There are other factors, as Philisides realizes, that enter into our estimation of the lover's experience. He defends his behavior to Mira by stating:

>   All my 'offence was love; with love then must
>   I be chastened,
>   and with more by the laws that to revenge do
>   belong.
>   If that love be a fault, more fault in you to
>   be lovely;
>   love never had me oppressed, but that I saw
>   to be loved.
>
>   (342, 26–30)

When Pyrocles and Musidorus are forced to account for their "offences" before Euarchus in the fifth book, this is also the heart of their defense. In Philisides' case as in the princes', the claim at once fails to absolve him of responsibility for his actions, and is impossible and unwise entirely to reject.

The native Arcadians dominate the last portion of the fourth eclogues as Agelastus sings two elegies on the death of Basilius. We pass from the private grief of Philisides to the public sorrow of a community of shepherds, following the progress of the fourth book and *The Old Arcadia* as a whole. Urania's absence is proceeded by Mira's banishment of Philisides; in Basilius's death we are confronted by the most permanent—or so it seems—of all of these losses. By placing the amorous complaints of the stranger shepherds in the context of a funeral, regardless of the additional symbolic weight that they are made to carry, Sidney succeeds in liberating them from the ordinary constraints of the love lyric; the mere fact that the absence of Urania and the banishment by Mira are associated with the kind of loss for which death is responsible deepens our sense of the tragedies incurred and provides a universality to the experiences that they might not otherwise possess. Intensely felt personal sorrows achieve a generalized significance. A different process takes place in this third myth of the loss of justice. We are made to experience not an expansion but a constriction of personal grief. There is a reason for this.

The central tradition of the pastoral elegy as it developed in antiquity and the Renaissance is represented by lyrics like Moschus's "Lament for Bion." In its orthodox version the classical elegy is the expression of a precariously maintained balance. Over the course of the poem a state of idealized sorrow is successfully achieved with the overthrow of despair. But the achievement is tentative since that state is made to appear in continual danger of collapse with a slide backward into perilous uncontrol. Intense private feelings of grief are delicately poised against a consciousness of the general human condition and a serene awareness of the immortality to be achieved through art and sometimes through God. In this central tradition, the lament is made for an actual person, one whom the poet ordinarily represents as his friend. As Poggioli writes, "the pastoral of death" is "a pastoral of friendship: it is only by grieving over a dead friend that a bucolic poet may safely hint that the death principle rules both world and self."[28] This is the tradition of Spenser's "November" eclogue and of Milton's *Lycidas*, but not of Sidney's elegies.

These are not laments for a real individual. Even if one adopts the perspective of the Arcadian shepherds who sing them, it would be mistaken to suggest that the poems are written for the flesh-and-blood Basilius. They are community laments. The very fact that Sidney chooses to have Agelastus deliver them, a shepherd about whom we know almost nothing, rather than Geron or Dicus, indicates the impersonal quality that he is striving to achieve in the poems. These are public laments for a public figure, who has been purged of all of the accidental features of personality. If a tension remains in Sidney's elegies between private feelings of grief and public expressions of sorrow, the private emotions are suppressed here, not so much because they threaten loss of control (although they do make that threat), but because they are inappropriate to and less noble than the public occasion that inspires them. Emotions are dignified as they are transformed into ritual. The ritualistic nature of Sidney's elegies serves to locate them within their proper tradition. Although inspired in part by Sannazaro's eleventh eclogue, a poem inspired in turn by Moschus, Agelastus's eclogues take their descent from the impersonal, stylish, mythological elegies of Bion and Theocritus. Judged according to the standards of this tradition, Sidney's elegies are among the several unheralded triumphs of the eclogues.

Of course, there are good reasons for purging Basilius of the accidental features of his personality. They are hardly the stuff out of which panegyrics are made. In fact, over the course of the romance, we have seen altogether too many examples of the duke's foolish behavior to accept without pause the shepherd's praise of him as "our earthly saint" (345, 15). We are meant to pause at this sudden shift in perspectives but not in order to reject Agelastus's laments as the inflated claims of a bumpkin. To do so is to establish a false dichotomy between the "real" Basilius, whose follies have appeared throughout the romance, and the "fictional" Basilius, whom Agelastus praises as an exemplar of the just ruler. What is taking place in these eclogues is subtler and considerably more interesting. Basilius's status as a symbol of injustice is distinguished from his position in the actual world as a duke who perpetrates injustice. The identity singled out by

Agelastus is no less "real" than the character that he displays as a man.[29] Perhaps it is even more real, since only in this role is Basilius perceived by the Arcadian shepherds. By means of this dichotomy, Sidney gives renewed emphasis simultaneously to the ideal of justice and to its absence from Arcadia.

This is the third myth of the loss of justice in the final set of poems, but it is the first occasion on which the topic is dealt with explicitly. Agelastus concludes his opening elegy by exclaiming:

> Justice, justice is now, alas, oppressed;
>   Bountifulness hath made his last conclusion;
>   Goodness for best attire in dust is dressed.
>
> (348, 13–15)

The justice whose oppression Agelastus complains of is largely political. He laments the loss of "well settled order" and "public . . . quiet" maintained under Basilius's rule: "While he did live, far, far was all disorder" (348, 23–25). Even in their most violent laments, the "quiet hearts" of the native shepherds preserve a proper regard for moral order. If he complains against mankind's cruel exclusion from nature's regenerative processes, Agelastus stops far short of convicting the heavens of cosmic injustice. Sidney allows no repeat of Plangus's assault against the gods; the stars have, not a mutable course, but an "inconstant constant race" (346, 2).

Agelastus fulfills to the letter the responsibilities of the elegaic poet as they are described in Sidney's *Apology*. He bewails "the weakness of mankind and the wretchedness of the world," and he does so while compassionately accompanying—in a phrase already quoted— "just causes of lamentation."[30] Agelastus himself refers several different times to "this justest cause of plaint," "this just lamentation," and his "just complainings" (345, 11; 347, 29; 346, 1). The death of a ruler merits grief. Agelastus fully lives up to his reputation among the Arcadians for "austerely maintained sorrowfulness" (284). The austerity with which he triumphs over grief elevates him as a model of Stoic fortitude and an exemplar of how to respond to adversity.

Agelastus concludes his laments with a sestina that can best be described as a coda to his opening elegy. This is an impression that Sidney has gone to some trouble to create. The first of the two eclogues ends, "And farewell prince, whom goodness hath made glorious" (348, 37); his sestina begins, "Farewell O sun, Arcadia's clearest light" (349, 4). In moving from one eclogue to the other there is no change in subject, only a marked heightening of style and increase in lyric intensity. Agelastus's status as an Athenian senator turned shepherd accounts for the sophistication of the literary form and the elevated rhetoric that Sidney allows him to utilize.

The fact that Sidney incorporates Agelastus's complaints into a sestina supplies one additional mark of his artistic intelligence and creative ingenuity. Until *The Old Arcadia*, the sestina had never, to my knowledge, been employed for any purpose other than writing love poetry. Sidney discovered its rich potential for the elegy. (In any case, Spenser appears to have thought so.) By making use of the sestina, he imparts both a greater emotional impact to Agelastus's laments and a greater sense of his mastery over those emotions. He succeeds in molding sorrow into a static, carefully structured unit of feeling. Sidney manages to create this impression by making a few skillful manipulations in the form. All of the verses are end-stopped; no sloppy emotions spill over these line endings. At the same time, the poem is given a stately rhythmic progression by Sidney's liberal use of anaphora. Like so many of the eclogues, this is a poem that displays its artificiality openly. In this instance, Sidney succeeds in justifying his elaborate artistry in an especially effective way since Agelastus's elegy is ultimately about the importance of symbolic forms: the importance of Basilius as a symbol of justice, and the importance of poetry as a means of providing relief.

Sidney displays his usual carefulness in selecting the sestina's repeating end-words. The six nouns chosen are a characteristic mixture of metaphorical vehicles and abstractions signaling Basilius's significance within the Arcadian community: "light," "treasure," "might," "pleasure," "direction," "affection." The poem reasserts the central importance of just "pleasure" within the Arcadian community. Considerable care has also gone into Sidney's selection of the primary metaphor of Agelastus's sestina. Agelastus bids farewell to Basilius, his metaphorical sun, just as the community of Arcadian shepherds is watching the real sun set. (Sidney is careful to inform us that they are on the western side of the mountain.) Furthermore, he employs the same metaphor for his loss as Strephon and Klaius made use of to describe the departure of Urania and as Philisides applies while describing his banishment from Mira. The continuity of imagery is significant since it reinforces our awareness of the continuity of subject matter. In all three cases, what Agelastus, Philisides, and Strephon and Klaius have suffered is a loss of quiet, which is also, and more importantly, a loss of justice.

Sidney incorporates different kinds of coherence into his three myths of the loss of justice, ranging from similarities in theme to orderly progressions in subject matter (the movement from private to public concerns, from temporary to permanent losses), but even these obvious attempts at establishing unity seem curiously incomplete. The fourth eclogues are strangely isolated from the narratives that surround it. Even as Sidney's shepherds supply in their withdrawal to the mountainside an unanticipated depth and universality to the romance's consideration of justice, their songs are made to appear peculiarly remote from the immediate concerns of the plot. Philisides, Agelastus, Strephon, and Klaius accomplish one major business of the pastoral by lamenting the absence of justice, but their poems seem, paradoxically enough, almost beside the point. The unity of the fourth eclogues will appear no less precarious when we expand our approach to the poems in the last portion of this study. As we shall see in part IV, the theme of art and nature does not provide final coherence to the laments, but it does explain the reasons for its absence. Only when we have learned to regard the fourth eclogues, and *The Old Arcadia* as a whole, as an ongoing, unfinished (even unfinishable) gesture to obtain justice, rather than as a simple complaint for its absence, will an understanding of the pastoral be possible.

PART IV
Poetic Justice

9
Nature and Art in *The Old Arcadia*

THE major questions posed by *The Old Arcadia* cannot be answered by attending only to the events of the narrative or to the conflicting attitudes expressed by the princes, the native Arcadians, and the stranger shepherds in the entertainments. Too much that is essential to Sidney's pastoral design, to his desire to procure justice and contentment for himself and his readers, is lost unless we learn to distinguish his critical voice within these fictions as he comments upon the processes of his art. We need to be alert not only to what the pastoral *says* (to the themes that it explores) but to what it *does* (to the changes that it seeks to effect in the minds of its readers.) In short, the self-reflexive qualities of Sidney's art require attention. For his activity as a poet offers *The Old Arcadia*'s best illustration of how to respond to changing fortunes. Styles of song become metaphors for states of mind.

The princes, the native Arcadians, and the stranger shepherds share a single goal: all of them attempt to use song to achieve contentment. Historically, this is a strong motive force of pastoral. Sidney's characters do not sing the same kind of songs—in large part because their ideas about contentment are so different. They do not inhabit the same natural world—or, at least, they do not look upon nature in the same way. They do not even present a single statement that defines an ideal poetic or an ideal relationship with nature. But they do agree about the importance of singing, and this is a crucial point. Considered in balance, their songs offer abundant evidence that the most important vehicle in achieving contentment, and the justice that Sidney represents as inseparable from it, is poetry—not any kind of poetry, not the poetry of the princes, the stranger shepherds, or the native Arcadians, but the special variety that Sidney creates out of all of them. The object of this portion of my study is to define that special variety and to describe how Sidney's version of pastoral attempts to harmonize justice and contentment. In making that definition, as I concentrate on the final two aspects of the idle life (styles of song and ways of contemplating the natural world), I shall complete my analysis of how Sidney conceives and how he strives to create a just life for himself and his readers.

In a romance that begins with a near-tragic act of misreading as Basilius misinterprets the Delphic oracle, and that ends with such a peculiar coincidence of art and providence, poetry is bound to assume a large importance. Considerable attention is given to the subject in the prose portions of *The Old Arcadia*, although, not surprisingly, it is in the lyric world of the eclogues, a world devoted wholly to song, that Sidney makes his most detailed explorations of the topic. The kind of focus given to poetry ranges from specific recommendations about literary style (the romance provides a series of models for the development of Elizabethan verse) to particular criticisms of other literary traditions: I have already noted a number of Sidney's objections to the values and methods of Italianate and Christian pastoral. More important in this context is Sidney's concern with the functions of poetry, with its use as a didactic tool, a means for impressing moral ideas upon refractory young shepherds, with its importance as an instrument of persuasion, a vehicle for procuring the affections of a reluctant mistress, and with its value as a therapeutic device, a way of achieving relief from the agonies of frustrated desire. Its three major functions correspond, neatly enough, to the three main groups of eclogue characters: the native Arcadians interest themselves largely in teaching, the princes in moving their mistresses, and the stranger shepherds in finding relief.

What Sidney sets out to do in *The Old Arcadia*, considered from a historical vantage, is to combine the major function of poetry in Christian pastoral, the didactic, with that of Italianate pastoral, the therapeutic. To these two functions he adds his own emphasis upon poetry's persuasive powers.[1] Again, Sidney's art is better, he implies, because it is more inclusive and syncretic. But his Arcadian poetry is more than the sum of its parts. In the process of making a version of pastoral that attempts to teach, persuade, and provide a measure of relief for himself and for his audience, Sidney creates a special brand of poetry that operates by concord to produce justice and contentment. While fashioning *The Old Arcadia* into a defense of poetry, the most important feature of the idle life, Sidney creates, as many of his predecessors did, a defense of pastoral.

This is to be a qualified defense, however. Viewed from a slightly different angle, Sidney's perspective on art and nature seems decidedly skeptical about song's potential to reconcile man to his world. There are no Vergilian shepherds here boasting that "carmina vel caelo possunt deducere lunam" ("Songs can even draw the moon down from heaven"); and it would be impossible to conceive that anyone in Sidney's world would agree with Sannazaro's Eugenio that "al mondo mal non è senza rimedio" ("there is no ill in the world without a remedy").[2] Few large claims for the powers of poetry are advanced explicitly. Like most English writers of the 1570s, and like the Christian pastoralists who precede him, Sidney is aware of the ease with which the imagination is subject to abuse and the dangers attendant upon its loss of control. This awareness led him within his fictional defense of poetry to include a critique of the misuse of the imagination. Only by means of the right use of poetry, as Sidney makes us aware, can the individual be reconciled to his world. When the art is abused—and it is frequently abused—discontent and alienation from nature are the result. Before examining *The Old Arcadia*'s special brand of poetic justice, it will be necessary to attend to its critique of the dangers of the imagination, a critique that will take us into largely unexplored aspects of Sidney's aesthetic thinking.[3]

A study of Sidney's poetics can neither begin nor end with a study of his *Apology for Poetry*. From *The Lady of May* to the revised *Arcadia*, critical concerns about the nature of poetry and its capacity to shape moral understanding assume primary importance. The *Apology* remains the single most helpful work in evaluating Sidney's conception of the poet's powers, particularly as they are exercized in remedying defects in man and nature, but the very fact that the *Apology* was written as a public defense of the poet strictly limited its usefulness in detailing the art's darker operations—and as Sidney knows, there is much to detail. In the fictional world of *The Old Arcadia*, these limitations were absent, as we enter a landscape where song corrupts more frequently than it cures. Out of self-love come the poetic "fancies" that the impassioned imagination attempts to impose upon nature. In *The Old Arcadia* the psychological distortions of the impassioned mind are linked to the poetic logic of romanticizing fiction to provide what is simultaneously a lesson in reading and a lesson in evaluating modes of thought.

i. The Perils of Fancy

The Old Arcadia is filled with examples of the misuse of the imagination—a faculty that Sidney calls most often the "fancy." At the outset of the romance, Basilius is criticized for taking Philanax's advice "for confirmation of fancies [rather] than correcting of errors" (6) [as support for his decision to retire to the lodges]. The native Arcadians are praised for having "their fancies opened to so high conceits" (4). *Fancy* is an important word in the pastoral because of its frequent use, and because of its flexibility in permitting Sidney to establish an easy commerce between aesthetic and psychological activities. Poems do more than act upon the mind; they show how the mind is acting.

Sidney focuses his critique of the dangers of the imagination largely on the experiences of the princes, and largely upon the issues of desire and persuasion. The poet is most likely to abuse his art when he begins to persuade, to operate upon the infected will with the powers of his erected wit: the potential for deception both for the self and for the audience is enormous. (Of course, by persuading the poet also achieves his greatest successes.) Sidney's ambivalence about the princes' experiences in love, as they threaten moral and political chaos to Arcadia, extends to an ambivalence about the kinds of imaginative tools they employ to sing their way into the hearts of their mistresses. As attempts to create a heightened mode of praise and persuasion for the satisfaction of amorous desires, the princes' songs are consistently used to indicate potential perils of the fancy in alienating man from nature and from the virtue and contentment that a life led in harmony with nature supplies.

Sidney takes advantage of the pastoralist's traditional freedom to present the natural world as if it were at once an objective fact, external to man, and a subjective state, a projection of the individual's psychological condition.[4] He does so, in a characteristically untraditional way, by forcing individual groups of characters to live almost entirely within one realm or the other. Arcadia is a schizophrenic landscape. On the one hand, we have the example of the native Arcadians whose natural world is made up of solidly objective trees that are a reflection of what appears to them, at least, as equally solid objective standards of morality. The native shepherds view the world as if it were a secular version of the Christian pastoralist's book of nature. Arcadia offers an endless supply of moral injunctions for their didactically intentioned songs. When Geron, an elderly Arcadian shepherd, wants to teach Mastix a lesson against slander, he creates a myth about how the swan lost its voice. When he wants to lecture Philisides on the inconstancy of women, he illustrates his arguments with maxims drawn from the natural world:

> He water ploughs, and soweth in the sand,
> And hopes the flick'ring wind with net to hold,
> Who hath his hopes laid up in woman's hand.
>
> (73, 22–24)

Some of their "readings" from the book of nature oversimplify and distort the text, like this last piece of misogyny, and they do not often have much success in persuading others about the "truth" of their teachings, but the native shepherds do manage to maintain an admirable degree of harmony with their world. Situated in the remote and comparatively untroubled realm of the eclogues, the shepherds maintain an impressive independence from the moral and political corruptions of the narrative. They are reasonable men living in a reasonable universe. Their world sets a standard against which we can measure the perilous transformations worked upon the landscape by the princes, by the stranger shepherds, and by Sidney himself.

For an image of nature subjectively conceived, we turn to the experiences of *The Old Arcadia*'s lovers. As the narrator remarks, love is "the refiner of invention" (12). From the moment in which he becomes entranced by a mistress, the lover enters a private landscape that differs radically from the "objective" nature of the native shepherds. After Cleophila falls in love, Sidney writes:

> Then was his chief delight secretly to draw his dear friend [Musidorus] a-walking to the desert of the two lodges where he saw no grass upon which he thought Philoclea might hap to tread but that he envied the happiness of it; and yet, with a contrary folly, would sometimes recommend [compare] his whole estate to it. (12)

From the lover's point of view, nature lacks consistency. As variable as his psychological states, nature appears, on one occasion, infinitely more fortunate than himself (because his mistress walks upon it), and on another, infinitely as wretched (because it is walked upon by him).

How does Sidney expect the reader to respond to his lovers' subjectively conceived landscapes? Should they be dismissed as unreal or untrue? Answering these questions involves much more than an evaluation of the princes' status as lovers; in accounting for their transformations of the landscape, we are ultimately asked to judge the nature and responsibilities of poetic imagination itself. Once Pyrocles has fallen in love, his world takes on a different and highly literary appearance as he enters the kind of world that one would expect a mind stored with fashionable pastoral notions to create. He exclaims to Musidorus:

Do you not see how everything conspires together to make this place a heavenly dwelling? Do you not see the grass, how in colour they excel the emeralds. . . ? And see you not the rest of all these beautiful flowers, each of which would require a man's wit to know, and his life to express? (15)

Musidorus, of course, sees nothing of the kind: he has not yet fallen in love. He proceeds to ridicule Pyrocles by marveling at "the excessive praises you give to this desert" (16). If we are willing to laugh along with him, it would be a mistake to label Musidorus's reply as an instance of "realistic" deflation. Sidney is not willing to allow us to dismiss Pyrocles' private world so easily. Musidorus goes on to remark about the Arcadian landscape: "And even Tempe, in my Thessalia, where you and I . . . were brought up together, is nothing inferior unto it" (16–17). This is Sidney in one of his most sphinxlike postures. To suggest that Arcadia is only as beautiful as the vale of the muses is hardly to destroy its idyllicism. Instead of deflating the ideal by the real, and dismissing the validity of Pyrocles' subjective nature in the process, he balances with good comic aplomb one literary myth against another. By doing so Sidney leaves the reader in considerable uncertainty about just how idyllic the Arcadian landscape really is, and correspondingly, about just how much truth is contained in Pyrocles' fanciful version of it.[5]

The process that Sidney outlines for us in this episode is clear: the lover transforms the world into an image of his desires. In Pyrocles' case, "each thing he saw seemed to figure out some part of his passions" (12). The lover inhabits a fictional landscape and struggles to have that landscape "come true." A small illustration of this process occurs in Pyrocles' change of name: by becoming Cleophila, turning Philoclea's name into himself, he makes a linguistic adjustment prepare the way for a transformation of self and status.

Sidney allows us to perceive the lover's metamorphosis of nature simultaneously as a particular kind of mental activity that is peculiar to the impassioned individual and as a particular kind of poetic activity that is peculiar to certain modes of literary creation. The lover's transformations of the landscape are exactly equivalent to those of the poet. Musidorus makes the connection between them explicit.

But I think you will make me see that the vigour of your wit can show itself in any subject; or else you feed sometimes your solitariness with the conceits of the poets whose liberal pens can as easily travel over mountains as molehills, and so (like well disposed men) set up everything to the highest note—especially when they put such words in the mouth of one of those fantastical mind-infected people that children and musicians call lovers. (17)

The "unfallen" Musidorus is as suspicious of art as he is of amorous affairs—peculiar qualities in a youth who has been raised in the vale of the muses.

Insofar as all poets in Sidney's world are "guilty" of setting up everything to the highest note, of fashioning golden worlds that show what should be rather than what is, the prince's remarks have a general relevance. They form a troubling contrast to the aggressively optimistic poetics of the *Apology*. For both Sidney and Cleophila set out to work ideal transformations upon the landscape. Consider the *Apology*'s most important statement of the poet's power to remedy defects in man and nature [created nature]: "man's wit with the efficacy of Nature [creating nature] . . . bringeth things forth far surpassing her doings."[6] While singing near-Edenic praises of the poet's golden world, Sidney clearly resembles one of Musidorus's "well-disposed men." It is possible to draw an even closer connection between the powers of wit attributed by Sidney to the poet and the vigorous wit which Musidorous mockingly attributes to Cleophila. To the degree that we are allowed to believe that Cleophila is not merely a "philosopher" but an "Astronomer" of fancies (as the prince claims), that his love is genuinely noble and heavenly, the poetic transformation that he works upon the landscape, while attempting to bring it into harmony with an ideal, is entirely justified—justified, that is, by the golden-world aesthetics of the *Apology* (28). For if the mistress *is* the source of all virtue in the world, he operates in accordance with Nature by using his poetry to bring about the fulfillment of his love. Sidney is far from anxious to deny the mind's power to apprehend images of absolute virtue and the value inherent in the poetic attempt to transform the world into an image of virtue.

But we do not often see the princes' amorous affairs from such a favorable point of view. We are rarely without suspicion that Dorus and Cleophila may, after all, be mere solipsists, inhabiting a never-never land constructed out of fictions that multiply as fast as their desires, alienating them from Nature, rather than allowing them to cooperate with it. Sidney does not side with Musidorus in his war against poetry, but Musidorus represents a side of Sidney—one that is uncommonly suspicious of the high claims advanced by lovers and poets (particularly by poets who are lovers). In *The Old Arcadia*, the mind's capacity to idealize its experience is equaled only by its capacity for self-deception. This is the importance of Musidorus's criticism of his newly enamored friend and the explanation for Sidney's deep suspicion of romanticizing poets. The high-flying wit of the *Apology*'s maker cannot finally be squared with the vigorous wit displayed by Cleophila. The prince belongs to a special category of poets, one that interprets the artist's responsibility to present what should be according not to the demands of virtue, but to the dictates of personal desires: the only "should be" for Cleophila is the satisfaction of his romantically idealized lust for Philoclea. We can therefore distinguish the prince's fanciful transformations from the kind recommended in Sidney's criticism, but the fact remains that the metamorphosis of a brazen landscape into the golden world of poetry is a far more problematic task than at first appears in the *Apology*. For when the liberty of the poet's conceit is exercised not in the apprehension of ideal images of virtue, but in illusory fictions that have merely the appearance of virtue, poetry becomes an enormously powerful tool for abuse. In the absence of fixed standards by which to determine the validity of the individual's ideal visions, poetic activity becomes dangerously uncertain. The golden world is easily changed into a solipsistic landscape, replete with perils for the self and for the audience. It is far safer to be a reasonable shepherd living in a reasonable world; the native Arcadian lacks the power to construct golden worlds, by refusing to work transformations upon nature, but he also avoids the perils of fancy.

Dicus defines the limits of the poet-lover's potential solipsism when he tells Dorus:

> For who doth hold his love in estimation,
> To witness that he thinks his thoughts delicious,
> Seeks to make each thing badge of his sweet passion.
> (137, 14–16)

The lover is not the only solipsist in Sidney's world. Far from it. Any passion, "sweet" or sour, is capable of working a similar effect upon the mind. Dametas, *The Old Arcadia*'s stupidest rustic and its most comic speaking picture of passion, is said to have "included all the world within his sheepcote" (272). After Plangus has blasphemed against the gods for torturing his beloved Erona, he is criticized by Boulon for a similar fault:

> Alas, while we are wrapped in foggy mist
> Of our self-love (so passions do deceive)

> We think they [the gods] hurt when most they
>   do assist.
>
> (148, 31–33)

The "wise counselor" is right on target. What I have been calling solipsism, Sidney refers to again and again as a particular form of impassioned self-love. When Cleophila convinces Gynecia that he is in love with her, luring her into a nighttime tryst with Basilius, the narrator comments, providing universality to the experience:

> For such, alas, are we all! In such a mould are we cast that, with the too much love we bear ourselves being first our own flatterers, we are easily hooked with others' flattery. (206)[7]

This peculiar variety of solipsistic self-love is ultimately responsible for most of the disorders in Sidney's world, for out of self-love come the desires that the impassioned individual attempts to impose upon nature. The world in which he strives to represent those desires is represented, at one moment, as the interior of his mind projected outward, and at another, as the fictional setting of his songs. Idealizing romantic poetry is merely an externalization of the impassioned imagination, an extension of self-love into poetic form. The importance that Sidney attached to divorcing poetry from self-love is more than adequately illustrated by his introduction to the *Apology*. After commenting upon the extraordinary claims for horsemanship made by John Pietro Pugliano, Sidney writes: "if I had not been a piece of a logician before I came to him, I think he would have persuaded me to have wished myself a horse. But thus much at least with his no few words he drave into me, that self-love is better than any gilding to make that seem gorgeous wherein ourselves are parties."[8]

At the end of the second eclogues, when Dorus is celebrating the delights of solitariness, he remarks that nature contains no "danger to thyself, if be not in thyself" (166, 22). Although he overlooks such discomforting realities as rebels and wild beasts, there is an important sense in which his observation is correct. As he tells Pyrocles at the end of the fourth book, "I well know there is nothing evil but within us; the rest is either natural or accidental" (318). The particular "evil" that the princes are discussing with the new-found fortitude that they acquire in prison, is uncontrolled passion. The implications of Musidorus's idea are as fascinating as they are far-reaching. For what Sidney implies in both these passages and throughout *The Old Arcadia*, is that passions, as a self-generated evil, are a kind of fiction. This does not make Sidney a nominalist; quite the reverse. Passions are all the more powerful, all the more "real," for being the product of an infected fancy. It is because they are generated from inside man and because they are concerned only with their own satisfaction that Sidney provides so much attention to self-love and the selfness of affection. Uncontrolled passions are the worst kinds of fictions; they deceive, corrupting the mind with desires that it is either impossible or unlawful to satisfy. As Love indicates in Dorus's psychomachia, man has no ailments, no discontents, "if he naught do desire" (80, 4).

The fact that Sidney chooses to identify passion as a particular kind of fiction explains his willingness to link the mental processes of the lover with the poetic logic of romanticizing fiction. It also helps to explain why poetry is a subject of such importance in *The Old Arcadia*'s exploration of the just life. If we are to understand and control the fictions generated within our minds, our passions, we must become, if not good poets, at least good readers of poetry.

Dorus and Cleophila run the risk as poet-lovers of cutting themselves off from nature by transforming the landscape into what may turn out to be an illusory and corrupting world. If their poems succeed in creating a nature that is responsive to man—and Arcadia is always willing to echo their complaints—the commerce between the lover and the landscape created by his desires is not so comforting as this fact would suggest. The song of a more experienced singer, the echo poem delivered by Philisides during the second eclogues, provides a paradigm of the impassioned mind's relationship to nature and the dangers inherent in it. As an echo poem the eclogue reinforces our awareness of the responsiveness of the world inhabited by the lover. In addition, the fact that Philisides sings Echo's lines as well as his own indicates the degree to which his landscape is self-created. The poet makes his own echo. The character of the myth is also telling. Philisides replaces Narcissus, the traditional representative of self-love, as Echo's interviewer, indicating once again the origins of the impassioned mind's transformation of nature and the source of fancy's perilous fictions.

The most important part of the dialogue between Philisides and Echo occurs in the central section of the song, as the poet-lover asks:

> But when I first did fall, what brought most fall
>   to my heart?   Art.
> Art? What can be that art which thou dost mean by thy
>   speech?   Speech.
> What be the fruits of speaking art? What grows by
>   the words?   Words.

> O much more than words: those words served more
> to me bless.   Less. (161, 20–27)

Nature contradicts the logic of passion. What Sidney comically portrays in these lines is the consternation of the romanticizing poet upon discovering that his fictions, far from providing the contentment he had hoped for, have actually compounded his sufferings. If passions are a kind of fiction, fictions can also be used to multiply passions, increasing thereby the mind's discontent.[9]

Philisides' echo poem illustrates a second danger from the way in which the poet-lover manipulates "fancy": as Sidney indicates, words may sometimes produce only words when the structures of relief conventionally available to the poet break down. By placing his hopes for contentment in a mistress, the lover risks frustration of a magnitude that poetry, Sidney suggests throughout *The Old Arcadia*, cannot always relieve.[10] In the second book Cleophila addresses his lute, exclaiming "how much thou art deceived to think that in my miseries thou couldst ease my woes, as in my careless times thou wert wont to please my fancies!" (93). The explanation for his song's inability to supply relief is important. Cleophilia goes on to remark:

> The evil is inward, my lute, the evil is inward; which all thou dost doth serve but to make me think more freely of. . . . The discord of my thoughts, my lute, doth ill agree to the concord of thy sweet strings. (93)

The impassioned mind lacks the balance that is music's essential attribute, just as it appears sometimes to lack the means to restore balance.

Philisides' echo poem comically illustrates one last peril inherent in the poet-lover's relationship to nature: passions are easily changed into sorrow. This fact accounts for the greatest misfortune that the lover faces while transforming the world into an image of his desires. For when his desires are frustrated, as on occasion they must be, his sufferings are increased by finding himself at the center of a hostile landscape only too ready to portray his agonies. Consider Echo's acerbic responses to Philisides. *The Old Arcadia*'s nymph is not the purveyor of contentment and the symbol of poetic harmony that she is in Vergil's *Eclogues*, when Gallus boasts "non canimus surdis, respondent omnia silvae" ("we sing to no deaf ears; the woods echo every note"), or the soothing spirit whom Sannazaro's Carino claims "mi risponde pietosa, murmurando al suono degli accenti miei" ("answers me in sympathy, murmuring to the sound of my words").[11] Echo's appearances in *The Old Arcadia* are a sign of the lover's continued sufferings in a distorted landscape resounding with his griefs. Cleophila's lament in the second book offers a clear illustration of this process:

> My thoughts, imprisoned in my secret woes,
> With flamy breath do issue oft in sound:
> The sound to this strange air no sooner goes
> But that it doth with echo's force rebound
>   And make me hear the plaints I would refrain:
>   Thus outward helps my inward griefs maintain.
>
> (118, 21–26)

Griefs can be increased as well as maintained, leading to the agonies of Strephon and Klaius's mental landscape and to Plangus's "cries to skies, and curses to the ground" (147, 6). Echo, we remember, sends Philisides packing to the devils.

This is exactly what Geron had warned Philisides against. During their debate, while criticizing the youth for multiplying his sorrows, "Thy wit dost use still still more harms to find," Geron makes explicit the nature of the imaginative process that permits this multiplication to occur:

> Then each conceit that enters in by sight
> Is made forsooth a jurat of his woes:
> Earth, sea, air, fire, heav'n, hell, and
>   ghastly sprite.
> Then cries to senseless things which neither
>   knows
> What aileth thee, and if they knew thy mind
> Would scorn in man (their king) such feeble
>   shows.
>
> (73, 7–12)

He objects to a kind of poetic style because that style at once signals and worsens a dangerous relationship between the mind and the natural world.

No wonder Geron advises Philisides: "Then let thy mind with better books be tamed" (75, 19). This is an astonishing recommendation from a shepherd—all the more so for being exactly to the point. As Sidney whimsically indicates, Philisides, like the princes, has been feeding his mind with the wrong kind of fictions, dieting too heavily upon romantically idealizing poets—poets, we assume, like the Petrarchists and the Italianate pastoralists. There are limits to the poet's abilities and there are risks in transforming the landscape into an image of his desires. Sidney attacks Italianate pastoral where it is most vulnerable: in its encouragement of self-absorption. When the poet helps passions to multiply, feeding the will and starving the wit, he produces discontent, alienating man from nature.

So far, all of the attention given to Sidney's critique of the imagination has been focused upon the consequences of its misuse for the poet-lover as he attempts to impose his desires upon nature. It needs to be pointed out that there are consequences for the audience as well, especially when the audience is the object of persuasion. In the third book of *The Old Arcadia,* appropriately enough, as the characters pursue various kinds of contentment, Sidney makes his most amusing and perceptive analysis of the poet's ability to deceive. In this case, Dorus and Cleophila act the part of the "bad" poets, weaving fictions that succeed in corrupting Dametas's household on the one hand and the royal couple on the other.

Dametas, Miso, and Mopsa are deluded by fictions: a childish treasure story, a fabliau for the jealous wife, and a ridiculous mythological narrative that Sidney describes as a "far-fet tale" (194). Basilius and Gynecia are taken in by similar means: a bit of pornography and an absurdly exaggerated melodrama relating Cleophila's adventures among the Amazons. Throughout both sets of episodes Sidney's language persistently forces us to view the princes' manipulations as the practices of an artist. As Cleophila succeeds in deceiving Gynecia, we are informed about his "pretended device" and his "open invention" (221). The prince even refers to himself as "the author of this device" (223). When Dametas discovers "his hope of wealth turned to poor verses," while digging for his fictional gold, Sidney's narrator comments that he has been "punished in conceit, as in conceit he had erred," drawing a direct connection between the kinds of fictions with which the mind deceives itself and allows itself to be deceived by others, and the literary fictions of the "bad" poet (265–66). Dorus and Cleophila succeed, as base romantic poets succeed, Sidney hints, because they appeal to the passions of their "readers," puffing up their hopes in an illusory form of contentment. What I described in the third chapter as a small allegory of how fortune operates in the world is revealed simultaneously as an illustration of the workings of the impassioned imagination and the processes of deceptive fiction. The bad poet behaves like fortune.

This is *Mirror for Magistrates* poetry with a difference: all of the falls from high estate suffered in the fourth and fifth books of *The Old Arcadia* are the products of illusion. There are no "real" estates to fall from. Dametas suffers by placing his hopes for contentment in gold that he never had and that he never should have aspired after. In Sidney's world, discontent is the product of fictions spawned by self-love.

Cleophila arranges his "invention" in the cave in order to produce "a pretty merriment" (228). By luring the royal couple into adulteries in the dark, he attempts to stage a farce. Basilius goes to the tryst in search of a delightful comedy; Gynecia, for a passionate romance; and in the end, providence arranges that the events serve as the ground-plot of a morality play. Fictions are extraordinarily difficult to control, as Cleophila discovers here and as Sidney had recently had an opportunity to learn because of Elizabeth's behavior at the end of *The Lady of May*.[12] Nowhere else in *The Old Arcadia* is the elusiveness of fiction more evident than in the problems of persuasion faced by the princes in the Arcadian eclogues—problems that are largely the result of their misuse of the imagination.

The lover and the poet have a common purpose: the need to exercise their powers of persuasion.[13] For this reason lovers in *The Old Arcadia* turn so often to poetry. Spenser's Colin Clout breaks his pipe after falling in love; Sidney's lovers, we are sometimes led to assume, would display only a minor interest in their pipes were they not devoted to the service of a mistress (or attempting to recover from such a devotion). Significantly enough, Lalus refuses to sing with Philisides after his marriage, "since he had gotten his desire" (159).

The difficulties of poetic expression that Dorus and Cleophila encounter are increased considerably by the circumstances in which they find themselves during the first and second eclogues. Sidney's dramatic strategy is crucial in focusing attention upon their problems of persuasion. We are never allowed to forget the complex framework within which each of these songs is performed. Inside the fiction a series of poets interact with audiences who make their presence felt in specific ways; they hiss, quarrel, and swoon. Disguised as a shepherd and an Amazon, the princes must attempt to convince Pamela and Philoclea of their worthiness as lovers without allowing Basilius, Gynecia, or any of the others present to discern their real motives. They must succeed in persuading, while not appearing to persuade.

As youths who have been raised in the vale of Tempe, one of whom is called "the gift of the muses" and the other of whom is dressed in the "likeness" of Clio, Dorus and Cleophila do not always have the kind of poetic success that one might anticipate (84, 27). Eliciting an emotional response from his listeners is easy, as Cleophila discovers, but assuring that he will procure the right response from the right person proves virtually impossible. During the entertainments, time after time the prince is frustrated to find that it is Basilius or Gynecia, rather than Philoclea, who has been enraptured by his voice. No sooner does Cleophila conclude a song on his poetic difficulties, such as "My muse what ails this ardour," than Basilius goes into a mad frenzy of love, thanking the gods that "they had preserved his life so long as to hear the very music they themselves used in an earthly body" (164). Dorus's songs, on the other hand, are almost always concluded with silence. Neither Pamela nor anyone else appears particularly moved by them.

What appears to the princes as a source of distress, Sidney treats comically. We are amused by their poetic failings and by the mishaps and entangled affections to which those failings give rise, but Sidney intends to do more than to amuse, he also means to instruct. There are reasons for the severe problems of persuasion faced by the princes. One major difficulty that the poet confronts is the unpredictability of language. Not only are his fictions slippery, but the very words that he uses cannot always be depended upon to move the individual to do what is desired at a desirable time. It is particularly troublesome, as Dorus discovers while lamenting his unrequited love, to convince his mistress of the full human reality of his grief:

> Such weight it hath which once is full possessed
> That I become a vision,
> Which hath in other's head his only being
> And lives in fancy's seeing.
>
> (63, 10–13)

What the prince is complaining about is the kind of change produced by his poetry, in which he, as a hot-blooded lover, is replaced by an insubstantial creature within the cold confines of his beloved's imagination. This is hardly the kind of poetic commerce he had been hoping for. This same insubstantiality of fiction disturbs Philisides when he asks:

> Can those eyes now yield to the kind conceit of a sorrow,
>   which ink only relates, but ne laments, ne replies?
> Ah, that, that do I not conceive.
>
> (341, 32–34; 342, 1)

These lovers attempt to overcome an even greater difficulty, since not only do their woes appear to be imaginary but the very imaginative framework in which they are contained proves to be a source of positive pleasure to their mistresses. Astrophil's understanding motivates Dorus's lament:

> Well may a pastor plain, but alas his plaints be not esteemed.
> Silly shepherd's poor pipe, when his harsh sound testifies
>   our woes,
> Into the fair looker-on, pastime, not passion, enters.
>
> (84, 3–6)

Much to the consternation of the lovers, fiction, Sidney reveals, is always a potential source of delight. This is the crucial point, for although all poets are bound to experience problems of persuasion, the princes compound their difficulties by attempting to make use of song for a purpose that it cannot fulfill: poetry can persuade by delighting; it can persuade with "siren's sweetness drawing the mind to the serpent's tale of sinful fancy," as Sidney writes in the *Apology;* but it cannot present the hot-blooded, fleshy realities that the princes would like it to convey.[14]

Of course, the princes do finally manage to sway the affections of their mistresses, and in Dorus's case poetry has a great deal to do with his success. The means he employs to obtain Pamela's heart are as comic as they are revealing. It is appropriate that Sidney should combine his princely shepherd's moment of poetic triumph with an anatomy of the pastoral process. While courting Pamela, Dorus pretends to make love to Mopsa, *The Old Arcadia*'s homeliest rustic. Sidney presents the seduction scene as a model of an essential pastoral process: in the case of the bucolic love poem, the pretense of making love to a sophisticated lady as if she were a shepherdess, under the guise of preferring simple countrified beauty to the elegance of a paramour; in the case of pastoral literature as a whole, the pretense of stooping, when the activity of the whole mind is bent upon rising to some higher value or to some more ideal style of life.[15] (One rises by stooping.) Sidney has no illusions about the pastoralist's claims to simplicity: Dorus's assertions about the honesty of his natural affection are balanced against the artfulness of his rhetorical methods, just as Sidney shows an ambivalence about a genre in which the means of achieving "perfections" should lie in seduction—which may be only another way of pointing to his ambivalence about fiction itself (102).

Dorus triumphs because he accomplishes what Astrophil attempts without success when pleading with Stella, "I am not I, pity the tale of me": the transformation of self into seductive fiction. There are substantial advantages to insubstantiality. If poetry allows pastimes rather than passions to enter the beloved's fancy, then it is necessary to present oneself as a pastime. This is precisely what Dorus sets about doing, first, as he weaves a melodramatic Greek romance on his pre-Arcadian adventures, and then, as he metamorphoses himself into a pastoral allegory, by assuring Pamela, while pointing to his shepherd's costume: "that this estate is not always to be rejected, since under that veil there may be hidden things to be esteemed" (106). What he has hidden is his princely status. After finding that his speeches "had given alarum to her imaginations," Dorus achieves his final success by singing Pamela a pastoral lyric, bringing her in the process "to a dull yielding-over her forces (as the nature of music is to do)" (106–7). The teenage seducer plies his date with popcorn.

Sidney concludes the scene with a final piece of irony that helps to illuminate the ambivalence he intends to convey toward the princes' lovemaking and singing. Only the ignorant rustic manages to preserve her virtue. As Mopsa tells Pamala, "for all his quaint speeches, she would keep her honesty close enough" (108). (Note the Chaucerian pun in the mouth of the rustic.) Dorus can convince a princess but not a shepherdess. If a certain kind of refined sensibility is necessary for responding to the pleasures of poetry and the apprehending of ideals to which those pleasures can lead, that same sensibility makes one vulnerable to seduction by dangerous passions.

Sidney is a peculiarly honest pastoralist—honest, because he presents a clear understanding of what his art cannot do: of its powerlessness, due to the difficulties inherent in language, always to be able to persuade the right person at the right time, or always to be able to persuade the right person to do the right thing. In spite of the aggressively optimistic poetics of the *Apology*, he is intensely aware of the limitations of fiction. Sidney also gives an unusually forthright analysis of what the poet does badly, when misusing his art: of poetry's capacity for constructing solipsistic worlds that corrupt as they multiply desires, alienating man from nature and trapping him within a painfully responsive landscape. The poet's powers are not only limited, but they are capable of producing harm. This is an analysis that Sidney grounds firmly in his moral concerns about the impassioned mind. The poet's fictions are important, ultimately, because they tell us about the fictions inside us. Nonetheless, we should beware of allowing ourselves to be taken in by Sidney's "honesty": as a pastoralist, he uses pretense even here. While making his critique of the misuse of fancy, he demonstrates its right use; while showing how fictions can produce discontent, he reveals how they may also attempt to produce the true contentment of a just life.

ii. "Jump Concord": Poetry and Justice

While Sidney prepares for the eclogues at the end of the first book, he supplies a short but detailed description of the Arcadians' theater. His description presents a simplified image of the aesthetic aims of his entertainments, just as he employs his entertainments, in turn, as less complicated fictions clarifying the aesthetic intentions of the romance as a whole. The theater has, then, important implications for the entire *Old Arcadia*. Calling its setting "a place of great delight," and praising its "sweet brook" and "abundant flowers," Sidney goes on to write:

> Round about the meadow, as if it had been to enclose a theatre, grew all such sorts of trees as either excellency of fruit, stateliness of growth, continual greenness, or poetical fancies have made at any time famous. In most part of which trees there had been framed by art such pleasant arbours that it became a gallery aloft, from one tree to the other, almost round about, which below yielded a perfect shadow, in those hot countries counted a great pleasure. (46)

Sidney's description is filled with the tell-tale signs of a poet talking significantly about his own poetry. "A perfect shadow," "a great pleasure," "a gallery," "poetical fancies," "art"; this is the language of criticism, language bent on transforming an ordinary theater into an aesthetic showcase. As in almost every preceding pastoral romance, the cooperation evidenced here between nature and art serves as a model of poetic perfection. Sidney's image is strictly traditional. What results from the combination of shepherdly arts and Arcadian nature is "a perfect shadow," poetry's true mimesis. This perfection is reinforced by the theater's circular structure. Twice in two sentences we are told that it is situated "round about."[16]

The Renaissance poet never so adamantly advances the claims of his art as when they are in danger of being overshadowed by the unlabored creativity of nature. For the pastoralist the natural world (created nature) is a foil, a backdrop against which he can assert superior artistic skills. At the same time Nature (creating nature) is a convenient agent to which he can attribute the effectiveness of those skills. Sidney pretends cooperation in order to achieve mastery. In his defining image, trees make up the foundation of the artificially constructed gallery in much the same way, he implies, as the artist depends upon the natural world, which he ultimately rises above in producing perfect pleasures. In transforming the meadow into a theater, art perfects nature for man's delight. Even the fame of the meadow's trees, as the result of combined vegetative and poetical qualities, Sidney wittily observes, is an instance of the harmonious relationship between nature and art. As in all pastoral catalogues of this kind since Ovid's *Metamorphoses*—those in Sannazaro's *Arcadia* and Spenser's *Faerie Queene* immediately come to mind—Sidney's trees are symbols of past literary creations.[17] This is a meadow, not a forest—a fact that points to the smaller, more restricted world of the eclogues. He emphasizes the variety of poetic traditions contained within the songs (they include "all such sorts of trees") and his selectivity in ordering them within the framework of his art: only those trees which are excellent, stately, or at the very least enduring, have been planted in his literary meadow. The pastoral inclusiveness that he boasts of is the product of balancing literary traditions and, more important, of harmonizing the two elements that comprise all creation: nature and art.

This much, again, is entirely traditional. Clarifying what is distinctive about *The Old Arcadia*'s treatment of art and nature, and, in turn, what is distinctive about Sidney's aesthetic, requires that we examine his description of the theater from a slightly different angle. For his description contains one important piece of evidence for how diverse elements—on the largest scale for how nature and art—are able to cooperate in producing beauty and pleasure. Sidney informs us that

> the meadow itself yielding so liberally all sorts of flowers . . . seemed to nourish a contention betwixt the colour and the smell whether in his kind were the more delightful. (46)

The suggestion that the pastoral delight of the meadow is in some way related to the "contention" between the diverse elements it contains has analogues throughout *The Old Arcadia*. When Sidney describes Philoclea's beauty, he writes that: "the sweet cast of her black eye . . . seemed to make a contention whether that in perfect blackness, or her skin in perfect whiteness, were the most excellent" (37). Cleophila praises the Arcadian landscape in a similar manner when he asks Musidorus: "Do you not see the grass, how in colour they excel the emeralds, everyone striving to pass his fellow—and yet they are all kept in an equal height?" (15). Again, the concord achieved among a variety of contending elements is what produces beauty. The idea that beauty is the product of contention, the harmony achieved by balancing a group of diverse elements, is a commonplace of Renaissance aesthetics—one that Sidney toys with and freely adapts for his own purposes in all of these passages. It is so commonplace, one suspects, because the idea frequently finds expression in classical and Continental philosophy, particularly among the Platonists. Pico, a Florentine Neoplatonist, defines the concept of *concordia discors* in this way:

> this may be offered as the true definition of Beauty, namely, that it is nothing else than an amicable enmity and a concordant discord. . . . For this reason it is said by the poets that Venus loves Mars, because Beauty, which we call Venus, cannot subsist without contrariety; and that Venus tames and mitigates Mars, because the tempering power restrains and overcomes the strife and hate which persist between the contrary elements.[18]

Sidney's notion of beauty is related. The Arcadian lovers sometimes attribute the beauty of their idealized mistresses to a *concordia discors*, we remember: Plangus calls Erona the child of Mars and Venus, and Philisides represents Mira as the benefactress of Venus's beauty and Diana's chastity. Even Cleophila's Amazonian hairdo is beautified by contention: "his hair . . . lay upon the upper part of his forehead in locks, some curled and some, as it were, forgotten, with such a careless care, and with an art so hiding art, that he seemed he would lay them for a paragon whether nature simply, or nature helped by cunning, be the more excellent" (26). Cleophila's "paragon" is a teasing model of comparison: his hair is beautiful because of the rivalry that it reflects between the contending powers of art and nature.

Pico's formulation of the concept of *concordia discors* was widely known, perhaps because it is so perspicuous, but the idea was by no means limited to the Platonists and Neoplatonists. It is associated most persistently with the one philosopher whom Sidney mentions by name in the eclogues, Heraclitus. He is a pre-Stoic who understands that: "Just as language may be riddling, ambiguous, paradoxical, so in the world opposites coexist, unity is a product of diversity, harmony a consequence of strife. . . ."[19] As it is articulated by Heraclitus and the Neoplatonists, the concept of *concordia discors* has far-reaching implications for the artist. While balancing the opposing worlds of art and nature in creating beauty, the poet asserts his power over the created universe in organizing and conveying within his art a unified image of its diversity.[20]

Seen in light of this tradition, the description of the eclogue theater implies impressively large claims for poetry, almost as large as the assertions of the romantically idealizing poets whom Sidney ridicules from time to time. If his treatment of art and nature is intended to suggest such meanings (and there are meanings that Sidney's *sprezzatura* compels him to suggest rather than to state), he labors to make the connection between this rather exalted and familiar conception of *concordia discors* and the poetics of *The Old Arcadia* as specific as possible. Sidney gives a unique application to the concept of *concordia discors*, as one distinguishing feature of his artistic process, by transforming a cultural commonplace into a device for restoring the golden world within. In the course of giving new meaning to the notion of *concordia discors*, Sidney succeeds in fashioning a distinctive poetic for himself as he makes original and powerful claims for the capacity of art to reform nature.

The third eclogues contain the passage of greatest importance for understanding how these claims are made. In Philisides' beast fable, Sidney fashions a creation myth that operates simultaneously as a myth of the Fall: the beasts who confer presents upon mankind are quickly subjected to tyrannical abuse in an allegory of private and public injustice. Man's creation and his Fall are intimately linked. Sidney combines these myths into a single fable because only by understanding that the individual and the state are created out of a diverse body of contending elements can we recognize the reasons for man's fallen condition. In the state of nature, the beasts enjoy "a harmless empire" as long as they succeed in preserving "order" among their different members (256, 19, 14). Sidney clarifies the principle upon which his allegory operates by attributing this advice to Languet:

> He said the music best thilke powers [the heavenly] pleased
> Was jump concord between our wit and will,
> Where highest notes to godliness are raised,
> And lowest sink not down to jot of ill.
>
> (255, 22–25)

The ideal balance between the wit and will operates as a definition of justice, as a golden mean that sets a standard of behavior for the state, the family, and the individual. In turn, the concord that Languet recommends, as a kind of "music" with high notes and low, is made exactly parallel to the action of poetry conceived as *concordia discors*. Poetry and justice are complementary activities: concord is the metaphor that joins them. The balance needed for a just life in the state, the family, and the individual is produced by the same activity that is utilized in poetry: a reconciliation between opposites, a harmonious balance between opposing elements, in this case between the wit and the will.

Sidney's example is not selected haphazardly. That he considered this opposition to be at once the single most important condition of our existence and the special object of the poet's attention is made plain by the poetics of his *Apology*. Sidney's golden-world aesthetic supplies conclusive evidence that the relationship between poetry and justice suggested by Languet's metaphor of musical concord is to be understood as an informing principle of his art. In the *Apology* Sidney details the powers of the poet in two separate stages: he describes the poet's relationship, first, to the natural world, and then to mankind in order to demonstrate the artist's ability to remedy defects in both.

The poet is distinct from all other artists who have "the works of Nature" for their "principal object," such as the moral philosopher and the lawyer, because "ranging within the zodiack of his own wit," he "doth grow in effect into another nature, in making things either better than Nature bringeth forth, or, quite anew, forms such as never were in Nature, as the Heroes, Demigods, Cyclops, Chimeras, Furies, and such like. . . ."[21] Sidney reaps the advantages of the pastoralist's traditional paradox: the simultaneous superiority of his art to nature and his harmonious cooperation with it. In order to describe the remedial effects of this cooperation between art and nature, he employs a traditional image from classical mythology: the natural "world is brazen," we are told, but "the poets only deliver a golden."[22] The image is carefully selected. The golden world of Hesiod, Aratus, Vergil, and Ovid furnishes the basis for a new Renaissance poetic that improves upon the natural world, but whose most important force is measured by its power over individual men and minds.

In the second part of his argument, Sidney goes on "to man," for whose benefit poetry's "uttermost cunning is employed."[23] This is where his real interests lie. Once again he establishes the poet's superiority to the natural world, but this time he does so by demonstrating that fiction not only creates better men than nature, men like Vergil's Aeneas and Xenophon's Cyrus, but that it bestows a "Cyrus upon the world to make many Cyruses."[24] The poet's golden world remedies the defects of man in the natural world by offering him exemplars of ideal virtue upon which to model himself, "if [he] will learn aright," that is, "why and how that maker made him."[25] Sidney's conditional clause is of such importance, as he goes on to indicate, because men are so constructed that if left to their own devices they will not learn aright. This is the crucial stage of the argument, for it is here that Sidney calls attention to the main defect in man's nature that the poet's art is designed to remedy. As in Philisides' beast fable, Sidney defines man's primary disorder as a conflict between the wit and the will, a conflict that results from another mythic Fall. He writes, "with no small argument to the incredulous of that first accursed fall of Adam: . . . our erected wit maketh us know what perfection is, and yet our infected will keepeth us from reaching unto it."[26] In the course of juxtaposing his remarks about the cooperation possible between art and nature with his statements about the results of "that first accursed fall of Adam" (the corruption of the will), Sidney implies that the poet's wit has a role in helping to alleviate the worst effects of that Fall. Poetry in the *Apology*, like musical concord in *The Old Arcadia*, assumes a therapeutic function in restoring man to a state of virtuous contentment lost in his Fall into disorder and division. When the artist cooperates properly with nature, the wit attempts to restore the now corrupted will to goodness. This is the poet's true business. He labors to restore a golden world within. Just as Vergil transformed the golden age from an unreachable past into a good to be realized in Rome's future, so Sidney reinterprets the golden world by transforming it out of space and time into a psychological condition to be produced within the individual by the action of poetry.

If the destruction of the golden age deprived man of justice, what did Adam and Eve lose in Eden? Answering this question helps to explain how Languet arrived at his principle of musical concord and how Sidney came to link in *The Old Arcadia* the actions of poetry and justice. In a century unrivaled for its theological controversies, there is universal agreement among Catholics and Protestants about the name given to the original state of man before the Fall. If man fell into original sin, he declined from a condition described from Thomas Aquinas onward as "justitia . . . originalis."[27] In man's natural state, Luther writes, "no leprosy of sin adhered either to his reason or to his will": Adam had been created "just, pious and holy" by God.[28] Calvin agrees. Man was originally gifted with "wisdom, virtue, holiness, truth and justice"; "he had his affections kept within the bounds of reason, all his senses tempered in the right order. . . ."[29] Most revealing of all, however, for understanding Languet's notion of musical concord is the commentary on Genesis by Andraeus Rivetus, a Dutch Calvinist who provides the best exposition of the Renaissance Protestant position on "justitia originalis." His commentary is revealing because of Rivetus's admirable clarity about the term's precise significance. Original justice is not to be understood in legal terms: there are no law courts in Eden. It is not a particular virtue, as temperance or prudence is; it is not even an aggregate or complex of virtues ("aggregatum seu complexum"). Rather, original justice is a certain kind of rectitude produced in the whole man by the order of his parts and the best disposition of his faculties ("sed potiùs rectitudinem quandam, quae in toto homine, ex partium & potentiarum ejus ordine & optima dispositione consurgebat").[30] What Languet calls "jump concord between the wit and will," Rivetus describes, again and again, as the "optima appetitus et rationis harmonia" ("the best harmony between appetite and reason").[31] For Rivetus as for Languet, justice is a kind of music in man's soul, emanating out of the original concord of its now discordant parts. What distinguishes Languet from Rivetus is his transformation of a piece of descriptive theological terminology into practical moral advice: the individual must work to restore a state of justice within himself by balancing his wit against his will. In turn, what distinguishes Sidney from Languet is his metamorphosis of moral advice into a poetic principle: only the poet is gifted with sufficient powers to restore the golden world within, because only the poet can move man's will to pursue the good that his wit envisions—though even he may fail.

In the *Apology*, Sidney quickly proceeds "to a more ordinary opening" of the subject, fearing that "these arguments will by few be understood, and by fewer granted."[32] (No wonder he is timid: these are scarcely orthodox arguments!) He allows the *Apology*'s emphasis upon the poet's ability to fashion persuasive images of virtue and vice to explain his power to help in correcting the problems of the infected will. The focus of *The Old Arcadia* is similar. What Sidney suggests here is that the poet attempts to solve the problem of wit and will by establishing "jump concord" between them; there is no room for imprecision; the balance must be "jump," exact. In *The Old Arcadia*, persuasion takes its place as one, especially important component within a more comprehensive poetic.

While Sidney defines the ideal function of poetry as a cooperation between the opposing worlds of art and nature that results in the creation of contentment, he gives that definition more specificity and relevance (both to the world of events and to the world of his art) by showing the poet's special ability to establish concord between the wit and will that results in the production of justice. These are two ways in which he asks us to examine the same activity. The poet's wit is the art that restores to a state of justice man's naturally diseased will.

The central metaphor of Sidney's poetic justice adds greater clarity to the didactic, persuasive, and remedial functions of *The Old Arcadia*'s art.[33] Sidney's "concord" supplies the basis for an unusual kind of didactic poetry in which new understandings are achieved by balancing opposing viewpoints. We have not been able to look to any one of these groups, the native Arcadians, the princes, or the stranger shepherds, for the "right" set of notions about how to adjust the demands of reason and passion. Sidney's method of judging suggests a better way: in the process of balancing the rival claims of the wit and the will, we achieve the justest possible understanding of them. Reasonable moderation is wisdom. In *The Old Arcadia*, a certain kind of mental activity ultimately becomes more important than specific moral propositions in achieving justice. The same balance of mind that Sidney displays as a poet, he labors to instill in his audience by means of the dialectical structure of the eclogues. In the course of evaluating the large body of diverse moral propositions within them, balancing the claims of the princes and the stranger shepherds against those of the Arcadians, we learn to think justly.

"Jump concord" can also be understood as the central metaphor in a poetry of persuasion. For concord accounts for the poet's ability to delight, and it is by delight that the will is persuaded to do good. It is the same appreciation of how pleasure is generated, moving the will and inspiring the wit, that motivates Cleophila's remark to Dorus:

> Happy be those mishaps which, justly proportion holding,
> Give right sound to the ears, and enter aright to the judgement.
>
> (83, 11–12)

Concord's effectiveness in supplying delight helps to explain Sidney's constant activity throughout *The Old Arcadia* in balancing opposing literary styles and in shifting rapidly between conflicting moods: juxtaposing Nico and Pas's humorous classical song contest against Plangus's somber continental love complaint, the native measures of Philisides' beast fable against the classical meters of his verse epistle. The conjunction itself is delightful.

Finally, Sidney's metaphor can also be understood as the central activity of a therapeutic poetry. This is an important fact within a pastoral romance designed not merely to teach the reader how to avoid misfortune, but to procure the contentment that only justice will bring. "For the practice of music, I mean real music, is beneficial to all men, but to Arcadians it is a necessity."[34] Polybius introduces his account of Arcadia as a digression intended to explain the savagery of a particular group within the Arcadian nation, savagery that he directly attributes to its disregard for music. Sidney's emphasis upon the remedial powers of pastoral song has an important historical precedent. But the poetic activity that Polybius represents as an essential element in preserving the virtue and tranquillity of the Arcadians, Sidney portrays as a necessity for all men in achieving the just life.

As we have seen, the notion of *concordia discors* is a commonplace that Sidney might have encountered in any number of classical and contemporary texts. There is only one work, however, that we can be certain that Sidney knew intimately in which this concept assumes major importance. In his essay "On Tranquillity of Mind," Plutarch quotes with approval Heraclitus's notion that "the harmony of the universe, like that of a lyre or a bow, is by alternatives"; his commentary on Heraclitus is helpful in explaining Sidney's understanding of concord:

> in mortal affairs there is nothing pure and unmixed. But as in music there are low notes and high notes, and in grammar there are vowels and consonants, yet a musician or a grammarian is not the man who dislikes and avoids the one or the other, but rather the man who knows how to use all and to blend them properly, so also in human affairs, which contain the principles of opposition to each other . . . we should not be disheartened or despondent in adversity, but like musicians who achieve harmony by consistently deadening bad music with better and encompassing the bad with the good, we should make the blending of our life harmonious and comfortable to our own nature.[35]

Just as Sidney does, Plutarch makes use of music as a metaphor for concord. He passes easily between aesthetic and moral questions to demonstrate that what produces harmony in art also produces what an Arcadian shepherd might call quiet of mind. (Plutarch uses music as an illustration in a moral argument; Sidney's argument is about "music" [poetry] just as much as it is about justice.) He also makes explicit what is implied by Sidney's metaphor and practice as a pastoralist: the artistic and moral need to be inclusive, to have an understanding of the diversity of things, ranging from the erected wit to the infected will. But the most significant feature of Plutarch's argument, and the one that tells us most about Sidney's therapeutic poetry, is that he represents *concordia discors* as an artistic and psychological activity that protects man against adversity largely, it appears, by helping to remedy misfortune's worst effects, containing and reconciling them in balance with the good. Finally, Plutarch describes this process as one that leads to harmony with nature—a nature that he interprets according to the laws of reason and virtue. By following Plutarch's example in grounding his definition of poetry upon concord, Sidney provides his readers with a model of how to make a just response to adversity in accordance with the laws of nature, Stoically defined. The individual achieves harmony in himself by establishing harmony between the wit and the will. As Nature argues in Dorus's lyric, "a man's self/Gives haps or mishaps, e'en as he ord'reth his heart" (79, 30–31).

Plutarch's concern with obtaining contentment by balancing reason and passion looks forward to the concept of original justice as it is expounded by Languet and by Renaissance commentators on Genesis, just as it looks backward toward a long Platonic tradition in which justice is defined as a "kind of mental health or beauty or fitness."[36] As Plato writes in *The Republic:* "Justice, therefore, we may say, is a principle of this kind; its real concern is not with external actions, but with a man's inward self, his true concern and interest. The just man will not allow the . . . elements which make up his inward self to trespass on each other's functions or interfere with each other, but, by keeping all . . . in tune, like the notes of a scale (high, middle, and low, and any others there be), will in the truest sense set his house to rights, attain self-mastery and order, and live on good terms with himself."[37] Political justice is mainly an extension of this principle of concord from the private to the public sphere. What Plato, Languet, Rivetus, and Sidney all have in common is an understanding of justice as a virtuous and pleasurable harmony created in the individual by the correct ordering of his faculties. Plutarch's version of musical concord assumes such importance in the context of *The Old Arcadia* because of his emphasis upon its effectiveness in remedying misfortunes—an emphasis that Sidney's personal and public life made especially compelling.

It is no accident that the concept of "jump concord" is advanced at the outset of a beast fable illustrating the consequences of injustice for the state and the individual: the remedy precedes the condition for which it is intended. Nor is it an accident that Philisides is the singer of the poem: Sidney, too, is in search of relief. When he wrote to his brother in 1580, informing him that *The Old Arcadia* would be sent by February, Sidney urged him to

> take a delight to keepe and increase your musick, yow will not beleive what a want I finde of it in my melancholie times.[38]

It should now be possible to describe how Sidney employed poetry to supply that "want," both for himself and for his audience.

Sidney depends on the symbolic action of the eclogues, rather than upon the kinds of explicit claims made in Italianate pastoral, in order to assert the power of his poetry. This is another instance of early Elizabethan reticence and yet another way of distancing himself from the likes of Sannazaro. At the outset of all four sets of entertainments, Sidney provides an emblem of the poet's ability to achieve concord in making a reconciliation between opposites as a way of illustrating the activity of his fiction as a whole. The *concordia discors* of the entertainments becomes, in turn, the principal device for achieving the harmony of *The Old Arcadia*'s concluding book. The clearest example of this process is supplied by the dances with which the first and second eclogues begin.

For the Elizabethans, dance had a rich symbolic potential. According to John Davies's Antinous, who was also aware of its seductive potential, everything from the motion of the spheres to "sacred Orgies," "Parliaments of peace," and "learned Arts," "A lively shape of Daunceing seems to beare."[39] Its significance was as a picture of *concordia discors*. As Antinous informs Penelope:

> Concords true picture shineth in thys Art,
> Where divers men and women ranked be,
> And every one doth daunce a severall part,
> Yet all as one, in measure doe agree,
> Observing perfect uniformitie:
>   All turne together, all together trace,
>   And all together honor and embrace.[40]

Sidney could have found an equal amount of praise for the concord imaged by dancing in Sir Thomas Elyot's *The Book named the Governor*. Elyot attributes the origins of dance to its effectiveness as a therapeutic device. At the very outset of his discussion of the educational benefits of the art, he relates two stories of its discovery, one from classical mythology, the other from the Bible, which tell how music and dance relieved the melancholy of Saturn and cured the vexed spirit of Saul.

The male and female in Davies's emblem of *concordia discors* are replaced in Sidney's first two sets of eclogues by the fortunate and unfortunate shepherds, on the one hand, and by the spokesmen for reason and passion on the other. In both dances there is a clearly defined movement from initial opposition or conflict to final harmony. In the contest between the fortunate and unfortunate shepherds, this movement is represented by the transition from stichomythic lines at the outset to the "joining" of voices at the ending (58). The struggle between the passionate and reasonable shepherds begins as an armed conflict between two opposing forces; gradually they are brought to a "nearer" approach, and finally they "embrace" as the dance concludes with friendship "instead of fighting" (136). The *concordia discors* that Sidney establishes between fortune and misfortune and between passion and reason is more than a didactic image of opposing conditions, or a delightful emblem of contrarieties; it is an effort to bring about the kind of reconciliation and relief that is promised by the dramatic movement of the dances. In these poems Sidney provides a symbolic illustration of the activity of the eclogues and the romance as a whole: the concord established between the reasonable and the passionate shepherds is only a miniature version of the *condordia discors* achieved between individual singers like Lalus and Dorus, and, on a slightly higher scale, between opposing qualities in man like wit and will, and, on the highest level, between the opposing elements in creation, art and nature.

There is no better example of *concordia discors* than marriage and no better medium in which to assert the poet's power to reconcile opposites than in an epithalamium. In marriage man has an institution that makes the second eclogues' reconciliation between the wit and the will possible. The numerological structure of the third eclogues is, itself, an embodiment of the principle, since five is the union of odd and even numbers, reflecting the conjunction of the male and female in marriage.[41] Dicus gives direct expression to the notion of concord when he urges Lalus and Kala to "Live one in two, a well united pair" (246, 2); and Geron, as we have seen, demonstrates the degree to which marriage can be regarded as a therapeutic tool when he describes it to Histor as the

>sweet and surest mean
>Our foolish lusts in honest rules to stay.
>
>(260, 8–9)

Examined in light of Sidney's conception of concord, Dicus's marriage song becomes more meaningful. Its meticulously balanced structure with five introductory and five concluding stanzas centered around a medial paean to virtue assumes a more purposeful significance as a demonstration of the poet's ability to reconcile opposites: the "good" qualities in the first half of the lyric—love, peace, modesty, and pleasure—are balanced against the "evils" in the second half—lust, churlishness, pride, and jealousy. There is nothing unusual in the Arcadian eclogues about a native shepherd using song as a means of procuring reconciliation or relief. In the first eclogues, Geron informs Philisides that "sweet tunes do passions ease," while urging him to:

> . . . discover us thy grief.
> Oft comes relief when most we seem in trap.
>
> (72, 26–27)

There is also nothing unusual about the fact that a native shepherd with his Stoical ethos should look to nature (or advise someone else to look) as a way of obtaining relief. Again, Geron's debate with Philisides supplies an illustration, as he advises the wayward youth to ease his passions by cultivating an "active mind":

> In hunting fearful beasts do spend some days,
> Or catch the birds with pitfalls, or with lime,
> Or train the fox that trains so crafty lays.
> Lie but to sleep, and in the early prime
> Seek skill of herbs in hills, haunt brooks near
>   night,
> And try with bait how fish will bite sometime.[42]
>
> (75, 22–27)

What is especially distinctive about Dicus's epithalamium is the implication contained in its pattern of injunctions and exorcisms, as the lovers are compared to "turtles fair," "lilies pure," and "rivers sweet," that song has a magical power to charm nature into making its similes come true, into providing good fortune to Lalus and Kala (246, 1, 19, 28). Magic is a metaphor for the action of poetry in producing contentment.

While demonstrating the poet's ability to produce contentment by reconciling opposites, Dicus's epithalamium illustrates the activity of the third eclogues as a whole in making use of marriage as a symbol of concord and a metaphor for the operation of justice. The symbolic character of the bridal pair is significant: Lalus, the shepherd whose poetic abilities are most prominent, marries Kala, the shepherdess whose name means "beauty." The poet is united with beauty, reason balanced with passion, as an image of the "justest love" produced by concord (245, 31).

The third eclogues make it look so easy, almost as if the just life were the product of a recipe straight from Kala's pastoral kitchen: bad fortune is spiced with good, will with wit, nature with art. One of the difficulties in presenting a process as complex as poetry or justice in terms of a simplified image is that it tends to lose its dynamism, to become distorted by a veneer of domestic complacency. Sidney is aware of this fact, and this is one explanation both for his reservations about the Stoic ideal of the quiet life and, paradoxically, for his motives in embodying a vision of achieved contentment in an event staged by the native Arcadians: the realization of full content can only be presented as a bucolic image because it can only occur in a world as simple as the shepherds'. The reconciliations that the poet is able to bring about in the realm of events, although genuine, as the harsher struggles of the first and second eclogues have already indicated, are much less exalted in degree. Dicus and Dorus are never reconciled; Plangus remains disconsolate; Geron is trailed off stage by gales of laughter. This is one reason for Sidney's insistence upon jarring our memories from time to time into recognizing that his images of the poet and poetic beauty, seen from a slightly different angle, are merely a babbling rustic and a big-busted shepherdess. Their full content is a fiction. But ironic recognitions are no substitute for a real assessment of the poet's capabilities. In order to complete that task, Sidney needed to test those abilities within the darker landscape of the fourth eclogues.

The fourth eclogues begin with Geron's Vergilian complaints upon the demise of Arcadia. As we have seen, Sidney makes use of these allusions to evoke a particularly rich variety of elegiac music and to prepare for the prophetic resonance of "Ye goat-herd gods." There is another reason for their presence. For in the ninth *Eclogue*, the one most readily called to mind by Geron's ravening soldiers, Vergil poses the major questions with which Sidney is concerned: what kind of protection can poetry provide against misfortunes, what kind of relief for its worst effects? As two shepherds journey toward the city, they lament the ravagement of the landscape and the eviction of Arcadians from their homes. Vergil permits Moeris to state what is ultimately unthinkable for most pastoralists, that poetry is futile against these kinds of injuries.

> sed carmina tantum
> nostra valent, Lycida, tela inter Martia, quantum
> Chaonias dicunt aquila veniente columbas.[43]

(But amid the weapons of war, Lycidas, our songs avail as much as, they say, the doves of Chaonia when the eagle comes.)

By the end of the eclogue the power of song is reasserted, but in a hesitant and tentative manner. Lycidas attempts to comfort his companion by saying

> aut si, nox pluviam ne colligat ante, veremur,
> cantantes licet usque (minus via laedit) eamus;
> cantantes ut eamus, ego hoc te fasce levabo.[44]

(Or if we fear that night may first bring on rain, we may yet go singing on our way—it makes the road less irksome. That we may go singing on our way, I will relieve you of this burden.)

Song is compassionate energy. If Vergil sometimes makes us aware that poetry appears powerless against the hostile world of events, he is not finally willing to abandon his hope for its effectiveness. Sidney follows his example.

"Ye goat-herd gods" is a poem about loss, but it is also an attempt at restoration. It is a prophetic allegory of the mind's aspiration to justice, but one that is incomprehensible until concord's role in the action of the poetry is understood. The same kind of magical inclusiveness that permits Sidney to make use of the sestina as an emblem of the need for temperance and of the attempt to obtain it also permits him to incorporate into its design a picture of the dangers of uncontrolled fancy and an illustration of the power of the imagination to provide the contentment that justice brings.

Strephon and Klaius suffer what I have previously described as the poet-lover's worst tragedy: a frustration of desire resulting in the transformation of the natural world into a subjectively conceived landscape echoing with despair. Unrequited passion has forced them to live among "monstrous mountains" and valleys filled with "foul affliction" (329, 6–7). Even music sometimes appears by multiplying the echoes within that landscape to compound their sufferings. Toward the end of the poem Strephon curses "the fiddling finders-out of music," and Klaius fears that he will "grow mad with music" (330, 9, 18). Far from receiving explicit support as a means of supplying relief, song appears in much of the sestinas's rhetoric as simply another especially perilous form of torture.

But there is a different and, I think, ultimately truer perspective from which to view the sestina's poetic action, one that is incorporated into its symbolic structure. The key to "Ye goat-herd gods" lies in its repeating end-words. The six nouns are arranged in a carefully delineated pattern of matched opposites: "mountains" contrast with "valleys," "morning" with "evening." The arrangement of the first stanza reinforces these contrasts, just as it makes clear that although "forests" and "music" are not similarly opposed, they take their place, as we shall see, within a more comprehensive balancing scheme:

> *Strephon.* Ye goat-herd gods, that love the
>   grassy mountains,
> Ye nymphs, which haunt the springs in pleasant
>   valleys,
> Ye satyrs, joyed with free and quiet forests,
> Vouchsafe your silent ears to plaining music
> Which to my woes gives still an early morning,
> And draws the dolour on till weary evening.
>
> (328, 23–28)

It is crucial to note that the only end-word that does not correspond to a physical object or to an exclusively natural phenomenon is "music," and it is music that is found in the sestina's first stanza mediating between the opposing worlds of space ("mountains," "valleys," "forests") and time ("morning," "evening").[45] It assumes this position again in the central stanza of the poem and in the concluding coda, as a symbol of the potential power of song to achieve concord between the two opposing dimensions that constitute the totality of experience.

This grandiose metaphysical gesture of *concordia discors* parallels the activity of the shepherds in attempting to achieve relief by balancing present agonies against past content (after all, that is why they sing) and at another stage of the allegory, in striving to achieve justice by making use of song to construct a portrait of Urania. The same mountains and forests that define throughout much of the sestina the limits of the lovers' mental landscape are employed in its final two stanzas, as the shepherds' music begins to take effect, in creating an image of the ideal beloved.

> *Strephon.* For she, whose parts maintained a
>   perfect music,
> Whose beauties shined more than the blushing
>   morning,

> Who much did pass in state the stately
>   mountains,
> In straitness passed the cedars of the forests,
> Hath cast me, wretch, into eternal evening,
> By taking her two suns from these dark valleys.
> *Klaius.* For she, with whom compared the Alps
>   are valleys,
> She, whose least word brings from the spheres
>   their music,
> At whose approach the sun rase in the evening,
> Who, where she went, bare in her forehead
>   morning,
> Is gone, is gone from these our spoiled forests
> Turning to deserts our best pastured mountains.
>
> (330, 19–30)

It is possible to interpret these final stanzas as a triumph of poetic concord, a triumph of the poet's ability, by reconciling opposites in nature, to achieve a vision of absolute justice.[46] It is preferable to interpret them as a prophecy of triumph that remains only potential, as a goal of the poet's immediate and continuing activity: "Our morning hymn this is, and song at evening" (330, 33). Sidney's assurances, like Vergil's, are tentative. Potential carries with it the possibility of failure—always a real possibiilty in Sidney's world—the chance that the attempt to realize a subjectively conceived ideal will lead to the frustration of desire and to the agonizing condition in which music is madness.

Examined in this light, Urania's symbolic character takes on new significance. She is not only, as the muse of astronomy, an image of heavenliness, and as Venus Urania, a representation of divine beauty; she is also, as a figure "whose parts maintained a perfect music," an ideal of celestial harmony (330, 19). This much has already been pointed out by Sidney's critics.[47] It is the implications of these facts that have gone unnoticed. By merging Urania with Astraea, Sidney is finally able to coalesce into a single image the subjects that he has labored to join throughout the romance: poetry and justice. Of equal importance is his success in making this link while revealing that both operate by means of a single process. Celestial harmony, like the music of the spheres that Urania's "least word" controls, is produced by *concordia discors* (330, 26). Again, it is upon concord that poetry and justice depend.

Sidney's borrowings from Gil Polo and Sannazaro now appear

more purposeful. The elaborate system of syntactic parallels that he adapted from "Pues ya esconde el sol" and that he imposed upon Sannazaro's sestina form demonstrates its appeal as a useful means of establishing concord, of making harmony out of the discordant passions of Strephon and Klaius in their struggle to achieve justice and contentment. At the same time, these borrowings are a covert signal to the reader of Sidney's intention of reconciling the two most important traditions in the history of pastoral: the moral austerity of Gil Polo and the Christian bucolic and the aestheticism of the Italianate tradition.

The same kind of balance that is found in "Ye goat-herd gods" appears as a structural principle throughout the fourth eclogues. Each poem in this group of complaints is paired with another: "Ye goat-herd gods" appears with "I joy in grief"; Philisides' dream vision with his verse epistle; and Agelastus's formal elegy with his farewell song. One discord is balanced against another. The double sestina with which the fourth eclogues begin is matched by the sestina at their conclusion.

A similar structural principle is evident within other individual complaints. This fact is easier to observe in Strephon and Klaius's second lament, where we find the shepherds' griefs juxtaposed within a circular structure that contains as it attempts to relieve them—a circular structure that is highlighted, as we have already seen, by the corona device and the repetition of its first and last lines. Even the figurative language of the poem embodies a kind of *concordia discors*.[48] "I joy in grief, and do detest all joys," is an extended series of paradoxes in which the contrary elements of the lovers' experiences, past content and present agony, are yoked in violent harmony.

A similar process is visible in the transition between Agelastus's concluding elegies. Only upon Basilius's "death" is there any suggestion of disharmony between the native shepherds and the world that they inhabit. The loss of their duke carries with it the realization that there are limits to man's ability to find himself at home in nature. Agelastus laments:

> Time ever old and young is still revolved
> Within itself, and never taketh end;
> But mankind is for ay to naught resolved.
> . . . .
> Ah, let us all against foul nature cry;
> We nature's works do help, she us defaces.
> (347, 10–12, 23–24)

His complaints are violent but restrained, and as Agelastus moves into his second lament, Sidney makes it increasingly obvious that song operates to produce that restraint. The complexity of the sestina form, with its stately anaphoric progression, is a measure of his success in using "outward wailing" to "seal up" what he describes in his first Arcadian poem as "inward grief" (284, 15). The sestina produces reconciliation as well as restraint. In the course of transforming the "farewell prince" of the opening complaint into the "Farewell O sun" of the concluding poem, transposing the duke into metaphor, Agelastus's art succeeds in reestablishing a significant degree of concord between man and nature: one important point about a setting sun is that it implies an eventual rising. The darkness of the fourth eclogues implies, as another *concordia discors* writ large, the lightness of the third: the pastoral system is self-enclosed and infinitely reflexive. Agelastus makes us look ahead to a new duke, and in the trial concluding the romance, Sidney fulfills that expectation in an entirely unexpected way.

When Vergil allowed Moeris and Lycidas to discuss song's power to provide relief in the world of real events, he did so, as the Elizabethans knew, because he wondered about the ability of his own poetry to provide relief for Rome and himself. The problems that crowd against the boundaries of the first and ninth *Eclogues* are those of an uncomfortably actual world. A similar sense of urgency is felt in the fourth eclogues not only among the Arcadian shepherds who elevate themselves above a landscape engulfed in moral and political chaos, but by Sidney himself as he looks out from retirement at Wilton toward an England that he believed to be threatened by awesome political misfortunes. As we have seen, Sidney feared Elizabeth's demise as the greatest threat to public quiet. The turmoil that descends upon the Arcadian state with Basilius's death is a reflection of Sidney's greatest fears for England. (The similarity is in situation, not in character; Basilius is not an allegorical mask for Elizabeth.) By giving expression to his worst fears in a fictional context that allows them to be safely resolved, Sidney exorcizes those fears. There is a pinch of magic here in the implication that fictions can control the future. But there is a pound of solid didactic advice to go with it. By indicating that a major cause of these chaotic aftershocks lies in the unjust relationship between the prince and the aristocracy, Sidney shows his contemporaries how to avoid making his most threatening fictions come true. (The didactic element in his poetry of justice also works to protect against misfortune.) Beneath the guise of its prose fable and the covert shapes of its eclogues, *The Old Arcadia* makes a critical analysis of the dangers besetting England from Tudor absolutism. Basilius's withdrawal from political life and self-imposed isolation from his aristocratic advisers are a reflection of Sidney's displeasure with a Queen who had similarly isolated herself from the able advice of her nobility—in ignoring the admonitions of the Leicester party against the Alençon marriage, in failing to adopt a more militantly Protestant foreign policy, and in encouraging (sometimes even in forcing) too many of her best educated courtiers, like Sidney himself, to expend their talents idly in absence from the court. It is wonderfully ironic how Sidney, writing in retirement, seemingly turns the charge of isolation against Elizabeth. *The Old Arcadia* represents, then, a strong protest against these injustices—a protest made even stronger by Sidney's acute political analysis of the consequences for the state when a just balance is not maintained between the monarch and the aristocracy.

There are private concerns to be considered as well. After Dorus's first lament in *The Old Arcadia,* Cleophila "felt a great impression of pity withal," Sidney informs us, since

> all persons that find themselves afflicted easily fall to compassion of them who taste of like misery, partly led by the common course of humanity, but principally because, under the image of them, they lament their own mishaps; and so the complaints the others make seem to touch the right tune of their own woes. (43)

In *The Old Arcadia*'s world, everyone eventually finds himself afflicted and everyone laments. Sidney provides a concrete example of the same process on a larger scale during the second eclogues. After Histor concludes his poeticized version of Plangus's complaints for Erona, the narrator observes:

> So well did Histor's voice express the passion of Plangus that all the princely beholders were stricken into a silent consideration of it; indeed everyone making that he heard of another the balance of his own troubles. (152)

By discovering in the fictional images with which they are confronted, portraits of their own emotional condition, it is fair to assume, the eclogues' audience does exactly what Sidney anticipates his audience of readers will do. The universality of the eclogues' concerns encourages, even guarantees, this kind of identification; in their struggles between reason and passion, their celebrations of contentment, and their complaints on abandonment and death, the reader discovers speaking pictures that he can transform into an image of his own experiences. As Sidney realizes, we come to Arcadia not only for escape but for catharsis, an aesthetically safe landscape in which to relieve our misfortunes.

Sidney realizes this so well because his presence in Arcadia is motivated by similar desires. The freedom that he allows his reader he also reserves for himself. It is no accident that Philisides occupies the central position in all four sets of eclogues. The events of the romance are persistently referred back to a personal frame of reference, however obliquely. Under the image of the persona, Sidney laments his own misfortunes, fights his own struggles against passion, rehearses the injustices and the joys that he has experienced. No other conclusion can be drawn from the aesthetic assumptions that govern the work. Consider for a moment the fictional biography that Sidney provides Philisides in the fourth eclogues. Born in Samothea, educated in the "natural knowledge of things," and "exercized with horsemanship, weapons, and suchlike . . . qualities," Philisides returns from travels abroad only to have his "course of tranquillity" diverted by love for Mira (334–35). He has come to Arcadia, as he tells Strephon and Klaius, "to choke mine own ill fortunes" (341). By modeling Philisides' life so closely and parodically on his own—however one interprets the confrontation with Mira (as his passion for a woman or his unsuccessful wooing of the Queen)—Sidney encourages the reader to find a similar motivation for his presence in Arcadia. This much seems apparent, but the fictional process is subjectively extended farther than these facts suggest. Not only Philisides, but all of the eclogues' characters, from Geron and Dicus to Strephon and Klaius, are what Sidney calls in the dedicatory letter to the Countess, his mental "monsters." Ultimately, the four sets of eclogues can be viewed as a theater of the poet's mind, as a grand psychomachia in which speaking pictures are balanced, one against another, by the imagination. This fact best explains the strangely insistent interiority of Sidney's fiction, its obsessive preoccupation with states of mind.

There is a considerable extent to which Sidney's private experiences are used to organize the romance. Only in light of this understanding can some of its vitally important idiosyncrasies be appreciated: for instance, Sidney's peculiar association of the heroic life with the innocent world of presexual adolescence and pastoral with the realm of experience and dangerous sexuality. As the dream vision of the fourth eclogues appears to indicate, these associations have their roots in Sidney's private experiences. As creatures spawned by his fancy, the eclogue characters are fictions that Sidney manipulates in order to accomplish what Philisides describes as his goal in coming to Arcadia: the choking of "mine own ill fortunes" (341). He follows the advice of Plutarch and Languet to the letter, as he balances good fortunes against bad, wit against will. Sidney sets out to gain quiet of mind by establishing concord among the discordant fictions of his own mental landscape.

It needs to be pointed out that there is a healthy measure of comedy in these activities. When each member of an audience turns someone else's complaints into the balance of his own troubles, treating fictions in the manner that the poet-lover treats trees—as tools for his solipsistic delights—the possibility of misreading is strong. While seeking relief, the reader may overlook the didactic intent of the song. Dorus and Cleophila clearly do not understand the warnings against excessive passion provided by Plangus's complaints.

In a similar fashion, we are amused by the posture struck by Philisides throughout the eclogues as he lies

> at the foot of a cypress tree, leaning upon his elbow, with so deep a melancholy that his senses carried to his mind no delight from any of their objects. (71)

If his solipsism makes him partly comic, it should be recognized that Sidney has the uncanny ability to poke fun at serious pursuits, without in any way diminishing their seriousness. Sidney distances himself significantly from his self-portrait: by laughing at Philisides, he makes his own search for relief seem less melodramatically grave; but more important, his laughter serves to indicate his awareness of the dangers inherent in that search, and to impart that awareness to his audience. The reader comes to Arcadia, like Philisides, in search of therapy, and is forced to discover, by entering into the world of the eclogues, that relief is more than a matter of sentimental indulgence. Therapy is only one element in Sidney's poetic justice, though his poetry is finally therapeutic. The wit must be informed and the will must be moved if the contentment that the just life alone provides is to be realized. One activity in the mind and in the poem inevitably implies and demands the other. Poetic justice is single.

The fourth eclogues do not resolve the issues of *The Old Arcadia*. In the vision of Urania, the laments for Basilius, and Philisides' complaints against exile, the poems offer gestures of reconciliation that are completed—if Sidney ever fully completes them—in the trial concluding the romance. It is to that event that we must now turn.

iii. Book Five: Poetry and Providence

The fifth book begins with Euarchus's entrance into Arcadia. He is the good ruler who attempts to restore quiet to the state by repairing the "dangerous division of men's minds" (351). Sidney points to this division in the book's opening sentence, recalling its appearance in the first and second eclogues, as the major cause of Arcadian misfortunes. When Philanax invites him to remain in the country, it is with the hope that Euarchus will be able to give "quiet" to "so many thousand," and to lay "a sufficient foundation of tranquillity" (361). His justice, it is expected, will be therapeutic. Euarchus is the third and last character from Sidney's introductory apologue to be brought to life within the pastoral. Like Basilius and Philanax, he finds that the world of verisimilar fiction is more complex than the landscape of the moral fable, just as he discovers that it is also more intractable to the efforts of the just man.

As Sidney's exemplar of the good ruler, Euarchus embodies the values that are central to the life-style of the native shepherds and to *The Old Arcadia* as a whole: a pastoral emblem places him beneath a tree as proof of his humble recognition that "the beginning and end of his body was earth" (357). The same ethos that has been used in the eclogues to test the characters' experiences throughout the romance is employed appropriately enough by the judge at the concluding trial. We are impressed by the "greatness of . . . mind" that allows him to recognize that "the reward of virtue" is "in itself"; by his ability to achieve a mean between extremes in being "neither beguiled with the painted gloss of pleasure nor dazzled with the false light of ambition"; and by his dedication to "constancy" (357–58). But his primary virtue is justice. Philanax speaks of the "true fame of that just prince, Euarchus," a fame, we are told, that is due more to the "trials of his equity" than to his "victories" (353, 351). That "jump concord" should present itself as the central feature in the activity of that justice points to the unity of Sidney's design. When Euarchus is asked to participate as a judge at the princes' trial, it is because he is expected "to unite our disunions" (354).

On the night before the trial, Sidney turns his attention from the public sphere to the private. The example set by Euarchus's behavior in how to make an ideal response to misfortune in the state is followed by three portraits of individual attempts to master private adversity. These are the trials-before-the-trial. Again, as in the fourth book, Sidney chooses to arrange these incidents schematically as illustrations in a larger didactic design. He progresses in a straight line from the least to the most noble response—only, in this case, there are no comic portraits of Dametas and his family to interrupt the mounting tragic movement of the romance.

Gynecia's despair is first. Sidney informs us that she "did crucify her own soul" with the thought of her "guiltiness" (366). He adds an irreligious element to her griefs, emphasizing her "blasphemous repining against . . . creation" (367). We are fascinated by the intensity of Gynecia's despair (she does nothing without intensity) and by Sidney's portrayal of the divided mind's commerce with destructive fictions of its own making.

Pamela and Philoclea, as Sidney informs us, are "No less sorrowful, though less rageful" (368). Their response to adversity is more admirable than Gynecia's, but it is hardly ideal: "they had not consented to so much evil, and so were at greater peace with themselves" (368). He draws attention to their "crying and wringing of hands" and to their "unquiet grief" (369). Sidney extends his schematic presentation of this theme even to distinguishing between the degree of patience possessed by each princess. If Pamela's "stronger disdain against her adversity" comes as no surprise, it is a mark of Sidney's sophisticated treatment of the subject that her greater strength should also produce "the greater torment, because it doth the more resist to his oppressor" (370). We pity the princesses as they attempt to console each other, but we reserve our admiration for the princes.

Pyrocles and Musidorus are presented as models of how to make a just response to private adversity. We find them in prison "fortifying courage with the true rampire of patience," appearing to be "governors of necessity than servants to fortune" (370). Their behavior is consistent with the Stoic fortitude that they acquire during the fourth book. After Pyrocles blames the heavens, in a moment of weakness, for lacking "just proportion," Musidorus assures him that there is "nothing done by the unreachable ruler of them, but hath an everlasting reason for it" (371). He is defending the justice of the cosmos. Musidorus goes on to state:

> And to say the truth of those things, we should deal ungratefully with nature if we should be forgetful receivers of her good gifts, and so diligent auditors of the chances we like not. We have lived, and have lived to be good to ourselves and others. Our souls (which are put into the stirring earth of our bodies) have achieved the causes of their hither coming. They have known, and honoured with knowledge, the cause of their creation. And to many men (for in this time, place, and fortune, it is lawful for us to speak gloriously) it hath been behoveful that we should live. (371)

In the style of virtuous pagans, Pyrocles and Musidorus proceed to affirm the existence of a life after death and to debate whether memory is retained throughout eternity.[49] Although these discussions have attracted much attention from Sidney's critics, it has never been understood that the princes contemplate and debate these matters as a way of preserving quiet of mind. This is their principle concern. Again, it is a passage from Plutarch's "On Tranquillity of Mind" that supplies the relevant gloss: "But he who understands somehow or other the nature of the soul and reflects that the change it undergoes at death will be for the better, or at least not for the worse, has no small provision to secure tranquillity of mind for facing life—fearlessness towards death."[50] As Musidorus's song makes plain, the princes hold

> . . . the bliss of peaceful mind,
> Since this we feel, great loss we cannot find.
>
> (374, 3–4)

Gynecia's blasphemy produces despair: their piety brings contentment. While contemplating immortality and while balancing their good fortunes against their bad, as embodiments of Plutarch's principles, the princes provide an example of how to maintain constancy in misfortune, at the same time that they achieve harmony with that nature whose "works be good" (373, 25). It is "lawful" for them to boast of their virtues "in this time" because while boasting Pyrocles and Musidorus are able to maintain a just balance between their fortunes, good and bad.

There is not even a hint of irony in the princes' meditations. If their self-congratulatory speeches seem less than fully appropriate for the Amazon and shepherd who made impassioned assaults upon their beloveds, helping to throw the Arcadian state into chaos, they are entirely suitable for the virtuous princes who articulate them—perhaps even for the princes who reject no part of their experiences as Amazon and shepherd. This is a question that the trial will decide. Their conversations are fully consistent with Sidney's design to reestablish and to increase to new proportions our admiration for them.

The trial that concludes *The Old Arcadia* forms a portion of this larger argument about how to make a just response to adversity. Throughout its proceedings Sidney encourages us simultaneously to view the action of the trial as the events of a stage play. At the outset of the fifth book, while informing him about the calamities that have occurred in Arcadia, Philanax urges Euarchus "to imagine . . . that here is before your eyes the pitiful spectacle of a most dolorously ending tragedy" (360). Euarchus does more than "imagine"; he proceeds to stage the trial as if it were a drama, while the judgments that he hands down nearly ensure that it becomes a tragedy. While preparing for the "spectacle," Euarchus orders Philanax:

> to draw out into the midst of the green (before the chief lodge) the throne of judgement seat in which Basilius was wont to sit. . . . For Euarchus did wisely consider the people to be naturally taken with exterior shows far more than with inward consideration of the material points; and therefore in this new entry into so entangled a matter he would leave nothing which might be either an armour or an ornament unto him; and in these pompous ceremonies he well knew a secret of government much to consist. (374–75)

He has no doubt about the utility of ornament and no hesitancy about employing the persuasive power of symbolic forms, in spite of his later inability to be swayed by them himself. Euarchus is not only the judge; he is the stage director. Our sense of the dramatic character of the trial is increased considerably by the narrator's detailed attention to the entrances of the participants and their elaborate costumes. We know what the actors look like, how they are arranged on the stage, and by means of what Samuel Wolff has described as *"pathetic optics,"* Sidney keeps us constantly aware of how the audience responds to the various orations, as a clear indication of how our emotions are being swayed.[51] This is Sidney's final speaking picture.

The metaphor of "trial as drama" is one of vital importance, since it signals Sidney's intention at the end of *The Old Arcadia* to bring together the two primary subjects of the romance, poetry and justice, and to do so in a context that shows their relevance to a world seemingly controlled by fortune. Once more, the dramatic character of these proceedings points toward a larger metaphor in which we are able to understand the trial as a miniature version of the five-act romance that it concludes. (Sidney refers to the major divisions in his story, we remember, as books or acts.) When Euarchus orders Philanax to carry Basilius's "judgement seat" onto the "green," we have an emblem of the action of the entire pastoral in locating justice at the center of Arcadia. In addition, we might view that "seat" as a reminder that we have also been sitting in judgment upon the "green," that is, upon the validity of the pastoral experience (the princes', Sidney's, and our own), just as we have been using, to complicate the image one stage further, the standards of the "green," of Nature Stoically defined, in order to make those judgments. The trial both mirrors the work as a whole, illustrating *The Old Arcadia*'s central processes and themes, and passes judgment upon it. In the course of doing so, it needs to be made plain, we are all very nearly condemned.

The trial's preliminary events, with the sentencing of Philoclea and Gynecia, constitute a calculated assault upon our sympathies, alienating them from Philanax in favor of the victims of his "unjust justice." When Pyrocles enters the spectacle, he is "led by Sympathus" (376). His companion's name indicates our continued sympathy for him. The prince shows himself willing to stretch the truth by insisting upon Philoclea's innocence, as he informs the court that "my coming into her chamber was wholly unwitting unto her," but the fact that he does so at the peril of his own life increases our admiration for the selflessness of his love and the intensity of his devotion (380).[52] It is a mark of Sidney's continued willingness to treat his princes humorously that Pyrocles responds with such disarming humanity to Philoclea's commitment to a nunnery; he is glad of the sentence since "none should obtain the after-enjoying that jewel whereon he had set his life's happiness" (381). Our reaction is different. It would be a mistake to underestimate the degree to which we are startled by the punishment of a fictional character who has been the source of considerable delight over the course of the romance. This is the kind of punishment that we would expect from Ben Jonson's comic satires but not from pastoral. At the very least, the sentence reflects badly upon the kinds of aesthetic pleasures that we have allowed ourselves, especially in the prurient delights of the bedroom scene. Sidney is taking pastoral inclusiveness to the limits, stretching the boundaries of the genre to the breaking point—nearly beyond. There are more shocks to come.

The sentencing of Gynecia provides a good illustration of how Sidney assaults and otherwise manipulates our sympathies. She is far from guiltless, but at the same time she is not guilty of Basilius's murder. When Philanax "incontinently" steps forward, "showing in his greedy eyes that he did thirst for her blood," our compassion for her is increased, particularly when we remember the torture to which her conscience subjects her (381). As she tells the court, "I have been too painful a judge over myself to desire pardon in others' judgement" (382). Philanax's role in these events is crucial. By saying the worst that can be said about the defendants—and this is true of the princes as well as Gynecia—exaggerating to outrageous proportions the reservations that we have had about the behavior of these characters, he exorcizes whatever desire we possessed to see them punished. Gynecia is simply not guilty of "execrable wickedness"—although she may have been *capable* of such wickedness (381). At the same time, while acting the part of the vindictive prosecutor, Philanax deflects from Euarchus most of the spite that is produced by the trial's harsh judgments. After all, he is the one presenting the case against the defendants. Euarchus does nothing more than make a dispassionate verdict upon the facts as they are presented to him.

We are startled by Gynecia's sentence both because of its viciousness (she is to be buried alive) and because it allows her to obtain what appears to be a final moment of dignity as she demonstrates "resolute constancy" in the face of death (384). We are also startled to find a clear suggestion of the limitations of human justice; she is condemned for a crime that she did not commit.

Performances by the three star actors occupy the center of the trial, as Philanax, Pyrocles, and Musidorus deliver their main speeches. In a spectacle that serves as a microcosm of the romance, the actors turn playwrights, constructing a series of miniature dramas intended to explain the events of *The Old Arcadia*.[53] As in the work as a whole, a variety of different fictions is brought into balance in order to sharpen our critical perspective upon the action. Sidney's pastoral "variableness" continues to the end.

Philanax is the first to take the stage. Returning to his original metaphor, he warns Euarchus that Pyrocles' "enormities" are such that he will imagine them to be "some tragedy invented of the extremity of wickedness than a just recital of a wickedness indeed committed" (386). He betrays his own strategy. For Philanax proceeds to weave out of the threads of *The Old Arcadia*'s plot a tragic melodrama designed to incriminate Pyrocles as a villain bent from the very outset upon seizing power in Arcadia, murdering Basilius, and corrupting Philoclea—all in complicity with Gynecia. In his account, the prince is transformed into

> the arrantest strumpet in luxuriousness, the cunningest forger in falsehood; a player in disguising, a tiger in cruelty, a dragon in ungratefulness. (390)

There is a measure of truth in each of these epithets but the entire group so grossly distorts the facts of the romance that it serves largely to outrage our sense of justice and to increase our sympathy for the princes.[54] In Philanax's speech, Sidney makes one of his shrewder critical observations by insuring that tragic melodrama takes its place alongside the tortured fictions of the *Arcadia*'s poet-lovers as the product of the impassioned imagination. An excess of morally righteous passion makes for bad poetry and bad justice, just as an excess of immoral passion does.

Pyrocles responds to these charges by interpreting the action of *The Old Arcadia* as if it were a romantic comedy that had unaccountably been spoiled in the final act. He explains his presence and behavior in Arcadia as the products of his quest for Philoclea's favors at the same time that he expects the virtue of his love to win forgiveness for what he modestly terms his "offence, towards the young lady" (394). As he tells the court, "But in fine I offered force to her; love offered more force to me" (394). Our ambivalence about the value of the princes' love renders the persuasiveness of Pyrocles' defense less than complete.

While his fortunes in the main trial continue to fluctuate uncertainly, Pyrocles is clearly triumphing in a second and equally important trial: like all of the other participants in these proceedings, his ability to maintain quiet in adversity is being tested. Although Pyrocles begins his speech, after listening to Philanax's malice, "with some impatience," he concludes by "declaring a resolute patience in whatsoever should be done with him" (391, 395). He wavers, but manages to maintain his constancy.

Musidorus has less success than Pyrocles both in creating a believable version of the romance and in preserving a quiet mind in adversity. He is, after all, the less noble of the two princes, and only with great effort does he restrain himself from physically assaulting Philanax. He matches the prosecutor's rage with rage of his own, while fabricating an interrupted and incoherent account of the romance as a drama of youthful heroism unrewarded. Dorus the shepherd belies his fiction. After reminding the court of their success in killing the lion and the bear and quelling the Phagonian rebellion, Musidorus joins Pyrocles in falling back upon the power of love as his ultimate defense, claiming that "our doing in the extremest interpretation is but a human error . . ." (402).

Sidney incorporates these miniature dramas into the trial as a means of verifying the worth of his pastoral technique, especially as an instrument of justice. While asking us to judge these fictions against the narrative that we have just concluded, he reminds us of the sophistication of his own art. For instance, by comparing the motives that Philanax supplies to the actors in his tragedy with those of *The Old Arcadia*'s characters, we are made conscious of how scrupulously logical Sidney's methods have been. Philanax's melodrama appears more like a parody than a version of the romance. Time after time, episodes into which Sidney has poured his richest insights about the mind and its desires are travestied by hackneyed reconstructions; Pyrocles' descent into the cave is made ridiculous by being turned into devil-worship, an attempt to please "infernal powers" having a dully literal existence (388). The dramas of Pyrocles and Musidorus are not much better. Pyrocles' emphasis upon the love plot trivializes *The Old Arcadia*, and the incoherence of his cousin's tale renders the work virtually meaningless. Each of these fictions is too limited to account for the complexities of the pastoral; as a consequence, they are also too limited to provide a just assessment of the princes' Arcadian experiences. They cannot supply the balance upon which real justice and good poetry depend. For that, a more inclusive fiction is required, one that is better than a simple tale of moral rebellion, an amorous adventure, or a heroic story because it is capable of containing and utilizing those fictions, as *The Old Arcadia* does, within a comprehensive framework of judgment.

After these performances, Euarchus brings the trial to a conclusion (or so he thinks) by passing sentence upon the princes. The manner in which he renders his judgments is important. For Euarchus does very much what Sidney would have his readers do: he attempts to arrive at a just assessment of the princes' Arcadian experiences by balancing the various fictions with which he is presented. After determining that Pyrocles and Musidorus should be judged in spite of their claims to nobility, Euarchus considers "how to judge well" (404). His answer is plain from this method of proceeding, as he states: "Now the action offereth itself to *due balance* betwixt the accuser's twofold accusation and their answer accordingly applied" (404, emphasis added).

We are disturbed to find the princes condemned to death. The groans from the Arcadian audience are a reflection of our own. Once more we are disturbed to find them condemned by means of a process that lies at the very heart of *The Old Arcadia*: Euarchus's concord. The entire work appears for a moment to have turned upon itself as a rejection of the pastoral experiences of the princes and, by implication, of ourselves. We too have come to the woods for the dangerous delights that Euarchus's sentences so roundly condemn. At the very least, this is a peculiar stageplay to perform in Arcadia.

One of the difficulties that the metaphor of "trial as drama" poses throughout these proceedings is the impossibility of perceiving Euarchus as a poet. The very notion boggles the imagination. Sidney refuses to allow us to view him as anything more than a kind of stage director, for Euarchus's province is fact, not fiction. He may share the ethos of the Arcadian shepherds but he does not have their passion for song—and this is a crucial distinction. For Euarchus is no friend to the idle life. He comes to Arcadia for the purpose of ending Basilius's pastoral retirement, convinced, as he is, that "inward gifts . . . were bestowed by the gods . . . to be beneficial and not idle" (362). Like Kalodoulus, he would be surprised to discover the existence of shepherds as virtuous as Geron and Dicus. Euarchus is no friend to the idealized eroticism at the center of the princes' idle life; while his belief in "right love" as a "sweet and heavenly uniting of the minds" is easily reconciled with the kind of passion that the princes aspire to in their nobler moments, his conviction that "it can never slide into any action that is not virtuous" renders his ideal admirably remote from the amorous affairs of Pyrocles and Musidorus (407).

It is impossible to view Euarchus as a poet, apart from the inherent silliness of the idea, because he employs concord as a limited tool for ferreting out legal evidence. The sentence is to be reached "not by a free discourse of reason and skill of philosophy, but must be tied to the laws of Greece and municipal statutes of this dukedom" (404). Euarchus goes on to justify his methods by pointing out that

> because philosophical discourses stand in the general consideration of things, they leave to every man a scope of his own interpretation; where the laws, applying themselves to the necessary use, fold us within assured bounds, which once broken, man's nature infinitely rangeth. (404)

Euarchus does precisely what the good ruler should do in sentencing the princes according to the laws of Greece. But exactly to the degree that we are unable to perceive Euarchus as a poet (since he restricts the amount of balance which reason can utilize), we are also unable to acknowledge his justice. He is hampered both by his legalism and by his position in the trial. For while Euarchus can only hand down judgment upon the princes' experiences on the basis of fictions created by Philanax, Musidorus, and Pyrocles, the reader is able to assess those experiences by comparing the trial's miniature dramas with the full narrative. Sidney has made us more capable of rendering a just decision than *(mirabile dictu)* Euarchus, the just ruler himself— and this is no small proof of the didactic effectiveness of his poetry.

But our position as readers is not nearly so comfortable as these facts imply. The trial is Sidney's most perplexing and aggressive fiction—perplexing, because of the complex set of reversals it forces us to witness, and aggressive, because it is specifically designed to foster discord between our emotional and rational responses to the events. On the one hand, as the objects of the massive amounts of sympathy created for Pyrocles and Musidorus during the last two books of *The Old Arcadia,* we are outraged by the death sentences. After witnessing their fortitude in prison, hearing their expressions of selfless devotion to the princesses, watching them as they are abused by Philanax's malice, we are tempted from the sidelines to join Kerxenus and Sympathus in howling for their release. This is a temptation that is best suppressed. For Sidney warns his readers when Euarchus warns the Arcadians: "do not easily judge of your judge" (365). He allows no room for sentimentalizing the events of the romance.[55] Judged by the laws of Arcadia, Pyrocles and Musidorus are guilty and ought to be punished; the preservation of public quiet demands it. Our private desires are juxtaposed against our appreciation of public responsibility, our will against our wit.

The process that we are witnessing is plain: Euarchus, the just ruler who attempts to supply concord, is himself absorbed into a larger balance—one that juxtaposes him, as a representative of reason, against Sympathus, the symbol of passion. At the same time, in the course of creating this seemingly irreconcilable discord between our desires to see the princes exonerated and our understanding of their guiltiness under Arcadian law, Sidney makes us aware that Euarchus's legalism does not constitute justice. If justice renders, according to one interpretation, "to everyone his own," the princes do not deserve to be executed (378).[56] Their innate nobility of character and their fortitude offer sufficient proof of that. They must also be found guiltless according to a second interpretation of the virtue, one that Pyrocles articulates, significantly enough, when threatened by the "dead pitiless laws" with which Philanax confronts him (304). If the prince is correct in asserting that justice depends upon "examining the depth of hearts" and "hath not his judgement fixed upon the event," that is, that true justice takes the motivations for human actions into account, both he and Musidorus must be held innocent (311). Their intentions have been unceasingly virtuous. But who, alas, can judge by intentions?

We have come full circle. As Kalodoulus interrupts the trial in order to reveal the princes' identities, we are again confronted by the questions with which this study began. Sidney raises our hopes for a good old-fashioned romance ending, immediately frustrates them as Euarchus refuses to alter his sentence, and then, a few pages later, ultimately fulfills those hopes as Basilius comes back to life. After examining *The Old Arcadia* and its eclogues in some detail, we should be able to indicate what this pattern means.

The doubleness of Sidney's reversal is important, first, because it permits him to conclude his trial-within-the-trial by creating a dramatically persuasive image of Stoic quiet. More rigorously than any of the other characters', Euarchus's ability to maintain constancy in misfortune is put to the test as he discovers that he has sentenced his son and nephew to death. Even though he is given an opportunity to alter his decision amidst the "roaring lamentations" of the crowd, he refuses, and in the course of doing so, manages to retain his commitment to "sacred rightfulness" (412, 411). As he points out: "If rightly I have judged, then rightly have I judged mine own children . . ." (411). No matter what we might think of its justice, his decision is as admirable as it is astonishing. Only to a degree are the princes able to match his behavior. Musidorus pleads for his cousin's life after being "stirred up with rage of unkindness" (412). Pyrocles also begs for his friend's life, but he does so while reminding Musidorus of "their resolution of well suffering all accidents" (413). The princes go some distance toward fulfilling that resolution, but it is Euarchus who establishes the highest standard of fortitude and patience:

> with such a sad assured behaviour as Cato killed himself withal, when he had heard the uttermost of that their speech tended unto, he commanded again they should be carried away. (414)

This is how Sidney would have his readers respond to misfortune. Euarchus's quiet of mind, highlighted by an allusion to Cato, the greatest of Stoics, is the fulfillment of the ideals of the native shepherds.

There is a second reason for the doubleness of Sidney's reversal. By making use of such a heavy-handed piece of romance gimmickry not once but twice within the space of ten pages (he is following Heliodorus), Sidney forces us to perceive as the deliberate and open manipulations of an artist what is simultaneously revealed as the operation of providence.[57] When Basilius awakes, he discovers with new-found insight that "all had fallen out by the highest providence" (416). This much we have already established. It is now possible to understand that what looked like the accidental happenings of fortune is really the action of God's art in producing justice (he too works by indirection)—and there is no question that when the princes are rewarded with the hands of Pamela and Philoclea, justice has been done. This is the point of Sidney's biblical parallels. In the movement between the Mosaic legalism of Euarchus and the forgiveness offered by the "newly resurrected Basilius" (even the phrase is comic), we have a fictional parody of the transition between the old dispensation and the new. That Basilius's awakening should suggest Christ's—even for a moment—is a typically Sidneian piece of audacity. It is audaciously suggested because Sidney is making use of a sacred analogy for a secular situation. The duke's return to life is not an allegory of the new dispensation; instead, it is *like* the new dispensation because it carries with it real justice that gives to "everyone his own," according not to the surface of events, but to "the depth of hearts." By means of this second reversal, as other critics have noticed, Sidney forces the reader to recognize that our ability to make accurate judgments is limited, just as the operation of human justice is inadequate when compared to the art of divine justice.[58]

But we had better not be too quick to narrow the boundaries of what is humanly possible. For there is another equally significant set of implications in Sidney's juxtaposition of art and providence. Not only does he suggest that there is an art to providence; he also indicates that the artist works like providence. Again, the analogy is audacious, but as Sidney writes in the *Apology* while discussing "the heavenly Maker of that maker": "Neither let it be deemed too saucy a comparison. . . ."[59] His suggestion is the logical extension of an already established simile. If the "bad" poet operates like fortune in deceiving the fancy to aspire after false kinds of contentment, the "good" poet acts like providence in establishing real justice in a world of his own creation. In part because he knows the motivation of his characters, the poet is able to design his fiction to conclude with "what should be," in place of life's drabber finale, "what is."

Euarchus's status in *The Old Arcadia* is clarified by this knowledge. Without the ability of providence or the poet (at least in his fictions) to have certain knowledge of human intentions, he acts as an ideal ruler in depending upon the assured foundation of the law to render judgment. Sidney is not proposing that poets replace judges in the Elizabethan courtroom. Far from it. What he sets out to demonstrate is that the justice of the law is inferior to the justice of the poet, that Euarchus is subordinate to himself. If the poet's justice is limited to the world of his fictions, that is not, after all, such a severe limitation. For the poet teaches man what real justice is, persuading him in the process to achieve it.

At the conclusion of *The Old Arcadia*, providence and the poet cooperate in producing justice by means of a grand *concordia discors*. Sidney signals his intentions within the same sentence that announces Basilius's awakening:

> But Philanax and Kerxenus, whose eyes honest love (though to diverse parties) held most attentive, leapt to the table, and putting off the velvet cover, might plainly discern, with as much wonder as gladness, that the duke lived. (415)

The duke's rebirth unites "diverse parties" in "gladness," indicating the concord that Sidney strives to achieve between the divided responses of the reader. The desire that we share with Kerxenus to see the princes released is revealed in the action of providence as a desire for justice of a higher kind than the law that Philanax invokes with so much force—a justice that the biblical analogy suggests is both the abrogation and the fulfillment of that law. Basilius's awakening establishes concord between our wit and will, uniting the dangerous divisions of men's minds and bringing quiet to the private and public spheres.

It is well to point out that Sidney accompanies this high-sounding activity with a whimsical sleight-of-hand signaling another complementary *concordia discors*. For his announcement of Basilius's awakening is followed by a story about the origin of the sleeping potion administered to the duke. The tale is pure cock and bull: Gynecia's grandmother, it happens, used the same drink to entrap her lover into marriage, a farcically inappropriate fabrication that Sidney manages to appropriate for his own ends. For the potion ultimately responsible for *The Old Arcadia*'s romance ending, as we discover, is "a drink made by notable art, and as it was thought not without natural magic" (415).[60] With characteristic indirection, Sidney points to the concord achieved between art and nature, a concord reflected in the princes' marriages and even in the names of their children, Pyrophilus and Melidora. The final detail is gratuitous, but this is, after all, the fifth book, and the harmony of Lalus's wedding has already taught us what to expect from the number five. It is equally characteristic of Sidney that the same tale should reveal so plainly that just beyond this ideal cooperation of art and nature there is the potential of delusion and the dangerous gratifications of impassioned fancy.

The Old Arcadia is Sidney's defense of pastoral, a defense that is no less genuine for the regularity with which it undermines our expectations about the nature of the pastoral experience and the persistence with which it forces us to question the values connected with it. Kalodoulus is right to be suspicious about the perils of the Arcadian life-style. Sidney provides multiple illustrations of the ways in which its major preoccupations can be travestied: Musidorus's love turns to lust as he prepares to assault Pamela; Pyrocles' poetic talents turn to seduction as he lures the royal couple into the cave; the landscape of Strephon and Klaius is transformed into an image of mental agony as their passionate desires are frustrated. In the testimony of Philanax and the sentences of the trial, Sidney shows us, in an alternative fiction, what the pastoral experience could have led to as a way of completing his critique of Sannazaro and the tradition of Italianate pastoral. There was nothing new in the 1570s about an attack upon Continental forms of bucolic literature. Sidney had been anticipated in this by Barclay and Googe, among others. What is different about *The Old Arcadia* is its discovery of an ethically informed structure capable of utilizing the aesthetically intriguing but morally dangerous fictions of classical and Italianate pastoral as the means for making complex criticism.

The Old Arcadia is a defense of pastoral because within it the traditional values of the genre are redefined rather than rejected. Making use of the freedom conventionally available to the Renaissance writer, Sidney clips the bucolic hedge to his own liking. He permits the green world to supply contentment and relief from misfortune, but only after we have learned that the green world is governed by the laws of reason and virtue, and that relief is the product of a special kind of concord. If Sidney had a precedent in the Horatian tradition for emphasizing that it is by means of a particular kind of mental activity (which is also a poetic activity) that a just life is created, he incorporates that emphasis into a bucolic context.

There are several advantages to adopting this interpretation of *The Old Arcadia*. Of most importance is the fact that it effectively answers the objections that have been raised against reading the romance as a pastoral by demonstrating that those objections are founded upon a misunderstanding of Renaissance pastoralism in general and Sidney's version of it in particular. The concept of a Stoic pastoral explains how it is possible for a bucolic poem to have an ethical foundation based on justice. It accounts for the presence of a hierarchical political structure in the romance, and by identifying its ethical and hierarchical features as the products of the fiction's essential pastoral mechanism—the pretense that following Nature is equivalent to leading a life in nature—it establishes the coherence of the whole. As a result this reading prevents us from having to discard the title and the setting of *The Old Arcadia* as irrelevant bits of escapist faddism. At the same time, it restores to critical prominence the almost exclusively pastoral literary traditions that the romance developed out of and in response to. This interpretation also has the advantage of highlighting the central role that the eclogues play in *The Old Arcadia*, as pastorals within a pastoral, simplified versions of the complex action of the romance in which different varieties of the idle life are measured as just responses to misfortune. They form a comprehensive critique of the quiet mind, and an urgent quest for it. Finally, this is an interpretation that stands in fundamental agreement with Sidney's aesthetic ideas as they are presented in the *Apology*, with his interest in the ethical treatises of Cicero, Aristotle, and Plutarch, with his education under Languet, and with his need to respond to profound public and private misfortunes. In *The Old Arcadia*, Sidney made available to his contemporaries a powerfully evocative literary image: a pastoral place providing both delight in beauty and knowledge about how to live justly. It is an image on which Spenser, Drayton, Shakespeare, and the rest of the English Renaissance pastoralists built a tradition.

Notes

Abbreviations

AUMLA	AUMLA; Journal of the Australasian University Language and Literature Association
CE	College English
CL	Comparative Literature
ELH	ELH; A Journal of English Literary History
ELN	English Language Notes
ELR	English Literary Renaissance
ES	English Studies; A Journal of English Letters and Philology
HLB	Huntington Library Bulletin
HLQ	Huntington Library Quarterly
JEPG	JEPG; Journal of English and Germanic Philology
JHI	Journal of the History of Ideas
JMRS	Journal of Medieval and Renaissance Studies
MLN	Modern Language Notes
MLR	The Modern Language Review
MP	Modern Philology
N&Q	Notes and Queries
PLL	Papers on Language and Literature
PQ	Philological Quarterly
RES	Review of English Studies
SCJ	Sixteenth Century Journal
SEL	Studies in English Literature
SLI	Studies in the Literary Imagination
SP	Studies in Philology
STC	A Short-Title Catalogue of Books Printed in England, Scotland, and Ireland. . . , 1475–1640. Comp. A. W. Pollard and G. R. Redgrave. London: The Bibliographical Society, 1926.
TSLL	Texas Studies in Literature and Language
UTQ	University of Toronto Quarterly

Preface

1. *The Poems of Sir Philip Sidney*, ed. William A. Ringler (Oxford: Clarendon Press, 1962), xxxviii.

2. Jon S. Lawry, *Sidney's Two* Arcadias: *Pattern and Proceeding* (Ithaca and London: Cornell University Press, 1972), 59.

3. The eclogues must be examined in the context of *The Old Arcadia*, rather than the revised version of the romance, because only in this work can we be certain that the arrangement of the poems was made by Sidney himself. His editors were responsible for the ordering of the eclogues in *The New Arcadia*. See, however, Sukanta Chaudhuri, "The Eclogues in Sidney's *New Arcadia*," RES, n.s., 35, no. 138 (May 1984): 185–202. Chaudhuri argues that the editors of the 1590 *Arcadia* found the eclogues "in a much more advanced stage of authorial revision . . . than has hitherto been supposed," though they do *not* have "a final, authorially conclusive order and setting" (194).

4. Stephen J. Greenblatt, *Renaissance Self-Fashioning: From More to Shakespeare* (Chicago and London: University of Chicago Press, 1980), 2.

5. Greenblatt, *Renaissance Self-Fashioning*, 9.

6. Ibid., 8.

7. Ibid., 4.

8. Thelma N. Greenfield, *The Eye of Judgment: Reading* The New Arcadia (Lewisburg: Bucknell University Press, 1982), 11.

9. Ibid., 22.

10. Ibid., 33.

11. Nancy Lindheim, *The Structures of Sidney's* Arcadia (Toronto, Buffalo, and London: University of Toronto Press, 1982), 4.

12. Ibid., 81.

13. Ibid., 77.

14. Richard Mallette, *Spenser, Milton, and Renaissance Pastoral* (Lewisburg: Bucknell University Press, 1981), 15.

15. Ibid., 15.

16. Ibid., 159.

17. Ibid., 44.

18. Ibid., 30.

19. D. M. Rosenberg, *Oaten Reeds and Trumpets: Pastoral and Epic in Virgil, Spenser, and Milton* (Lewisburg: Bucknell University Press, 1981), 18.

Chapter 1. Justice, Contentment, and the Idle Life

1. Sir Philip Sidney, *The Countess of Pembroke's Arcadia* (The Old Arcadia), ed. Jean Robertson (Oxford: Clarendon Press, 1973), 408. All further quotations will be from this edition and will be documented in the text.

2. Sidney's "narrowly moralistic" critics generally assume that *The Old Arcadia* is an antipastoral, and would, I think, be very much in harmony with Kalodoulus's bias against Arcadia. See Elizabeth Dipple, "Harmony and Pastoral in *The Old Arcadia*," ELH 35, no. 3 (September 1968): 309–28; and Franco Marenco, "Double Plot in Sidney's Old Arcadia," MLR 64, no. 2 (April 1969): 248–63. Andrew D. Weiner argues for the "severity and absoluteness of [*The Old Arcadia's*] moral judgments" (*Sir Philip Sidney and the Poetics of Protestantism* [Minneapolis: Univ. of Minnesota Press, 1978], x). Lindheim argues, by contrast "Sidney's treatment of his heroes there [in *The Old Arcadia*] is, I suggest, more complex and sympathetic than we have recently been led to believe" (139).

3. Kenneth Thorpe Rowe, "Romantic Love and Parental Authority in Sidney's *Arcadia*," *The University of Michigan Contributions in Modern Philology*, no. 4 (April 1947), 16;

Richard A. Lanham, *The Old Arcadia,* in *Sidney's* Arcadia (New Haven and London: Yale Univ. Press, 1965), 375; Elizabeth Dipple, "The 'Fore Conceit' of Sidney's Eclogues," *Literary Monographs* 1 (1967): 13-14; see also Elizabeth Dipple, " 'Unjust Justice' in the *Old Arcadia,*" SEL 10, no. 1 (Winter 1970): 83-101; Margaret E. Dana, "The Providential Plot of the *Old Arcadia,*" SEL 17, no. 1 (Winter 1977): 39-57. This last article contains a useful survey of the criticism of the trial scene. See also Richard C. McCoy's remarks on *The Old Arcadia's* "confused and elliptical ending" (*Sir Philip Sidney: Rebellion in Arcadia* [New Brunswick: Rutgers Univ. Press, 1979], 10, 52-53).

4. Critics who have written well on the fortune theme in connection with the revised version of the romance are John F. Danby, *Poets on Fortune's Hill: Studies in Sidney, Shakespeare, Beaumont and Fletcher* (rev. title, *Elizabethan and Jacobean Poets,* 1964; London: Faber and Faber, 1952), and Mark Rose, *Heroic Love: Studies in Sidney and Spenser* (Cambridge, Mass.: Harvard Univ. Press, 1968). See also Greenfield, *Eye of Judgment,* 111-17. Much less attention has been given to the presence of this theme in the original *Arcadia.* Scholars who are satisfied with analyzing the amatory intrigues of the romance, or with pointing to the debates between reason and passion, run the risk of trivializing *The Old Arcadia.* With her emphasis upon the "folly and delight" of love as the pastoral's main theme, Dorothy Connell seems particularly vulnerable to this kind of criticism; see *Sir Philip Sidney: The Maker's Mind* (Oxford: Clarendon Press, 1977), 127.

5. The first readers of the *Arcadia* were particularly sensitive to the fortune theme. In 1581 Thomas Howell published a poem in his *Devises* in praise of a "most excellent Booke, full of rare invention." The third stanza focuses on what Howell considers to be the *Arcadia's* moral:

> How much they erre, thy rare event bewrayes,
> That stretch their skill the Fates to overthrow:
> And how mans wisedome here in vaine seekes wayes,
> To shun high powers that sway our states below.
>   Against whose rule, although we strive to runne,
>   What Jove forefets, no humaine force may shunne.

Howell's Devises, 1581, ed. Walter Raleigh (Oxford: Clarendon Press, 1906), 44. One other contemporary critic was undoubtedly acquainted with the original version of the romance: Fulke Greville. Although he refers to the revised text of the *Arcadia,* it is important to remember his testimony that it was Sidney's purpose

> to limn out such exact pictures, of every posture in the minde, that any man being forced in the straines of this life, to pass through any straights or latitudes of good or ill fortune, might—as in a glasse—see how to set a good countenance upon all the discountenances of adversitie and a stay upon the exorbitant smilings of Chance.

The Life of the Renowned Sir Philip Sidney, in *The Works in Verse and Prose Complete of . . . Fulke Greville, Lord Brooke,* ed. Alexander B. Grosart, 4 vols. (London: C. Tiplady and Son, 1870), 4:19.

6. See Harry Levin, *The Myth of the Golden Age in the Renaissance* (Bloomington: Indiana Univ. Press, 1969), and Patricia A. Johnston, *Vergil's Agricultural Golden Age: A Study of the Georgics* (Leiden: E. J. Brill, 1980).

7. Aratus Solensis, *Phaenomena, The Aratus Ascribed to Germanicus Caesar,* ed. and trans. D. B. Gain (London: Athlone Press, 1976), 112-19; trans. p. 56.

8. Hesiod, *Works and Days,* in *The Homeric Hymns and Homerica,* trans. Hugh G. Evelyn-White (London: William Heinemann; Cambridge, Mass.: Harvard Univ. Press, 1936), 230-31; trans. p. 21.

9. Ovid, *Metamorphoses*, trans. Frank Justus Miller, 2 vols. (London: William Heinemann; Cambridge, Mass.: Harvard Univ. Press, 1926), 1. 129: ". . . pudor verumque fidesque"; trans. 1:11.

10. Ovid *Metamorphoses* 1. 149–50; trans. 1:13.

11. See Robert E. Stillman, "Justice and the 'Good Word' in Sidney's *The Lady of May*," *SEL* 24, no. 1 (Winter 1984): 23–38.

12. Virgil, *Eclogues, Georgics, Aeneid I–IV*, trans. H. Rushton Fairclough (London: William Heinemann; Cambridge, Mass.: Harvard Univ. Press, 1924). *Georgics* 2. 510; trans. p. 151. On politics and justice in Vergil's *Eclogues*, see Paul Alpers, *The Singer of the Eclogues: A Study of Virgilian Pastoral* (Berkeley: Univ. of California Press, 1979), 200–222.

13. Virgil *Eclogues* 4. 52; trans. p. 33.

14. Ibid., 4. 14; trans. p. 31.

15. Edmund Spenser, *The Faerie Queene*, in *The Complete Poetical Works . . .*, ed. R. E. Neil Dodge (Boston and New York: Houghton Mifflin, 1908), 6. 10. 19. See also Judith H. Anderson, "'Come, let's away to prison': Fortune and Freedom in *The Faerie Queene*, Book VI," *Journal of Narrative Technique* 2, no. 2 (May 1972): 133–37; Dorothy Woodward Culp, "Courtesy and Fortune's Chance in Book 6 of *The Faerie Queene*," *MP* 68, no. 3(February 1971): 254–59; Michael N. Dixon, "Fairy Tale, Fortune, and Boethian Wonder: Rhetorical Structure in Book VI of *The Faerie Queene*," *UTQ* 44, no. 2(Winter 1975): 141–65.

16. I am indebted here to Bruno Snell's *The Discovery of the Mind: The Greek Origins of European Thought*, trans. Thomas G. Rosenmeyer (Oxford: Blackwell, 1953); see also Michael C. J. Putnam, *Virgil's Pastoral Art: Studies in the* Eclogues (Princeton: Princeton Univ. Press, 1970), for good discussions of Vergil's transformations of Theocritus.

17. For a helpful short history of the subject, see Paul H. Johnstone, "In Praise of Husbandry," *Agricultural History* 11, no. 2(April 1937): 80–95.

18. See Virgil *Georgics* 2. 458–74.

19. See *Q. Horati Flacci Opera*, ed. Edward C. Wickham (Oxford: Clarendon Press, 1901, 1967), *Carminum Liber* 2. 10. 5–6; trans. Joseph P. Clancy, *The* Odes *and* Epodes *of Horace: A Modern Verse Translation* (Chicago: Univ. of Chicago Press, 1960), 85.

20. As Maren Sophie-Røstvig points out, Horatian man is happy because he has learned to moderate his desires, to refuse to expose himself "to the dangers and hazards that beset the path of the ambitious" (*The Happy Man: Studies in the Metamorphosis of a Classical Ideal, 1600–1700* [Oslo: Akademisk Forlag; Oxford: Basil Blackwell, 1954], 72).

21. *Psalms of David*, in Ringler, ed., *The Poems of Sir Philip Sidney*, 270: 11–12. For helpful discussions of the Christian tradition in Renaissance pastoral, see Patrick Cullen, *Spenser, Marvell, and Renaissance Pastoral* (Cambridge, Mass.: Harvard Univ. Press, 1970); and Nancy Jo Hoffman, *Spenser's Pastorals:* The Shepheardes Calendar *and "Colin Clout"* (Baltimore and London: The Johns Hopkins Univ. Press, 1977).

22. Renaissance georgic and Horatian poetry, as well as early English eclogues, are filled with shepherds, farmers, and retired gentlemen enjoying good fortune in the countryside. See Marcellus Palingenius, *The Zodiake of Life*, trans. Barnabe Googe (New York: Scholars' Facsimiles and Reprints, 1947), 71–72; Sir Thomas Wyatt's satire to John Poins in *Collected Poems . . .*, ed. Kenneth Muir (Cambridge, Mass.: Harvard Univ. Press, 1949), 190: 92–99; *The* Eclogues *of Alexander Barclay*, ed. Beatrice White, Early English Text Society, o.s., vol. 175 (London: Oxford Univ. Press, 1928), Ecl. 1. 1065–76, 1087–1122; Barnabe Googe, *Eglogs, Epytaphes, and Sonettes, 1563*, ed. Edward Arber, English Reprints (London and Edinburgh: Muir and Paterson, 1871), 62–64.

23. Iacopo Sannazaro, *Arcadia,* in *Opere volgari, a cura di Alfredo Mauro* (Bari: Laterza, 1961), 131. The English translation is from Ralph Nash, *Arcadia and Piscatorial Eclogues* (Detroit: Wayne State Univ. Press, 1966), 153.

24. Sannazaro, *Arcadia,* 132; trans. Nash, 154.

25. This is a controversial point that I shall substantiate at some length in chapter 2.

26. Joseph R. Jones, " 'Human Time' in *La Diana,*" *Romance Notes* 10, no. 1(Autumn 1968): 141. On the fortune theme, see also Bruce W. Wardropper, "The *Diana* of Montemayor: Revaluation and Interpretation," *SP* 48, no. 2 (April 1951): 135–37.

27. See Walter R. Davis, *A Map of* Arcadia: *Sidney's Romance in its Tradition,* in *Sidney's* Arcadia, 34–44.

28. For a helpful analysis of Gil Polo, see A. Solé-Leris, "The Theory of Love in the Two *Dianas:* A Contrast," *Bulletin of Hispanic Studies* 36 (1959): 65–79.

29. Gaspar Gil Polo, *Diana Enamorada,* ed. Rafael Ferreres (Madrid: Espasa-Calpe, 1953), 260. The English included in later translations incorporated into my text is from *A Critical Edition of Yong's Translation of George of Montemayor's* Diana *and Gil Polo's* Enamoured Diana, ed. Judith M. Kennedy (Oxford: Clarendon Press, 1968).

30. The fortune theme links all of the works that can lay claim to being major sources of *The Old Arcadia.* The two significant nonpastoral influences on Sidney's romance are books 8 and 11 of *Amadis de Gaule* and Heliodorus's *An Aethiopian Romance.* As Samuel Lee Wolff points out, in Heliodorus the "main events are controlled by a divine intention, and shadow forth, however dimly, the ways of the gods" (*The Greek Romances in Elizabethan Prose Fiction* [New York: Columbia Univ. Press, 1912], 116). John O'Connor has recently argued for the existence of a similar point of view in the *Amadis:* "Over all events in the romance rules the hierarchy of supernatural power—God, Fortune, the magicians—and the reader is constantly reminded that despite confusion in the narrative surface the world of *Amadis* is ordered by a purpose ultimately divine" (Amadis de Gaule *and its Influence on Elizabethan Literature* [New Brunswick: Rutgers Univ. Press, 1970], 129). Sidney's reading seems to have been considerably less haphazard than has sometimes been assumed.

31. Biographical criticism has its dangers. With a twist in one direction, the facts of Sidney's life can set the pattern for Denkinger's saint—the heroic knight and lover, cruelly slain before attaining the height of his glory; with a twist in the other, they produce the design for Lanham's sinner—the incompetent and neglected courtier, transformed by a petty battlefield accident into an ornament for his age (Emma Marshall Denkinger, *Philip Sidney* [London: George Allen and Unwin, 1932]; Richard A. Lanham, "Sidney: The Ornament of his Age," *Southern Review: An Australian Journal of Literary Studies* 2, no. 4 [Fall 1967]: 319–40). For a commentary on some of these dangers, see Alan Hager, "The Exemplary Mirage: Fabrication of Sir Philip Sidney's Biographical Image and the Sidney Reader," *ELH* 48, no. 1 (Spring 1981): 1–16.

A second and more important problem in relating Sidney's works to his life is in doing justice simultaneously to the personal urgency out of which his writings spring and to the public character of those writings in which the private responses of a Renaissance courtier are transformed into works of art whose significance and power are meant to be universally available.

32. Malcolm W. Wallace, *The Life of Sir Philip Sidney* (Cambridge: Cambridge Univ. Press, 1915), 195.

33. Greville, *Life,* 4: 42.

34. For the former argument, see James M. Osborn, *Young Sir Philip Sidney, 1572–77* (New Haven and London: Yale Univ. Press, 1972), 500; for the latter, see Lanham, "Sidney: The Ornament of his Age," 327.

35. Languet to Sidney, 5 March 1574, Osborn, *Young Sir Philip Sidney*, 155.

36. *The Correspondence of Philip Sidney and Hubert Languet*, ed. William Aspenwall Bradley (Boston: The Merrymount Press, 1912), 159.

37. Osborn, *Young Sir Philip Sidney*, 537. I have modernized the spelling of Renaissance texts here and throughout the book by changing "i" to "j" and "u" to "v" where appropriate.

38. Languet to Sidney, 24 September 1580, Bradley, ed., *Correspondence*, 203.

39. Osborn, *Young Sir Philip Sidney*, 155. In the same year he warns Sidney about "an enormous fleet which is being fitted out in Spain," and tells him that "you English, they will fall upon first, as the chief authors of their misfortunes." Languet to Sidney, 18 April 1574, Bradley, ed., *Correspondence*, 63.

40. Sidney to Languet, 11 February 1574, Bradley, ed., *Correspondence*, 40.

41. Sidney to Languet, 28 May 1574, Bradley, ed., *Correspondence*, 73.

42. Sidney to the Count of Hanau, 12 June 1575, Osborn, *Young Sir Philip Sidney*, 309.

43. Languet to Sidney, 22 October 1577, Bradley, ed., *Correspondence*, 129.

44. Languet to Sidney, 14 June 1577, Bradley, ed., *Correspondence*, 122. See also Languet to Sidney, 20 September 1578, Bradley, ed., *Correspondence*, 170–71.

45. Sidney to Languet, 10 March 1578, Bradley, ed., *Correspondence*, 163.

46. Bradley, ed., *Correspondence*, 188.

47. Sidney to Henry Sidney, 25 April 1578, *The Complete Works of Sir Philip Sidney*, ed. Albert Feuillerat, 4 vols. (Cambridge: Cambridge Univ. Press, 1912–26), 3:122.

48. Languet to Sidney, 7 January 1574, Osborn, *Young Sir Philip Sidney*, 129.

49. Languet to Sidney, 28 November 1577, Bradley, ed., *Correspondence*, 140–41.

50. Sidney to Languet, 21 April 1576, Osborn, *Young Sir Philip Sidney*, 419.

51. Osborn, *Young Sir Philip Sidney*, 540.

52. Sir Philip Sidney, *An Apology for Poetry; or, the Defence of Poesy*, ed. Geoffrey Shepherd (London and Edinburgh: Thomas Nelson and Sons, 1965), 95.

53. Denkinger, *Philip Sidney*, 162; see also Michel Poirier, *Sir Philip Sidney: Le chevalier poète élizabéthain* (Lille: Bibliothèque universitaire de Lille, 1948), 168.

54. A. C. Hamilton, *Sir Philip Sidney: A Study of His Life and Works* (Cambridge and New York: Cambridge Univ. Press, 1977), 50.

55. Neil L. Rudenstine, *Sidney's Poetic Development* (Cambridge, Mass.: Harvard Univ. Press, 1967), 46. Richard McCoy takes a different approach. In *The Old Arcadia* Sidney dramatizes a conflict between "obedient submission to authority and the recalcitrant urges of desire," and this conflict, McCoy argues, has its origins in Sidney's own life (ix). "Submission still prompts feelings of frustration, defiance, and painful inadequacy, while self-assertion arouses guilt and confusion. The conflicts of the period prove as intractable for him in literature as they do in life, and his ambivalence and uncertainty prevent him from following his ideas through to any conclusion" (10). McCoy grants Sidney less artistic control and independence than my reading of *The Old Arcadia* can support.

56. To ask what a poem *does*, instead of what it *says*, as Stanley Fish writes, is to view the text "no longer as an object, a thing-in-itself, but an *event*, something that *happens* to, and with the participation of, the reader." As Fish goes on to argue, "the value of such a procedure is predicated on the idea of meaning as an event [as opposed to meaning as pure content], something that is happening between the words and in the reader's mind, something not visible to the naked eye, but which can be made visible . . . by the regular introduction of a 'searching' question (what does this do?)" ("Literature in the Reader: Affective Stylistics," in *Self-Consuming Artifacts: The Experience of Seventeenth-Century Literature* [Berkeley: Univ. of California Press, 1972], 386, 389). More

influential in my reading of *The Old Arcadia*, as will become clear in part IV, is Sidney's insistence in the *Apology* on the poet's responsibility to make real changes in the mental landscapes of his readers: Sidney anticipates Fish's claims for meaning as an event. In Sidney's view, poetry performs actions; it does not simply make statements.

57. Kenneth O. Myrick, *Sir Philip Sidney As a Literary Craftsman* (1935; reprint, Lincoln: Univ. of Nebraska Press, 1965), 27.

58. Renato Poggioli, *The Oaten Flute, Essays on Pastoral Poetry and the Pastoral Ideal* (Cambridge, Mass.: Harvard Univ. Press, 1975), 11.

59. Abraham Fleming, *The Bucolikes of Publius Virgilius Maro* . . . (London: John Charlewood, 1575; STC 24816), 35.

60. Abraham Fleming, *The Bucoliks. Georgiks. All Newly Translated* . . . (London: Thomas Woodcocke, 1589; STC 24817), A4.

61. Fleming, *The Bucolikes of Publius Virgilius Maro* . . ., 4, 29.

62. Fleming, *The Bucoliks. Georgiks* . . ., A3.

63. "The life of Virgill," in Thomas Twyne, *The xiii Bookes of Aeneidos* (London: William How, 1584; STC 24802), A5.

64. E. K., "To the most excellent and learned both orator and poete, Mayster Gabriell Harvey . . .," in Spenser, *Faerie Queene*, 7.

65. Edward Dyer [?], *Sixe Idillia* . . . *Chosen out of* . . . *Theocritus, and translated into English Verse* (Oxford: Joseph Barnes, 1588; STC 23937), A4.

66. Languet to Sidney, 28 January 1574, Osborn, *Young Sir Philip Sidney*, 139.

67. Sidney to Languet, 4 February 1574, Osborn, *Young Sir Philip Sidney*, 143.

68. Sidney to Languet, 28 May 1574, Osborn, *Young Sir Philip Sidney*, Osborn, 193.

69. 18 October 1580, Feuillerat, ed., *The Complete Works of Sir Philip Sidney*, 3:133.

70. Sir Philip Sidney, *The Lady of May*, in *Miscellaneous Prose of Sir Philip Sidney*, ed. Katherine Duncan-Jones and Jan Van Dorsten (Oxford: Clarendon Press, 1973), 29.

71. *Astrophil and Stella*, in Ringler, ed., *The Poems of Sir Philip Sidney*, no. 18, 8–9.

72. *Apology*, 95.

Chapter 2. Pastoralism and Generic Definition

1. *Idea, The Shepheards Garland, Fashioned in nine Eglogs* (1593), in *The Works of Michael Drayton*, ed. J. William Hebel, 4 vols. (Oxford: Shakespeare Head Press, 1931–41), Egl. 1:58–60.

2. See *The Poems of William Browne of Tavistock*, ed. Gordon Goodwin, 2 vols. (London: G. Routledge, 1894), 2:8.

3. Ibid., 2:11. Joint praise for Sidney and Spenser also appears in Thomas Collins, *The Teares of Love: or Cupids Progresse* (London: G. Purslowe, 1615; STC 5567), 47.

> *Sidney* and *Spencer,* be you aye renoun'd
> No time hath pow'r your Pastorals to confound.

4. See also Helen Cooper, *Pastoral: Medieval into Renaissance* (Ipswich: D. S. Brewer; Totowa, N.J.: Rowman and Littlefield, 1977), 150–52.

5. Richard Barnfield, *The Affectionate Shepherd* (1594), ed. James O. Halliwell, Early English Poetry, vol. 20 (London: The Percy Society, 1845), 37.

6. Francis Meres, *Palladis Tamia* (1598), in *Elizabethan Critical Essays*, ed. G. Gregory Smith, 2 vols. (Oxford: Clarendon Press, 1904), 2:321.

7. George Puttenham, *The Arte of English Poesie* (1589), in G. Gregory Smith, ed., *Elizabethan Critical Essays*, 2:65.

8. Richard Carew, *The Excellency of the English Tongue* (ca. 1595–96), in G. Gregory Smith, ed., *Elizabethan Critical Essays*, 2:292.

9. *Howell's Devises, 1581*, 45.

10. Gabriel Harvey, *Pierce's Supererogation* (1593), in G. Gregory Smith, ed., *Elizabethan Critical Essays*, 2:263. The other three are "amorous Courting," "sage counselling," and "valorous fighting."

11. Angel Day, *Vpon the Life and Death of . . . Sir Phillip Sidney* (London: Robert Waldegrave, 1586; STC 6409), 4. It is uncertain which version of the *Arcadia* Day is referring to.

12. For more examples, see the elegies included in *Exequiae illustrissimi equitis d. Philippi Sidnaei, gratissimae memoriae ac nomini impensae* (Oxford: Joseph Barnes, 1587; STC 22551), especially "Stellati Pastoris. . . ."

13. Matthew Roydon, "An Elegie. . . ," in *The Phoenix Nest, 1593*, ed. Hyder E. Rollins (Cambridge, Mass.: Harvard Univ. Press, 1931), 12:1–6.

14. William Browne, bk. 2, song 2, ll. 257, 248.

15. Ibid., l. 275. It was not until later in the seventeenth century that the *Arcadia* was referred to as a heroic poem. Sir William Alexander in the *Anacrisis* (1634?) seems to have been the first to assert that the work is like an epic since it contains "such things as both in War and in Peace were fit to be practised by Princes" (*Critical Essays of the Seventeenth Century*, ed. J. E. Spingarn, 3 vols. [Bloomington and London: Indiana Univ. Press, 1968], 1:188). Edwin A. Greenlaw argues that the "*Arcadia* was regarded as an heroic poem" ("Sidney's *Arcadia* as an Example of Elizabethan Allegory," in *Anniversary Papers by Colleagues and Pupils of George Lyman Kittredge* [New York: Russell and Russell, 1913, 1967], 330). In every instance the evidence offered in support of this remark represents a distortion of the contemporary critical comments that he cites. For instance, Fraunce mentions the *Arcadia* along with the *Iliad*, the *Odyssey*, and the *Aeneid*, as Greenlaw notices, but the mention occurs in a passage that also cites the *Eclogues*, the *Georgics*, and a group of other pastoral works. Meres includes the *Arcadia* in a group of texts that mingle poetry and prose, but he does not—and this is the crucial point—include the romance in his category of heroic writings. However, as we have seen, Meres does include Sidney among the pastoralists. The passages that Greenlaw cites from Harrington and Harvey require no comment here. In neither instance is there any reason to suppose that the author believed the *Arcadia* to be a heroic poem. Greenlaw's remarks are quoted with approval by Marcus S. Goldman in *Sir Philip Sidney and the Arcadia*, Illinois Studies in Languages and Literatures 17, nos. 1–2 (Urbana: Univ. of Illinois Press, 1934), 151.

16. The beginnings of a movement away from a pastoral interpretation of the *Arcadia* coincided with a growing disregard for the importance of the eclogues. When at the close of the nineteenth century, in reference to the composite version of the romance, the claim that Sidney's shepherds "are only there for decoration" found acceptance, it was feasible to exclaim "with how little reason the 'Arcadia' is sometimes placed in the category of bedizened pastorals . . ." (J. J. Jusserand, *The English Novel in the Time of Shakespeare*, trans. Elizabeth Lee [London: T. Fisher Unwin, 1889], 236, 249). Once the shepherds and the Arcadian setting were reduced to a set of shaggy stage props, the eclogues could be ignored entirely. Moreover, if pastoral is something easy and vulgar, Sidney had to be rescued from it—or at the very least, he had to be shown to have quickly rescued himself. The discovery of *The Old Arcadia* by Bertram Dobell and its publication by Albert Feuillerat confronted Sidney's modern critics with the difficulty of explaining and justifying the changes that the romance underwent from one version to the next. With the help of some selectively interpreted passages from the *Apology* and Italian Renaissance criticism, it was feasible for Kenneth Myrick and his followers to

transform *The New Arcadia* into a heroic poem. In this way Sidney's literary career was made to embody an astonishingly rapid Vergilian progression from base pastoral to noble epic.

When it was still popular to downgrade the original version of the romance in comparative studies with the revised text, on the basis of its supposed intellectual and artistic immaturity, *The Old Arcadia* was most frequently referred to as a pastoral—a label that carried distinctly negative connotations, especially in contrast to the new-found heroic status of its successor. As a result, a defense of *The Old Arcadia*'s integrity, and its eventual transformation into a heroic poem in its own right, became irrevocably attached to a dismissal of its pastoral elements as "stage-setting." Once again, this effort to remove the work from its pastoral context entailed the neglect of its eclogues as important functioning elements in its design. The interpretation of *The Old Arcadia* as a heroic poem leaves no room for its eclogues. See Myrick, "The *Arcadia* as an Heroic Poem," chap. 4.

It is not difficult to find harsh criticisms of the eclogues in twentieth-century scholarship. They have been devalued as "exercises" (Theodore Spencer's "The Poetry of Sir Philip Sidney," *ELH* 12, no. 4 [December 1945]: 256), and as "experiments" (Mona Wilson, *Sir Philip Sidney* [London and Southampton: Duckworth, 1931], 129). Ernest A. Baker has asserted that "few of these metrical pieces are readable . . ." (*The History of the English Novel*, 10 vols. [London: H. F. & G. Witherby, 1924–39], 2:86). Hector Genouy has written more politely that "Sidney est mal à l'aise dans ce genre de poésie" (*L'* Arcadia *de Sidney dans ses rapports avec l'*Arcadia *de Sannazaro et la* Diana *de Montemayor* [Paris: Henri Didier, 1928], 119). Walter W. Greg was more blunt, referring to their style as "wholly unworthy of its author" (*Pastoral Poetry and Pastoral Drama* [London, 1906; reprint, New York: Russell and Russell, 1959], 153). In more recent years they have been described by Robert Kimbrough as the prisoners of context, the best of which are mere *"tours de force"* (*Sir Philip Sidney*, Twayne's English Authors Series [New York: Twayne, 1971], 102); and by Simone Dorangeon as mere decorative additions to the romance in *L'églogue anglaise de Spenser à Milton* (Paris: Didier, 1974), 176. Most often, Sidney scholars simply choose to ignore them.

17. See Laurence Lerner, *The Uses of Nostalgia, Studies in Pastoral Poetry* (New York: Schocken Books, 1972), 105–8. These are attributes of the romance that lead Lerner to call it an "antipastoral," though he appears to be thinking largely of the revised version.

18. For a review of the multiple generic features of the work, see Lanham, *The Old Arcadia*, 358–83. A handy recent summary of the various generic interpretations offered by Sidney's critics appears in Robert W. Parker, "Terentian Structure and Sidney's Original *Arcadia*," *ELR* 2, no. 1 (Winter 1972): 61–78. Parker is yet another exponent of the theory that Sidney's pastoral is a "Heroic poem," even though he believes, together with Alan D. Isler ("Heroic Poetry and Sidney's Two *Arcadias*," *PMLA* 83, no. 2 [May 1968]:368–79), that the "Elizabethan conception of heroic poetry, in terms of structure, method, and convention, is too vague to be meaningful" (63). Why there is such enthusiasm for placing a label upon the romance, which even its proponents regard as meaningless, is difficult to understand. For a more recent argument that *The Old Arcadia* can claim "at least in *cinquecento* terms . . . the title of epic," see P. Jeffrey Ford, "Philosophy, History, and Sidney's *Old Arcadia*," *CL* 26, no. 1 (Winter 1974): 34. Clark L. Chalifour argues that the work is a comedy in "Sir Philip Sidney's *Old Arcadia* as a Terentian Comedy," *SEL* 16, no. 1 (Winter 1976): 51–63. The work has recently been discussed briefly as a pastoral romance in Paul A. Scanlon, "Sidney's *Old Arcadia*: A Renaissance Pastoral Romance," *Ariel* 10, no. 4 (October 1979): 69–76. See also Donald V. Stump, "Sidney's Concept of Tragedy in the *Apology* and in the *Arcadia*," *SP*

79, no. 1 (Winter 1982): 41–61 and Stephen J. Greenblatt, "Sidney's *Arcadia* and the Mixed Mode," *SP* 70, no. 3 (July 1973): 269–78.

19. My debts in this portion of my chapter are larger than I can indicate. Two scholars who have placed considerable emphasis on the degree to which the pastoralist interests his audience in the processes of his fiction as fiction are Humphrey Tonkin in *Spenser's Courteous Pastoral, Book Six of* The Faerie Queene (Oxford: Clarendon Press, 1970), 192, 284, and Harold E. Toliver in *Pastoral Forms and Attitudes* (Berkeley: Univ. of California Press, 1971), 1–19. See also Harry Berger, Jr., "The Renaissance Imagination: Second World and Green World," *Centennial Review* 9, no. 1 (Winter 1965): 36–78; James Neil Brown, "Elizabethan Pastoralism and Renaissance Platonism," *AUMLA* 44 (November 1975): 247–67; Patrick Cullen, *Spenser, Marvell, and Renaissance Pastoralism* (Cambridge, Mass.: Harvard Univ. Press, 1970); William Empson, *English Pastoral Poetry* (1935 ed., *Some Versions of Pastoral;* reprint, Freeport: Books for Libraries Press, 1972); Northrop Frye, "Varieties of Literary Utopias," *Daedalus* 94 (1965): 323–47; S. K. Heninger, Jr., "The Renaissance Perversion of Pastoral," *JHI* 22, no. 2 (April–June 1961): 254–61; Frank Kermode, ed., *English Pastoral Poetry from the Beginnings to Marvell* (New York: W. W. Norton, 1952, 1972); Hallett D. Smith, *Elizabethan Poetry: A Study in Conventions, Meaning and Expression* (Cambridge, Mass.: Harvard Univ. Press, 1952); and Raymond Williams, *The Country and the City* (New York: Oxford Univ. Press, 1973).

20. Drayton, Egl. 8:1–2.

21. Longus's pastoral romance, *Daphnis and Chloe,* is an important exception to the rule.

22. Francesco Petrarcha, *Petrarch's Bucolicum Carmen,* trans. Thomas G. Bergin (New Haven: Yale Univ. Press, 1974), Ecl. 10:41, 46–47; trans. p. 145.

23. Petrarcha, Ecl. 10:359–60; trans. p. 179.

24. Petrarcha, Ecl. 10:364–65; trans. p. 179.

25. I do not wish to claim, however, that generic definition is in any sense unique to the pastoral. Epic writers from Vergil to Milton make use of similar techniques. But pastoral lends itself especially well to this kind of activity, both because of the extreme self-consciousness with which pastoralists from the genre's very beginnings look back to earlier models of writing and because of the readiness with which different conceptions of nature (the primary motive behind all pastoral definitions) are translated into different styles of poetry. For similar notions about how to approach questions of genre in Shakespeare's plays, see Howard Felpernin, *Shakespearean Representations: Mimesis and Modernity in Elizabethan Tragedy* (Princeton: Princeton Univ. Press, 1977).

See also Paul Alpers's argument that "pastoral works are representations of shepherds, who are felt to be representative of some other or of all other men. But since all the terms in this definition are subject to modification or reinterpretation, pastoral is historically diversified and transformed" ("What is Pastoral?," *Critical Inquiry* 8, no. 3 [Spring 1982]: 456). For a study of generic redefinition in the wider context of Continental Renaissance literature, see Thomas M. Greene's analysis of "heuristic imitation" in *The Light in Troy: Imitation and Discovery in Renaissance Poetry* (New Haven and London: Yale Univ. Press, 1982), 37–48.

26. Hallett D. Smith, *Elizabethan Poetry,* 10. Louis Adrian Montrose also uses the concept of "negotiation" in order to define the pastoralist's main activity; see " 'Eliza, Queene of shepheardes,' and the Pastoral of Power," *ELR* 10, no. 2(Spring 1980): 153–82. But Montrose limits his critique (brilliant as it is) to a study of "social relationships," and ignores what I consider to be the shepherd-poet's frequently more important ethical and aesthetic negotiations with the literary past (153). See also Montrose's recent essay, "Of Gentlemen and Shepherds: The Politics of Elizabethan Pastoral

Form," *ELH* 50, no. 3 (Fall 1983): 415–59. I am in complete agreement with his argument that the study of pastoralism "cannot confine its inquiry to matters of literary taxonomy and thematics, to what pastorals 'are' or what they 'mean'; it must also ask what pastorals *do*, and by what operations they perform their cultural work" (416). At the same time, we cannot arbitrarily limit our understanding of "cultural work" to the pastoral's political functions and thereby neglect its important aesthetic, psychological, and moral activities. These, too, are matters of culture.

27. Puttenham, *Arte of English Poesie*, 2: 40. See also Lindheim, *Structures of Sidney's Arcadia*, 63.

28. Sannazaro, *Arcadia and Piscatorial Eclogues*, 79, trans. Nash, 101. All further citations to these works will be documented in the text.

29. David Kalstone writes: "The tenth prose recounts a myth of the descent of pastoral poetry" (*Sidney's Poetry: Contexts and Interpretations* [Cambridge, Mass.: Harvard Univ. Press, 1967], 37). What Sannazaro is attempting can better be referred to as a history.

30. So frequent are its literary allusions that Genouy refers to the *Arcadia* as "le manuel le plus complet de pastoralisme . . ." (53); see also Mia I. Gerhardt, *Essai d'analyse littéraire de la pastorale* (Assen: Van Gorcum, 1950), 100–110.

31. Walter R. Davis points out this connection in "Actaeon in Arcadia," *SEL* 2, no. 1(Winter 1962): 100.

32. Longus, *The Story of Daphnis and Chloe. A Greek Pastoral . . .*, trans. W. D. Lowe (Cambridge: Deighton Bell, 1908), 11.

33. Samuel Lee Wolff is entirely correct in pointing out, however, that: "*They* are simple enough, but *we* are not; and Longus knows it" (131).

34. See Kalstone, *Sidney's Poetry*, 23–39. He is particularly good on the relationship between Petrarch and Sannazaro.

35. Kalstone calls the *Arcadia* "a paradise for poets," (12); Peter V. Marinelli uses the same phrase to describe the work in *Pastoral* (London: Methuen, 1971), 46. Luigi Monga points to the power of verse in controlling the passions, but believes the romance ends with desperation (*Le Genre pastoral au xvi siècle: Sannazar et Belleau* [Paris: éditions universitaires, 1974], 55–60). Rachel Bromberg seems much closer to the truth when writing: "Death disposes of his Neopolitan girl, but [Sincero] may still indulge in lament. By monumentalizing his grief, the lament helps to relieve him of it. Art makes up for what nature cannot give" (*Three Pastoral Novels* [Brooklyn: Postar Press, 1970], 37). A. C. Hamilton claims, by contrast, that the *Arcadia* "shows man's alienation from Nature in his isolated and divided state" (44). See Longus's account of his aesthetic aims: "I have written a story in four books . . ., a joy forever to mankind to heal their sickness and soothe their grief . . ." *Daphnis and Chloe* (5).

36. In a rich and suggestive article Paul Alpers emphasizes the considerable degree to which pastoral is concerned with the ability of song to reconcile man to his world ("The Eclogue Tradition and the Nature of Pastoralism," *CE* 34, no. 3 [December 1972]: 352–71); in Theocritus, Thomas G. Rosenmeyer writes, "song is nothing less than the documentation of the native nobility of man" (*The Green Cabinet: Theocritus and the European Pastoral Lyric* [Berkeley and Los Angeles: Univ. of California Press, 1969], 147); on Vergil's celebration of the poet's power to assert "control over the world that reflects human desires," see Eleanor Winsor Leach, *Vergil's* Eclogues, *Landscapes of Experience* (Ithaca: Cornell Univ. Press, 1974), 242.

37. Barclay *Eclogues* 2. 324. Further references to this work will be documented in the text.

38. Dorangeon, *L'églogue anglaise*, 108.

39. Wilfred P. Mustard, "Notes on the Eclogues of Alexander Barclay," *MLN* 24, no. 1 (January 1909): 8–10.

40. See John R. Schultz, "The Method of Barclay's *Eclogues*," *JEGP* 32 (1933): 549–71, on the English character of the poems.

41. See Paul E. Parnell, "Barnabe Googe: A Puritan in Arcadia," *JEGP* 60 (1961): 273–81, for a good analysis of another Christian pastoralist's struggle to avoid the dangers of pagan literature.

42. The best of the most recent analyses of "plain" style aesthetics is Douglas L. Peterson's *The English Lyric from Wyatt to Donne: A History of the Plain and Eloquent Styles* (Princeton: Princeton Univ. Press, 1967).

43. Cullen is particularly good on the country-city contrasts in what he terms "Mantuanesque pastoral," *Spenser, Marvell, and Renaissance Pastoral*, 19–26.

44. See Dorangeon on nature in the Christian pastoral, *L'églogue anglaise*, 108.

Chapter 3. As Critic and Poet, Sidney Defines *Pastoral*

1. James E. Congleton, *Theories of Pastoral Poetry in England, 1684–1798* (Gainesville: Univ. of Florida Press, 1952), 16.

2. *Apology*, 116.

3. Poggioli, *Oaten Flute*, 201. To argue, as he does, that this reference implies that justice is an "aristocratic privilege" is to miss the point.

4. Geoffrey Shepherd calls the comparison "puzzling" (186). There is good reason to be puzzled, but we had better avoid misreadings. Shepherd argues that the point of Sidney's comparison is that "even in the greatest political struggle of the past all that comes down to the present has *the appearance of a trivial dispute*, the intensity of contending is forgotten and only the outcome is recalled" (emphasis added). Sidney's point is considerably stronger: the dispute *is* trifling.

5. Virgil *Eclogues* 7.16.

6. See Dipple, "Harmony and Pastoral . . .," 311–13. She also mentions Sidney's debts here to Polybius, but her conclusions are quite different.

7. It is possible that Sidney underplays the idyllic features of pastoral in the *Apology* passage because of his wish to heighten its ethical content for a specific polemical purpose demanded by the occasion.

8. Polybius, *The Histories*, trans. W. R. Paton, 6 vols. (New York: G. P. Putnam's Sons; London: William Heinemann, 1922), 4.20. 1–3; trans. vol. 2:349.

9. Basil Willey, *The Religion of Nature* (London: Lindsey Press, 1957), 19. See also C. S. Lewis, *Studies in Words* (Cambridge: Cambridge University Press, 1960), 58–62; R. G. Collingwood, *The Idea of Nature* (Oxford: Clarendon Press, 1945).

10. A similar point is made by Arthur O. Lovejoy and George Boas in *Primitivism and Related Ideas in Antiquity* (Baltimore: The Johns Hopkins Univ. Press, 1935), 13.

11. On Cicero's role in this history, see Gerard Watson, "The Natural Law and Stoicism," in *Problems in Stoicism*, ed. A. A. Long (London: Athlone Press, 1971), 216–38; and Lovejoy and Boas, *Primitivism*, 252–53.

12. Tonkin, *Spenser's Courteous Pastoral*, 182; for ideas about nature in the Renaissance, see also Douglas Bush, *Prefaces to Renaissance Literature* (Cambridge, Mass.: Harvard Univ. Press, 1965), 44–64; John F. Danby, *Shakespeare's Doctrine of Nature: A Study of King Lear* (London: Faber and Faber, 1949), 15–53; Hiram Haydn, *The Counter-Renaissance* (New York: Charles Scribner's Sons, 1950), 461–554; Theodore Spencer, *Shakespeare and the Nature of Man*, Lowell Lectures (New York: Macmillan, 1942), 1–50;

and Edward Tayler, *Nature and Art in Renaissance Literature* (New York and London: Columbia Univ. Press, 1964).

13. Lois Whitney finds a similar view of nature in *The New Arcadia* in "Concerning Nature in *The Countess of Pembrokes Arcadia*," *SP* 24, no. 2 (April 1927): 207–22. Sidney enjoys having his characters invoke the law of nature as a standard of virtuous behavior even on behalf of arguments that he may dislike and in moments of evident hypocrisy. Cleophila's defense of chastity to Basilius as "the truest observance of nature," reverberates with ironies that he is scarcely in control of (220). In a similar fashion, Basilius may be right to suggest that nature's "never failing laws" teach "gratefulness and mercy," but these virtues will hardly bear the sexual twist that he hopes Cleophila will give them (219).

14. For a definition of Epicurean pastoral, see Rosenmeyer, *Green Cabinet*, 3–30. Attention to Stoic elements in Sidney's *New Arcadia* appears in Danby's *Poet's on Fortune's Hill*, 55–73, and Davis's *A Map of* Arcadia, 63–65, 76–83; both emphasize the Christian character of Sidney's Stoicism. See also Poirier, *Sir Philip Sidney*, 82–83. While claiming that Sidney is a Stoic, Mark Rose in *Heroic Love* attacks these critics for their religious interpretations, arguing that the *New Arcadia* is entirely secular in design, 59–73. Rose is correct to insist upon the specifically and guardedly nonreligious character of the romance. Lanham calls attention to Stoic elements in *The Old Arcadia*, 284–88. In reference to Kalander's personal manners and estate in the *New Arcadia*, Toliver writes: "It is obviously a stoic version of Arcadia" (50). His use of the term does not accord with the definition that I shall supply for it.

15. "On Moral Virtue," in *Plutarch's* Moralia, trans. W. C. Helmbold, 14 vols. (Cambridge, Mass.: Harvard Univ. Press; London: William Heinemann, 1939, 1962), 450 E; trans. 6:75.

16. Robert Hoopes, *Right Reason in the English Renaissance* (Cambridge, Mass.: Harvard Univ. Press, 1962), 44.

17. Haydn, *Counter-Renaissance*, 474. He defines the Stoic view of nature in much the same way. See also Elizabeth Armstrong, *Ronsard and the Age of Gold* (Cambridge: The University Press, 1968), "Lucretius, Seneca, Natural Law," 121–34.

18. Cicero, *De Officiis*, trans. Walter Miller (Cambridge, Mass.: Harvard Univ. Press; London: William Heinemann, 1913, 1961), 3. 3. 13; trans. p. 281.

19. *Apology*, 105.

20. *Apology*, 134; *Certain Sonnets*, 14.

21. Ringler calls attention to the biographical relevance of the change in his notes, *The Poems of Sir Philip Sidney*, 428.

22. Bradley, ed., *Correspondence*, 159–60.

23. With its closing ironies softened, Seneca would undoubtedly have been pleased by the argument, as this passage from his *De Tranquillitate Animi* illustrates: "The mind must be given relaxation; it will arise better and keener after resting. As rich fields must be forced—for their productiveness, if they have no rest, will quickly exhaust them—so constant labour will break the vigour of the mind, but if it is released and relaxed a little while, it will recover its powers" (*Moral Essays*, ed. John W. Basore [Cambridge, Mass.: Harvard Univ. Press; London: William Heinemann, 1931, 1952], 17. 5–6; trans. 2:281).

24. Osborn, *Young Sir Philip Sidney*, 538–39.

25. On the close relationship between Aristotle and the Stoics, see A. A. Long, "Aristotle's Legacy to Stoic Ethics," *Bulletin of the Institute of Classical Studies* (Univ. of London), 15 (1968): 72–85, and the same author's *Hellenistic Philosophy: Stoics, Epicureans, Sceptics* (London: Duckworth, 1974), 150–52. Sixteenth-century neo-Stoics frequently quoted Cicero in support of their doctrines: see Jason Lewis Saunders, *Justus*

Lipsius: The Philosophy of Renaissance Stoicism (New York: Liberal Arts Press, 1955), 80–84. This is not very surprising in light of the fact that Cicero in his *De Officiis* is profoundly influenced by the later Stoic philosopher Panaetius. Panaetius also exerted a strong influence upon Plutarch's treatise "The Tranquillity of the Mind," as D. A. Russell points out (*Plutarch* [London: Duckworth, 1972], 25). In fact, until recently, Plutarch was ordinarily classed among the Stoics. As R. H. Barrow indicates, "most of his teaching any Stoic would have accepted . . .," (*Plutarch and his Times* [Bloomington: Indiana Univ. Press, 1967], 103). The fact that Renaissance intellectuals believed that he had a great deal in common with the Stoics (and some viewed him as a Stoic) is more important for my purposes than Daniel Babut's recent exhaustive critique attempting to prove that he did not, *Plutarch et le stoïcisme* (Paris: Presses universitaires de France, 1969).

26. *Apology*, 101.

27. See Walter R. Davis, *Idea and Act in Elizabethan Fiction* (Princeton: Princeton Univ. Press, 1969); he argues that the central motive of Elizabethan fiction is "the testing of ideas of value by means of experience," vii. See also Lindheim, *The Structures*, 63.

28. Long, *Hellenistic Philosophy*, 174.

29. Given this belief—one that is shared by the Arcadian shepherds—Sidney's motives for placing his fiction in a pre-Christian world become clearer. In the preface to his *Six Excellent Treatises*, Sidney's friend de Mornay justifies the inclusion of such pagans as Cicero, Plato, and Seneca in his work by arguing that men who understand moral truths by "naturall judgement" will serve to arouse modern Christians from their drowsy nests (Philippe de Mornay, *Six Excellent Treatises of Life and Death* [London: Mathew Lownes, 1607; STC 18155], A 4–A 5).

30. See Lovejoy and Boas, *Primitivism*, 152.

31. Seneca, *Ad Lucilium Epistulae Morales*, trans. Richard M. Gummere, 3 vols. (New York: G. P. Putnam's Sons; London: William Heinemann, 1917), Ep. 90. 16–17; trans. 2:405.

32. Lovejoy and Boas, *Primitivism*, 119.

33. See Basil Willey, *The English Moralists* (London: Chatto and Windus, 1964), 66–72. James Sanforde begins his translation of *The Manuell of Epictetus* by asking that it be read "with a quiet minde voide of all care and solicitude" (London: H. Bynneman, 1567; STC 10423), Aii.

34. Francesco Petrarca, *De Vita Solitaria Secondo Lo Pseudo-Autografo Vaticano 3357*, ed. Antonio Altamura (Napoli: Dino Amodio, 1943), 25–26; trans. Jacob Zeitlin, *The Life of Solitude* (Urbana: Univ. of Illinois Press, 1924), 115. Petrarch's fervor inspired an Elizabethan, Roger Baynes, to translate his treatise in 1577, a treatise that was dedicated, interestingly enough, to Sidney's friend Edward Dyer: *The Praise of Solitarinesse* (London: Francis Coldocke and Henry Bynneman, 1577; STC 1651).

It might be simpler to refer to the Epicurean and Stoic pastoralists in terms of Poggioli's distinction between the pastoral of happiness and the pastoral of innocence, but to do so would obscure the philosophical origins of these two distinct versions and the all-important foundation of their respective attitudes upon particular interpretations of nature.

Chapter 4. From Prose to Poetry

1. *Apology*, 116.

2. Gil Polo may have suggested the idea of entr'acte entertainments to Sidney, even

though he does not set his poems apart from the narrative so distinctly. See Judith M. Kennedy, *Critical Edition of Yong's Translation,* xxxi–xxxix.

3. See Parker for insightful commentary on what he calls the logic of Sidney's "syllogistic" plot, "Terentian Structure," 77–78.

4. See Myron Turner, "The Disfigured Face of Nature: Image and Metaphor in the Revised *Arcadia,*" *ELR* 2, no. 1 (Winter 1972): 116–35.

5. Sannazaro's creation of the Renaissance prose pastoral had consequences that he did not understand and that—given his commitment to the amoral lyricism of Theocritean pastoralism—he had no intention of exploiting. For his division of the pastoral romance into prose and poetry made possible the later ascendancy within sixteenth-century pastoral not only of prose, but of a tough-minded narrative style that writers like Gil Polo and Sidney could adapt more easily to prose than to poetry.

6. See John A. Galm, *Sidney's Arcadian Poems,* Institut für Englische Sprache und Literatur: Elizabethan and Renaissance Studies, no. 1 (Salzburg: Universität Salzburg, 1973), 16–22.

7. See Robert L. Montgomery, Jr., *Symmetry and Sense: The Poetry of Sir Philip Sidney* (Austin: Univ. of Texas Press, 1961), 9–47.

8. *Apology,* 140.

9. See Lanham, *The Old Arcadia,* on the "dialectical method" of Sidney's narrative, 327–31.

10. See John W. Cunliffe, "Italian Prototypes of the Masque and Dumb Show," *PMLA* 22 (1907): 140–56; E. K. Chambers, *The Elizabethan Stage,* 4 vols (Oxford: Clarendon Press, 1923), 1:185; and Marvin T. Herrick, *Italian Comedy in the Renaissance* (Urbana: University of Illinois Press, 1960), 26–59.

11. Antonfrancesco Grazzini, *La Strega,* ed. Michel Plaisance (Abbeville: Imprimerie F. Paillart, 1976), 55.

12. Herrick, *Italian Comedy,* 62.

13. See Thornton Shirley Graves, "The 'Act Time' in Elizabethan Theatres," *SP* 12, no. 3 (July 1915): 103–34.

14. Dieter Mehl, *The Elizabethan Dumb Show: The History of a Dramatic Convention* (London: Methuen, 1965), 17.

15. A variety of functions have been attributed to the eclogues by Sidney's critics. Mona Wilson in *Sir Philip Sidney* argues that their chief purpose is "to relieve the monotony of the narrative" (139); Spencer brings a different perspective to bear: Sidney "was not only educating himself, he was educating a whole generation" in styles of writing, "The Poetry of Sir Philip Sidney" (255); Ringler writes in his edition of the poems that they "set the tone and establish the themes that control the action of the main narrative" (xxxviii); Ford in "Philosophy, History" emphasizes their role in criticizing what he believes is "the increasing abnormality" of the princes' behavior (49); Galm's focus in *Sidney's Arcadian Poems* is similar: ". . . they provide criticism and guidelines for the interpretation of the action" (22); according to Lawry, they supply "a high Platonic overview of mortal toils, together with a hushed, sympathetic awareness of mortal griefs," *Sidney's Two* Arcadias (60); Dipple's major argument in "The 'Fore Conceit' of Sidney's Eclogues" is virtually identical: "Through their existence and world they teach a Neo-Platonic idea that will later supplant that basic indictment which is the moral end of the *Old Arcadia*" (14). In *A Map of* Arcadia, Davis has given the best account of the thematic function of the eclogues in his statement that ". . . the shepherd's world . . . [is] a kind of 'ocean' of possibility, where different views of man's nature, concerns, and goals are held in solution" (112). Rosenberg attributes to Spenser in *The Shepheardes Calendar* a similar kind of inclusiveness of literary styles and attitudes, *Oaten Reeds,* 62–63.

16. See Empson, *Some Versions of Pastoral*, 27.
17. See Lawry, *Sidney's Two* Arcadias, for an argument that the eclogues are organized in "five-step movements" (89).
18. See Ringler, ed., *The Poems of Sir Philip Sidney*, xxxviii–xl.

Chapter 5. Book One: The Divided Mind

1. Fortune may force Pyrocles to fall in love, but Pyrocles is responsible for his behavior as a lover. Perhaps it was Sidney's religious training that encouraged him to permit determinism and moral responsibility to coexist in the fiction as mutually supportive propositions.

2. The princes' debate has provoked most of the criticism of the first book. The earlier tendency among Sidney's critics was to see Musidorus as the clear "winner" in the dispute; Reinard Willem Zandvoort contends that his opinions are an expression of Sidney's "inmost conviction" (*Sidney's* Arcadia: *A Comparison Between the Two Versions* [Amsterdam: N. V. Swets & Zeitlinger, 1929], 150). This reading has been challenged in one instance by the argument that Pyrocles has the better of the two positions: "love has opened his spirit to a realm of feelings altogether inaccessible to Musidorus" (Rudenstine, *Sidney's Poetic Development*, 19). Kimbrough contends in *Sir Philip Sidney* that ". . . the narrator . . . keeps us from taking sides so that the immediate effect is comic and entertaining" (73). Most of Sidney's recent critics appear to agree that neither of the princes has a monopoly on the truth, and most would be suspicious, presumably, of Hamilton's claim in his *Sir Philip Sidney* that "the reader must attend to what is said, not to who says it or why" (140). For a recent "hard" reading of the scene (anti-Pyrocles), see Clifford Davidson, "Nature and Judgment in the *Old Arcadia*," *PLL* 6, no. 4 (Fall 1970): 348–65.

3. Pyrocles and Musidorus idealize their eroticism but one can find little evidence here or elsewhere for what Dipple calls their "enlarging and intensely personal neoplatonic desire for heavenly beauty" ("Metamorphosis in Sidney's *Arcadias*," *PQ* 50, no. 1 [January 1971]: 51).

4. The attack of the lion and the bear is usually interpreted as a symbol of the outbreak of disruptive passions in Arcadia. See, for example, Dipple's "Harmony and Pastoral. . . ," 323.

5. It may be more than a coincidence that the songs at the end of the first book of Gil Polo's *Diana Enamorada* are also concerned with the question of unreciprocated love. See also John P. Cutts, "More Manuscript Versions of Poems by Sidney," *ELN* 9, no. 1 (September 1971): 3–12; he supplies what is possibly a "lost" stanza from the poem, 6.

6. See Margaret E. Dana, "Heroic and Pastoral: Sidney's *Arcadia* as Masquerade," *CL* 25, no. 4 (Fall 1973): 308–20.

7. See Daniel Javitch, *Poetry and Courtliness in Renaissance England* (Princeton: Princeton Univ. Press, 1978), 80–82, for an interesting discussion of the relationship between pastoral and synecdoche.

8. Ringler argues that it is Lalus who "loses" the contest because Dorus is able to surpass him by introducing into the rhyme scheme complications that the shepherd is unable to follow (386); Rudenstine contends that it is Lalus who "wins" since Dorus first abandons complex *sdrucciola* rhymes for a simpler pattern (81). I do not believe that the eclogue contains clear evidence for deciding on a winner.

9. A similar point is made in Robert Eril Levine, *A Comparison of Sidney's* Old *and* New Arcadia, Institut für Englische Sprache und Literatur: Elizabethan and Renaissance Studies, no. 13 (Salzburg: Universität Salzburg, 1974), 21.

10. See Robert P. Miller, "Venus, Adonis, and the Horses," *ELH* 19, no. 4 (December 1952): 249–64.

11. For a different opinion, see Lanham, *The Old Arcadia*: "When Dicus comes to sing his song, one finally feels that he has hit upon a sane man . . ." (212); Marenco agrees, "Double Plot," 262, as does Davidson, "Nature and Judgment," 356.

12. Gil Polo, *Diana Enamorada*, 26; trans. Yong, 251–52: ". . . feares, cares, jealousies, changes, and other infinite passions. . . ." The final lines of Alcida's poetic attack on Cupid ("No es ciego Amor . . .") correspond almost exactly to the first stanza of Dicus's tirade (25:18–20):

> Porque es Amor mentira de poetas,
> sueño de locos, ídolo de vanos:
> mirad qué negro Dios el que adoramos.

13. As Davis points out, the eclogues have a special dimension in time because of their use of traditional literary materials, "since any present event is seen as the recurrence in a new form of an old event" (*A Map of* Arcadia, 112).

14. See Winfried Schleiner's fine article, "Differences of Theme and Structure of the Erona Episode in the *Old* and *New Arcadia*," *SP* 70, no. 4 (October 1973): 377–91.

15. Dipple, therefore, is only partially correct when writing that Histor's story ". . . is finally much more alarming that Dicus' more forthright . . . attack on Cupid" ("The 'Fore Conceit,' " 24).

16. For an informative comparison of Geron and Philisides' debate with its source, Sannazaro's second eclogue, see Rudenstine, *Sidney's Poetic Development*, 36–39. See also his helpful discussion of Philisides as a precursor of Astrophil, "The Drama of Philisides," chap. 7.

17. Plutarch, "On the Control of Anger," 461A; trans. p. 139.

18. See Walter R. Davis, "Actaeon in Arcadia," *SEL* 2, no. 1 (Winter 1962): 102–6, for information about the ways in which the Actaeon myth was utilized during the Renaissance.

19. Thomas Moffett, *Nobilis; or A View of the Life and Death of a Sidney, and Lessus Lugubris*, ed. Virgil B. Heltzel and Hoyt H. Hudson (San Marino: The Huntington Library, 1940), 74.

20. Davis comments upon Dorus's lyric: "It places man alone in direct contact with the forces governing the universe, which, even in grinding him down, allow him the heroic reward, the dignity of despair" (*A Map of* Arcadia, 99). Dorus is not despairing; he is juggling imponderables for the amusement of his beloved.

21. See also the narrator's comment: ". . . for so it seemed that love had purposed to make in those solitary woods a perfect demonstration of his unresistible force, to show that no desert place can avoid his dart" (49).

Chapter 6. Book Two: The Consequences of the Divided Mind

1. See Whitney, "Concerning Nature," 217.

2. See Lanham, *The Old Arcadia*, 268. We are also made aware that Cleophila's presence has helped to spark the rebellion.

3. Ringler, ed., *The Poems of Sir Philip Sidney*, xxxix.

4. See Ford on the role of structural parallels in encouraging "philosophical analysis of a poetic action" ("Philosophy, History," 50).

5. Plutarch "On Moral Virtue" 447B; trans. pp. 55–57.

6. Lanham is mistaken to represent this conclusion as a mere "orthodox injunction": his remark dismisses without explaining (*The Old Arcadia*, 219). McCoy writes about the concluding lines: "The brief glimpse of the hereafter reveals only the cold stasis of death—the 'stark and dead congealment' that debate was intended to prevent" (*Sir Philip Sidney*, 51).

7. Dipple has a different view. She argues that the poem "does not touch our impression of Dorus' . . . songs or viewpoint" ("The 'Fore Conceit,' " 31).

8. Ringler, ed., *The Poems of Sir Philip Sidney*, 400.

9. The debate between Plangus and Boulon is also reminiscent of the dispute in Barclay's first *Eclogue* between Cornix, who questions God's justice, and Coridon, who reassures him of the beneficence of the divine plan; see l. 213–87.

10. I am in agreement with Rudenstine here, *Sidney's Poetic Development*, 40. See also Connell, *Sir Philip Sidney*, 40–41.

11. As Dipple writes, the princes ". . . have no understanding of or participation in the multiple destructive passions that all of Asia shows them" ("The 'Fore Conceit,' " 31).

12. "Dialogue d'un amoreux et d'Echo," in *Poésies françaises et latines de Joachim Du Bellay*, ed. E. Courbet, 2 vols. (Paris: Garnier, 1918), 1:13, 9.

13. Galm's point is a good one: "reason is finally reduced to the remote and ineffectual reply of [an] echo in Philisides' poem," (*Sidney's Arcadian Poems*, 122).

14. See Poggioli, *Oaten Flute*, 183–93.

Chapter 7. Book Three: Contentment and Justice

1. Davis, "Narrative Methods in Sidney's *Old Arcadia*," *SEL* 18, no. 1 (Winter 1978): 19.

2. My reading of this scene is close to Hamilton's: "the narrator shares the passion—and so then the reader—by feeling it with Musidorus" (39).

3. Davis, "Actaeon in Arcadia," 109.

4. See Lanham: "One cannot belittle the style of this scene. It is subtle, amusing, and touching" (*The Old Arcadia*, 283).

5. See Dorothy Jones, "Sidney's Erotic Pen: An Interpretation of One of the *Arcadia* Poems," *JEGP* 73, no. 1 (January 1974): 32–47.

6. Gil Polo, *Diana Enamorada*, 205; trans. Yong, 377.

7. Ibid., 225; trans. Yong, 390.

8. See Dipple, "The 'Fore Conceit,' " 34, and Galm, *Sidney's Arcadian Poems*, 151–82, for further emphasis on the third eclogues' moral criticism of the princes.

9. Hamilton goes even farther in arguing that ". . . the joyous marriage of the shepherds deepens our sympathy for the princes" (*Sir Philip Sidney*, 67)—maybe a bit too far.

10. *The Garden of Cyrus*, in *The Prose of Sir Thomas Browne*, ed. Norman J. Endicott (New York: W. W. Norton, 1967), 339.

11. Alastair Fowler, *Triumphall Forms: Structural Patterns in Elizabethan Poetry* (Cambridge: University Press, 1970), 148; see also Christopher Butler, "Numerological Thought," in *Silent Poetry: Essays in Numerological Analysis*, ed. Alastair Fowler (London: Routledge & Kegan Paul, 1970), 1–31.

12. This is one of the first examples of the epithalamic genre in English and one of the best of Sidney's early poems. It is by no means without precedent in the pastoral

tradition. Theocritus introduced the epithalamium into a bucolic context in *Idyll* 18, a poem on the wedding of Menelaus and Helen, and Gil Polo incorporated it into the pastoral romance in a song that provided Sidney with a partial model for his own. See Virginia Tufte, *The Poetry of Marriage: The Epithalamium in Europe and Its Development in England* (Los Angeles: Tinnon Brown, 1970), 152–56.

13. Dipple makes a similar point ("The 'Fore Conceit,'" 35).

14. Gil Polo, *Diana Enamorada*, 85; trans. Yong, 296.

15. Charles Muscatine, *Chaucer and the French Tradition* (Berkeley and Los Angeles: Univ. of California Press, 1957, 1969), 61.

16. See J. G. Nichols, *The Poetry of Sir Philip Sidney: An Interpretation in the Context of his Life and Times* (New York: Barnes & Noble, 1974), 3; for splendid criticism of Gynecia, see also Lindheim, *The Structures*, 54.

17. *Apology*, 106.

18. Sir Thomas Browne, *Garden of Cyrus*, 338. See also Alastair Fowler, *Spenser and the Numbers of Time* (New York: Barnes & Noble, 1964), 34–47.

19. Ringler, ed., *The Poems of Sir Philip Sidney*, 412–15.

20. Aristotle, *The Nicomachean Ethics*, trans. H. Rackham (Cambridge, Mass.: Harvard Univ. Press; London: William Heinemann, 1926, 1968), 8.10.5–6; trans. p. 493.

21. Aristotle *Ethics* 8. 12. 8; trans p. 503.

22. Galm discovered that the beast fable has a source in Samuel, but he does not probe the implications of that fact, *Sidney's Arcadian Poems*, 221–22.

23. This interpretation is by no means unique; see Ringler, ed., *The Poems of Sir Philip Sidney*, 412–15. There has been a great deal of discussion about the meaning of the final lines of the fable in which the beasts are told to "know your strengths and then you shall do well" (259, 16). Ringler is right in arguing that this is not a poem about rebellion, even though it has been frequently treated as such. For the best discussions of Sidney's "theory" of rebellion, see Fritz Caspari, *Humanism and the Social Order in Tudor England* (Chicago: Univ. of Chicago Press, 1954), 157–75; and Ernest William Talbert, *The Problem of Order: Elizabethan Political Commonplaces and an Example of Shakespeare's Art* (Chapel Hill: Univ. of North Carolina Press, 1962), 92–117. Sidney sanctioned rebellion only in a limited number of circumstances—for instance, in cases of gross tyrannical behavior—and apparently only when it was led by capable members of an aristocracy. See also William Dinsmore Briggs, "Political Ideas in Sidney's *Arcadia*," *SP* 28, no. 2 (April 1931): 137–61, and an unconvincing study by Irving Ribner, "Sir Philip Sidney on Civil Insurrection," *JHI* 13, no. 2 (April 1952): 257–65. For a more recent and more helpful reading of the beast fable as a poem "about repression and the restriction of free political commentary," see Annabel M. Patterson, "'Under . . . Pretty Tales': Intention in Sidney's *Arcadia*," *SLI* 15, no. 1 (Spring 1982): 17.

24. Dipple argues by contrast that the marriage ". . . is not typical of the real pastoral experience" ("The 'Fore Conceit,'" 37).

Chapter 8. Book Four: "Discontentation" and Injustice

1. See Lawry's argument that "The ending . . . demands Basilius" (*Sidney's Two Arcadias*, 137).

2. See Davis, *A Map of* Arcadia, 80, and Danby, *Poets on Fortune's Hill*, 56.

3. See, for instance, Philippe de Mornay, *A Woorke Concerning the Trewnesse of the Christian Religion*, trans. Sir Philip Sidney [?] and Arthur Golding (Delmar, N.Y.:

Scholars' Facsimiles & Reprints, 1976), 271. He quotes with approval Epictetus's praise of suicide without actually sanctioning it.

4. As Nancy R. Lindheim argues, the scene offers "no victory" for either Pyrocles or Philoclea, "Vision, Revision, and the 1593 Text of the *Arcadia*," *ELR* 2, no. 1 (Winter 1972): 136–47. A similar argument appears in Paul D. Green, " 'Doors to the House of Death': The Treatment of Suicide in Sidney's *Arcadia*," *SCJ* 10, no. 3 (Fall 1979): 17–27. By far the most interesting and sophisticated reading of this scene appears in Myron Turner, " 'Disguised Passion' and the Psychology of Suicide in Sidney's *Old Arcadia*," *PLL* 15, no. 1 (Winter 1979): 17–37. He focuses on the complex psychological transformation in Pyrocles, from shame at the prospect of being dishonored in Philoclea's eyes to the achievement of what Turner rightly calls a "towering tranquillity" (37).

5. At the outset of Virgil's *Eclogue* 9, Moeris laments:

> O Lycida, vivi pervenimus, advena nostri
> (quod nunquam veriti sumus) ut possessor agelli
> diceret: 'haec mea sunt; veteres migrate coloni.'
> nunc victi, tristes, quoniam fors omnia versat,
> hos illi (quod nec vertat bene) mittimus haedos.
>
> (9.2–6)

The tone and dramatic situation are similar.

6. Empson's study of "Ye goat-herd gods" appears in *Seven Types of Ambiguity* (London: Chatto and Windus 1930, 1949), 34–38; see Kalstone, *Sidney's Poetry*, 71–83. Other helpful discussions of the sestina appear in: Spencer, "The Poetry of Sir Philip Sidney," 251–58; Davis, *A Map of* Arcadia, 84–92; Dipple, "The 'Fore-Conceit,' " 40–46; Terry Comito's brilliant article, "The Lady in a Landscape and the Poetics of Elizabethan Pastoral," *UTQ* 41, no. 3 (Spring 1972): 200–218; and Alastair Fowler, *Conceitful Thought: The Interpretation of English Renaissance Poems* (Edinburgh: Edinburgh Univ. Press, 1975), 39–51. See also Robert E. Stillman, "Poetry and Justice in Sidney's 'Ye goat-herd gods'," *SEL* 22, no. 1 (Winter 1982): 39–50.

7. For a different view, see Katherine Duncan-Jones, "Sidney's Urania," *RES*, n. s., 17, no. 66 (May 1966): 123–32. See also Lily B. Campbell, "The Christian Muse," *HLB* 8 (October 1935): 29–70.

8. Duncan-Jones is the first critic to have mentioned Corinthians as a possible source for Sidney's "Ye goat-herd gods," "Sidney's Urania," 124–25. See also Heb. 12: 1.

9. *Apology*, 116.

10. Gil Polo, *Diana Enamorada*, 60; trans. Yong, 277.

11. Ibid., 62; trans. Yong, 278–79.

12. In an interesting and suggestive chapter on "Sestina Structure in *Ye Goatherd Gods*" [*Conceitful Thought*], Fowler does his best to distinguish between the characters of Strephon and Klaius, but the result seems to be less clarity, not more, 35–58. Fowler's approach to the poem has recently been extended farther by Gary L. Litt, in "Characterization and Rhetoric in Sidney's 'Ye Goatherd Gods,' " *SLI* 11, no. 1 (Spring 1978): 115–24.

13. Duncan-Jones, "Sidney in Samothea," 127.

14. Erwin Panofsky, *Studies in Iconology: Humanistic Themes in the Art of the Renaissance* (London, 1939; reprint, New York: Harper and Row, 1972), 142.

15. Ovid *Metamorphoses* 1. 149–50; trans. 1:13.

16. Frances A. Yates, *Astraea: The Imperial Theme in the Sixteenth Century* (London and Boston: Routledge & Kegan Paul, 1975), 32–33. For the frontispiece of Riccoli's astrolog-

ical treatise, *Almagestum novum* (1651), containing a picture of Astraea as Urania, see S. K. Heninger, Jr., *The Cosmographical Glass: Renaissance Diagrams of the Universe* (San Marino, Cal.: The Huntington Library, 1977), 67.

17. My paraphrase of Silvestris comes from a quotation in Richard Hamilton Green's "Alan of Lille's *De Planctu Naturae,*" *Speculum* 31 (October 1956): 668.

18. Fowler (*Conceitful Thought,* 47) identifies another apocalyptic passage in "Ye goatherd gods," comparing Strephon's verse, "The nightingales do learn of owls their music," to Isa. 34:14: "the satyr shall cry to his fellow; the screech owl also shall rest there, and find for herself a place of rest." The sestina abounds in biblically resonant imagery; see also Job 11:17; Jer. 21:13–14; Amos 5:8; Ezek. 31:8. For a Christian reading of the poem, see Weiner, *Poetics of Protestantism,* 139–42.

In this context, it is important to remember that mountains and valleys were traditionally interpreted during the Renaissance as signs of the "decay of nature." As Marjorie Hope Nicolson writes, the "lumps and warts" disfiguring the landscape's face were Renaissance man's best proof that "the innocent earth has been forced to bear man's curse. Nature has decayed with man, and the world degenerates and grows worse every day" (*Mountain Gloom and Mountain Glory: The Development of the Aesthetics of the Infinite* [Ithaca: Cornell Univ. Press, 1959], 104). Strephon and Klaius's exile among "monstrous mountains" is, therefore, one more sign of their fallen condition and one more indication of their need for everlasting justice.

19. This is a device in which Sidney may have become interested by reading another dialogue between Berardo and Tauriso included at the end of Gil Polo's third book, "Tauriso, el fresco viento," 110.

20. Katherine Duncan-Jones, "Sidney in Samothea: A Forgotten National Myth," *RES,* n.s., 25, no. 98 (May 1974): 174–77. See also W. L. Godshalk, "A Return to Sidney's Samothea," *RES,* n.s., 29, no. 115 (August 1978): 325–26.

21. *Holinshed's Chronicles of England, Scotland, and Ireland,* 6 vols. (London: J. Johnson, et al., 1807–08). 1: 429.

22. *Holinshed's Chronicles,* 1: 432.

23. Duncan-Jones, "Sidney in Samothea," 174.

24. The political satire contained in the eclogues of Petrarch and the Christian pastoralists suggests a modification of this claim, but I do not believe that it establishes a real precedent for Sidney's reversal of the usual political pattern of the pastoral romance.

25. Christine Rees, "Some Seventeenth-Century Versions of the Judgment of Paris," *N&Q,* n.s., 24, no. 3 (May–June 1977): 197–200.

26. Quoted in J. A. Van Dorsten, *Poets, Patrons, and Professors: Sir Philip Sidney, Daniel Rogers, and the Leiden Humanists* (London: Oxford Univ. Press; Leiden: University Press, 1962), 64.

27. Galm in *Sidney's Arcadian Poems* discusses the various candidates who have been proposed for Mira (his favorite is Queen Elizabeth), 218. See also Dennis Moore, "Philisides and Mira: Autobiographical Allegory in the *Old Arcadia,*" *Spenser Studies* 3 (1982): 125–37. Moore makes a plausible case for reading the Mira poems as an extended complaint by Sidney against the injustices he has received from Elizabeth. However, the possibility that Sidney may have represented in a single fictional character (Mira) frustrations both sexual and political needs to be considered seriously. There is no conclusive evidence as to whom Mira represents; for an extended discussion of these issues, see Dennis Moore, *The Politics of Spenser's* Complaints *and Sidney's* Philisides Poems, Institut für Anglistik und Amerikanistik: Elizabethan & Renaissance Studies, no. 101 (Salzburg: Universität Salzburg, 1982), 82–125.

28. Poggioli, *Oaten Flute*, 78. See also Mallette's discussion of competing traditions of the pastoral elegy, *Spenser, Milton, and Renaissance Pastoral*, 116–24.

29. Dipple draws a distinction between the "actual" and the "symbolic" Basilius in "The 'Fore-Conceit,'" 40.

30. *Apology*, 116.

Chapter 9. Nature and Art in *The Old Arcadia*

1. As Madeleine Doran points out: "To Horace's two ends of poetry, to profit and to delight, many renaissance critics added a third, to move. Moving might be thought of as an inevitable accompaniment of the other ends. . . . It came, apparently, from Cicero's formula for oratory: *docere, delectare, permovere,* and may be found in Pontano, Lionardi, Scaliger, Minturno, Sidney, and Jonson" (*Endeavors of Art: A Study of Form in Elizabethan Drama* [Madison, Milwaukee and London: Univ. of Wisconsin Press, 1954], 27). See also Rudenstine: ". . . persuasion lies at the heart of Sidney's entire theory of poetry," (*Sidney's Poetic Development*, 152).

My concern with the multiple functions of Sidney's art (persuasive, didactic, and therapeutic) stands in contrast to the approach recently adopted by Annabel Patterson, who chooses to limit the "intention" of Sidney's romance to "indirect didacticism"—what she later terms "socio-political commentary" (9, 15).

2. Virgil *Eclogues* 8.69, trans. p. 61; Sannazaro, *Arcadia and Piscatorial Eclogues*, 67, trans., 89. I do not mean to suggest that Sidney is somehow unique among pastoralists in attending to the limitations and dangers of poetry. He is not. But the fact that it is impossible to find in *The Old Arcadia* even a single character who voices large claims for the art is some measure of the unusual degree of his skepticism.

3. It has long been recognized that Sidney's concerns about the nature and function of poetry extend into his fictional works. Penny Pickett has written about *The Lady of May* as a study in rhetoric, "Sidney's Use of *Phaedrus* in *The Lady of May*," *SEL* 16, no. 1 (Winter 1976): 33–50. *Astrophil and Stella* has been used to examine Sidney's poetics by numbers of critics from Hallett Smith to Neil Rudenstine to Jacqueline T. Miller in her recent article, "'Love Doth Hold My Hand': Writing and Wooing in the Sonnets of Sidney and Spenser," *ELH* 46, no. 4 (Winter 1979): 541–58. For a study of contrasting ideas about poetry in Sidney's Psalms, see Gary F. Waller, "'This Matching of Contraries': Calvinism and Courtly Philosophy in the Sidney Psalms" *ES* 55, no. 1 (February 1974): 22–31. However, there has been very little recognition of the degree to which Sidney interests his readers in problems of poetry and the poetic imagination in *The Old Arcadia*. See Comito as one exception to this rule. See also Michael McCanles, who argues that Sidney thematizes the problem of reading in *The Old Arcadia* by focusing "on Basilius' failure as an interpreter of texts," in "Oracular Prediction and the Fore-Conceit of Sidney's *Arcadia*," *ELH* 50, no. 2 (Summer 1983): 238. If McCanles is right about this matter, he is less cautious to conclude: "If for Basilius what is at issue is how to conduct his own life, for the reader it is how to conduct his reading of Sidney's text" (238). No such easy distinction can be made in *The Old Arcadia* between a knowledge about how to read and a knowledge about how to live: Sidney makes one activity fully dependent upon the other.

4. Empson, *English Pastoral Poetry*, 136.

5. See Dipple, "Harmony and Pastoral," 316–18.

6. *Apology*, 101.

7. Basilius's behavior at the end of the second book supplies another pointed illus-

tration of self-love. When he misinterprets the oracle for the second time, we are told: "such is the selfness of affection that, because his mind ran wholly upon Cleophila, he thought the gods in their oracles did mind nothing but her" (133–34).

8. *Apology*, 95. For a very different discussion of self-love in the *Apology*, see Margaret W. Ferguson, "Sidney's *A Defence of Poetry*: A Retrial," *Boundary 2* 7, no. 2 (Winter 1979): 61–95. See also Margaret W. Ferguson, *Trials of Desire: Renaissance Defences of Poetry* (New Haven and London: Yale Univ. Press, 1983), 137–62.

According to Melanchthon (whose Protestantism was a major influence on Sidney), Adam's sin was essentially a sin of self-love: "Thus it happens that the soul being without celestial light and life is in darkness. As a result, it most ardently loves itself, seeks its own desires and wishes nothing but carnal things. . . . It cannot but be true that a creature whom the love of God has not absorbed, loves itself in the highest degree" (The Loci Communes *of Philip Melanchthon,* trans. Charles Leander Hill [Boston: Meador Publishing, 1944], 82–83). Poetry that extends from self-love, far from helping to raise humanity from its decayed state, only further confirms its fallen condition.

9. Geron establishes the Arcadian eclogues' strongest link between passion and fiction when he warns Philisides:

> Passion bears high when puffing wit doth blow,
> But is indeed a toy; if not a toy,
> True cause of ills, and cause of causeless woe.
> If once thou mayst that fancy gloss destroy
> Within thyself, thou soon wilt be ashamed
> To be a player of thine own annoy.
>
> (75, 13–18)

By describing Philisides' devices as a "fancy gloss," he recalls Dicus's criticism of the poets' "glosses of deceits" (65, 12).

10. Sidney frequently returns to the same point in connection with Basilius. See the Duke as minor romantic bard, 97.

11. Virgil *Eclogues* 10.8, trans. p. 71; Sannazaro, *Arcadia and Piscatorial Eclogues,* 61, trans., 83.

12. As most critics now agree, Elizabeth made the wrong decision at the end of *The Lady of May* in selecting Espilus rather than Therion as the winner in the dispute—much to Sidney's frustration. See Stephen Orgel, *The Jonsonian Masque* (Cambridge, Mass.: Harvard Univ. Press, 1965), 44–57 and Kalstone, *Sidney's Poetry,* 42–47. From personal experience, Sidney knew how difficult it is to persuade an audience (particularly a royal audience) to do the right thing at the right time. The freedom that the poet enjoys in manipulating the characters of his fictional world is far less available in his dealings with the recalcitrant beings of an intractable historical reality.

13. Connell also comments on the relationship between the lover and the poet in Sidney's fictions, *Sir Philip Sidney,* 45.

14. *Apology*, 123.

15. See Poggioli, *Oaten Flute,* 15.

16. Davidson argues, by contrast: ". . . the theater is generally merely a symbol for the world of the senses" ("Nature and Judgment," 353). "Merely" is a dangerously restrictive word to apply to any of Sidney's symbols. See also Frances A. Yates, *Theatre of the World* (Chicago: Univ. of Chicago Press, 1969), 58, 162–68.

17. Ovid *Metamorphoses* 10.86–125; *The Faerie Queene,* 1.1.8–9; Sannazaro's Prologue.

18. Quoted by Edgar Wind in *Pagan Mysteries in the Renaissance* (1958; reprint, New York: Barnes & Noble, 1968), 88–89.

19. See Long, *Hellenistic Philosophy*, 146.//
20. See Berger, "The Renaissance Imagination," 40.
21. *Apology*, 99–100.
22. Ibid., 100.
23. Ibid., 100. By emphasizing the importance of the poet's effort to reform the will, thereby highlighting the psychological dimensions of the art, I do not wish to deny that the ultimate end of knowledge remains for Sidney "well-doing and not . . . well-knowing only" (104). I concentrate on the therapeutic functions of Sidney's art, as the *Apology* does, because reforming the will is logically prior to virtuous action, and virtuous action depends upon the poet's success in persuading the will to goodness.
24. *Apology*, 101.
25. Ibid.
26. Ibid.
27. St. Thomas Aquinas, *Summa Theologiae*, 23 vols. (Cambridge: Blackfriars; New York: McGraw Hill, 1964–76), Ia.100.1.
28. *Lectures on Genesis*, in *Luther's Works*, ed. Jaroslav Pelikan and trans. George V. Schick, 24 vols. (Saint Louis: Concordia, 1958), 1:62. See also *What Luther Says: An Anthology*, ed Ewald M. Plass, 3 vols. (Saint Louis: Concordia, 1959), 2:877.
29. Jean Calvin, *Institutes of the Christian Religion*, ed. John T. McNeill and trans. Ford Lewis Battles, 2 vols. (Philadelphia: Westminster Press, 1960), 1:246, 188.
30. Andraeus Rivetus, *Theologicae et Scholasticae Exercitationes CXC In Genesin* (Lugduni Batavorum: Bonaventurae & Abrahami Elzevir, 1633), 32.
31. Rivetus, *Theologicae et Scholasticae Exercitationes*, 34.
32. *Apology*, 101. As D. H. Craig demonstrates so well, Sidney's "ideas about the poet are incompatible with Calvinism . . ." ("A Hybrid Growth: Sidney's Theory of Poetry in *An Apology for Poetry*," *ELR* 10, no. 2 [Spring 1980]: 190). Craig's conclusion convincingly undermines the central thesis of Weiner's recent study of Sidney, which represents his fictions as the product of a "Protestant" (and specifically Calvinistic) poetics. A second recent article on the *Apology* that is useful in clarifying the diverse intellectual traditions of Sidney's treatise is John C. Ulreich, Jr.'s "'The Poets Only Deliver': Sidney's Conception of Mimesis," *SLI* 15, no. 1 (Spring 1982): 67–84.
33. In this respect, I agree with Connell that a "key element" in Sidney's thought is "an ability to encompass and balance contradictions," (5). As A. Leigh DeNeef argues, in Sidney's view "the real lesson of poetry is not the virtue itself, whether of lover, prince, or friend, but the 'skill' by which that virtue is put into practice . . ." ("Rereading Sidney's *Apology*," *JMRS* 10, no. 2 [Fall 1980]: 162).
34. Polybius 4.20.3–7; trans. 2:349.
35. Plutarch "On Tranquillity of Mind" 474A–B; trans. pp. 219–21. There is nothing unusual about Plutarch's description of *concordia discors* as a therapeutic device. See Leo Spitzer, *Classical and Christian Ideas of World Harmony: Prolegomena to an Interpretation of the Word "Stimmung"* (Baltimore: Johns Hopkins Press, 1963), 16, 67. What is unusual about Plutarch's description is that he represents concord as a means that the individual can use to protect himself against misfortune.
36. Plato, *The Republic*, trans. Desmond Lee, 2d ed. (Baltimore: Penguin Books, 1974), 444d–444e; trans. p. 222.
37. Plato *Republic* 443c–444a; trans. p. 221.
38. Feuillerat, ed., *Complete Works of Sir Philip Sidney*, 3:133.
39. *The Poems of Sir John Davies*, ed. Robert Krueger (Oxford: Clarendon Press, 1975). "Orchestra. Or a Poeme of Dauncing," 111, st. 77. See Tonkin, *Spenser's Courteous Pastoral*, 188, 238–80.

40. Davies, *Poems of Sir John Davies*, 119, st. 110.

41. When Scudamour discovers Amoret in the temple of Venus, he also finds Concord, who "to afflicted minds sweet rest and quiet sends" (*FQ* 4.10.34).

42. Geron's lines are paralleled in the Christian lyric by Felix's advice to Faustus in Googe's sixth eclogue; see 53–54.

43. Virgil *Eclogues* 9.11–13; trans. pp. 66–67.

44. Ibid., 9.63–65; trans. pp. 70–71.

45. Fowler points to the division in Sidney's end-words between "features of the natural landscape" and "temporal measure," but he does not account for the unique status of "music" (*Conceitful Thought*, 43).

46. See Spencer's argument that the vision of Urania "clarifies and relieves the despairing darkness by explaining its cause" ("The Poetry of Sir Philip Sidney," 265). This reading finds more support in the sestina's symbolic form than Kalstone's emphasis upon the speaker's unrelenting despair, *Sidney's Poetry*, 77–83.

47. See Dipple, "The 'Fore Conceit' of Sidney's Eclogues," 42–43.

48. See Rosalie Colie, *Paradoxica Epidemica: The Renaissance Tradition of Paradox* (Princeton: Princeton Univ. Press, 1966), on the oxymoron as a form of *concordia discors*, 32.

49. Davis argues that Mornay's *A Woorke Concerning the Trewnesse of the Christian Religion* is "the immediate source of the entire prison scene" (*A Map of* Arcadia, 63). The date of its publication makes that claim unlikely in spite of Mornay's previous visit to England. A more probable "source" for these events might be Mornay's earlier, translated treatise, *The Defense of Death* (1577). In both instances, Mornay discusses concepts of mortality for the specifically announced purpose of discovering how much reason can find out unaided by faith and Christian revelation. Davis himself cites chapter 15 in the later work as the source of Sidney's prison scene, a chapter entirely concerned with "pagan" discussions of death. There is nothing exclusively Christian about the contents of the princes' debate.

50. Plutarch "On Tranquillity of Mind" 476A; trans. p. 233.

51. Wolff, *The Greek Romances*, 177, 181–89.

52. See Peter Lindenbaum, "Sidney's *Arcadia*: The Endings of the Three Versions," *HLQ* 34, no. 3 (May 1971): 205–18. With typical unconcern for Sidney's affective strategies, Lindenbaum argues that in stretching the truth here Pyrocles "threatens to become an outright villain" (209).

53. Davis was the first to describe these accounts as fictions. He does so, however, for the purpose of investigating Sidney's narrative strategy rather than the main themes of poetry and justice. See "Narrative Methods in Sidney's *Old Arcadia*," 30–33. Dana describes these mini-dramas as rival "theories" of the romance in "The Providential Plot," 51.

54. Lanham argues, by contrast, that: "It is only with Philanax that the reader can fully sympathize" (*The Old Arcadia*, 227).

55. Rudenstine seems to be guilty of such sentimentality when he argues that Euarchus's justice "now begins to triumph only at the expense of joy and life itself" (44). See also Myron Turner on Euarchus's failure to adopt a "relativistic attitude" toward reason in "Distance and Astonishment in the Old *Arcadia*: A Study of Sidney's Psychology," *TSLL* 20, no. 3 (Fall 1978): 325. It is impossible to escape the conclusion that the king's sentences are *right*—although they are not necessarily *just*.

56. See Dana: "Though all have erred in some degree, they certainly merit nothing like this" ("The Providential Plot," 52).

57. Sidney's trial is modeled in large part, as has long been recognized, on the ending of Heliodorus's *An Aethiopian Romance*.

58. See Dana, "The Providential Plot," 55–56.

59. *Apology*, 101.

60. Connell is the first critic to point out Sidney's conjunction of art and nature in this episode, although she sentimentalizes the tale somewhat by arguing that its purpose is to show the artist's power "to disarm those who would resist beauty . . ." (*Sir Philip Sidney*, 36). Two recent critics who also comment upon Sidney's manipulation of the readers' divided responses during the trial scene are Ann W. Astell in "Sidney's Didactic Method in *The Old Arcadia*," SEL 24, no. 1 (Winter 1984): 46–51 and Nancy Lindheim, *The Structures of Sidney's* Arcadia, 158.

Works Cited

Alexander, Sir William. *Anacrisis* (1634?). In *Critical Essays of the Seventeenth Century*, edited by J. E. Spingarn. 3 vols. Bloomington and London: Indiana Univ. Press, 1968.

Alpers, Paul. "The Eclogue Tradition and the Nature of Pastoralism." CE 34, no. 3 (December 1972): 352–71.

———. *The Singer of the Eclogues: A Study of Virgilian Pastoral*. Berkeley: Univ. of California Press, 1979.

———. "What is Pastoral?" *Critical Inquiry* 8, no. 3 (Spring 1982): 437–60.

Anderson, Judith H. " 'Come, let's away to prison': Fortune and Freedom in *The Faerie Queene*, Book VI." *Journal of Narrative Technique* 2, no. 2 (May 1972): 133–37.

Aquinas, St. Thomas. *Summa Theologiae*. 23 vols. Cambridge: Blackfriars; New York: McGraw-Hill, 1964–76.

Aristotle. *The Nicomachean Ethics*. Translated by H. Rackham. Cambridge, Mass.: Harvard Univ. Press; London: William Heinemann, 1926, 1968.

Armstrong, Elizabeth. "Lucretius, Seneca, Natural Law." In *Ronsard and the Age of Gold*, 121–34. Cambridge: The University Press, 1968.

Astell, Ann W. "Sidney's Didactic Method in *The Old Arcadia*." *SEL* 24, no. 1 (Winter 1984): 39–51.

Babut, Daniel. *Plutarch et le stoïcisme*. Paris: Presses universitaires de France, 1969.

Baker, Ernest A. *The History of the English Novel*. 10 vols. London: H. F. & G. Witherby, 1924–39.

Barclay, Alexander. *The Eclogues of Alexander Barclay*. Edited by Beatrice White. Early English Text Society, o.s., vol. 175. London: Oxford Univ. Press, 1928.

Barnfield, Richard. *The Affectionate Shepherd* (1594). Edited by James O. Halliwell. Early English Poetry, vol. 20. London: The Percy Society, 1845.

Barrow, R. H. *Plutarch and his Times*. Bloomington: Indiana Univ. Press, 1967.

Berger, Harry Jr. "The Renaissance Imagination: Second World and Green World." *Centennial Review* 9, no. 1 (Winter 1965): 36–78.

Briggs, William Dinsmore. "Political Ideas in Sidney's *Arcadia*." *SP* 28, no. 2 (April 1931): 137–61.

Bromberg, Rachel. *Three Pastoral Novels.* Brooklyn: Postar Press, 1970.

Brown, James Neil. "Elizabethan Pastoralism and Renaissance Platonism." *AUMLA* 44 (November 1975): 247–67.

Browne, Sir Thomas. *The Garden of Cyrus.* In *The Prose of Sir Thomas Browne,* edited by Norman J. Endicott. New York: W. W. Norton, 1967.

Browne, William. *The Poems of William Browne of Tavistock.* Edited by Gordon Goodwin. 2 vols. London: G. Routledge, 1894.

Bush, Douglas. *Prefaces to Renaissance Literature.* Cambridge, Mass.: Harvard Univ. Press, 1965.

Butler, Christopher. "Numerological Thought." In *Silent Poetry: Essays in Numerological Analysis,* edited by Alastair Fowler, 1–31. London: Routledge & Kegan Paul, 1970.

Calvin, Jean. *Institutes of the Christian Religion.* Edited by John T. McNeill and translated by Ford Lewis Battles. 2 vols. Philadelphia: Westminster Press, 1960.

Campbell, Lily B. "The Christian Muse." *HLB* 8 (October 1935): 29–70.

Carew, Richard. *The Excellency of the English Tongue* (ca. 1595–96). In *Elizabethan Critical Essays,* edited by G. Gregory Smith, 2 vols. Oxford: Clarendon Press, 1904).

Caspari, Fritz. *Humanism and the Social Order in Tudor England.* Chicago: Univ. of Chicago Press, 1954.

Chalifour, Clark L. "Sir Philip Sidney's *Old Arcadia* as a Terentian Comedy." *SEL* 16, no. 1 (Winter 1976): 51–63.

Chambers, E. K. *The Elizabethan Stage.* 4 vols. Oxford: Clarendon Press, 1923.

Chaudhuri, Sukanta. "The Eclogues in Sidney's *New Arcadia.*" *RES,* n.s., 35, no. 138 (May 1984): 185–202.

Cicero. *De Officiis.* Translated by Walter Miller. Cambridge, Mass.: Harvard Univ. Press; London: William Heinemann, 1913, 1961.

Colie, Rosalie. *Paradoxica Epidemica: The Renaissance Tradition of Paradox.* Princeton: Princeton Univ. Press, 1966.

Collingwood, R. G. *The Idea of Nature.* Oxford: Clarendon Press, 1945.

Collins, Thomas. *The Teares of Love: or Cupids Progresse.* London: G. Purslowe, 1615. STC 5567.

Comito, Terry. "The Lady in a Landscape and the Poetics of Elizabethan Pastoral." *UTQ* 41, no. 3 (Spring 1972): 200–218.

Congleton, James E. *Theories of Pastoral Poetry in England, 1684–1798.* Gainesville: Univ. of Florida Press, 1952.

Connell, Dorothy. *Sir Philip Sidney: The Maker's Mind.* Oxford: Clarendon Press, 1977.

Cooper, Helen. *Pastoral: Medieval into Renaissance.* Ipswich: D. S. Brewer; Totowa, N.J.: Rowman and Littlefield, 1977.

Craig, D. H. "A Hybrid Growth: Sidney's Theory of Poetry in *An Apology for Poetry.*" *ELR* 10, no. 2 (Spring 1980): 183–201.

Cullen, Patrick. *Spenser, Marvell, and Renaissance Pastoral.* Cambridge, Mass.: Harvard Univ. Press, 1970.

Culp, Dorothy Woodward. "Courtesy and Fortune's Chance in Book 6 of *The Faerie Queene.*" *MP* 68, no. 3 (February 1971): 254–59.

Cunliffe, John W. "Italian Prototypes of the Masque and Dumb Show." *PMLA* 22 (1907): 140–56.

Cutts, John P. "More Manuscript Versions of Poems by Sidney." *ELN* 9, no. 1 (September 1971): 3–12.

Dana, Margaret E. "Heroic and Pastoral: Sidney's *Arcadia* as Masquerade." *CL* 25, no. 4 (Fall 1973): 308–20.

———. "The Providential Plot of the *Old Arcadia.*" *SEL* 17, no. 1 (Winter 1977): 39–57.

Danby, John F. *Poets on Fortune's Hill: Studies in Sidney, Shakespeare, Beaumont and Fletcher.* London: Faber and Faber, 1952. Rev. title, *Elizabethan and Jacobean Poets,* 1964.

———. *Shakespeare's Doctrine of Nature: A Study of* King Lear. London: Faber and Faber, 1949.

Davidson, Clifford. "Nature and Judgment in the *Old Arcadia.*" *PLL* 6, no. 4 (Fall 1970): 348–65.

Davies, Sir John. *The Poems of Sir John Davies.* Edited by Robert Krueger. Oxford: Clarendon Press, 1975.

Davis, Walter R. "Actaeon in Arcadia." *SEL* 2, no. 1 (Winter 1962): 95–110.

———. *Idea and Act in Elizabethan Fiction.* Princeton: Princeton Univ. Press, 1969.

———. *A Map of* Arcadia: *Sidney's Romance in its Tradition.* In Richard A. Lanham and Walter R. Davis, *Sidney's* Arcadia. New Haven and London: Yale Univ. Press, 1965.

———. "Narrative Methods in Sidney's *Old Arcadia.*" *SEL* 18, no. 1 (Winter 1978): 13–33.

Day, Angel. *Vpon the Life and Death of . . . Sir Philip Sidney.* London: Robert Waldegrave, 1586. STC 6409.

DeNeef, A. Leigh. "Rereading Sidney's *Apology.*" *JMRS* 10, no. 2 (Fall 1980): 155–91.

Denkinger, Emma Marshall. *Philip Sidney.* London: George Allen and Unwin, 1932.

Dipple, Elizabeth. "The 'Fore Conceit' of Sidney's Eclogues." *Literary Monographs* 1 (1967): 3–47.

———. "Harmony and Pastoral in *The Old Arcadia.*" *ELH* 35, no. 3 (September 1968): 309–28.

———. "Metamorphosis in Sidney's *Arcadias.*" *PQ* 50, no. 1 (January 1971): 47–62.

———. "'Unjust Justice' in the *Old Arcadia.*" *SEL* 10, no. 1 (Winter 1970): 83–101.

Dixon, Michael N. "Fairy Tale, Fortune, and Boethian Wonder: Rhetorical

Structure in Book VI of *The Faerie Queene*." *UTQ* 44, no. 2 (Winter 1975): 141–65.

Doran, Madeleine. *Endeavors of Art. A Study of Form in Elizabethan Drama*. Madison, Milwaukee and London: Univ. of Wisconsin Press, 1954.

Dorangeon, Simone. *L'églogue anglaise de Spenser à Milton*. Paris: Didier, 1974.

Drayton, Michael. *Idea, The Shepheards Garland, Fashioned in Nine Eglogs* (1593). In *The Works of Michael Drayton*, edited by J. William Hebel, 4 vols. Oxford: Shakespeare Head Press, 1931–41.

Du Bellay, Joachim. "Dialogue d'un amoreux et d'Echo." In *Poésies françaises et latines de Joachim Du Bellay*, edited by E. Courbet, 2 vols. Paris: Garnier, 1918.

Duncan-Jones, Katherine. "Sidney in Samothea: A Forgotten National Myth." *RES*, n.s., 25, no. 98 (May 1974): 174–77.

———. "Sidney's Urania." *RES*, n.s., 17, no. 66 (May 1966): 123–32.

Dyer, Edward (?). *Sixe Idillia . . . Chosen out of . . . Theocritus, and translated into English Verse*. Oxford: Joseph Barnes, 1588. STC 23937.

Empson, William. *Seven Types of Ambiguity*. London: Chatto and Windus, 1930, 1949.

———. *Some Versions of Pastoral*. 1935. Reprint. *English Pastoral Poetry*. Freeport: Books for Libraries Press, 1972.

Exequiae illustrissimi equitis d. Philippi Sidnaei, gratissimae memoriae ac nomini impensae. Oxford: Joseph Barnes, 1587. STC 22551.

Felpernin, Howard. *Shakespearean Representations: Mimesis and Modernity in Elizabethan Tragedy*. Princeton: Princeton Univ. Press, 1977.

Ferguson, Margaret W. "Sidney's *A Defence of Poetry*: A Retrial." *Boundary 2* 7, no. 2 (Winter 1979): 61–95.

———. *Trials of Desire: Renaissance Defences of Poetry*. New Haven and London: Yale Univ. Press, 1983.

Fish, Stanley. "Literature in the Reader: Affective Stylistics." In *Self-Consuming Artifacts: The Experience of Seventeenth-Century Literature*, 383–427. Berkeley: Univ. of California Press, 1972.

Fleming, Abraham, trans. *The Bucoliks. Georgiks. All Newly Translated. . . .* London: Thomas Woodcocke, 1589. STC 24817.

———. *The Bucolikes of Publius Virgilius Maro. . . .* London: John Charlewood, 1575. STC 24816.

Ford, Jeffrey P. "Philosophy, History, and Sidney's *Old Arcadia*." *CL* 26, no. 1 (Winter 1974): 32–50.

Fowler, Alastair. *Conceitful Thought: The Interpretation of English Renaissance Poems*. Edinburgh: Edinburgh Univ. Press, 1975.

———. *Spenser and the Numbers of Time*. New York: Barnes and Noble, 1964.

———. *Triumphall Forms: Structural Patterns in Elizabethan Poetry*. Cambridge: University Press, 1970.

Frye, Northrop. "Varieties of Literary Utopias." *Daedalus* 94 (1965): 323–47.

Galm, John A. *Sidney's Arcadian Poems*. Institut für Englische Sprache und Literatur, Elizabethan and Renaissance Studies, no. 1. Salzburg: Universität Salzburg, 1973.

Genouy, Hector. *L' Arcadia de Sidney dans ses rapports avec l'Arcadia de Sannazaro et la Diana de Montemayor*. Paris: Henri Didier, 1928.

Gerhardt, Mia I. *Essai d'analyse littéraire de la pastorale*. Assen: Van Gorcum, 1950.

Gil Polo, Gaspar. *Diana Enamorada*. Edited by Rafael Ferreres. Madrid: Espasa-Calpe, 1953.

Godshalk. W. L. "A Return to Sidney's Samothea." *RES*, n.s., 29, no. 115 (August 1978): 325–26.

Goldman, Marcus S. *Sir Philip Sidney and the* Arcadia. Illinois Studies in Languages and Literatures, vol. 17, nos. 1–2. Urbana: Univ. of Illinois, 1934.

Googe, Barnabe. *Eglogs, Epytaphes, and Sonettes, 1563*. Edited by Edward Arber. English Reprints. London and Edinburgh: Muir and Paterson, 1871.

Graves, Thornton Shirley. "The 'Act Time' in Elizabethan Theatres." *SP* 12, no. 3 (July 1915): 103–34.

Grazzini, Antonfrancesco. *La Strega*. Edited by Michel Plaisance. Abbeville: Imprimerie F. Paillart, 1976.

Green, Paul D. " 'Doors to the House of Death': The Treatment of Suicide in Sidney's *Arcadia*." *SCJ* 10, no. 3 (Fall 1979): 17–27.

Green, Richard Hamilton. "Alan of Lille's *De Planctu Naturae*." *Speculum* 31 (October 1956): 649–74.

Greenblatt, Stephen J. *Renaissance Self-Fashioning: From More to Shakespeare*. Chicago and London: Univ. of Chicago Press, 1980.

———. "Sidney's *Arcadia* and the Mixed Mode." *SP* 70, no. 3 (July 1973): 269–78.

Greene, Thomas M. *The Light in Troy: Imitation and Discovery in Renaissance Poetry*. New Haven and London: Yale Univ. Press, 1982.

Greenfield, Thelma N. *The Eye of Judgment: Reading* The New Arcadia. Lewisburg: Bucknell Univ. Press, 1982.

Greenlaw, Edwin A. "Sidney's *Arcadia* as an Example of Elizabethan Allegory." In *Anniversary Papers by Colleagues and Pupils of George Lyman Kittredge*, 327–37. New York: Russell and Russell, 1913, 1967.

Greg, Walter W. *Pastoral Poetry and Pastoral Drama*. London, 1906. Reprint, New York: Russell and Russell, 1959.

Greville, Fulke. *The Life of the Renowned Sir Philip Sidney*. In *The Works in Verse and Prose Complete of the Right Honorable Fulke Greville, Lord Brooke*, edited by Alexander B. Grosart, 4 vols. London: C. Tiplady and Son, 1870.

Hager, Alan. "The Exemplary Mirage: Fabrication of Sir Philip Sidney's Biographical Image and the Sidney Reader." *ELH* 48, no. 1 (Spring 1981): 1–16.

Hamilton, A. C. *Sir Philip Sidney: A Study of His Life and Works*. Cambridge and New York: Cambridge Univ. Press, 1977.

Harvey, Gabriel. *Pierce's Supererogation* (1593). In *Elizabethan Critical Essays,* edited by G. Gregory Smith, 2 vols. Oxford: Clarendon Press, 1904.

Haydn, Hiram. *The Counter-Renaissance.* New York: Charles Scribner's Sons, 1950.

Heninger, S.K., Jr. *The Cosmographical Glass: Renaissance Diagrams of the Universe.* San Marino, Cal.: The Huntington Library, 1977.

———. "The Renaissance Perversion of Pastoral." *JHI* 22, no. 2 (April–June 1961): 254–61.

Herrick, Marvin T. *Italian Comedy in the Renaissance.* Urbana: Univ. of Illinois Press, 1960.

Hesiod. *Works and Days.* In *The Homeric Hymns and Homerica,* translated by Hugh G. Evelyn-White. London: William Heinemann; Cambridge, Mass: Harvard Univ. Press, 1936.

Hoffman, Nancy Jo. *Spenser's Pastorals:* The Shepheardes Calendar *and "Colin Clout."* Baltimore and London: The Johns Hopkins Univ. Press, 1977.

Holinshed, Raphael. *Holinshed's Chronicles of England, Scotland, and Ireland.* Edited by H. Ellis. 6 vols. London: J. Johnson, et al., 1807–08.

Hoopes, Robert. *Right Reason in the English Renaissance.* Cambridge, Mass: Harvard Univ. Press, 1962.

Horace. *The Odes and Epodes of Horace: A Modern Verse Translation.* Translated by Joseph P. Clancy. Chicago: Univ. of Chicago, 1960.

———. *Q Horati Flacci Opera.* Edited by Edward C. Wickham. Oxford: Clarendon Press, 1901, 1967.

Howell, Thomas. *Howell's Devises, 1581.* Edited by Walter Raleigh. Oxford: Clarendon Press, 1906.

Isler, Alan D. "Heroic Poetry and Sidney's Two *Arcadias.*" *PMLA* 83, no. 2 (May 1968): 368–79.

Javitch, Daniel. *Poetry and Courtliness in Renaissance England.* Princeton: Princeton Univ. Press, 1978.

Johnston, Patricia A. *Vergil's Agricultural Golden Age: A Study of the* Georgics. Leiden: E. J. Brill, 1980.

Johnstone, Paul H. "In Praise of Husbandry." *Agricultural History* 11, no. 2 (April 1937): 80–95.

Jones, Dorothy. "Sidney's Erotic Pen: An Interpretation of One of the *Arcadia* Poems." *JEGP* 73, no. 1 (January 1974): 32–47.

Jones, Joseph R. " 'Human Time' in *La Diana.*" *Romance Notes* 10, no. 1 (Autumn 1968): 139–46.

Jusserand, J. J. *The English Novel in the Time of Shakespeare.* Translated by Elizabeth Lee. London: T. Fisher Unwin, 1889.

Kalstone, David. *Sidney's Poetry: Contexts and Interpretations.* Cambridge, Mass.: Harvard Univ. Press, 1965.

Kennedy, Judith M. *A Critical Edition of Yong's Translation of George of Montemayor's* Diana *and Gil Polo's* Enamoured Diana. Oxford: Clarendon Press, 1968.

Kermode, Frank, ed. *English Pastoral Poetry from the Beginnings to Marvell.* New York: W. W. Norton, 1952, 1972.

Kimbrough, Robert. *Sir Philip Sidney.* Twayne's English Authors Series. New York: Twayne, 1971.

Lanham, Richard A. *The Old Arcadia.* In Walter R. Davis and Richard A. Lanham, *Sidney's* Arcadia. New Haven and London: Yale Univ. Press, 1965.

———. "Sidney: The Ornament of his Age." *Southern Review: An Australian Journal of Literary Studies* 2, no. 4 (Fall 1967): 319–40.

Lawry, Jon S. *Sidney's Two* Arcadias: *Pattern and Proceeding.* Ithaca and London: Cornell Univ. Press, 1972.

Leach, Eleanor Winsor. *Vergil's* Eclogues, *Landscapes of Experience.* Ithaca: Cornell Univ. Press, 1974.

Lerner, Laurence. *The Uses of Nostalgia, Studies in Pastoral Poetry.* New York: Schocken Books, 1972.

Levin, Harry. *The Myth of the Golden Age in the Renaissance.* Bloomington: Indiana Univ. Press, 1969.

Levine, Robert Eril. *A Comparison of Sidney's* Old *and* New Arcadia. Institut für Englische Sprache und Literatur, Elizabethan and Renaissance Studies, no. 13. Salzburg: Universität Salzburg, 1974.

Lewis, C. S. *Studies in Words.* Cambridge: Cambridge Univ. Press, 1960.

Lindenbaum, Peter. "Sidney's *Arcadia:* The Endings of the Three Versions." *HLQ* 34, no. 3 (May 1971): 205–18.

Lindheim, Nancy R. *The Structures of Sidney's* Arcadia. Toronto, Buffalo, and London: Univ. of Toronto Press, 1982.

———. "Vision, Revision, and the 1593 Text of the *Arcadia.*" *ELR* 2, no. 1 (Winter 1972): 136–47.

Litt, Gary L. "Characterization and Rhetoric in Sidney's 'Ye Goatherd Gods.'" *SLI* 11, no. 1 (Spring 1978): 115–24.

Long, A. A. "Aristotle's Legacy to Stoic Ethics." *Bulletin of the Institute of Classical Studies* (Univ. of London) 15 (1968): 72–85.

———. *Hellenistic Philosophy: Stoics, Epicureans, Sceptics.* London: Duckworth, 1974.

Longus. *The Story of Daphnis and Chloe. A Greek Pastoral.* Translated by W. D. Lowe. Cambridge: Deighton Bell, 1908.

Lovejoy, Arthur O., and George Boas. *Primitivism and Related Ideas in Antiquity.* Baltimore: The Johns Hopkins Univ. Press, 1935.

Luther, Martin. *Lectures on Genesis.* In *Luther's Works,* edited by Jaroslav Pelikan and translated by George V. Schick, 24 vols. Saint Louis: Concordia, 1958.

McCanles, Michael. "Oracular Prediction and the Fore-Conceit of Sidney's *Arcadia.*" *ELH* 50, no. 2 (Summer 1983): 233–44.

McCoy, Richard C. *Sir Philip Sidney: Rebellion in Arcadia.* New Brunswick: Rutgers Univ. Press, 1979.

Mallette, Richard. *Spenser, Milton and Renaissance Pastoral.* Lewisburg: Bucknell Univ. Press, 1981.

Marenco, Franco. "Double Plot in Sidney's Old *Arcadia.*" *MLR* 64, no. 2 (April 1969): 248–63.

Marinelli, Peter V. *Pastoral.* London: Methuen, 1971.

Mehl, Dieter. *The Elizabethan Dumb Show: The History of a Dramatic Convention.* London: Methuen, 1965.

Melanchthon, Philip. The Loci Communes *of Philip Melanchthon.* Translated by Charles Leander Hill. Boston: Meador Publishing, 1944.

Meres, Francis. *Palladis Tamia.* In *Elizabethan Critical Essays,* edited by G. Gregory Smith. 2 vols. Oxford: Clarendon Press, 1904.

Miller, Jacqueline T. " 'Love Doth Hold My Hand': Writing and Wooing in the Sonnets of Sidney and Spenser." *ELH* 46, no. 4 (Winter 1979): 541–58.

Miller, Robert P. "Venus, Adonis, and the Horses." *ELH* 19, no. 4 (December 1952): 249–64.

Moffett, Thomas. *Nobilis; or A View of the Life and Death of a Sidney, and Lessus Lugubris.* Edited by Virgil B. Heltzel and Hoyt H. Hudson. San Marino: The Huntington Library, 1940.

Monga, Luigi. *Le Genre pastoral an xvi siècle: Sannazar et Belleau.* Paris: éditions universitaires, 1974.

Montgomery, Robert L., Jr. *Symmetry and Sense: The Poetry of Sir Philip Sidney.* Austin: Univ. of Texas Press, 1961.

Montrose, Louis Adrian. " 'Eliza, Queene of shepheardes,' and the Pastoral of Power." *ELR* 10, no. 2 (Spring 1980): 153–82.

———. "Of Gentlemen and Shepherds: The Politics of Elizabethan Pastoral Form." *ELH* 50, no. 3 (Fall 1983): 415–59.

Moore, Dennis. "Philisides and Mira: Autobiographical Allegory in the *Old Arcadia.*" *Spenser Studies* 3 (1982): 125–37.

———. *The Politics of Spenser's* Complaints *and Sidney's Philisides Poems.* Institut für Anglistik und Amerikanistik, Elizabethan & Renaissance Studies, no. 101. Salzburg: Universität Salzburg, 1982.

Mornay, Philippe de. *Six Excellent Treatises of Life and Death.* London: Matthew Lownes, 1607. STC 18155.

———. *A Woorke Concerning the Trewnesse of the Christian Religion.* Translated by Sir Philip Sidney (?) and Arthur Golding. Delmar, N.Y.: Scholars' Facsimiles & Reprints, 1976.

Muscatine, Charles. *Chaucer and the French Tradition: A Study in Style and Meaning.* Berkeley and Los Angeles: Univ. of California Press, 1957, 1969.

Mustard, Wilfred P. "Notes on the Eclogues of Alexander Barclay." *MLN* 24, no. 1 (January 1909): 8–10.

Myrick, Kenneth O. *Sir Philip Sidney As a Literary Craftsman.* 1935, reprint, Lincoln: Univ. of Nebraska Press, 1965.

Nichols, J. G. *The Poetry of Sir Philip Sidney: An Interpretation in the Context of his Life and Times.* New York: Barnes and Noble, 1974.

Nicolson, Marjorie Hope. *Mountain Gloom and Mountain Glory: The Development of the Aesthetics of the Infinite.* Ithaca: Cornell Univ. Press, 1959.

O'Connor, John J. *Amadis de Gaule and Its Influence on Elizabethan Literature.* New Brunswick: Rutgers Univ. Press, 1970.

Orgel, Stephen. *The Jonsonian Masque.* Cambridge, Mass.: Harvard Univ. Press, 1965.

Osborn, James M. *Young Sir Philip Sidney, 1572–77.* New Haven and London: Yale Univ. Press, 1972.

Ovid. *Metamorphoses.* Translated by Frank Justus Miller. 4 vols. London: William Heinemann; Cambridge, Mass.: Harvard Univ. Press, 1926.

Palingenius, Marcellus. *The Zodiake of Life.* Translated by Barnabe Googe. New York: Scholars' Facsimiles and Reprints, 1947.

Panofsky, Erwin. *Studies in Iconology: Humanistic Themes in the Art of the Renaissance.* London: 1939; reprint, New York: Harper and Row, 1972.

Parker, Robert W. "Terentian Structure and Sidney's Original *Arcadia.*" *ELR* 2, no. 1 (Winter 1972): 61–78.

Parnell, Paul E. "Barnabe Googe: A Puritan in Arcadia." *JEGP* 60 (1961): 273–81.

Patterson, Annabel M. " 'Under . . . Pretty Tales': Intention in Sidney's *Arcadia.*" *SLI* 15, no. 1 (Spring 1982): 5–21.

Peterson, Douglas L. *The English Lyric from Wyatt to Donne: A History of the Plain and Eloquent Styles.* Princeton: Princeton Univ. Press, 1967.

Petrarca, Francesco. *The Life of Solitude.* Translated by Jacob Zeitlen. Urbana: Univ. of Illinois Press, 1924.

———. De Vita Solitaria *Secondo Lo Pseudo-Autografo Vaticano 3357.* Edited Antonio Altamura. Napoli: Dino Amodio, 1943.

———. *The Praise of Solitarinesse.* Translated by Roger Baynes. London: Francis Coldocke and Henry Bynneman, 1577. STC 1651.

———. *Petrarch's* Bucolicum Carmen. Translated by Thomas G. Bergin. New Haven: Yale Univ. Press, 1974.

Pickett, Penny. "Sidney's Use of *Phaedrus* in *The Lady of May.*" *SEL* 16, no. 1 (Winter 1976): 33–50.

Plass, Ewald M., ed. *What Luther Says: An Anthology.* 3 vols. Saint Louis: Concordia, 1959.

Plato. *The Republic.* 2d ed. Translated by Desmond Lee. Baltimore: Penguin Books, 1974.

Plutarch. *Plutarch's* Moralia. Translated by W. C. Helmbold, 14 vols. Cambridge, Mass.: Harvard Univ. Press; London: William Heinemann, 1939, 1962.

Poggioli, Renato. *The Oaten Flute, Essays on Pastoral Poetry and the Pastoral Ideal.* Cambridge, Mass.: Harvard Univ. Press, 1975.

Poirier, Michel. *Sir Philip Sidney: Le chevalier poète élizabéthain.* Lille: Bibliothèque universitaire de Lille, 1948.

Polybius. *The Histories*. Translated by W. R. Paton. 6 vols. New York: G. P. Putnams' Sons; London: William Heinemann, 1922.

Putnam, Michael C. J. *Virgil's Pastoral Art: Studies in the Eclogues*. Princeton: Princeton Univ. Press, 1970.

Puttenham, George. *The Arte of English Poesie* (1589). In *Elizabethan Critical Essays*, edited by G. Gregory Smith, 2 vols. Oxford: Clarendon Press, 1904.

Rees, Christine. "Some Seventeenth-Century Versions of the Judgment of Paris." *N&Q*, n.s., 24, no. 3 (May–June 1977): 197–200.

Ribner, Irving. "Sir Philip Sidney on Civil Insurrection." *JHI* 13, no. 2 (April 1952): 257–65.

Rivetus, Andraeus. *Theologicae et Scholasticae Exercitationes CXC In Genesin*. Lugduni Batavorum: Bonaventurae & Abrahami Elzevir, 1633.

Rose, Mark. *Heroic Love: Studies in Sidney and Spenser*. Cambridge, Mass.: Harvard Univ. Press, 1968.

Rosenberg, D. M. *Oaten Reeds and Trumpets: Pastoral and Epic in Virgil, Spenser, and Milton*. Lewisburg: Bucknell Univ. Press, 1981.

Rosenmeyer, Thomas G. *The Green Cabinet: Theocritus and the European Pastoral Lyric*. Berkeley and Los Angeles: Univ. of California Press, 1969.

Rowe, Kenneth Thorpe. "Romantic Love and Parental Authority in Sidney's *Arcadia*." *The Univ. of Michigan Contributions in Modern Philology*, no. 4 (April 1947): 1–58.

Roydon, Matthew. "An Elegie. . . ." In *The Phoenix Nest, 1593*, edited by Hyder E. Rollins. Cambridge, Mass.: Harvard Univ. Press, 1931.

Rudenstine, Neil L. *Sidney's Poetic Development*. Cambridge, Mass.: Harvard Univ. Press, 1967.

Russell, D. A. *Plutarch*. London: Duckworth, 1972.

Sanforde, James. *The Manuell of Epictetus*. London: H. Bynneman, 1567. STC 10423.

Sannazaro, Iacopo. *Arcadia*. In *Opere volgari, a cura di Alfredo Mauro*. Bari: Laterza, 1961.

———. *Arcadia and Piscatorial Eclogues*. Translated by Ralph Nash. Detroit: Wayne State Univ. Press, 1966.

Saunders, Jason Lewis. *Justus Lipsius: The Philosophy of Renaissance Stoicism*. New York: Liberal Arts Press, 1955.

Scanlon, Paul A. "Sidney's *Old Arcadia*: A Renaissance Pastoral Romance." *Ariel* 10, no. 4 (October 1979): 69–76.

Schleiner, Winfried. "Differences of Theme and Structure of the Erona Episode in the *Old* and *New Arcadia*." *SP* 70, no. 4 (October 1973): 377–91.

Schultz, John R. "The Method of Barclay's *Eclogues*." *JEGP* 32 (1933): 549–71.

Seneca. *Ad Lucillium Epistulae Morales*. Translated by Richard M. Gummere. 3 vols. New York: G. P. Putnam's Sons; London: William Heinemann, 1917.

———. *De Tranquillitate Animi*. In *Moral Essays*, edited by John W. Basore. 3 vols. Cambridge, Mass.: Harvard Univ. Press; London: William Heinemann, 1931, 1952.

Sidney, Sir Philip. *An Apology for Poetry; or, the Defence of Poesy.* Edited by Geoffrey Shepherd. London and Edinburgh: Thomas Nelson and Sons, 1965.

———. *The Complete Works of Sir Philip Sidney.* Edited by Albert Feuillerat. 4 vols. Cambridge: Cambridge Univ. Press, 1912–26.

———. *The Countess of Pembroke's Arcadia* (The Old Arcadia). Edited by Jean Robertson. Oxford: Clarendon Press, 1973.

———. *The Lady of May.* In *Miscellaneous Prose of Sir Philip Sidney,* edited by Katherine Duncan-Jones and Jan Van Dorsten. Oxford: Clarendon Press, 1973.

———. *The Poems of Sir Philip Sidney.* Edited by William A. Ringler, Jr. Oxford: Clarendon Press, 1962.

———, and Hubert Languet. *The Correspondence of Philip Sidney and Hubert Languet.* Edited by William Aspenwall Bradley. Boston: The Merrymount Press, 1912.

Smith, Hallett D. *Elizabethan Poetry: A Study in Conventions, Meaning and Expression.* Cambridge, Mass.: Harvard Univ. Press, 1952.

Snell, Bruno. *The Discovery of the Mind: The Greek Origins of European Thought.* Translated by Thomas G. Rosenmeyer. Oxford: Blackwell, 1953.

Solé-Leris, A. "The Theory of Love in the Two *Dianas*: A Contrast." *Bulletin of Hispanic Studies* 36 (1959): 65–79.

Solensis, Aratus. *Phaenomena, The Aratus Ascribed to Germanicus Caesar.* Edited and translated by D. B. Gain. London: Athlone Press, 1976.

Sophie-Røstvig, Maren. *The Happy Man: Studies in the Metamorphosis of a Classical Ideal, 1600–1700.* Oslo: Akademisk Forlag; Oxford: Basil Blackwell, 1954.

Spencer, Theodore. "The Poetry of Sir Philip Sidney." *ELH* 12, no. 4 (December 1945): 251–78.

———. *Shakespeare and the Nature of Man.* Lowell Lectures. New York: Macmillan, 1942.

Spenser, Edmund. *The Faerie Queene.* In *The Complete Poetical Works of Edmund Spenser,* edited by R. E. Neil Dodge. Boston and New York: Houghton Mifflin, 1908.

Spitzer, Leo. *Classical and Christian Ideas of World Harmony: Prolegomena to an Interpretation of the Word "Stimmung."* Baltimore: Johns Hopkins Press, 1963.

Stillman, Robert E. "Justice and the 'Good Word' in Sidney's *The Lady of May.*" *SEL* 24, no. 1 (Winter 1984): 23–38.

———. "Poetry and Justice in Sidney's 'Ye goat-herd gods.'" *SEL* 22, no. 1 (Winter 1982): 39–50.

Stump, Donald V. "Sidney's Concept of Tragedy in the *Apology* and in the *Arcadia.*" *SP* 79, no. 1 (Winter 1982): 41–61.

Talbert, Ernest William. *The Problem of Order: Elizabethan Political Commonplaces and an Example of Shakespeare's Art.* Chapel Hill: Univ. of North Carolina Press, 1962.

Tayler, Edward. *Nature and Art in Renaissance Literature.* New York and London: Columbia Univ. Press, 1964.

Toliver, Harold E. *Pastoral Forms and Attitudes.* Berkeley: Univ. of California Press, 1971.

Tonkin, Humphrey. *Spenser's Courteous Pastoral, Book Six of* The Faerie Queene. Oxford: Clarendon Press, 1970.

Turner, Myron. "The Disfigured Face of Nature: Image and Metaphor in the Revised *Arcadia.*" *ELR* 2, no. 1 (Winter 1972): 116–35.

———. "'Disguised Passion' and the Psychology of Suicide in Sidney's *Old Arcadia.*" *PLL* 15, no. 1 (Winter 1979): 17–37.

———. "Distance and Astonishment in the Old *Arcadia*: A Study of Sidney's Psychology." *TSLL* 20, no. 3 (Fall 1978): 303–29.

Tufte, Virginia. *The Poetry of Marriage: The Epithalamium in Europe and Its Development in England.* Los Angeles: Tinnon Brown, 1970.

Twyne, Thomas. "The life of Virgil." In *The xiii Bookes of Aeneidos.* London: William How, 1584. STC 24802.

Ulreich, John C., Jr. "'The Poets Only Deliver': Sidney's Conception of Mimesis." *SLI* 15, no. 1 (Spring 1982): 67–84.

Van Dorsten, J. A. *Poets, Patrons, and Professors: Sir Philip Sidney, Daniel Rogers, and the Leiden Humanists.* London: Oxford Univ. Press; Leiden: University Press, 1962.

Virgil. *Eclogues, Georgics, Aeneid I–IV.* Translated by H. Rushton Fairclough. London: William Heinemann; Cambridge, Mass.: Harvard Univ. Press, 1924.

Wallace, Malcolm. *The Life of Sir Philip Sidney.* Cambridge: Cambridge Univ. Press, 1915.

Waller, Gary F. "'This Matching of Contraries': Calvinism and Courtly Philosophy in the Sidney Psalms." *ES* 55, no. 1 (February 1974): 22–31.

Wardropper, Bruce W. "The *Diana* of Montemayor: Revaluation and Interpretation." *SP* 48, no. 2 (April 1951): 126–44.

Watson, Gerard. "The Natural Law and Stoicism." In *Problems in Stoicism*, edited by A. A. Long, 216–38. London: Athlone Press, 1971.

Weiner, Andrew D. *Sir Philip Sidney and the Poetics of Protestantism.* Minneapolis: Univ. of Minnesota Press, 1978.

Whitney, Lois. "Concerning Nature in *The Countess of Pembrokes Arcadia.*" *SP* 24, no. 2 (April 1927): 207–22.

Willey, Basil. *The English Moralists.* London: Chatto and Windus, 1964.

———. *The Religion of Nature.* London: Lindsey Press, 1957.

Williams, Raymond. *The Country and the City.* New York: Oxford Univ. Press, 1973.

Wilson, Mona. *Sir Philip Sidney.* London and Southampton: Duckworth, 1931.

Wind, Edgar. *Pagan Mysteries in the Renaissance.* 1958. Reprint. New York: Barnes & Noble, 1968.

Wolff, Samuel Lee. *The Greek Romances in Elizabethan Prose Fiction.* New York: Columbia University Press, 1912.

Wyatt, Thomas. *Collected Poems of Sir Thomas Wyatt.* Edited by Kenneth Muir. London: Routledge & Kegan Paul, 1949; reprint, Cambridge, Mass.: Harvard Univ. Press, 1963.

Yates, Frances A. *Astraea: The Imperial Theme in the Sixteenth Century.* London and Boston: Routledge & Kegan Paul, 1975.

———. *Theatre of the World.* Chicago: Univ. of Chicago Press, 1969.

Zandvoort, Reinard Willem. *Sidney's* Arcadia: *A Comparison Between the Two Versions.* Amsterdam: N. V. Swets & Zeitlinger, 1929.

Index

Actaeon, 160
Adam, 197, 251 n.8
Agelastus, 88, 96, 168, 169–71, 172, 209–10
Alençon, Duke of, 34, 36, 211
Alexander, Sir William, 236 n.15
Alpers, Paul, 232 n.12, 238 n.25, 239 n.36
Amadis de Gaule, 233 n.30
Amassis, 128
Amos, 249 n.18
Anderson, Judith H., 232 n.15
Andromana, Queen, 128
Antiphilus, 108
Apology for Poetry, The, 8, 9, 37, 44, 70, 90, 92, 106, 144, 236 n.16; the concept of "Idea" in, 74, 77; definition of "pastoral" in, 64–66, 68, 75, 123, 156; discussion of prose and poetry in, 82, 86; and the elegy, 157, 170; intellectual traditions of, 252 n.23; and the power of poetry, 23, 177, 181, 182–83, 190, 191, 196–98, 225, 228, 251 n.8, 252 n.23; and the theme of relief, 26, 27, 69, 196–98, 225
Aquinas, Thomas, 197
Arber, Edward, 232 n.22
Arcadian eclogues: coherence in, 95–97, 171–72; *concordia discors* in, 202–13; eclogue theater, 192–95; first eclogues, 102–16, 120; second eclogues, 120–32, 203–5; third eclogues, 137–49, 195; fourth eclogues, 155–72, 205–13; innovations in pastoral conventions in, 89–97; and *intermedii*, 91–93; multiple perceptions in, 87, 91; as pastoral withdrawal, 94–95; role of, in the *Arcadia*, 50, 81–97, 228, 243 n.15; Sidney's motives in creating, 86–89; and Sidney's poetics, 7–8, 192–213; and Sidney's reputation as a pastoralist, 48–49; structural patterns in, 120–24, 139–40, 209

Arcadian poems:
"A banished man, long barred from his desire," 134
"And are you there, old Pas? In truth I ever thought," 123–24
"A neighbour mine not long ago there was," 142
"Apollo great, whose beams the greater world do light," 85, 119–20
"As I behind a bush did sit," 124–27, 182–83, 186
"As I my little flock on Ister bank," 143–47, 195
"Come, Dorus, come, let songs thy sorrows signify," 103–6, 189
"Dorus, tell me, where is thy wanted motion," 122–23, 182
"Down, down, Melampus; what? your fellow bite?" 112–14
"Fair rocks, goodly rivers, sweet woods, when shall I see peace? Peace," 128–30, 184–87
"Farewell O sun, Arcadia's clearest light," 170–71, 210
"Feed on my sheep, my charge, my comfort, feed," 119
"Fortune, Nature, Love, long have contended about me," 114–15, 184, 201
"Get hence foul grief, the canker of the mind," 136
"If mine eyes can speak to do hearty errand," 115
"I joy in grief, and do detest all joys," 162–63, 209
"In faith, good Histor, long is your de-

Arcadian poems *(continued)*
  lay," 147–48, 203
  "Lady, reserved by the heav'ns to do pastors' company honour," 115, 118, 190, 199
  "Let mother earth now deck herself in flowers," 140–41, 204–5
  "My muse what ails this ardour," 130
  "Now thanked be the great God Pan," 85
  "Now was our heav'nly vault deprived of the light," 163–67
  "O night, the ease of care, the pledge of pleasure," 151
  "O sweet woods, the delight of solitariness," 130–32, 183
  "Over these brooks, trusting to ease mine eyes," 186
  "Poor painters oft with silly poets join," 106–7
  "Rason, tell me thy mind, if here be reason," 130
  "Since nature's works be good, and death doth serve," 216
  "Since that to death is gone the shepherd high," 168–70, 209–10
  "Since wailing is a bud of causeful sorrow," 210
  "Thou rebel vile, come, to thy master yield," 121–22, 202–3
  "Transformed in show, but more transformed in mind," 85–86
  "Unto the caitiff wretch whom long affliction holdeth," 167–68, 189
  "Up, up, Philisides, let sorrows go," 110–12, 186, 204
  "We love, and have our loves rewarded," 102–3, 202–3
  "What length of verse can serve brave Mopsa's good to show," 85
  "What tongue can her perfections tell," 85, 136
  "Who doth desire that chaste his wife should be," 142–43
  "Ye goat-herd gods, that love the grassy mountains," 156–63, 205–9
  "Ye living powers enclosed in stately shrine," 119
Aristotle, 9, 71, 72, 73, 74, 145–46, 228
Armstrong, Elizabeth, 241 n.17

Art, 168–69, 192–98, 224–26, 254 n.60. *See also* Nature; Poetry
Artaxia, 108, 128
Astell, Ann W., 254 n.60
Astraea, 160, 208
Astrophil, 43–44, 143, 190–91
Astrophil and Stella, 44, 48, 143, 190–91, 250 n.3
Athenaeus, 166

Babut, Daniel, 241–42 n.25
Baker, Ernest A., 237 n.16
Barclay, Alexander: and the Christian pastoral tradition, 55, 59–63, 65, 77, 227, 246 n.9; and pastoral pretense, 68; and pastoral relief, 70, 232 n.22; and politics, 166; Sidney's critique of, 90, 113. *See also* Christian pastoral
Barnfield, Richard, 48
Barrow, R. H., 241–42 n.25
Basilius: his adultery with Gynecia, 97, 136, 139, 142, 143, 183; "death" and rebirth of, 20, 23, 24, 83, 88, 150–52, 168–71, 209–10, 213, 218–19, 224–26; fall of, 70, 128, 151; and Dicus, 106–7; and fancy, 178; and the idle life, 44; his misreading of the oracle, 120, 176, 250 nn.3 and 7; and nature, 241 n.13; and Philanax, 126, 178, 214; as a ruler, 67, 119, 155, 217; and solitariness, 131; as symbol of justice, 171, 250 n.29; his withdrawal to Arcadia, 44, 87, 98–102, 119, 133, 211, 222
Baynes, Roger, 242 n.34
Beast fable, 95, 143–47, 195–96, 197, 199, 201–2
Beaumont and Fletcher, 153
Berger, Harry, Jr., 238 n.19, 252 n.20
Bion, 169
Boas, George, 240 nn. 9 and 11, 242 n.30
Boccaccio, 52, 59
Boulon, 126–27, 130, 152, 182
Briggs, William Dinsmore, 247 n.23
Bromberg, Rachel, 239 n.35
Brown, James Neil, 238 n.19
Browne, Sir Thomas, 139, 144
Browne, William, 47, 49
Bucolics, 27–28
Bush, Douglas, 240 n.12
Butler, Christopher, 246 n.11

270 INDEX

Calvin, Jean, 197
Campbell, Lily B., 248 n.7
Carew, Richard, 48
Caspari, Fritz, 247 n.23
Cato, 224
Certain Sonnets, 48, 72
Chalifour, Clark L., 237 n.18
Chambers, E. K., 243 n.10
Chapman, George, 139
Chaucer, Geoffrey, 144, 191
Chaudhuri, Sukanta, 230 n.3
Christian pastoral, 90, 104, 177, 178; and Barclay, 55, 59–63; and Geron's debate with Philisides, 110, 113; moral concerns in, 28, 69, 70, 74, 137, 209; and politics, 249 n.24; Sidney's critique of, 176
Cicero, 9, 71–72, 73, 74, 228, 241–42 n.25, 242 n.29, 250 n.1
Classical pastoral, 61, 227
Cleophila. *See* Pyrocles and Musidorus
Clio, 188
Colic, Rosalie, 253 n.48
Collingwood, R. G., 240 n.9
Collins, Thomas, 235 n.3
Comito, Terry, 248 n.6, 250 n.3
Concord, 38, 43, 145–49, 176, 192–226. See also *Concordia discors*; Music
Concordia discors, 194–226, 252 n.35, 253 n.48. *See also* Concord
Congleton, James E., 240 n.1
Connell, Dorothy, 231 n.4, 252 n.33, 254 n.60, 251 n.13
Contentment: and justice, 133–49, 155; loss of, 150–72; and marriage, 137–49; as a pastoral theme, 27–31, 97, 102, 105; and Sidney, 37–44. *See also* Idle life; Quiet mind; Relief
Cooper, Helen, 235 n.4
Cosma, 124
Craig, D. H., 252 n.32
Cullen, Patrick, 232 n.21, 238 n.19, 240 n.43
Culp, Dorothy Woodward, 232 n.15
Cunliffe, John W., 243 n.10
Cupid, 106–9, 110, 141, 148
Cutts, John P., 244 n.5

Dametas, 98, 104, 152; and comic relief, 85, 182, 215; and "discontentation," 150–51; and passion, 125, 133–36, 139, 187

Dana, Margaret E., 23, 244 n.6, 253 nn. 53 and 56, 254 n.58
Danby, John F., 231 n.4, 240 n.12, 241 n.14
Davidson, Clifford, 244 n.2, 245 n.11, 251 n.16
Davies, John, 202, 203
Davis, Walter R., 233 n.27, 239 n.31, 241 n.14, 242 n.27, 243 n.15, 245 nn. 13, 18, and 20, 247 n.2, 248 n.6, 253 nn. 49 and 53
Day, Angel, 49, 54
Defence of Poetry, The. See *Apology for Poetry, The*
DeNeef, A. Leigh, 252 n.33
Denkinger, Emma Marshall, 37, 233 n.31
Denny, Edward, 33, 36, 73, 112, 166
Devereux, Penelope, 166
Diana, 163, 166, 167
Dicus, 22, 76, 126, 149, 169, 212; as allegorical name, 93, 107; his assault on Cupid, 92, 106–7, 245 nn. 12 and 15, 251 n.9; his debate with Dorus, 122–23, 130, 182, 205; epithalamium by, 140–41, 147, 203–5; and Pas, 124; and passion, 87, 109, 114; and Philisides, 144; and unity in the eclogues, 89, 95; virtues of, 222, 245 n.11
Dipple, Elizabeth, 23, 230 n.2, 231 n.3, 240 n.6, 243 n.15, 244 nn. 3 and 4, 245 n.15, 246 nn. 7, 11, and 8, 247 nn. 13 and 24, 248 n.6, 250 nn. 29, 5, 253 n.47
Discontentation, 151–72
Divided mind: consequences of, 111–14, 117–32, 143, 215; and fortune, 98–102; and justice, 214; and love, 102–16; and marriage, 144. *See also* Passion
Dixon, Michael N., 232 n.15
Dobell, Bertram, 236 n.16
Donne, John, 162–63
Doran, Madeleine, 250 n.1
Dorangeon, Simone, 237 n.16, 240 n.44
Dorcas, 131
Dorus. *See* Pyrocles and Musidorus
Drayton, Michael, 47, 48, 51, 74, 228
Du Bellay, Joachim, 129
Duncan-Jones, Katherine, 164, 165, 248 nn. 7 and 8
Dyer, Edward, 42, 242 n.34

Echo, 96, 125, 129–30, 184–86
Eclogues. *See* Arcadian eclogues

Eden, 197–98
E. K., 41–42, 52, 64, 65
Elegy, 168–71, 205, 209–10
Elizabeth I (queen of England), 9, 32, 33, 34–35, 36, 42, 51, 147, 166, 167, 188, 210–11, 212, 249n.27, 251n.12
Elyot, Sir Thomas, 202–3
Emblem, 85–86, 102, 121, 156–57, 161–62, 202–3, 214
Empson, Wiliam, 7, 13, 94, 156, 238n.19, 244n.16
England, 33–35, 164, 165, 166
Epicurean pastoral, 69, 242n.34
Epithalamium, 140–41, 203–5, 246–47n.12
Erona, 108, 109, 110, 125. *See also* Plangus and Erona
Espilus, 9, 43, 251n.12
Euarchus, 20, 22, 24, 82, 99, 144, 168, 214, 216–25, 253n.55
Eve, 197
Ezekiel, 249n.18

Fancy, 177–92, 226
Felpernin, Howard, 238n.25
Ferguson, Margaret W., 251n.8
Feuillerat, Albert, 236n.16
Ficino, Marsilio, 166
First eclogues. *See* Arcadian eclogues
Fish, Stanley, 234n.56
Fleming, Abraham, 40–41
Ford, Jeffrey P., 237n.18, 243n.15, 245n.4
Fortune: emphasis on, in *The Old Arcadia*, 23–24, 98–102, 244n.1; and passion, 133–36 and providence, 117–32, 214–26; responses to, 150–55, 214–26; as Sidney's pastoral subject, 65–70; Stoic response to, 74–76
Fourth eclogues. *See* Arcadian eclogues
Fowler, Alastair, 140, 248nn. 6 and 12, 249n.18, 253n.45
Fraunce, Abraham, 48, 236n.15
Frobisher, Martin, 32, 35
Frye, Northop, 238n.19

Galm, John A., 243nn. 6 and 15, 246n.13, 247n.22, 249n.27
Gascoigne, George, 129
Genesis, 201
Genouy, Hector, 237n.16, 239n.30
Georgic pastoral, 28, 62

Gerhardt, Mia I., 239n.30
Geron, 22, 76, 118, 126, 169, 212, 222; as allegorical name, 93, 107; his complaint to his sheep, 156, 205; his debate with Histor, 137, 147–49, 203; his debate with Philisides, 88, 96, 106, 110–15, 127, 143, 151, 167, 179, 186, 204, 245n.16, 251n.9, 253n.42; and Mastix, 112–14, 178; and unity among eclogues, 89, 95
Gewen, Christopher, 48
Gil Polo, Gaspar, 84; *Diana Enamorada*, 29, 30, 83, 107, 165–66, 244n.5, 249n.19; and models for "Ye goat-herd gods . . ." 157–59, 208–9; and the theme of marriage, 137–38, 141, 246–47n.12; his use of prose and poetry, 82, 242n.2, 243n.5
Godshalk, W. L., 249n.20
Golden age, or golden world: and justice, 25–27; perils of creating, 181–82; restoring, through art, 37–38, 161, 195–98; Samothea as symbol of, 164–67; Vergil's myth of, 26–27, 43, 196–97
Goldman, Marcus S., 236n.15
Googe, Barnabe, 62, 227, 232n.22, 253n.42
Graves, Thornton Shirley, 243n.13
Grazzini, Antonfrancesco, 91
Green, Paul D., 248n.4
Green, Richard Hamilton, 249n.17
Greenblatt, Stephen, 8–9, 237–38n.18
Greene, Thomas M., 238n.25
Greenfield, Thelma N., 10–11, 231n.4
Greenlaw, Edwin A., 236n.15
Greg, Walter W., 237n.16
Greville, Faulke, 32, 37, 231n.5
Gynecia: her "adultery" with Basilius, 139, 142, 183; and Cleophila, 88, 124, 135–36, 183, 187, 188–89; and the death of Basilius, 83, 151–52, 163, 215, 216, 218–19, 226; and passion, 99, 117, 120, 141, 143

Hager, Alan, 233n.31
Hamilton, A. C., 37, 239n.35, 244n.2, 246nn. 2 and 9
Hardinge, Samuel, 47
Harvey, Gabriel, 48
Haydn, Hiram, 240n.12
Hebrews, 248n.8
Heliodorus, 224, 233n.30, 253n.57
Heninger, S. K., Jr., 238n.19, 248–49n.16

Henry VIII (king of England), 166
Heraclitus, 100, 194
Herrick, Marvin T., 243 n.10
Hesiod, 25, 26, 53, 56, 58, 196
Histor, 114, 118; his debate with Geron, 137, 147–48, 203; his tale of Plangus and Erona, 107–9, 125, 245 n.15; his tale of Plangus's lament to Boulon, 125–27; his tales of the princes, 125, 127–28, 152
Hoffman, Nancy Jo, 232 n.21
Holinshed, Raphael, 165
Hoppes, Robert, 71
Horace, 71–72, 77, 250 n.1
Horatian pastoral, 28, 227
Howell, Thomas, 48, 54, 231 n.5
Hymen, 140, 141

Idle life: and the divided mind, 115, 131–32; Dorus's celebration of, 130–32; Euarchus's view of, 222; evaluations of, 20–22; and marriage, 140; as metaphor for goodness, 69–70; pastoral versions of, 24–31; Sidney's view of, 37–38, 43–44, 68–70; and the Stoic view of nature, 70–76. *See also* Contentment; Quiet mind; Relief
Isaiah, 145, 161
Isler, Alan D., 237 n.18
Itlianate pastoral, 90, 99, 111, 113, 133; emphasis on contentment in, 69, 70, 77, 135, 176; and the princes, 101, 115; and relief through poetry, 70, 202, 209; Sannazaro's version of, 55–59, 60, 62; Sidney's critique of, 84, 187, 227

Javitch, Daniel, 244 n.7
Jealousy, 141–43
Jeremiah, 249 n.18
Jerusalem, 161
Job, 249 n.18
Johnston, Patricia A., 231 n.6
Johnstone, Paul H., 232 n.17
Jones, Dorothy, 246 n.5
Jones, Joseph R., 233 n.26
Jonson, Ben, 218, 250 n.1
Jove, 145–46
Jump concord. *See* Concord
Jusserand, J. J., 236 n.16
Justice: and the audience, 217–26; in the concluding trial, 19–24, 214–26; and concord, 195–226; and contentment, 27, 38, 69, 97, 125, 133–49, 155; and doctrine of "justitia originalis," 197–98; and fortune, 98–99; loss of, 155–72; and marriage, 137–49; and poetry, 9–10, 192–226; political, 155; Sidney's interest in, 9; as traditional pastoral theme, 24–27

Kala. *See* Lalus
Kalander, 241 n.14
Kalodoulus, 19–24, 58, 222, 223
Kalstone, David, 156, 239 nn. 29 and 35, 251 n.12, 253 n.46
Kennedy, Judith M., 242–43 n.2
Kermode, Frank, 238 n.19
Kerxenus, 19, 23, 223, 226
Kimbrough, Robert, 237 n.16, 244 n.2
Klaius. *See* Strephon and Klaius

Lady of May, The, 9, 26, 43, 48, 131, 177, 188, 250 n.3
Laelaps, 112
Lalus, 188; his contest with Dorus, 102–6, 115, 122, 203, 244 n.8; his love for Kala, 104, 105, 114, 142; his marriage to Kala, 22, 88, 138–39, 147–49, 155, 203–6, 226; and unity in the eclogues, 89
Landi, Antonio, 91
Languet, Hubert, 9, 228; in the beast fable, 95, 144–46, 195–96; and concord, 144–46, 148, 195–96, 197–98, 213; his correspondence with Sidney, 32–37, 42–43, 73, 166; and justice, 201
Lanham, Richard A., 23, 237 n.18, 241 n.14, 243 n.9, 245 nn. 11 and 2, 246 nn. 6 and 4, 253 n.54
Lawry, Jon S., 7, 243 n.15, 244 n.17, 247 n.1
Leach, Eleanor Winsor, 239 n.36
Lerner, Laurence, 237 n.17
Leuca, 124
Levin, Harry, 231 n.6
Levine, Robert Eril, 244 n.9
Lewis, C. S., 240 n.9
Lindenbaum, Peter, 253 n.52
Lindheim, Nancy, 10, 11, 230 n.2, 242 n.27, 247 n.16, 248 n.4, 254 n.60
Lionardi, Alessandro, 250 n.1
Lipsius, Justus, 153
Litt, Gary L, 248 n.12
Livy, 59

Long, A. A., 241 n.25, 252 n.19
Longus, 56, 57, 238 n.21, 239 n.35
Love: and contentment, 133–36; and the divided mind, 98–116, 117–20; as protection against misfortune, 122–24; and the transformation of nature, 179–87; versions of, in the first eclogues, 102–16; versions of, in the second eclogues, 122–24, 128–32. *See also* Marriage
Lovejoy, Arthur O., 240 nn. 9 and 11, 242 n.30
Luther, Martin, 197
Lydia, 108

McCanles, Michael, 250 n.3
McCoy, Richard C., 231 n.3, 234 n.55, 246 n.6
Mallette, Richard, 12, 250 n.28
Mantuan, 13, 28, 50, 52, 53, 59, 62, 63
Marenco, Franco, 230 n.2, 245 n.11
Marinelli, Peter V., 239 n.35
Marriage: as example of *concordia discorse*, 203–5; as image of the quiet mind, 137–49. *See also* Love
Marvell, Andrew, 12
Mastix, 93, 112–14, 132, 178
Mehl, Dieter, 92
Melampus, 112
Melanchthon, Philip, 251 n.8
Melidora. *See* Pyrophilus and Melidora
Menalcas, 19, 21
Meres, Francis, 48, 235 n.6, 236 n.15
Miller, Jacqueline T., 250 n.3
Miller, Robert P., 245 n.10
Milton, John, 12, 13, 169
Minturno, Antonio 250 n.1
Mira, 96, 163–68, 171, 194, 212, 249 n.27
Mirror for Magistrates, 39, 150, 188
Miso, 134, 136, 139, 151, 187
Moffett, Thomas, 113
Monga, Luigi, 239 n.35
Montemajor, Jorge de, 29, 30, 50, 82, 111, 164
Montgomery, Robert L., Jr., 243 n.7
Montrose, Louis Adrian, 238–39 n.26
Moore, Dennis 249 n.27
Mopsa, 118, 134, 136, 139, 151, 187, 190, 191
More, Sir Thomas, 8

Mornay, Philippe de, 153, 242 n.29, 247 n.3, 253 n.49
Moschus, 168, 169
Muir, Kenneth, 232 n.22
Muscatine, Charles, 142
Music, 38, 145, 195–202, 207–8. *See also* Concord
Musidorus. *See* Pyrocles and Musidorus
Mustard, Wilfred P., 240 n.39
Myrick, Kenneth O., 39, 236–37 n.16
Myth: of creation, 145, 195; of "death" and rebirth of Basilius, 169–72, 209–10, 224–26; of Echo and Phlisides, 128–30, 184–87; of the Fall, 9, 38, 195, 197–98; of the judgment of Paris, 163, 166–67; of the loss of Urania, 155–63, 207–8; of Samothea, 163–67, 212

Nature: alienation from, 178–92; and art, 192–202, 226; and morality, 63; responsiveness of, in Sannazaro, 58–59; Sidney's view of, 70–77; and Stoicism, 70–77; as a symbol, 249 n.18
New Arcadia, The, 10–12, 177
Nichols, J. G., 247 n.16
Nico and Pas, 123–24, 130, 137, 141–43, 199
Nicolson, Marjorie Hope, 249 n.18

O'Connor, John, 233 n.30
Old Arcadia, The: and the concluding trial, 19–24, 214–26, 253 nn. 55 and 57, 254 n.60; critical views of, 23–24, 37, 236–37 n.16; dedicatory letter in, 39–44, 68; as a defense of pastoral, 43–44, 176–77, 226–28; dramatic structure of, 91–95; the eclogues in, 82–97, 102–16, 120–32, 137–49, 155–72, 195, 202–13, 236–37 n.16; genre of, 48–50, 76–77, 236–37 nn. 15, 16, and 18; introduction to, 66–70; mixture of prose and poetry in, 81–97; multiple perceptions in, 11–12, 87, 100–101, 104; narrative style in, 82–89; the narrator in, 19, 21, 82, 87, 93, 112, 150, 154, 183, 211, 217, 244 n.2; and pastoralism, 10, 20–22, 50–63, 64–77, 217–28; as poetic gesture, 8, 9, 37–44, 172; and the reader, 11, 44, 132, 175, 184, 217–26; as Stoic pastoral, 71–77
Orgel, Stephen, 251 n.12
Osborn, James M., 233 n.34, 234 nn. 35, 37,

39, 42, 48, 50, and 51, 235 nn. 66, 67, and 68
Otanes, 108
Ovid, 25, 26, 65, 145, 160, 163–64, 193, 196

Palingenius, Marcellus, 232 n.22
Pamela, 98, 105, 224; attempted rape of, 20, 135, 227; Dorus's wooing of, 88, 101, 117–18, 188–89, 190–91; Musidorus's flight with, 87, 133–35; her response to adversity, 154, 215
Pan, 140
Panaetius, 241–42 n.25
Panofsky, Erwin, 160
Paris. *See* Myth
Parker, Robert W., 237 n.18, 243 n.3
Parnell, Paul E., 240 n.41
Pas. *See* Nico and Pas
Passion: and the abuse of imagination, 177–92; dangers of uncontrolled, 98–116, 117–32, 134–36, 141; and "discontentation," 151–72; and reason, 121–23, 126–32, 137, 145, 148, 167, 203, 223. *See also* Divided mind
Pastoral: Barclay's version of, 59–63; criticism of, in *The Old Arcadia*, 214–28; life, dangers of, 20–22, 83–84; and generic redefinition, 52–54; inclusiveness of, 12, 50–51, 155, 163, 218, 220–21; as litrary tradition, 13, 24–31, 50–63; paradoxical relationship to nature in, 178, 192–93, 196–98; and politics, 50, 65–68, 165–66, 227; pretense in, 51–52, 67–68, 74, 145; Renaissance, 12–13, 50–63, 227; Sannazaro's version of, 54–59; Sidney's redefinition of, 64–77; therapeutic intent of, 39–44, 57–59, 175–228. *See also* Bucolics; Christian pastoral; Classical pastoral; Georgic pastoral; Horatian pastoral; Italianate pastoral; Poetry; Stoic pastoral
Patterson, Annabel M., 247 n.23, 250 n.1
Paul, Saint, 56–57, 161
Pembroke, Countess of. *See* Sidney, Mary
Peterson, Douglas L., 240 n.42
Petrarch, Francesco, 52, 53–54, 58, 60, 68, 75, 242 n.34, 249 n.24
Phagonian rebellion, 119, 121, 123, 220
Philanax, 19, 100, 101, 110, 253 n.54; his attack on the princes, 21, 82, 223; and Basilius's rebirth, 226; and Euarchus, 214, 216–17; and passion, 152; his rebuke of Basilius, 98–99, 126, 178; and the trial, 218–21
Philisides, 22, 114, 123; his banishment from Mira, 167–68, 171, 172; and beast fable, 38, 95, 137, 143–47, 148, 195, 197, 199; his debate with Echo, 128–30, 184–87; his debate with Geron, 88, 110–12, 115, 178, 204, 245 n.16, 251 n.9; dream vision of, 163–67; laments for Mira, 120, 136, 155, 163–68, 194, 209; as Sidney's double, 96, 149, 201–2, 212–13; and unity in the eclogues, 96
Philoclea, 142, 193, 219, 224; Dametas's discovery of, 150, 152–54; and fortune, 99; and passion, 82, 117, 118–19, 120, 139; Pyrocles' love for, 20, 100, 136, 179–82, 188–89, 218, 220; her response to adversity, 82, 152–54, 215
Pickett, Penny, 250 n.3
Pico, 194
Plangus, 167, 205; complaints of, 92–93, 120, 130, 131, 170, 186, 199, 211, 213; his debate with Boulon, 125–28. *See also* Plangus and Erona
Plangus and Erona, 11, 108–9, 114, 132, 182, 194, 211
Plass, Ewald M., 252 n.28
Plato, 201, 242 n.29
Plutarch: and the balance of passion and reason, 121; and Barclay, 59; and concord, 200–201, 213, 252 n.35; and the quiet mind, 216, 228; Sidney's interest in, 9, 59; Stoic principles of, 71, 74
Poetry: and the abuse of imagination, 177–87; and Christian morality, 61–63; and deception, 187–92; and its functions, 176–77, 199–200; and injustice, 175–92; and justice, 9–10, 192–226; and nature, 178–202, 226; in *The Old Arcadia*, 81–97; persuasive power of, 132, 176, 187–92, 198–99, 250 n.1; and providence, 23, 24, 214–26; therapeutic power of, 7–10, 37–43, 57–59, 70, 171, 175–77, 192–228
Poggioli, Renato, 13, 40, 169, 242 n.34, 246 n.14, 251 n.15
Poirier, Michel, 37, 241 n.14
Politics: in the beast fable, 145–47; and comic relief, 123; injustice in, 155–72; in

the pastoral tradition, 50, 65–66
Poliziano, Angelo, 64
Polybius, 68, 69, 102, 200
Pontano, Giovanni, 250 n.1
Providence: and art, 224–26; and fortune, 117–32; and justice, 150–51
Pugliano, John Pietro, 183
Putnam, Michael C. J., 232 n.16
Puttenham, George, 48, 54, 235 n.7
Pyrocles and Musidorus (Cleophila and Dorus), 76, 123–24, 125, 139; as "bad" poets, 187–92, 227; and the coherence of *The Old Arcadia*, 96, 120; and concord, 193–94, 199; and the dangers of poetry, 179–84, 185; debate between, 99–102, 110; and Dicus, 122–23, 205; and the divided mind, 114–16, 117, 130–32, 133–36; and the eclogues, 85–89, 102–4; and fortune, 99–102; Histor's tales of, 11, 108–9, 120, 126–28; and Lalus, 104–6, 139, 203; and Philisides, 112, 125; and relief, 131–32, 175, 211, 213; responses of, to misfortune, 150–55, 215–16, 218, 219, 221; sentencing of, 19–24, 221–26; their wooing of Pamela and Philoclea, 117–20
Pyrophilus and Melidora, 226

Quiet mind: limits of, 155; and marriage, 137; and Philisides, 164; Sidney's evaluation of, 35–36, 213; as Stoic ideal, 224. *See also* Contentment; Idle life; Relief

Reason. *See* Passion
Rees, Christine, 249 n.25
Relief: Sidney's desire for, through the composition of *The Old Arcadia*, 37–44, 202; as traditional pastoral theme, 27–31. *See also* Contentment; Idle life; Poetry; Quiet mind
Revelation, 160
Ribner, Irving, 247 n.23
Riccioli, Cardinal, 160
Ringler, William A., 7, 120, 124, 145, 241 n.21, 243 n.15, 244 nn. 18 and 8, 247 n.23
Rivetus, Andraeus, 198, 201
Rixus, 43, 105
Rogers, Daniel, 166
Rose, Mark, 231 n.4, 241 n.14

Rosenberg, D. M., 12, 13, 243 n.15
Rosenmeyer, Thomas G., 239 n.36, 241 n.14
Rowe, Kenneth Thorpe, 23
Roydon, Matthew, 49
Rudenstine, Neil, 37, 42, 244 nn. 2 and 8, 245 n.16, 246 n.10, 250 nn. 1 and 3, 253 n.55
Russell, D. A., 241–42 n.25

Sallust, 59
Samothea, 156, 163, 164–65, 212
Samothes, King, 165
Samuel, 146–47
Sanforde, James, 242 n.33
Sannazaro, Jacopo: *Arcadia*, 28–30, 55–59, 65, 81–82, 101, 107, 165, 193, 243 n.5; and Barclay, 60, 62, 63, 77; as an Italianate pastoralist, 69, 75, 76–77, 113, 177, 202, 227; and models for "Ye goatherd gods . . ." in the *Arcadia*, 157, 208–9; and the pastoral tradition, 13, 28–30, 40, 41, 50, 53; and Sidney's *Arcadia*, 67, 68, 70, 76–77, 163, 185; and Sidney's eclogues, 89, 90, 111–12, 157, 163, 169, 245 n.16. *See also* Italianate pastoral
Saunders, Jason Lewis, 241–42 n.25
Scaliger, Julius Caesar, 64, 250 n.1
Scanlon, Paul A., 237 n.18
Schleiner, Winfried, 245 n.14
Schultz, John R., 240 n.40
Second eclogues. *See* Arcadian eclogues
Self-love. *See* Solipsism
Seneca, 39, 71, 77, 241 n.23, 242 n.29
Shakespeare, William, 8, 12, 66, 74, 228
Shepherd, Geoffrey, 240 n.4
Sidney, Sir Henry, 35, 100
Sidney, Mary, 36, 39, 42, 166, 212
Sidney, Sir Philip: and the composition of *The Old Arcadia*, 37–38, 42–44, 202; critical reputation of, as a pastoralist, 47–50; personal misfortunes of (1577–80), 31–33; and Philisides, 96, 112, 128, 149, 212; political concerns of, 33–35, 210; private interests of, in *The Old Arcadia*, 210–13; his retirement to Wilton, 36; and Stoicism, 72–74; on value of the quiet mind, 35–36. *See also Apology for Poetry, The*; Arcadian eclogues; Arcadian poems; *Astrophil and Stella*; *Certain Sonnets*; *Lady*

of May, The; New Arcadia, The; Old Arcadia, The
Sidney, Robert, 43, 202
Silvestris, Bernard, 160
Smith, Hallett D., 54, 238n.19, 250n.3
Snell, Bruno, 232n.16
Socrates, 24
Solé-Leris, A., 233n.28
Solensis, Aratus, 25, 26, 196
Solipsism, 181–92, 213, 250–51nn. 7 and 8
Solitariness, 130–32, 183
Song. *See* Poetry
Sophie-Røstvig, Maren, 232n.20
Spencer, Theodore, 237n.16, 240n.12, 243n.15, 248n.6, 253n.46
Spenser, Edmund: *Epithalamion*, 139; *Faerie Queene*, 27, 50, 58, 83, 193, 253n.41; pastoral in the works of, 12, 13, 27, 83; as a pastoralist, 40–42, 47, 48, 53, 228; *Shepheardes Calendar*, 41, 51, 52, 89, 112, 144, 166, 169, 188, 243n.15
Spitzer, Leo, 252n.35
Stella, 44, 191
Stillman, Robert E., 232n.11, 248n.6
Stoicism: and contentment, 141, 148; definition of, 71–76; difference from Epicureanism, 75; and pastoral repose, 74–77; as a response to adversity, 153–55, 170; Sidney's attitude toward, 71–74, 205; and suicide, 153–54
Stoic pastoral, 71–77, 81, 90–91, 104–6, 110, 227
Strephon and Klaius, 96, 130, 212; distinction between, 248n.12; their laments for loss of Urania, 156–63, 206–9; and loss of justice, 171, 172; mental landscape of, 186, 206–9, 227, 249n.18; as stranger shepherds, 22, 76, 155
Stump, Donald V., 237–38n.18
Suetonius, 41, 59
Suicide, 152–54, 248n.4
Sylvius, Aeneas, 61
Sympathus, 218, 223

Talbert, Ernest William, 247n.23
Tayler, Edward, 240–41n.12
Tempe, vale of, 188
Theocritus: and Barclay, 59–60; elegies of, 169; epithalaium in the *Idylls*, 246–47n.12; and the pastoral tradition, 52, 56, 58, 69, 75; and stasis in the *Idylls*, 84, 89; and the therapeutic power of the pastoral, 42, 57, 239n.36
Therion, 9, 251n.12
Third eclogues. *See* Arcadian eclogues
Toliver, Harold, 238n.19, 241n.14
Tonkin, Humphrey, 238n.19, 252n.39
Trial, 9, 19–24, 214–26. *See also* Justice
Trissino, Gian Girogio, 91
Tufte, Virginia, 246–47n.12
Turberville, George, 113
Turner, Myron, 243n.4, 248n.4, 253n.55

Ulreich, John C., Jr., 252n.32
Urania: loss of, 22, 156–57, 162–63, 168, 171; restoration of, through poetry, 207–8; symbolic functions of, 159–62, 208; vision of, 213, 253n.46

Van Dorsten, J. A., 235n.70, 249n.26
Venus, 159–60, 163, 166, 167, 194, 208
Vergil: and the myth of the golden age, 26–27, 43, 196–97; narrative elements in the *Eclogues*, 84; and *The Old Arcadia*, 67, 68, 185; and the pastoral tradition, 13, 49–60, 165, 177; and relief, 28–29, 40–41, 43, 177, 205–6, 208, 210, 239n.36; and Sidney's *Apology*, 65–66, 123, 156; and Sidney's eclogues, 89, 95, 112, 156, 161, 205–6, 208, 210
Vida, Marco Girolamo, 64
Virgo, Caelestis, 160

Wallace, Malcolm, 233n.32
Waller, Gary F., 250n.3
Wardropper, Bruce W., 233n.26
Watson, Gerard, 240n.11
Weiner, Andrew D., 230n.2, 249n.18, 252n.32
White, Beatrice, 232n.22
Whitney, Lois, 241n.13, 245n.1
Wickham, Edward C., 232n.19
Willey, Basil, 70, 242n.33
Williams, Raymond, 238n.19
Wilson, Mona, 237n.16, 243n.15
Wilton, 36–37
Wind, Edgar, 251n.18
Wit and will, 38; balance of, 195–226
Wolff, Samuel Lee, 217, 233n.30, 239n.33, 253n.51

Wyatt, Sir Thomas, 232 n.22

Xenophon, 196

Yates, Francis, 160, 251 n.16

Zandvoort, Reinard Willem, 244 n.2

DATE DUE

FEB 1 8 2003			

WITHDRAWN from the Alma College Library

DEMCO 38-297